EDUCATION
IN AMERICA

EDUCATION IN AMERICA

SECOND EDITION

James Monroe Hughes

Harper & Row, Publishers

NEW YORK, EVANSTON, AND LONDON

212393

CONTENTS

UNIT ONE   The Teacher in American Education

UNIT TWO   Ideas Influential in American Education

UNIT THREE The American School System

UNIT FOUR   Stimulating and Directing Growth
and Development

PREFACE

Education in America attempts to portray what the American people have done, are doing, and may be expected to do toward providing the nation with adequate education. Discussions have been addressed to two types of readers—beginning students in professional education, and laymen who for various reasons may wish to become intelligently informed about education as it has been and is being conducted in the United States.

The organization of the first edition has been maintained in this text. Some sections of the book, however, have been rewritten or augmented. Even since the second printing of the first edition, in 1962, the educational scene has changed markedly. To reflect such changes the data, charts, pictures, and other illustrations have also been revised. In Unit Four, "Stimulating and Directing Growth and Development," two new chapters have been added. The Unit now begins with a chapter entitled "Understanding Pupils"; and the treatment of methods has been expanded into two chapters—one on methods of teaching and one on instructional aids. The latter describes such current practices as team teaching, programmed learning, and use of closed-circuit television.

The sequence of the units may be changed without injury to the principal theme of the book. Some instructors who have used the book as a college text have preferred to begin with Unit II, "Ideas Influential in American Education." Some have preferred to postpone Unit I, "The Teacher in American Education," to the end of the course. Such interchange has not lessened the effectiveness of the text.

As before, the overview approach has been kept. The coverage is comprehensive and the discussions compact, allowing for expansion in any direction the instructor may deem desirable.

The author is indebted to many for help given both for this and for the previous edition. The sources of help have been so numerous it is not possible here to give individual acknowledgment. To all of them he expresses sincere thanks. Special acknowledgment and appreciation are due the National Education Association and its several departments, and especially Mr. Sam Lambert, Director of Research, and his staff, who have furnished a great deal of data and information.

J. M. H.

EDUCATION IN AMERICA

CHAPTER 1

Introduction

A professor of one of the social sciences always introduced his course to the students by explaining that his field of study is truly a highly respected, logically organized, and systematic discipline. He pointed out, by way of contrast, that the subject matter used in the study of professional education is not systematized and that the term, when used to describe a field of study, is so broad that it may include almost anything. Therefore, he concluded, professional education, commonly referred to as education, cannot qualify as a separate discipline. If, he pointed out, the student elected a course in physics or chemistry or algebra or economics, he would have some idea about what he was going to study. When he approached the subject of education, however, he could have no idea of what he was going to study because the term "education" is all-inclusive. Every subject in the school is there to help in the education of the student.

The professor had a point. Since his own course was offered for the purpose of educating the students, he could not see why another course should assume such an inclusive title as "education." Actually, his confusion grew out of what someone has labeled "the tyranny of words." We are victims of confusion, misunderstanding, and disagreement because a common word like "education" may be used as a broad or as a limited term. One may use it, as the professor of social sciences does, to include all aspects of formal schooling. We say that an individual has had a high-school education. In another sense "education" is used to apply to that which is related to the profession of education. Thus, we talk about a school of education and courses in education. We may also conceive of "education" as a very broad term including all the activities by which children learn the techniques, customs, and sentiments of the society in which they live. In order to reduce the degree of confusion, we must explain the meaning of the term as it is used herein.

In this discussion education refers to learning that is deliberate and formal and is organized and directed by the people of the United States. Whenever the discussion utilizes a broader, more inclusive meaning of education, the distinction will be made clear.

EDUCATION AND AN ENLIGHTENED CITIZENRY

The schools in the United States are particularly the special responsibility of the citizens. Even privately controlled schools exist and perform a valuable function only because of public policy. Even they must meet certain regulatory standards which are established by the public. Placing the educational destiny of the nation in the hands of its people requires an intelligent and well-informed public.

The American people are fully cognizant of the power of education and, hence, are concerned that their power over education not be minimized. They are aware that education received in the schools may change a whole social viewpoint in a single generation. As we shall see later, the American people shrewdly exercise their power over the schools in a short, direct line by establishing their basic control over the schools from the home, the community, and the local school district, and by dictating—probably through school election—who shall be in charge of the schools and how, and how much, money shall be spent. This means that it would be very difficult for any single political group in the 'United States ever to seize control over education throughout the nation. It is readily apparent that people who are inclined to keep their hands tightly on the reins and who insist on occupying the driver's seat should,

President Johnson signs legislation setting up a grant and loan program ($1.2 billion) to help colleges build classrooms, laboratories, and libraries. The Federal Government influences education in America through a constantly expanding program of financial aid. (United Press International)

if schools are to achieve good results, themselves be enlightened about the needs of education and have a clear notion about the general direction education should take.

MAGNITUDE OF THE EDUCATIONAL UNDERTAKING

An enlightened citizenry is also necessary because of the very magnitude of the educational enterprise. Indeed, almost everyone in the United States has some kind of relationship with education.

Each September, more than fifty million people of all ages enter some kind of school, some to attend full time, some to attend for only a single class. And as Figs. 1.1 and 1.2 show, this number grows each year. There are, moreover, many others who do not attend school who are involved in a variety of other ways—parents of school children, members of school boards, school trustees, school architects, builders of school buildings, keepers of grounds, investors

Few if any thoughtful people have denied that the art of teaching can be developed by practice, under suitable conditions. Thus, the members of the Massachusetts Board of Education, before they established the first normal school in the United States, subscribed to the statement that "No one can entertain a doubt that there is a mastery in teaching as in every other art. Nor is it less obvious that within reasonable limits this skill and this mastery may themselves be made the subject of instruction and be communicated to others." These words were written in 1838. The question then was: What is this skill and how can one communicate it to others? This question remains the hard core of the issue. . . .

At the outset, I think we can identify four components of the intellectual equipment that would be a prerequisite to the development of teaching skill. The first I shall call the "democratic social component." The second is an interest in the way behavior develops in groups of children and some experience of this development. A third is a sympathetic knowledge of the growth of children, by which I mean far more than physical growth, of course. A fourth might be called the principles of teaching. This last is almost equally applicable to a teacher with only one pupil (the tutor of a rich family in former times) as to a person attempting to develop an intellectual skill in a group of children.

My phrase "democratic social component" may need an explanation. To understand what I mean, we must consider everything that is involved in teaching in our elementary or secondary schools. We must constantly bear in mind that the schools in every nation have been and continue to be involved in more than imparting knowledge and developing skills. . . .

The second of my four components, which has to do with the development of behavior in groups of children, is not unrelated to the first. A concern with the values inherent in a "democratic social system" has intruded itself into questions that some social scientists

in school bonds. If we include the payers of school taxes and the voters on school matters, almost everyone in the United States is included. For such vast and widespread participation in a single institutional venture, lack of an enlightened citizenry would constitute a potential social calamity.

EDUCATION AND WELL-INFORMED TEACHERS

The public depends upon the trained professional teaching group for a mature and intelligent interpretation of what educa-

might say should involve only predictive generalizations based upon observations or experience. At all events, *a teacher must know something about the processes by which social behavior emerges in groups of children.* Technically one ought to be able to study this process dispassionately as a problem in social psychology. In fact, however, it has proved incredibly difficult to separate this question from one of another type: "What kind of social behavior do we wish to develop?"

My third and fourth components, a knowledge of the growth of children and the principles of teaching, emerge most clearly if one notes what good schoolteachers do. Let me ask you to run through a list of such "doings." First of all, obviously the teacher disseminates information, and it goes without saying that this information should be accurate and significant. . . .

But the elementary teacher, and to a lesser extent the secondary teacher, must select and organize materials without the guidelines marked by university research fields; that is, he teaches "science" not "qualitative analysis," "social studies" not "history of England in the seventeenth century." Moreover, the information must be presented in a form understandable by the very young; the conceptual and verbal skill of the educated adult cannot be assumed.

The public school teacher is also expected to adjust his methods of instruction to a student group that is highly heterogeneous with respect to intellectual ability, motivation, and previous educational achievement. This means that he must select from a wide range of instructional materials those most suited to the intellectual maturity of each youngster, and this maturity may vary as much as two or three years in normal development. . . .

From James B. Conant, *The Education of American Teachers* (New York: McGraw-Hill Book Company, Inc., 1963), pp. 113, 115, 116. Quoted by permission of McGraw-Hill Book Company.

tion in the United States should be, what its principal needs are, and what is necessary for the maintenance of an excellent system of schools. Only a well-informed, responsible teaching profession can supply this kind of information.

Furthermore, all theories of education—progressive or reactionary, liberal or conservative—assume that the classroom teacher is always in direct control. The dependence upon the instructor's initiative and discretion justifies the expectation that classrooms be manned by teachers who are well informed about the entire educational venture.

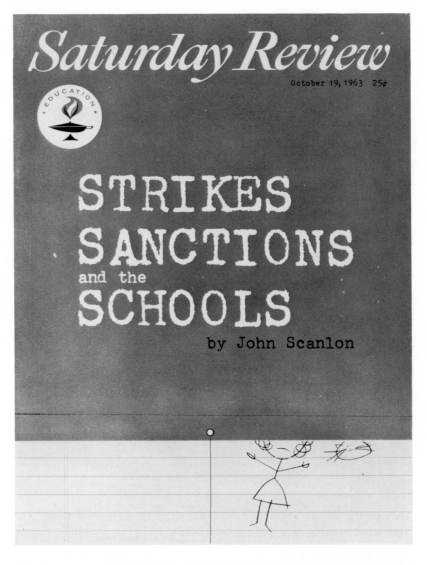

Magazines and newspapers keep the public informed about current educational topics. The *Saturday Review* devotes one issue each month to education. (Courtesy of *Saturday Review* and cover artist Irving Spellens)

While teachers play a role that requires considerable individual initiative, they also play a role that calls for a close relationship with many other persons. Throughout the day teachers are in close contact not only with the pupils in their own classrooms, but also with the pupils taught by other teachers. Further, they have personal

FIG. 1.1 PUBLIC SCHOOL ENROLLMENTS AND AVERAGE DAILY
ATTENDANCE, 1953-1954 to 1963-1964

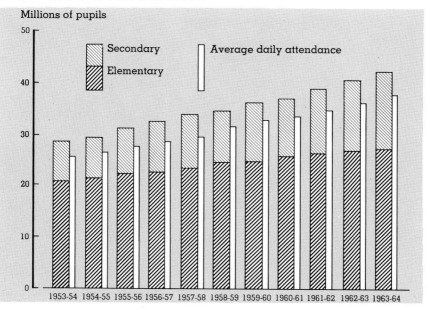

(Data from NEA Research Division, Research Report 1963–R12)

FIG. 1.2 PUBLIC SCHOOL ENROLLMENTS PERCENTAGE INCREASES
OVER 1953-1954

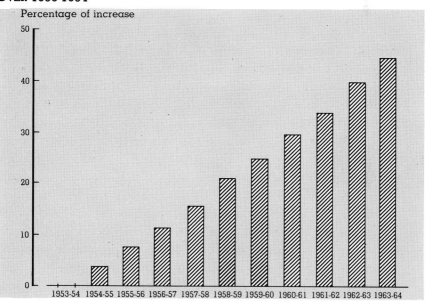

(Data from NEA Research Division, Research Report 1963–R12)

Fig. 1.3   Projected School Enrollment

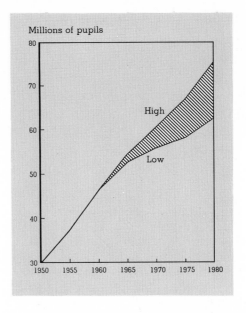

(Data from National Industrial Conference Board, *Road Maps of Industry*, No. 1338)

relationships with other teachers, with principals and supervisors, and with the pupils' parents. In no other profession do roles interlock so intimately; maintaining good relationships in all of these roles is an important factor in achieving marked teaching success. This demands that the teacher be well informed about education in general. It is not enough to know subject matter and to master methods and problems related only to the classroom. He must be equipped to recognize, adjust to, and influence the many forces at play in the process of education.

THE OVERVIEW APPROACH

Research concerning the relative effectiveness of various approaches to introductory college courses in specialized fields reveals that, for most specialized fields, the overview approach is superior. "Overview" as applied to introductory courses carries the idea that the coverage is extensive and that the topics selected are basic and

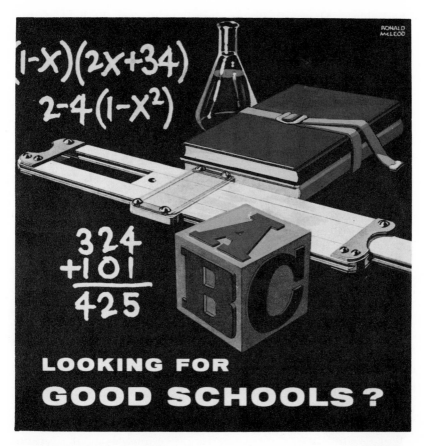

COME TO "UPSTATE, N.Y."
new market place of the world

Modern schools with excellent faculties help make Upstate, N.Y., a great place for families to raise their children. Here, you'll find some of the most complete and well planned educational facilities in the nation, from kindergarten to college. These schools provide industry and business with a large, stable supply of technicians and skilled workers.

POWERED BY
NIAGARA MOHAWK

NIAGARA MOHAWK

Business concerns recognize that good schools are an essential element to successful business enterprises. (Niagara Mohawk Power Company)

fundamental to later study. In many colleges students pursue one-year or one-semester introductory courses, each of which delineates a field of study, reveals the nature of major problems included in the field, describes the methods used, and elaborates on the more basic ideas. Above all, the purpose is to present the field of study so that the student may obtain accurate insights into its foundational elements. The approach, then, is sweeping and general rather than technical and specialized; the treatment is simple rather than complicated; the subject matter is introductory rather than terminal. Such an approach is particularly appropriate to an introduction to the study of education.

The overview technique followed in this book meets the needs of intelligent citizens who are interested in education and of those students who, as prospective teachers, desire to learn about education in the United States. The book supplies practical knowledge and theoretical understanding of American educational institutions and their problems.

Other teachers, principals, heads of departments, and supervisors can help teachers keep abreast of educational thought and practices. Here, a visiting department head explains a technique of student planning of class work. (Hays from Monkmeyer)

SELECTION OF MATERIAL

Certain principles have guided in the selection and rejection of both topics and materials.

First, it is assumed that the reader is taking his first systematic look at education in the United States. Perhaps he is a citizen who wishes to be informed enough about education to function as an intelligent parent or voter. Perhaps he is a taxpayer who wishes to know more about the educational venture he is obligated to support. The materials are selected and the discussions are fashioned with these kinds of readers in mind.

THE AMERICAN EDUCATIONAL ESTABLISHMENT, 1963/1964[a]

THE INSTITUTIONS		THE TEACHERS	
Elementary Schools	94,860	Public School Teachers	
Secondary Schools	30,000	Elementary	901,820
Universities, Colleges,		High School	607,460
and Junior Colleges	2,100	Nonpublic School	
Total Institutions	126,960	Teachers	190,000
		College and University Teachers	
		For resident degree-credit students	312,900
		Other teaching faculty (extension courses,	
THE LEARNERS		noncredit courses,	
Pupils in Elementary		etc.)	50,000
Schools (through grade 8)		Total teachers	2,062,180
Public Schools	29,400,000	ADMINISTRATORS	
Nonpublic (Private and		AND SUPERVISORS	
Parochial)	5,400,000	Superintendents of	
Other	200,000	Schools	13,130
Total Elementary	35,000,000	Principals and Super-visors	86,540
Secondary School Students		College and University Presidents	2,100
Public High Schools	10,700,000	Other College Ad-	
Nonpublic	1,300,000	ministrative and	
Other	100,000	library staff	48,400
Total Secondary	12,100,000	Total	150,170
College and University full- and part-time		BOARD MEMBERS	
students enrolled for credit toward degrees		Local School Board	
Public Institutions	2,631,600	Members	147,860
Private	1,754,400	State Board Members	840
Total	4,386,000	College and University Board Members	35,000
Grand Total En-rolled Students	51,486,000	Total	183,700

[a] As noted in the *Saturday Review*, September 21, 1963. Figures are based on latest available estimates from the U.S. Office of Education and the National Education Association.

Second, those phases of education have been selected that will give students of education the information and understanding they need to assist in making a vocational choice or some related decision.

Third, in some states a general, introductory education course is required for state certification for all who enter a teacher education program. The requirement is usually imposed by the state educational authority, an agency that will be described later. Even where such a course is not required for state certification it is assumed that every teacher will have some knowledge of the funda-

If the earth were struck by one of Mr. Wells's comets, and if, in consequence, every human being now alive were to lose all the knowledge and habits which he had acquired from preceding generations (though retaining unchanged all his own powers of invention, and memory, and habituation) nine tenths of the inhabitants of London or New York would be dead in a month, and 99 per cent of the remaining tenth would be dead in six months. They would have no language to express their thoughts, and no thoughts but vague reverie. They could not read notices, or drive motors or horses. They would wander about, led by the inarticulate cries of a few naturally dominant individuals, drowning themselves, as thirst came on, in hundreds at the riverside landing places, looting those shops where the smell of decaying food attracted them, and perhaps at the end stumbling on the expedient of cannibalism. Even in the country districts, men could not invent, in time to preserve their lives, methods of growing food, or taming animals, or making fire, or so clothing themselves as to endure a northern winter. An attack of constipation or measles would be invariably fatal. After a few years mankind would almost certainly disappear from the northern and temperate zones. The white races would probably become extinct everywhere. A few primitive races might live on fruit and small animals in those fertile tropical regions where the human species was originally evolved, until they had slowly accumulated a new social heritage. After some thousands of generations they would probably possess something which we should recognize as a language, and perhaps some art of taming animals and cultivating land. They might or might not have created what we should call a religion, or a few of our simpler mechanical inventions and political expedients. They probably would not have re-created such general ideas as "Law" or "Liberty"; though they might have created other general ideas which would be new to us.

From Graham Wallas, Our Social Heritage (New Haven, Conn.: Yale University Press, 1921), pp. 16–17. Quoted by permission of Yale University Press.

mental features of education as they are incorporated in the various school systems throughout America.

Fourth, the materials of the book are selected to serve as a foundation for more advanced study in professional education.

PLAN OF THE BOOK

The materials of the book are organized around four aspects of education referred to as "units." Each unit can be studied more or less independently of the others. Unit One focuses upon the classroom teacher—describing what he does, how he qualifies, how he is related to his profession, how he formulates his professional philosophy, and how he is affected by being part of an institution.

Unit Two focuses upon ideas that have been influential in shaping the course of American education. Discussed first are the ideas that were propagated by three significant European social movements—the Athenian cultural movement, the Christian religious movement, and the broad-scale intellectual movement, the Renaissance, particularly the Italian Renaissance. This is followed by a discussion of the ideas of outstanding European thinkers and writers. Treated next are ideas that flowed from the American frontier movement. Then follows a discussion of the impact of the contemporary social scene upon education. The emphasis here is upon those ideas that have been and continue to be influential in shaping the course of American education.

Unit Three focuses upon the American school system. Five chapters are devoted to the organization of American education. These deal, respectively, with local aspects of the administration and organization of public school systems, state school systems, federal educational activity, nonpublic schools, and units of school organization.

Unit Four focuses upon the pupils in the school and the processes of stimulating and guiding their growth and development. Attention is directed specifically to understanding the pupils, aims, subject matter, methods of teaching, and instructional aids. Unit Four concludes with a fairly brief discussion of some future fields of study. This is designed to help the student who expects to continue in further study of education.

Education is considered a partnership between teachers and the community. The P.T.A. is a semiprofessional organization whose chief purpose is to make this partnership effective. The National Congress of Parents and Teachers had a membership of approximately 12 million at the beginning of the 1964 school year. (National Congress of Parents and Teachers)

SUMMARY

Numerous meanings are given the term "education." In the text, except where indicated otherwise, education refers to that aspect of learning that is deliberate and formal and is organized and directed by the people of the United States.

The schools are particularly the responsibility of American citizens. Such responsibility calls for an enlightened citizenry. Since citizens must look to the teachers in the schools for mature and intelligent interpretations of what education in the United States should be and what its principal needs are, the teaching profession also must be a well-informed body of people.

It is the purpose of this introductory study of education in the United States to provide the reader with sufficient knowledge of the educational picture in America so that he can at least qualify as one who understands the general nature of the educational venture in the United States and can sense the needs of education and constructively advance the cause.

The plan of the book is dictated by an overview approach. Materials are organized in four units. Unit One focuses upon the classroom teacher; Unit Two, upon the ideas that have been effective in shaping the character of American education; Unit Three, upon the American school system; and Unit Four, upon the pupils in the school and the processes of stimulating and guiding their growth.

The Teacher in

Merrim from Monkmeyer

American Education

CHAPTER 2

What teachers do

We begin with a study of the work of the key figure in the educational picture—the teacher. In Unit One five questions about the teacher are considered. What do teachers do? How must they qualify? What are the principal characteristics of the profession to which they belong? How does a teacher formulate his professional philosophy? And how are his obligations affected by the nature of the institution in which he works? Since none of the questions lends itself to brief analysis, a separate chapter is devoted to each. First, what do teachers do?

THE BASIC FUNCTION OF A TEACHER

The familiar statement that the principal function of the teacher is to stimulate and direct learning activities constitutes a fairly accurate, simple, and definitive description of what teachers do. Though it must be followed with a more detailed analysis if we are to acquire an adequate description of the occupation, the statement, nevertheless, is helpful as a point of departure from which our analysis may proceed. It conveys the idea that the teacher is the key figure in the drama of the education of a child. He is in control of many of the manageable features of the educative process. The results of the process certainly are determined by the wisdom of his control.

The word "stimulation" is equally as significant as the word "direction." A teacher may be in control of the classroom and may greatly influence what is learned. What any child learns depends upon how he, personally, interacts with his environment. "Stimulation" emphasizes that a teacher's job is not limited to guidance and direction and control. It also includes inciting the pupils to action. It involves providing a foundation upon which is built self-direction and the advance toward a higher level of maturity. The teacher's job is to modify the stimuli in the environment so that they have a favorable educational impact upon the learners.

COMPLEX NATURE OF THE WORK OF TEACHERS

Such scientists as physiologists, psychologists, and social biologists, who devote their lives to a study of the human organism, maintain that their subject matter is the most intricate of all. Few people will contradict this claim. The problems involved are complex and baffling in their elusiveness and intangibility. The best efforts of the most gifted minds are needed to solve them. To influence large numbers of these growing complex systems of living energy to develop in worthwhile, desirable directions can, by no possible stretch of the imagination, be considered a simple task that can be satisfactorily performed by almost any normal person.

LIMITATIONS ON INTERPRETATIONS OF TEACHERS' WORK

Gaps in Knowledge

One factor that limits our interpretation of what teachers do and should do is a lack of fundamental knowledge about the nature of the human organism. It is significant, for instance, that those who work in the fields referred to as the life sciences have never adequately defined what life is. Their efforts to measure the amount of life an organism possesses have been unsatisfactory. They are resigned to describing life and, sometimes, to measuring some of its manifestations. Life and death and cell growth and the nature of individuality and emotions can be cited as only a few of the many unknowns. Furthermore, complete explanations of such processes as learning, perceiving, reasoning, and imagining aren't available to the educator.

Voids in knowledge are, of course, common to all fields of study. For example, when Newton stated the laws of gravitation, he exempted certain natural phenomena such as light, electricity, and magnetism from his interpretation. What gravitation is remains an unknown. The whole field of cosmology, the general science of the universe, is characterized by much that is unexplained. Since such gaps exist in our knowledge of the physical aspects of human environment—aspects that can be measured—it is not surprising that so many gaps exist in our knowledge of human organisms, an area that does not lend itself to experimentation and quantification.

Despite the gaps and the many obstacles to narrowing them, useful knowledge of human behavior has been accumulated. The gaps are stressed here because students are sometimes disturbed when final answers cannot be given to some educational problems. Beginning teachers, particularly, are apt to be confused by the tendency among those who teach education to reason along theoretical lines. Where one does not have facts and the principles or "laws" abstracted from facts, one must turn to theories. Yet it is the presence of unsolved problems that helps make teaching such an intriguing occupation.

Influence of Past Experience

The individual's interpretation of what he reads about education is inevitably colored by his past school experiences. This is both a helpful and a limiting factor. Such experiences, however, afford only a partial view of what teachers do. From the pupil's desk, ordinarily in front of the teacher, the point of perspective is limited and the conclusions drawn may not be entirely dependable. However, certain attitudes toward teachers and teaching, favorable and unfavorable, are built through these experiences and tend to persist. Thus, we begin our study of what teachers do with certain, probably varied, predispositions. In making our interpretations, we must take these predispositions into account.

Tendency to Oversimplify

The student is taught to rely upon the *simplicity postulate* when working on a problem in the field of physics. This postulate asserts that of two alternatives the one that can be more simply stated is likely to be more acceptable. The principle of simplicity is often applied to our thinking about problems of teaching. When two educational theories are proposed, we tend to accept the one that is simpler, that more nearly accords with our previous experiences, and that promises to be more fruitful in its application. The simplicity postulate holds in education as it does in other fields of learning, but oversimplification sometimes presents the teaching profession with its most frustrating situations. Simplification is desirable only when it follows careful and expert analysis. The tendency generally leads to good habits of thinking. In interpreting the work of the teacher, however, it can be unwisely used and lead to harmful results.

Often influential citizens who are relatively uninformed about education will make statements such as, "I am opposed to federal aid to education," or "Teachers should fail more pupils in the interest of higher achievement standards." Their statements appeal to many partly because they are simple, positive, direct answers about what schools should be and what teachers should do. Those who have carefully and diligently studied the problems, however, are not always sure of the solutions. They wish to weigh various alternatives with thoughtful care.

Unobservable Elements

Interpretations based upon studies of teachers' work must recognize that there are elements in this work that are not revealed by any form of investigation. One is the qualitative factor. This will be discussed after an examination of the nature and extent of teachers' duties.

CLASSIFYING TEACHERS' DUTIES

Need for Classification

Classification is a basic method used for studying the similarities and differences among objects in the universe. Those objects that have similar characteristics are assigned to the same category. This is perhaps the oldest and simplest method for arriving at order in the world of knowledge. By noting similarities among the activities in which teachers engage, we can, in some measure, reduce many of them to a class and then speak of them as a single activity. Thus we can discuss guidance as a single activity even though we know that guidance actually consists of a large number of individual activities.

Exactness in classification of a teacher's duties would be helpful but does not seem possible. Educational terminology is not fully standardized, and, even more important, teaching activities do not fall into readily classifiable categories. Lines of demarcation between classifications are often blurred. They frequently overlap. No classification is, therefore, to be considered final or authoritative.

If we had generally accepted definitions of educational terms, more uniform classifications of activities would be possible. In an effort to promote a kind of standardization of terms to be helpful not only in classifying but in the education field generally, a dictionary of the specialized vocabulary of professional education has been produced.[1] Such standardization is particularly important to the student who needs to know that professional writers and instructors in education use the same words to convey like meanings. More work is needed in this area of standardization. There is, however, more or less general agreement with respect to some of the classifications of teacher activities.

Classifications

In general, teacher functions have been broadly grouped into five classifications: (1) classroom instruction, (2) guidance, (3) staff functions, (4) community duties, and (5) professional activities. The classifications are, of course, arbitrary. Everything a teacher does might be classified as related to classroom instruction or to guidance.

1. Classroom Instruction

This is the foremost duty of the teacher; it comprises the bulk of his activities. It involves all the duties that the teacher performs in directing group and individual learning. Teachers direct dis-

[1] Carter V. Good, *Dictionary of Education* (2d ed.; New York: McGraw-Hill Book Company, Inc., 1959), 704 pp.

Good health manifest in vigor and energy and enthusiasm is an important teacher asset. (Wide World)

cussions, make assignments, listen to reports and recitations, direct reading, show films, check workbooks, and plan and check work, often at home evenings. You know from your own experiences that this most important function is discharged in a great variety of ways, and you can appreciate better now that it reflects most accurately the philosophy of the teacher and of the school and that it is most readily modified by the social environment of the teacher and by the physical resources made available to him. Extended observation of classroom instruction is necessary for a picture that will reflect practically every facet of the total school situation.

2. Guidance

Every teacher is a counselor to his pupils. Duties in this classification consume much time and energy. Often they are incidental to instruction. Sometimes they are definitely scheduled, perhaps weekly conferences with an individual pupil over a period of time. The teacher may find it necessary to counsel pupils outside of school hours. Counseling may also involve parent conferences, home visits, or interviews with supervisors, principals, or other teachers. The teacher must be adept at group guidance, too. Almost every day he must assist the entire class, a committee group, or some other group in making choices and decisions.

In some schools teachers have a number of periods a week which they devote to counseling. Some schools provide special help for teachers in the performance of this function—deans, social case-workers, school psychologists, testing departments, and others.

Regardless of the organizational plan, however, most guidance is directed by the classroom teacher. It is the teacher who must work with the specialist in helping a pupil make an adjustment. It is the teacher who must utilize what the specialists supply to help guide and counsel a pupil. It is the teacher who does most of the investigating, testing, interviewing, follow-up, and record making that are involved. But the satisfactions that accrue to the teacher as a result of success in pupil guidance are commensurate with the effort involved.

Teaching and guidance are inseparable functions. When the teacher directs a pupil in developing a chemistry project for a con-

Classroom teaching yields many satisfactions to the successful classroom teacher. His challenges are such that he continues to study and grow. This classroom teacher has lost none of his love for teaching after forty-two years of continuous experience. (Better Schools Advertising Council)

test, he instructs the pupil in the chemistry involved and guides him in making a mature approach to a competitive situation, in independently completing self-assigned work, and in developing good study habits. The distinction between instruction and guidance cannot be a sharp one. When a teacher reprimands a pupil for discourteous behavior, is he directing classroom instruction or engaging in guidance? Much guidance is incidental. No guidance is unimportant.

3. Staff Functions

The classroom teachers, collectively, are responsible for the greatest part of the administration of a school. The classroom is the administrative unit in the school, and the teacher is primarily responsible for the administration of its affairs. But classrooms are not isolated, independent units of school administration. The school is the larger unit, an organization with a principal who is responsible for achieving a reasonable measure of coordination of the staff members' efforts. Teachers are organized into a system to work as a unit and to plan together.

As a member of an organized staff the teacher is obliged to attend faculty, departmental, or grade-level meetings; to work on curriculum committees; and to assist with such school functions as plays, parties, and concerts. The teacher must make announcements, issue bulletins, collect fees. He must keep attendance records, make monthly enrollment reports, prepare report cards, and record health, behavior, and achievement data. He must make inventories; order, distribute, and collect supplies; and assign lockers. He must supervise play periods and lunchrooms and proctor children in the halls. These are just examples of the kinds of duties added to the teacher's work because his classroom is the unit of administration and he is a member of a staff whose work must be coordinated. Many of the duties are routine and mechanical. All of them are time-consuming.

It is in the area of these auxiliary activities that teachers tend to be most vocal in their complaints. The complaints arise not because the importance of the work is unrecognized but because the duties tend to be numerous and exceedingly time-consuming. Usually they must be made to fit into a rigid schedule. Sometimes the teacher cannot see that certain records are utilized sufficiently to warrant the time they take to be made out. Often meetings are

This teacher is teaching a young child to read. She not only knows how to teach reading but is also skilled in selecting and wisely using the proper teaching aid. In this case she is using a tape recorder. (William R. Simmons, Ford Foundation)

held after school hours and seem unduly prolonged to a tired teacher. At times responsibilities such as lunchroom supervision and hall proctoring seem to be unfairly distributed.

Parent or mature student help is sometimes used to assist the teacher with such duties. Teachers have more time for classroom instruction and guidance functions when they are relieved of some such job as fee collecting.

4. Community Duties

The ideal elementary or secondary school in the United States is a neighborhood institution, where the teachers are valued members of a community. The responsibility for the education of the pupils is shared by the school with the community. The community largely controls the school. It decides who is to be educated. By controlling the purse strings it determines, for instance, whether there will be summer schools, nursery schools, and classes for various atypical children. The community influences what the schools can attempt to do. For instance, if community mores are opposed to social dancing, the school cannot offer instruction in social dancing. The people connected with the school can, of course, by exerting influence on the Parent-Teacher Association and other community groups, work to change community attitudes.

It is difficult to isolate a teacher's duties because he is a member of a community. As we have said before, all the classifications of duties overlap. Perhaps producing the concert is the music teacher's job because he is a faculty member—but perhaps it falls on his shoulders because he is a member of a community of interested lay people.

Certain teaching duties such as participating in the Parent-Teacher Association seem to be related to the teacher's community membership. In many communities the teacher is expected to have a church affiliation. He might very well have many of the community relationships regardless of his teaching connection. The point is that, as a teacher, he is *expected* to have them, to be a community participant. His free choice is somewhat curtailed.

Besides the responsibility for contributing to the community, the teacher usually has the opportunity and privilege of using various community resources. Individuals with unique skills, special talents, or interesting backgrounds of experience can, at appropriate times, be enlisted to supplement the regular work of the classroom or to contribute to some professional activity, perhaps curriculum planning. Museums, historical societies, courts, and industrial organizations are examples of another kind of community resource that can also be used. Teachers feel free to use suitable and available human and material community resources because they, as well as their schools, are a part of the community.

5. Professional Activities

Certain other tasks fall to teachers because they are affiliated with various local, regional, state, and national professional organizations—organizations dedicated to promoting good education and to advancing teacher welfare. A teacher may add markedly to his work load by sharing in the preparation of a study of salaries and a faculty salary schedule for the local board of education; by participating in the development of a state convention program for English teachers; by writing an article for a professional journal describing his success in the classroom with some novel approach or device; or by serving as a discussion member on a program for the local professional fraternity. This kind of work is usually assumed voluntarily by the teacher, and the extent of an individual's time and energy invested varies with his interest, zeal, and ability. Even those who take no responsibility for leadership devote considerable time to attending meetings and reading professional publications. All teachers are interested in welfare matters related to teaching load, retirement, pensions, salaries, certification, and tenure.

As a rule, teachers also are expected to advance professionally by pursuing college study, either after school hours during the year or during the summer vacation period. A master's degree is not a terminal point. In some places advancement on a salary scale depends upon the accumulation of specified hours of additional college credit.

ALLOCATION OF TIME

To a teacher each school day is a challenge, not only because of the constancy of important and varied activity, but also because of the element referred to earlier as the unobservable, but nevertheless real, qualitative factor. A teacher must learn many things about each pupil and, in terms of these, formulate daily aims, select subject matter, decide upon procedures to follow, and choose appropriate teaching aids. One who teaches effectively with a free and easy grace has expended considerable time and energy in achieving the background that makes his performance possible.

No two days' work are precisely the same for any teacher, nor is a day's work for each of two teachers ever identical. This is evident from the descriptions on pages 34–35 of the work of five different teachers. Certain broad classifications of duties are, however, common to most teachers. Earlier studies averaged the time that a large number of teachers from all grade levels devoted to various activities. The studies showed, in general, that half of the teachers spent eight hours or more daily on teaching duties, and that other activities—conferring with parents, preparing materials, correcting papers,

The teacher's role involves many interrelationships. The warmth and friendliness with which the above teacher greets a pupil and his mother is a good start toward a pleasant and mutually profitable relationship. (Merrim from Monkmeyer)

keeping records, making reports, attending meetings—took as much of a teacher's time as did activities classified as classroom instruction.

Figs. 2.1 and 2.2 show how, on the average, elementary and high school teachers divide the school week. It should be noted that while elementary school teachers spend an average of 48.5 hours on the performance of their duties, half of them spend more than this. High school teachers fare a little better by virtue of the fact, perhaps, that 93 percent of the high school teachers devote more than half their time to teaching in a single field.

Such practices as lengthening the school day, requiring additional study by teachers for promotional credit, enlarging class size, increasing pupils' home study, and expecting teachers to share more in formulating administrative policies that closely concern them

Many school systems provide home and hospital instruction for pupils suffering from extended illness. This boy keeps up with his school work with the help of regular assignments and periodic conferences with his teacher. (Shelton from Monkmeyer)

have added to the teachers' work day despite attempts to alleviate the situation by providing such help as expert supervision, lay readers, special classes for slow learners, and opportunity rooms for

FIG. 2.1   HOW THE ELEMENTARY SCHOOL TEACHER DIVIDES THE WEEK (AVERAGE WORK WEEK OF 48 HOURS, 30 MINUTES)

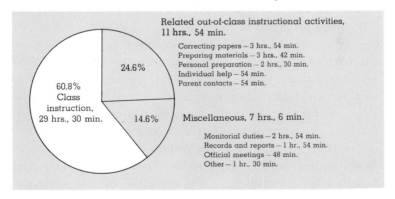

Related out-of-class instructional activities, 11 hrs., 54 min.

Correcting papers — 3 hrs., 54 min.
Preparing materials — 3 hrs., 42 min.
Personal preparation — 2 hrs., 30 min.
Individual help — 54 min.
Parent contacts — 54 min.

24.6%

60.8%
Class
instruction,
29 hrs., 30 min.

14.6%

Miscellaneous, 7 hrs., 6 min.

Monitorial duties — 2 hrs., 54 min.
Records and reports — 1 hr., 54 min.
Official meetings — 48 min.
Other — 1 hr., 30 min.

(Data from NEA Research Division, Research Monograph 1963–M2)

FIG. 2.2 HOW THE HIGH SCHOOL TEACHER DIVIDES THE WEEK (AVERAGE WORK WEEK OF 45 HOURS, 54 MINUTES)

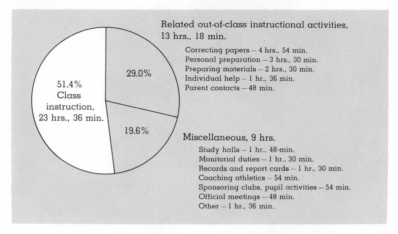

Related out-of-class instructional activities, 13 hrs., 18 min.

Correcting papers — 4 hrs., 54 min.
Personal preparation — 3 hrs., 30 min.
Preparing materials — 2 hrs., 30 min.
Individual help — 1 hr., 36 min.
Parent contacts — 48 min.

29.0%

51.4%
Class
instruction,
23 hrs., 36 min.

19.6%

Miscellaneous, 9 hrs.

Study halls — 1 hr., 48 min.
Monitorial duties — 1 hr., 30 min.
Records and report cards — 1 hr., 30 min.
Coaching athletics — 54 min.
Sponsoring clubs, pupil activities — 54 min.
Official meetings — 48 min.
Other — 1 hr., 36 min.

(Data from NEA Research Division, Research Monograph 1963–M2)

the poorly adjusted. There is little evidence to indicate that the teacher's working day will be lighter in the future.

Beginning teachers, perhaps dismayed at the span of duties allocated to the average teacher, will gradually learn that, with the skill that comes with experience, teachers learn to discriminate and to budget and organize their time efficiently. As in other professions, experience and study usually lead to capacity to work with more ease and to fulfill responsibilities with less strain.

STUDY OF TEACHERS' WORK

There are two approaches to a study of the work of teachers. The first is an intensive study of the work of one, or of a few teachers. This approach has certain advantages. It enables one to study the work of a highly skilled teacher who works at a given level of education, of one who teaches a special subject, or of one who works in a particular kind of environmental setting. The second approach is an extensive study of the work of a large sampling of teachers teaching at several levels of education and in many kinds of situations. This approach also has certain advantages. It gives breadth to the findings, reveals the possible range of duties, and gives, perhaps, a more accurate picture of the kinds of duties performed by teachers. A more realistic and complete account of what teachers do results from a combination of both methods of study. Therefore, we shall first note the results from studying the work of individual teachers and then follow with the more extensive findings of the wider sampling.

Studying Individuals

Two procedures may be followed in studying the work performed by a selected individual or individuals: directly observing what they do, and obtaining from the teachers themselves verbal descriptions of what they have done over a definite period of time. The two procedures lead to slightly different conclusions. Both methods contribute useful information.

1. Direct Observation

By observing a teacher at work for several successive days, one may secure a more vivid and realistic picture of what he does than by any other method. This is especially true if many of his activities are observed.

It is important to realize that this method has its limitations. In learning about the work done by one teacher, we may not directly observe all that he does, such as preparing for the day's teaching, counseling with pupils or parents, or reading the written assignments handed in by pupils. Also the value of the observation is related to the maturity, the insights, and the understandings of the observer. What an experienced teacher concludes from an observation tends to be quite different from what a novice or a layman concludes.

Still, this method is especially helpful to the beginning student, for thus he can learn what and how to observe. He learns to discriminate, to get a feeling for what the teacher's job is in a particular subject, at a given level of teaching, or in a single aspect of his work.

2. Verbal Description

Some of the shortcomings of direct observation are overcome by having teachers describe their work in simple, direct statements. This method has certain advantages. A teacher can accurately describe his own work, and he is more likely to select what is most important in his job. A description of the work of individual teachers tends also to emphasize the many differences in the work that various teachers do. Descriptions are also valuable in revealing some of the subtle, more qualitative aspects of the teacher's work. The following examples illustrate some of the features of teaching.

A first grade teacher says:

There are thirty-eight children in my room. It would take thirty-eight pages of typewritten material to describe the work I do. [A lengthy, although condensed, description of classroom work then follows, closing with this statement.]

Now a few words about the "extras." I attend faculty meetings, committee meetings, meetings of the Parent-Teacher Association, district meetings and, well, just meetings. These are always held during school time.

I operate the movie projector, the slide projector, and the hectograph machine. I prepare the seat work by hand and run it off on the hectograph, and sometimes I make drawings from typewritten material which I prepare. I keep records of daily attendance, daily work, test grades, and monies collected. I prepare monthly summary sheets of attendance, monthly supply orders, lists of supplies to be put away, and book inventories. I fill out health records, quarterly report cards, cumulative records, and other office records required at the end of the semester and, occasionally, make special reports. I also prepare plan books for the work of each day.

A third grade teacher writes:

No two days of work are ever alike. I view my job as that of working with children—all kinds of children—striving to help them make worthwhile progress each day. In order to do this I try to understand each child and try to find ways of helping him adjust to me and to his many classmates. I try also to know all of the parents, to find out how they live and what their interests are. Yes, I even enjoy talking to Mrs. Hill who insists that her son has a right to break other children's crayons whenever his heart desires. It is only by being able to talk to her that I have hopes of showing her what our common problems are. Teaching is such a natural, easy way of living, in spite of the many things there are to teach and do, like making impromptu talks to parents, selling taffy apples, growing a community garden, and learning about the insects that are garden pests. . . .

A junior high school teacher says:

My functions are to teach music to four classes on the sixth, seventh, and eighth grade levels. Each of these music classes meets twice a week, eight periods of music in all. The remainder of the teaching week is spent with my homeroom, the eighth grade. I teach the following subjects in my homeroom: arithmetic, social studies, reading, composition and related language arts, and health. The school day begins at eight thirty and runs until three fifteen. Sometimes it merely creeps. The genuine teaching duties are stimulating and highly rewarding for the most part. The numerous nonteaching duties and clerical duties definitely take the edge off the pleasure of being a teacher. . . .

A physical education teacher describes her work:

I teach physical education to boys and girls eight to fourteen years of age. I teach thirty-five class periods a week, twenty-eight of which are devoted to regular physical education activities, four to co-recreational programs for the seventh and eighth grade pupils, one to a gymnastics class, one to the school safety patrol which I sponsor, and one to keeping my records and equipment in good order. In addition I assist with the annual paper drive, present an assembly program once a year, direct the color guard, take charge of the boys' entrance, and serve as a member of the audio-visual aids committee, as cochairman of the community resources committee, as chairman of the standards of achievement committee, and as instructor at our school's after-school social center. I also serve as recording secretary and member of the executive board of the teachers' union. My listing of duties might leave the impression that teachers do quite a bit. They do!

Another teacher writes:

I am a teacher of industrial arts in an industrial arts department in a high school of twenty-six hundred pupils. I teach two classes of industrial arts pupils. The shop is general shop, each experience extending over six weeks. The two classes alternate experiences. I also teach two classes of sophomore printing of twenty-two pupils each. There are some juniors and seniors in these two groups. The pupils are of all kinds of abilities and offer all kinds of reasons for being in the class—from an intense interest to nothing-else-to-take. I also have an advanced vocational class which does much of the production printing of the school. . . .

The linotypes and presses require repair and maintenance that must be cared for by the teacher. The costs of jobs must be figured, charged, and recorded. Supplies of paper, ink, and other materials must be replenished as needed. Telephone calls on the status of the newspaper and other jobs frequently interrupt the work of the classes. Club sponsors and office personnel come into the shop often. Copy is handed in late, and finished jobs are expected overnight.

I like printing and I like teaching. There are no boring moments. . . . Each week I take home some work—papers to be corrected, orders to write, costs to be figured, jobs and projects to be planned. Each week I return to the school for an average of three hours to keep abreast of the work at the school shop that cannot be done during the day and, of course, cannot be taken home.

Before entering college I worked at the printing trade and I still do during the summer months. I keep in touch with the trade, earn additional income, and have the assurance that I can tell the principal "good-by" tonight and go out tomorrow and take my pick of ten jobs which pay more than teaching and require less work. But, then, I wouldn't be helping young people! I'd just be helping myself!

Personal description of a teacher's duties shows that the work of an individual teacher is unique. Instead of emphasizing similarities in the work of teachers, such descriptions tend to bring out the differences. Even when the same activity is reported, the approach, the time invested, and the manner of performing it tend to vary. One teacher, as a result of his interests, may emphasize some activities far more than others. The teacher's philosophy, interests, and abilities are related to the proportion of time invested in any activity. Usually the more favored activities are more efficiently performed.

A carefully written and fairly complete description of the work of a single teacher sets forth what the teacher believes important to report, not what the investigator thinks is important to observe. It gives a reasonably accurate picture of each teacher's work, but does not afford as definite a summation of duties as some of the other methods of study.

Studying Large Samplings by the Method of Vocational Analysis

This method has been borrowed from industry and the armed services where it has been used as a sort of measuring stick to select individuals who, in terms of personality and training, have the greatest promise of success with certain kinds of work.

In general, the method consists of three steps: (1) the duties involved in a particular vocation are itemized; (2) the relative difficulty of performing each of the duties is determined; and (3) the knowledge, skills, and habits necessary to a successful pursuit of the vocation are then determined. Appropriate instructional materials can then be prepared to teach an individual to meet successfully the demands of the job. Each of the steps calls for considerable interpretative skill. The method has proved very valuable for providing information about all the vocations—information that has been especially useful to those who formulate training programs.

The method should be used, however, with full recognition of its limitations. One shortcoming can be illustrated from the findings of one vocational analysis project. This project analyzed reports from over 6,000 classroom teachers who enumerated what they did while on their jobs. The activities reported numbered around 200,000! Those activities considered to be most significant were selected for more intensive study. They still numbered 1,001 items. They could not be further reduced and still give a realistic picture of the work of teachers. The list of duties is so extensive that it is of little value in providing a typical picture.

Although largely inappropriate for studying the work of any given teacher, the vocational analysis method has revealed certain general features of the work of teachers as a group. It has shown that the range of activities teachers engage in is enormous and that many of these activities are difficult and time-consuming. It has made clear why teachers, if they desire to become expertly proficient, must continue to study throughout their professional careers. Competence is not quickly developed. There is a continuously mounting hierarchy among the skills to be acquired. One competence becomes the foundation for building another, higher level of competence. Skills, however, are not accumulated as one fits bricks into a mounting wall.

Incidentally, educators have applied the vocational analysis method to the activities in which adults generally engage. These activities have then been classified and the results made the basis for planning the school curriculum. In Unit Four, in the study of aims, this approach is examined in more detail.

In enlarging the sampling, the various investigators have not found it practicable to make a complete vocational analysis. The various studies have used certain specialized techniques, each of which gives an incomplete but nevertheless helpful picture of the teacher's work. The more common techniques include the questionnaire, direct observation, verbal description, and time analysis.

1. The Questionnaire

The questionnaire is a device frequently used in the analysis of teaching. Many carefully selected and skillfully phrased questions are directed to the teacher. Each question can be answered simply, sometimes with a single word like *yes* or *no,* or a number. The questions are prepared in advance by the investigator and cover those aspects of the teacher's work that the investigator selects for study.

Questionnaire studies are convenient to tabulate, record, and summarize. The questionnaire is especially appropriate in determining what practices are current. Because of this, studies of teacher activities based on questionnaires are often called *status* studies. They have been helpful in revealing what activities give most difficulty, recur most often, and seem to persist over long periods of time. They are well adapted to showing what problems are peculiar to teaching a given subject or to teaching at a given grade level. The English teacher, the shop teacher, the kindergarten teacher, the eighth grade teacher—each encounters a range of varying problems. Even when the problems are approximately the same at different educational levels, dealing with each of them involves a different kind of teacher activity.

Questionnaires, like each of the other techniques, have certain weaknesses of which one must be aware when interpreting the information they provide. For example, if a teacher has a behavior problem in his classroom he cannot by a simple answer tell how he solved it. He may report how many behavior problems he has had, but his answer gives no indication of how serious each of them has been or how much time and energy he has given to the solution of each. If an English teacher makes a vivid presentation of a beautiful poem, gives it a striking interpretation, he cannot report on a questionnaire precisely what he did. Nor can he accurately report all the time he spent in preparation. The findings of a good questionnaire are revealing, but the picture provided is never complete.

2. Direct Observation

Direct observation may be applied to a group of teachers in much the same way that it is applied to an individual teacher. In this case an observer may extend the number of direct observations, or a team of observers may observe teachers working at different levels and in varying situations. Direct observation of the group has the same limitations as direct observation of the individual. As a method of mass study it suffers further because it is exceedingly time-consuming.

3. Verbal Description

The method of obtaining individual descriptions can be expanded to include any number of teachers teaching at any level of education or teaching any given subject. It is somewhat difficult to summarize verbal descriptions, and the interpretation of the results presents a special problem. The sampling, however, may be as wide as the investigator wishes to make it.

4. Time Analysis

The time analysis of activities may be used as an extension of the questionnaire, direct observation, or the analysis of individual

Where the teacher is, there is the classroom. These students, on a class trip to Washington, D.C., are studying firsthand the national government at work. Students often study their local and state governments on similar field trips. Parents frequently assist the teacher on such trips. (Wide World)

descriptions. The time given to the performance of a certain activity is recorded. As an observer notes what activity a teacher engages in, for instance, he also uses a stop watch and makes a record of the exact time spent on the activity. Or teachers may report on questionnaires their estimates of time they devote to the various activities they perform.

THE QUALITATIVE ELEMENT

Each of the techniques of discovering and reporting what a teacher does gives a picture of the work from a somewhat different perspective. In all the information gathered, however, one important element of the teacher's work, perhaps the most important feature, is more or less omitted—is almost simplified out of existence. This is the qualitative factor mentioned earlier. It is the one element that is, in large part, responsible for the great differences in

From earliest times to the present, great thinkers have directed their thinking toward the education of children. In 1416, a renowned discoverer of ancient learning, Poggio, found the complete text of Quintilian's *Institutes of Oratory* at a Swiss monastery in a dump heap in one of the towers of the abbey. The two books came to be viewed as summarizing all the pedagogical wisdom of the ancients. The following quotation from Quintilian shows the trend of his thinking about the successful qualities of the good teacher.

Let him therefore adopt a parental attitude to his pupils, and regard himself as the representative of those who have committed their children to his charge. Let him be free from vice himself and refuse to tolerate it in others. Let him be strict but not austere, genial but not too familiar: for austerity will make him unpopular, while familiarity breeds contempt. Let his discourse continually turn on what is good and honorable; the more he admonishes, the less he will have to punish. He must control his temper without however shutting his eyes to faults requiring correction: his instruction must be free from affectation, his industry great, his demands on his class continuous but not extravagant.

Reprinted by permission of the publishers from Marcus Fabius Quintilianus, *The Institutio Oratoria of Quintilian*, with English translation by H. E. Butler (Cambridge, Mass.: Harvard University Press, Loeb Classical Library edition, 1921), Vol. I, Book II, ii, paragraph 5, p. 213.

what teachers do. Two teachers covering the same subject may make identical assignments, but the two assignments are not qualitatively the same and may have differing effects upon how the pupils feel and what they learn. The same is true of giving tests, assigning marks, or any other activity.

Through observation we may sense this qualitative characteristic, or teachers' descriptions may reveal its presence; but no statistical tabulation, classification, or report can completely capture it. In making conclusions about what teachers do, using all the sources of information, we must recognize the importance of this factor and avoid oversimplification.

Qualitative differences stem from many factors, some of which do not lend themselves to ready analysis. The freedom that teachers in American schools have to use their own judgments about what shall be taught, how it shall be taught, and how the classroom should be managed is but one example. Teachers differ greatly in personality and in the kind of personal and professional philosophy that guides their teaching. They differ in social background, in edu-

At the close of a grading period, after a day's work, completion of pupil records is one of the time-consuming, routine teacher duties. (Hays from Monkmeyer)

cation, and in many other ways. They teach in vastly different situations. All such factors contribute to the encouragement of the qualitative differences so characteristic of teaching. As we discuss such subjects as the philosophy and aims of the teacher, subject matter, methods of teaching, and other topics, we shall become increasingly conscious of the causes and of the effects of the ever-present qualitative differences that are characteristic of teachers' work.

SUMMARY

What knowledge of the work of the teacher has Chapter 2 revealed? In commencing our overview of education in the United States, what details about what schoolteachers do can we now fill in?

In seeking to discover what teachers do, studies that use the method of vocational analysis are one source of information. We get a picture with a different perspective by turning to a teacher's own description of what he does. Another readily available source of fruitful information is direct observation, which allows us to capture some of the "feel" of the teaching, to get an appreciation of the essence of the pupil-teacher and other classroom relationships that elude tabulation and reporting, and to focus our study on a single teacher or particular factor.

From the many studies made we discover that the work of the teacher is highly complex and his duties cover a great range. For convenience, we group teacher activities into five classifications: (1) classroom instruction, (2) guidance, (3) staff functions, (4) community duties, and (5) professional activities. Such classifications are neither definite nor rigid in their boundaries. They are made in order to facilitate our thinking and to simplify our understanding.

It is evident that in reporting what teachers do it has not been possible to include the qualitative differences that mark the activities of any two or more teachers. This elusive and intangible element is present in all features of the entire school picture. It is influenced most dramatically by the teacher's philosophy, personality, training, and experience as manifest in his values, beliefs, and ideals.

In conclusion, then, we recognize that teaching is a collective name for many kinds of work and that it involves many kinds of activities. Describing the work that teachers do is somewhat analogous to analyzing the constituents of a bowl of soup. The soup is a mixture of a large number of ingredients. Not only are the ingredients separate; they are also heterogeneous in character. Each ingredient changes its original characteristic when it becomes part of the final dish. The ingredients that go to make up teaching are numerous, and, like the ingredients in the soup, they are heterogeneous in character. The work of the teacher, then, does not lend itself to simple description such as would be the case if we were describing the duties of a cook in baking a cake or of an operator in using a lathe. This study of what teachers do in American schools can be no more than preliminary—preliminary to further study, to a more detailed analysis, and to a broadening of interpretation that will continue throughout the book.

QUESTIONS

1. What are some reasons why the work of one teacher is never exactly like the work of another?

2. How do your own experiences in school contribute to or handicap your better understanding of the work of a classroom teacher? In what respects are your experiences probably atypical?

3. In describing a teacher's work, how can one give due recognition to the factor of excellence of performance?

4. What attitude should a beginning teacher assume toward the performance of routine duties?

5. What are some purposes served by classifying all that teachers do into broad categories? What undesirable effects may also result?

6. In the school, what are the functions of such specialists as the supervisor, guidance director, and school psychologist? How is the teacher's work affected by specialists in the school?

7. What has caused recent tendencies to increase the work load of classroom teachers?

PROJECTS

1. Interview a classroom teacher concerning the kind and amount of work he has done over a period of one week.

2. Observe a teacher teach a single class and describe the kind of preparation you think he made before teaching the class.

3. Write an essay of not more than five hundred words explaining why most teachers find teaching school an interesting and challenging occupation.

4. Write a letter to some highly successful teacher asking him to explain to you and the class the aspects of teaching he finds most challenging and the aspects he finds least challenging. Ask what advice he would like to give to one seriously considering entering the teaching profession.

3

How teachers qualify

How do teachers qualify to discharge their vital and varied responsibilities? Why and how do the states assure that teachers shall have minimum qualifications? How do teacher education institutions prepare teachers? What skills should one cultivate in order to be a successful teacher? What part do personality traits play in teaching success? How may an individual assess his potential teaching success?

QUALIFICATIONS IMPOSED BY SOCIETY

The teaching profession is different from other professions in that it is the *only* tax-supported profession; it is controlled and supported by the public. Society imposes certain minimum qualifications that individuals must meet before they are admitted to teaching. This policy of control over the teachers is exercised in part because society recognizes that the schools are vital to its welfare, survival, and progress. Society depends upon the schools for the transmission of many of the essentials of our culture. Many indispensable beliefs and skills and techniques are made available to

All the state universities have schools of education that are adequately housed, staffed, and equipped. Most conduct demonstration schools. This building, housing the offices of the faculty of the School of Education at Indiana University, is fairly typical. The School has a large enrollment of both undergraduate and graduate students. The number and kinds of services rendered are great and varied. The influence of such schools upon education in America can scarcely be assessed. (Indiana University)

children through the schools. Without transmission and preservation of such features, our culture could not survive. Society is aware that the responsibility is so important that it should be entrusted only to competent individuals, and it is to this end that society sets up some qualifications for teachers that it believes will assure a degree of teaching competence.

Society exercises a measure of control over teacher qualifications also in part because the public is determined to do what it can to insure that the huge amount of money invested in the schools be spent wisely. Society requires that the great single item in school costs—salary for school personnel—be paid only to individuals who have met minimum requirements. It hopes, thereby, to assure an adequate return for the money invested.

By imposing standards for admission to teaching, society also provides teachers with a measure of security and stability. It thereby adds to the attractiveness of teaching for capable people. By adding rewards of status and financial advantages to those within the profession who meet more exacting or more specialized professional requirements, encouragement is provided for development along lines that society considers desirable.

The state is the unit of government generally responsible for safeguarding minimum educational standards. Naturally, details of control over the qualifications of teachers vary from state to state. But by and large, state control is accomplished through two practices: certification of the teachers and accreditation of the institutions that educate the teachers. Certification brings the individual under the scrutiny of the state while accreditation gives the state an opportunity to influence the nature and quality of education the teacher receives. Control over teacher qualifications is the end sought in both cases.

Certification

In frontier times when local school boards certified teachers, the standards were, of course, very superficial, almost nonexistent. Later, district and county boards or their designated school authority took over the task of licensing teachers. In some states, by the end of the century, the county superintendent of schools periodically administered competitive examinations covering the various subjects taught in the elementary and high schools and issued certificates only to those who "passed" the examinations. Little or no emphasis was placed upon college attendance, and in some states graduation from the eighth grade was the only prerequisite. Since the beginning of the century upgrading the teaching profession has been a continuing policy, and controlling entrance to the profession through licensing has been one means of accomplishing this. In line with the principle that the state is the unit of school administration, local licensing of teachers has been discontinued, and now in all fifty states the state authority has taken over this function.

Selected high school students tutor their elementary school counterparts and thus experience a "feel" for what is involved in learning and teaching. (Seattle School District)

Although an improvement over licensing teachers by local school authorities, centralizing licensing of teachers in the state educational authority has not eliminated the perplexing problems due to lack of uniformity in standards among the states. Despite a great variation among the states, however, there is general agreement about the following:

1. Authority for the certification of teachers is centralized in the state department of education.
2. Certificates are issued for definite subject fields or a specified grade level.
3. Certificates must be renewed periodically.
4. A bachelor's degree is a minimum requirement for a teaching certificate.
5. Specific courses in education and a definite number of semester hours in a subject matter teaching field or fields are required.

Reference to the map, Fig. 3.1, shows that in 1964 all the states required the bachelor's degree for entrance to high school teaching and 44 states required it for entrance to elementary school teaching. Three states required a fifth year of training for a high school teaching certificate. Although not shown by the map, there has been a tendency to increase the subject matter requirements for teaching at all grade levels.

Judging from present trends in certification, the standards of competence demanded for entrance to the teaching profession will continue to rise, perhaps slowly because in some regions citizens still have the attitude typical of the frontier and expressed well by the often quoted statement attributed to George Bernard Shaw: "Those who can, do; those who can't, teach."

Certification of teachers is but one avenue to upgrading teaching competence. As the following discussion shows, accreditment of institutions preparing teachers is another. A third is for the profession itself, through its own professional organizations, to assume responsibility for guaranteeing the public adequate standards of competence. A fourth is for the individual institutions that train teachers to assume a greater degree of responsibility for improving their teacher education.

Accreditation

In exerting control over the qualifications of teachers by a process of accreditation of teacher education institutions, the state authority demands that a college or university to be accredited must offer a prescribed kind of teacher education program. This is actually an extension of control by certification. After setting up training qualifications for teaching, the state requires that the teacher education institutions provide the facilities and curriculums that will permit students to fulfill the stipulated requirements.

Some college staff members resent state accrediting policies. They argue that the state has encroached upon functions that belong to the institutions, that formulating a program for teacher education should be left to the discretion of the institutions, that the state's dictation of the program shows a lack of confidence in the ability of those who administer higher institutions. They do not maintain that the final control of the education of teachers in the state is not a proper function of the state. Rather, the argument is over whether the state makes wise use of its accrediting authority.

The accreditment of institutions seems to be peculiar to American higher education and is, perhaps, an outgrowth of our system of government. Teaching is only one of many fields subject to accreditation, and the official state authority is not the only agency to accredit, or pass upon whether a teacher-training institution is fully qualified to prepare teachers. Different criteria are used by various

FIG. 3.1   MINIMUM REQUIREMENTS OF STATES FOR LOWEST
REGULAR TEACHING CERTIFICATE FOR BEGINNING
ELEMENTARY-SCHOOL TEACHERS, AS OF JULY 1, 1964

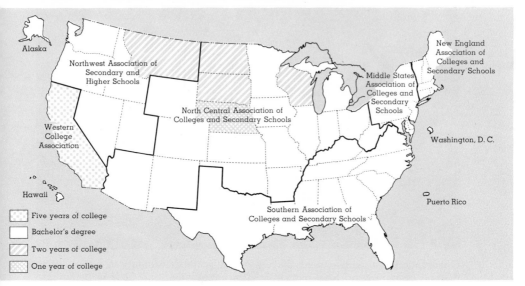

(Data from *A Manual on Certification Requirements for School Personnel in the United States*, issued by the National Commission on Teacher Education and Professional Standards, National Education Association, 1964)

agencies. Although, except for a state department of education, each of the accreditation agencies is an extralegal authority, the lists they prepare of acceptable institutions are usually accepted by legal bodies as equivalent to the lists prepared by legal authorities.

Among the many agencies outside the state authority that make decisions that have a bearing upon the qualifications of teachers, two influential national and regional associations are selected as illustrative.

The North Central Association of Colleges and Secondary Schools is an example of a *voluntary* regional accrediting organization that influences standards in a multistate region. Rigid standards, often higher than those set by the states, must be met by any school before it may become a member of this association. So influential has the association become that, to the general public, a school that does not hold membership is an inferior educational organization. The association has also tried to guard against the efforts of some organized groups to lower teacher qualifications.

Observation and subsequent discussion of pattern teaching is an effective method of improving teaching skills. The pattern teaching here is being presented by a third grade teacher. (Seattle School District)

The association has not concerned itself with standards for elementary education; these standards have remained completely under state control. Since the North Central Association and similar regional associations include colleges and secondary schools only, their accreditation practices have tended to add to the prestige of high school teachers and, in some ways, to lower the prestige of elementary teachers. In general, however, the effect of accrediting associations of this kind has been salutary. They have not attempted to infringe on the state's right to set standards. They have sought only to raise the standards of education given in public and nonpublic schools.

In 1949 the presidents of a number of colleges and universities became concerned with the growing number of accrediting agencies for higher institutions and they established the National Commission on Accrediting. In the words of the Executive Secretary, "the commission is serving as a coordinating agency through the labyrinth of accreditation; it is continually making suggestions for improvement in this frequently misunderstood educational activity. . . ." At the present writing, membership of the commission includes more than 1,200 colleges and universities located in many sections of the United States, and 7 national organizations such as the Association of American Universities. Serving as a coordinating agent, the commission recognizes 6 regional associations and 23 professional associations. Among the professional associations recognized is the influential National Council for Accreditation of Teacher Education, usually called the NCATE. The NCATE was established by the NEA in 1952.

In 1956 the National Commission on Accrediting officially recognized the NCATE as most directly responsible for determining the accreditation procedures for teacher education programs. The plan is to have this association evaluate and accredit a qualified teacher education program. The states would then automatically license all graduates who successfully complete the accredited program. At the present writing 24 states have agreed to this.

All the problems of accreditation have not been solved nor can a complete analysis be made here. Efforts are being made on a broad scale to discover proper methods of guaranteeing academic standards, of encouraging, even coercing, institutions to maintain certain minimum standards in the education of teachers, and of coordinating and approving the activities of the many voluntary agencies involved in accreditation of teacher education programs.

TEACHER PREPARATION

For years all the states have attempted to improve the quality of education by improving the programs of teacher training, by assuming the authority for accrediting teacher education institutions, and by imposing more demanding certificate requirements. A college degree has, in most states, become a requirement for entrance to teaching. Furthermore, degree candidates must take specific courses deemed essential for teacher preparation.

Although there is some difference of opinion concerning the details of a desirable program of teacher education, there is general agreement that it should be at least four years in length and, ideally, that it should be a five-year program. There is also general agreement that the program should be *balanced*—made up of three broad classifications of subject matter: (1) background education—the broad cultural setting, (2) specialized subject matter, and (3) courses in professional education.

Background Education

There is no disagreement about the fact that a teacher should have a broad cultural background, should be a "cultured" person. There are, however, two schools of thought regarding how a prospective teacher can best achieve this. The traditional approach is to accomplish a "liberal" education by study in traditional fields. That there has been widespread dissatisfaction with this kind of effort to provide a satisfactory background for teachers in preparation is indicated by the fact that so many colleges have experimented with new types of courses and with improved methods of teaching.

Most of the experiments have followed an approach based upon a belief that the broad cultural background can be achieved more effectively through "general" education. Instead of pursuing study in traditional fields and taking courses designed partly to be a portion of the course of study for specialists in that subject area, a prospective teacher takes a course or courses that include subject matter from a number of closely related fields. These courses, variously called "integrated," "basic," "orientation," "survey," or "core" courses, encompass resources from all fields within a broad area. For instance, a course called "Basic Science" might be taught by a professor of mathematics together with a professor of biology, a professor of chemistry, and a professor of geology. A course called "Modern Society" might encompass resources from history, sociology, political science, economics, and psychology.

Agreement has never been reached as to whether the objectives of preparing a teacher with a broad cultural background are more successfully met through the "liberal education" approach or through the "general education" approach. No valid way of determining the extent to which the objectives of a broad cultural background are being achieved has been devised.

Regardless of the organization of the subject matter, the quality of the background afforded the prospective teacher depends upon the quality of teaching the student receives in college.

Specialized Subject Matter

For prospective high school teachers, specialization in a particular field is obligatory. The state usually requires from 24 to 36 semester hours of work in a given subject or field for certification.

Years of special training are necessary to become an art teacher. (Illinois State University)

This amounts to from three to four years of continuous study. Leaders concerned with improving present high school programs urge states to require that teachers prepare themselves in broad fields corresponding to the major areas taught in secondary schools. Some colleges have responded to such requests. Some of them, for instance, permit students to complete majors in areas like general science and social studies. These subjects harmonize with the classifications of subject matter found in secondary and elementary schools. Some offer courses like "Mathematics for the Intermediate Teacher" or "Basic Mathematics."

Deciding the best type of specialized preparation for elementary teachers presents special difficulties to the colleges. School officials frequently expect an elementary teacher to be prepared in every basic and special field of the elementary curriculum besides being competent in the areas of child growth and development and human relations. Some state authorities have made the elementary school certification requirements so specific that the curriculum of the colleges has been practically dictated by a state educational authority.

Whatever the final answer to the question of required specialized training, there is wide agreement that the fields included in

Student teaching is a college professional course highly valued by prospective teachers. Under the supervision of a sympathetic, experienced teacher, this student is teaching a chemistry course for the first time. After a few trials the expectant, somewhat curious attitude shown in the faces of the pupils will disappear and the student teacher will become accepted as a regular part of the school organization. (Seattle School District)

the teacher education program should be carefully selected for the purpose of improving potential teaching competences. In other words, although the specialized content of the teacher education program should be balanced in relation to the broad cultural courses and the professional courses, it should also be designed to give the teacher professional competence in those special fields of study which he intends to teach.

Professional Preparation

While the academic education of a teacher, including general and specialized courses, is basic, it is not the whole of his essential preparation. Much of the professional knowledge and skill that is necessary for entrance to teaching must be acquired in professional courses given in college. These courses are, in many states, specified in state regulations, and thereby some uniformity about this portion of the prospective teacher's program is assured. However, there is much difference of opinion about what part of the total time of training should be devoted to professional education and whether courses should begin with the freshman year or at some later stage in the program. Professional courses are sometimes considered to be so theoretical as to make them more suitable for graduate than undergraduate study.

The Commission on Teacher Education recommends that "strictly professional elements should be allocated from one-eighth to one-sixth of the time available in a four- or five-year program of teacher preparation." Most colleges accept this division of time. Usually out of the total of 120 semester hours of college work required for graduation, from 15 to 20 semester hours of professional courses, including special methods and student teaching, are required for high school teachers and from 20 to 30 hours for elementary teachers. Colleges differ, however, in their specific requirements and in the nature of the content and organization of professional courses.

In the area of teacher preparation perhaps the greatest agreement is in the matter of practical experience. It is uniformly agreed that the individual and class assignments of a prospective teacher should include observations in the classrooms, that the prospective teacher should participate in a wealth of activities with children in both school and community situations, and that he should engage in actual student teaching. It is only through supervised full-time work with pupils over a period of time that a student gains a "feel" for the teacher's task and can assess his own potentialities in relation to the task. Student teaching usually comes in the senior year. Despite agreement that teaching should be included in a prospective teacher's program, there is no general agreement on how much time students should spend teaching, in which fields they should teach, and when they should begin teaching.

Sometimes, usually during a fifth year of preparation and as a part of graduate study, a program of teaching internship is offered. This is teaching, full- or part-time, in a regular public school classroom with the approval and under the close supervision of the teacher education institution. The program provides an opportunity to combine theoretical with practical work while completing requirements for a master's degree. Some feel, however, that a beginning teacher who has complete teaching responsibility for a group of children needs to give all his time to teaching during his initial years and that the effort to combine teaching with graduate study and seminar attendance works to the disadvantage of both the practical and theoretical phases of an internship plan. Whether an internship plan is a part of the teacher program or not, the trend is toward planning the total teacher preparation program in terms of five years' work.

SELECTION OF PROSPECTIVE TEACHERS

The current shortage of teachers makes a consideration of selection somewhat theoretical. One cannot make choices when the number of suitable candidates is too limited. In the long run, the number of capable people who will be attracted to teaching will increase only if teaching standards are high enough to win respect and if prestige, security, and financial rewards are attractive to qualified people.

Unfortunately, research has provided neither the measures for making predictions of success nor a scientific basis for deciding how selections should be made. We cannot, for instance, with accuracy define what successful teaching is, or specifically identify the personality traits that are the attributes of the successful teacher. Our selection must therefore be largely subjective and must be based on such sources of information as interviews, letters of recommendation, standard tests, physical examinations, marks in college courses, and the like. Even with data concerning scholastic achievement, special aptitudes, attitude toward teaching, and experience with youth groups, we still cannot, with assurance, predict in advance what teaching ability an individual possesses. Subjective judgments are liable to considerable error. This does not mean, however, that we cannot recognize that some factors are more favorable to producing teaching success than others.

Perhaps the most important qualifying factor in determining success is the individual's interest in teaching. Unfortunately, it cannot be measured. A student who has an interest in teaching, ideally founded on some kind of firsthand experience in working with children and youth, will be motivated to plan wisely with his advisers in selecting the most fruitful teacher education program. He will be alert to the opportunities to develop necessary basic

The new teacher enters upon her work with poise and confidence, knowing that she is adequately prepared and fully qualified. (Hays from Monkmeyer)

abilities appropriate to the field of his choice. If his institution does not offer the necessary opportunities, he will discover them in some other institution.

The selection of students to pursue the teaching profession is a process that continues during the entire period of preparation. It is not one act completed when the student is admitted to college. Continuous study *by* the student is accompanied with continuous study *of* the student so that a redirection of the student's program can be made at any time when warranted. The student's welfare is kept in mind but so also is the welfare of all those whom he may teach. Counseling by the professional staff is an important aspect of selection. An attempt is made to aid the student in matching his potentialities with his choice of teaching field and to eliminate only those who obviously possess disabling qualifications such as, for instance, emotional instability or low ability to succeed in academic work. In selection, the college staff emphasizes positive factors related to the growth and education of the student rather than the negative factor of denial of the right to continue.

Although all higher institutions have admission officers, the process of making a reasonable selection of potential teachers is a responsibility of the staffs that prepare them. In this way teachers themselves influence the standards applied to the selection of those who will qualify and enter the profession.

PLACEMENT OF TEACHERS

After completing the teacher preparation program and qualifying for certification, the prospective teacher faces the important step of placement. All teacher education institutions counsel their students about placement and recommend them for positions. Most of them maintain placement bureaus. Graduates are assisted in writing letters of application and in making personal applications. It is, however, the superintendent of a local school system, a school trustee, or someone else officially charged by a local school system with the responsibility of employing the staff who makes the final offer.

Commercial teachers' agencies, organizations that make a business of placing teachers and that charge a commission for their services, also may be utilized by the student. If a candidate wishes to teach in a certain school system, it is considered ethical to write a letter of inquiry that includes information about his training, experience, and interests.

PERSONAL QUALIFICATIONS

Problem of Generalization

We have indicated that it is impossible to define in detail the personality characteristics of the successful teacher. One must use terms that are general, that call for considerable subjective interpretation, and that are related more or less to standard virtues about which there can be little disagreement. We can, for instance, agree that a sympathetic personality is desirable. Can we define a sympathetic personality? Can we agree on the specific traits that must always, or generally, be identified with this personality? Numerous studies of what constitutes first-rate teaching have re-

APPLYING FOR A TEACHING POST
1871

"Want to be a school-master, do you? You? Well, what would *you* do in Flat Crick deestrick, *I'd* like to know? Why, the boys have driv off the last two, and licked the one afore them like blazes. You might teach a summer school, when nothin' but children come. But I 'low it takes a right smart *man* to be a school-master in Flat Crick in the winter. They'd pitch you out of doors, sonny, neck and heels, afore Christmas."

. . . The impression made by these ominous remarks was emphasized by the glances which he received from Jack Means' two sons. The older one eyed him from the top of his brawny shoulders with that amiable look which a big dog turns on a little one before shaking him. Ralph Hartsook had never thought of being measured by the standard of muscle. This notion of beating education into young savages in spite of themselves dashed his ardor.

From Edward Eggleston, *The Hoosier Schoolmaster: A Story of Backwoods Life in Indiana,* 1871.

TODAY

While the policies with respect to employment vary considerably from district to district, the following practices are not uncommon.

1. Most teacher education institutions now help the student to obtain his initial appointment. Many colleges have placement offices that specialize in teacher placement. They collect information about the student, counsel him, and direct him in his attempts to obtain his first teaching position.

2. Some superintendents of schools visit the colleges and personally seek out and employ the student. Many administrators look upon this as their best opportunity to improve the quality of teaching in their school systems.

3. Many school systems print attractive brochures about the schools and the community that are sent to all applicants for teaching positions. The administrative policies of the school system are plainly set forth.

The trend in the employment of teachers is toward having the school seek the teacher rather than having the teacher seek the school.

sulted in a list of virtues expressing more of a hope than an expectation.

The difficulty of defining personal qualifications necessary to teaching success is further compounded because, strictly speaking, teaching is not a single occupation. It is a large family of occupations. Opportunities for specialization in teaching are numerous. Obviously the requirements for a third-grade teacher will not be identical with those for a teacher at the graduate school level, for a teacher-librarian, or for a teacher of physically handicapped children. Even positions that appear, at first, to be the same may make widely varying demands depending upon variations in total school responsibilities and the makeup of the pupil enrollment.

Minimum personal qualifications required are influenced, too, by the times. In one generation, one set of qualifications is deemed sufficient, while in another, such qualifications are considered inadequate. Radio, television, movies, maps, globes, improved textbooks—all help to change the character of teaching and to modify teacher requirements. New knowledge about such matters as individual differences, special abilities, or the nature of growth change the nature of teaching, modify the standards of successful teaching, and influence the personal qualifications needed.

Studies

Despite the difficulties, numerous studies have been made in an effort to shed some light on our understanding of what characteristics, in general, seem to be related to teaching success. The studies have been principally of two kinds—those that approach the problem by asking pupils to report the characteristics of the teachers they considered most successful and those that base conclusions on reports from school administrators and professors of school administration.

One investigator analyzed the opinions of a total of 30,000 pupils.[1] He discovered that those characteristics most persistently cherished by pupils were: fairness, cheerfulness, businesslike procedures when teaching, ability to obtain pupil response, and skillful methods of teaching. Under the classification of fairness, for example, the pupils wished that praise and criticism be based upon fact, that the teacher show no favoritism, that grading be fair, that the opinions of pupils be respected, and that the teacher reveal at all times a willingness to help pupils. Pupils did not like teachers who consistently found fault, nagged, scolded, used sarcasm, and otherwise reacted negatively to that which the pupils were attempt-

[1] Dwight E. Beecher, *The Evaluation of Teaching* (Syracuse, N.Y.: Syracuse University Press, 1949), pp. 41–63.

Teachers in preparation are often required to complete tasks they will have their pupils perform. In so doing they can anticipate and appreciate some of the difficulties their pupils may meet. These student teachers are operating a teaching machine they will subsequently use with pupils. (The School of Teaching Arts, University of Portland)

ing to do. They seemed greatly to appreciate the teacher who had what they thought to be a wholesome sense of humor.

Studies based on reports from school administrators and professors of school administration are legion. In general, the most impressive fact emphasized by the findings is that only a very low correlation between any single personality trait and teaching success can be discovered.

Studies by psychologists have been devoted to the relation of personality traits to success in various lines of endeavor. They have emphasized that a combination of traits is vitally related to performance. However, it is not always possible to state what this combination actually is. Indeed, many different combinations may be equally successful. A weakness in one trait may be compensated for by strength in another. In focusing attention upon the individual it is easy to forget this and to overemphasize the importance of some one outstanding personality trait.

Because it is impossible to identify any single ability or trait

Many studies have been made to discover what traits or personal qualities pupils consider characteristic of the teachers they like best and those they like least. A pioneering investigation by Professor F. W. Hart of the responses of several thousand high school students is summarized in the following table.

HIGHEST RANKING TRAITS OF THE "BEST LIKED" TEACHERS

1. Is helpful with school work, explains lessons and assignments clearly and thoroughly, and uses examples in teaching.
2. Cheerful, happy, good-natured, jolly, has a sense of humor and can take a joke.
3. Human, friendly, companionable, "one of us."
4. Interested in and understands pupils.
5. Makes work interesting, creates a desire to work, makes class work a pleasure.
6. Strict, has control of the class, commands respect.
7. Impartial, shows no favoritism, has no "pets."
8. Not cross, crabby, grouchy, nagging, or sarcastic.
9. "We learned the subject."
10. A pleasing personality.

HIGHEST RANKING TRAITS OF THE "LEAST LIKED" TEACHERS

1. Too cross, crabby, grouchy, never smiles, nagging, sarcastic, loses temper, "flies off the handle."
2. Not helpful with school work, does not explain lessons and assignments, not clear, work not planned.
3. Partial, has "pets" or favored students, and "picks on certain pupils."
4. Superior, aloof, haughty, "snooty," overbearing, does not know you out of class.
5. Mean, unreasonable, "hard boiled," intolerant, ill mannered, too strict.
6. Unfair in marking and grading, unfair in tests and examinations.
7. Inconsiderate of pupils' feelings, bawls out pupils in the presence of classmates, pupils are afraid and ill at ease and dread class.
8. Not interested in pupils and does not understand them.
9. Unreasonable assignments and home work.
10. Too loose in discipline, no control of class, does not command respect.

From F. W. Hart, *Teachers and Teaching* (New York: The Macmillan Company, 1934), pp. 131, 250–251.

that is principally responsible for success or to determine whether training will lead to the development of some required combination of abilities, our discussion of personal qualifications is developed in terms of five broad classifications of qualities: (1) native intelligence, (2) social intelligence, (3) special abilities, (4) physical traits, and (5) facility of expression. These classifications have often been divided and subdivided. They are, however, fairly representative of classifications generally accepted.

Native Intelligence

Intelligence tests, perhaps the best measure of native ability known to us, seem to measure the individual's aptitude for scholastic work, verbal learning, and problem solving. Teaching involves considerable mental work. Other things being equal, then, it may be assumed that native intelligence is related to success in teaching. Studies indicate that, at least to some extent, this is true. The degree of relationship, however, is unknown. The most that can be said is that success in teaching is related to a number of factors of which intelligence seems to be one.

As discussed in Chapter 16, intelligence tests are applicable only to children under 16 years of age. It is the custom to supplement them in the early years with achievement tests, and after the elementary school, to rely wholly upon various kinds of standardized achievement tests, the assumption being, of course, that test scores on achievement tests are closely related to native intelligence.

The importance of native intelligence, or of any other trait, is always relative to the total personality. Perhaps scores on intelligence tests can be best used to establish a critical minimum point, say the point that marks the average of the intelligence scores made by the population at large. The higher the scores one makes on such a scale, the more certain it is that he possesses enough intelligence to succeed at teaching. Below a certain minimum point other personality factors cannot sufficiently compensate.

In deciding the level or field of teaching in which one has the best chances of success, those fields that call for a higher level of scholastic work, that demand greater facility in expression, and that call for a greater application of ability at problem solving will tend to require a higher minimum native intelligence.

Scholastic achievement as revealed in marks received in school is related to native intelligence and will give a prospective teacher a clue to his native intelligence. One who has great difficulty in his own school work probably should not teach.

Social Intelligence

Teaching is always concerned with helping people to grow in maturity and develop desirable responses to various social situations. Behavior is primarily social. The one who teaches others must himself, to a reasonable degree, possess what the psychologists call social intelligence. He must exhibit social competence. Social intelligence cannot, of course, be separated from native intelligence or from any of the other personality traits.

The social competences associated with successful teaching include capacity for leadership, tactfulness in working closely with others, sensitivity to the needs and wants of those with whom one works. There are no techniques to measure the degree to which an individual possesses social intelligence. Only through intimate personal acquaintance can one make a subjective appraisal of what the effectiveness of training and experience in the development of this qualification might be.

Special Abilities

It is not difficult to recognize individuals who have unusual artistic ability, musical ability, mathematical ability, mechanical ability, or some other similar special ability. Certain people, for example, delight in working with numbers and develop mathematical skills with ease. Obviously, a special ability would enhance an individual's interest and success in teaching any subject related to his special ability.

Physical Traits

Because teaching taxes physical strength, it is generally accepted that physical vigor and good health are necessary to teaching effectiveness. Supply of energy, appearance, and quality of voice are all believed to have some bearing upon the quality of teaching. There is little evidence, however, that any particular type of physical structure or amount of physical vigor is essential to success in teaching. As is true with all the other traits, various physical traits must all be considered in relation to each other and to the entire personality.

Facility of Expression

Regardless of the field or the level of a teacher's work, he is always aided by his fluency in the use of symbols or upon what is sometimes called his verbal ability. The demand for this ability is almost constant although some teaching positions place a higher premium upon it than others. Explaining, expressing original thought, interpreting, advising, giving directions—the effectiveness of these and many other activities depends, in part, upon the teacher's facility of expression. This is an ability that can be developed, largely through training and persistent practice. The teacher who is apt in his choice of words and phrases, who gives vivid illustrations, who speaks "trippingly on the tongue" is a teacher who has a quality among his repertoire of qualifications that is valuable indeed.

Combination of Abilities

None of the abilities classified above and designated basic in teaching is an entity. Success in teaching seems to be related to all of them, but the degree of relationship for all teachers can only be guessed. The relationship undoubtedly varies with the entire teaching situation including the teaching field and the grade level. In some teaching situations a woman of small stature and great intelligence would have less chance of success than a less intelligent man built like a professional heavyweight boxer. Situation makes a difference. The concept of what a fine teacher is continuously takes on new meaning in different times and places.

PREDICTING TEACHING SUCCESS

In considering whether it would be wise for an interested individual to enter teaching, it is well to consider all the qualities—native intelligence, social intelligence, special abilities, physical traits, and facility of expression. Four years of college study, carefully planned to meet the individual's particular needs and earnestly pursued, can contribute significantly to improving the combination of traits that characterize the student when he first enters the program.

A pleasant, friendly personality is needed to teach well. (Roy Stevens, Ford Foundation)

The most accurate way to predict success in teaching and to test abilities and combinations of abilities is through experience in student teaching or in activities closely related to teaching—working with children in clubs, teaching Sunday school, or counseling in boys' or girls' camps. How one works in the classroom and shoulders teaching responsibility will, in say three years' time, establish whether one possesses the basic abilities needed for successful teaching. Even here, however, an initial failure does not prove that success is impossible. Some great teachers have been failures in their initial attempts.

SUMMARY

By setting standards for teachers as a condition for granting teaching certificates, the state attempts to protect the public against substandard education and the teaching profession from infiltration of the inferior and the poorly prepared. States also control the quality of teaching through their accreditation policies for teacher education institutions. In addition, schools themselves have banded into voluntary associations that cut across state lines and that have established standards for the schools to meet as conditions to membership. Their standards do not apply to levels of education below the high school.

In qualifying, the prospective teacher receives his college education through three classifications of subject matter. One is referred to as courses for background education. Another is made up of specialized courses that are related to what the teacher will teach. In the third are professional courses that point directly to the vocation of teaching. While progress has been made toward improving courses pursued by prospective teachers, marked agreement as to what the curriculum should be has yet to be reached.

Native intelligence, social intelligence, special abilities, physical traits, and facility of expression seem to be positively related to success in teaching. There is, however, no stereotype of the successful teacher. The key to success is not found in one or several personality traits but in the combination of all the traits in a total personality.

QUESTIONS

1. What advantages may accrue to the teaching profession from the imposition of minimum standards of qualification by society?
2. When may minimum standards of qualification be inimical to the cause of good education?
3. In what ways may a state legislature misuse its authority to establish minimum standards of qualification for teachers?
4. How can the legislatures of the various states deal with the problem of encouraging free interflow of teachers between states?
5. Why have voluntary accrediting agencies arisen in the different geographical sections of the country?
6. Why have voluntary accrediting agencies concerned themselves mainly with standards at the high school and college levels? How has the teaching profession been affected by this policy?
7. Why have the colleges in America not agreed upon what constitutes a satisfactory background education?
8. What are some of the difficulties colleges face in offering suitable content courses for elementary teachers? For junior high school teachers? For, say, teachers of social studies in senior high schools?
9. What are the principal differences between the content of a professional education course and a specialized content course?
10. How can stricter selective policies be made effective in the occupational field of teaching?
11. What is the responsibility of American society in upgrading its teaching profession?
12. In view of the fact that there are over 2,000,000 teachers in the teaching profession, how selective, in your opinion, can teacher education institutions become?

13. Considering the number of teachers in the teaching profession, what responsibilities do college teachers need to assume for the development of outstanding teaching skills?

PROJECTS

1. Study the official certification requirements for teaching in your state. Give your personal evaluation of the requirements in: (*a*) background education, (*b*) specialized subject matter, (*c*) professional subject matter.
2. Describe an outstanding teacher you have known in terms of his personal qualifications for teaching.
3. For one week note your own speech inadequacies. Outline for yourself a speech improvement program. Follow this program for one week and make a note of the results. You may substitute another qualification if you desire.
4. Write your reactions to the Conant recommendation which reads as follows:

   For certification purposes the state should require only (a) that a candidate hold a baccalaureate degree from a legitimate college or university . . . ; (b) that he hold a specially endorsed teaching certificate from a college or university which, in issuing the official document, attests that the institution as a whole considers the person adequately prepared to teach in a designated field and grade level.

5. Contrast the effect of the Illinois certification requirement with the effect of the requirement as recommended by Conant. The Illinois requirement reads as follows:

   Graduates of Illinois institutions of higher learning in approved entitlement programs for elementary, high school, or special certificates and graduates as recommended by out-of-state NCATE institutions use the programs certified by the institution, providing application is made within a period of three years following graduation.

CHAPTER   4

The teacher
and his profession

This chapter is concerned with such questions as: What is a profession? How do professional groups differ from other vocational groups? How does the teaching profession differ from other professions? How are teachers affected by being members of the teaching profession? What standards are imposed on teachers? How were the professional standards that apply to teaching derived?

America's social well-being and its future progress depend, in considerable degree, upon that small proportion of its population that is commonly classified as professional. While no one of the professions is more important to the national welfare than any of the others, it is true that the achievements of all are dependent upon how efficiently the teaching group performs its functions. All, including the teaching profession, must rely upon the education their members receive from the teachers in the schools.

The American public and its teachers are "natural partners." And as teachers must be aware of the implications of membership in their profession, so the public must recognize the impact that the profession has on general welfare. Together, they must work toward policies that strengthen both.

WHAT IS A PROFESSION?

Difficulties of Definition

In attempting to define a profession, to set up criteria to distinguish a profession from other occupational groups, significant difficulties are encountered. The word "profession" is loosely used. Even in a college textbook in sociology, for instance, the gambling profession and other illicit professions are mentioned. When we speak of certain professions as "full-fledged," we imply that some are more professional than others. Many vocational groups claim professional status and the number continues to increase. The oldest of the professions—medicine, law, and the ministry—have been joined by other groups seeking and achieving, in some degree, recognition as professions: teachers, engineers, pharmacists, dentists, nurses, social workers, architects, and, more recently, journalists, accountants, and others. The boundary between professional and nonprofessional occupational groups is, in fact, so hazy that the Bureau of the Census has refrained from defining the term "profession."[1]

The attitudes of the American people toward a vocational group, like the journalists for instance, determine whether the desires and efforts of the group to be accorded professional status will be successful. If the public recognizes the importance of the group, has an uncommon regard for the training, knowledge, and skill that membership in the group requires, and highly respects the relatively few people who engage in the occupation, then they may accord with the desire of the occupation to have the title of profession.

In one sense, then, the public decides when a group is a profession. The number of groups recognized as professions changes somewhat in relation to the demands for particular services. For instance, national statistics on employment opportunities reveal current shortages in engineering and an unfilled demand for physicists and

---

[1] For an able explanation of the common elements between professions and other leading occupations, see Talcott Parsons, *Essays in Sociological Theory* (rev. ed.; New York: The Macmillan Company, 1954), Chap. 2, "The Professions and Social Structure."

chemists. Members of these fields are striving for recognition as professions. That their services are in strong demand adds to the promise of success in achieving professional status.

Despite the confusion over the meaning of the word "profession," there are certain characteristics typical of, and more or less unique with, professions.

Organization

Like some other occupational groups, a profession is an organization that regulates admission of members, exerts controls over them, and secures for them certain rights and privileges. Historically, professions have been initiated when those practicing a technique or craft that required special training desired to be set apart and identified as the persons so specially equipped. For this purpose they formed associations, limiting membership to individuals with minimum qualifications. By excluding the unqualified, they guaranteed their own competence and secured public recognition of their competence. In addition, they set up standards of conduct required for continued membership. In this way they sought to guarantee honor and exclude not only the incompetent but also the unscrupulous. Having established their membership, the professions sought next to improve the status of their members. Since the relation between status and remuneration is a close one, the professions gave attention to remuneration among other factors.

Nature of Work

The dictionary says that the body of persons in a profession is engaged in a calling that involves special mental and other attainments. The word "calling" conveys the idea of a vocation that summons or appeals to those who enter because they recognize the social importance of the work to be done. This recognition helps them to do the work better and to get satisfaction from doing it well. Again we see that the line of demarcation between a profession and another vocational group need not be clear-cut. Certainly a vocational group may also be social-minded and, on the other hand, a professional group may de-emphasize its social responsibility. In general, however, it is the professional group that gives greatest deliberate stress to its opportunities and responsibilities to render service that contributes to public welfare.

The teacher-to-be is willing to devote much time and thought and money to adequate preparation partly because he recognizes that the work of the teaching profession is socially significant—that teaching is a calling. As a calling, a profession should seek improvements of benefit to the public as zealously as it seeks improvements of benefit only to the profession or to individuals within the profession. A profession is distinguished from other vocational groups in this stress upon social perspective, in its emphasis upon the dedication of its members to public service.

A profession is somewhat distinguished also in that it involves work that is generally more mental than manual. Members of a profession must seek a constant flow of ideas from the seminar, from the laboratory, from communication within the profession. Such intellectual demands call for a liberal education as a part of the preservice preparation. Teachers and those in other professions, too, must have broad and basic understandings. Every teacher should strive to secure a broad cultural education, not only in order to live a rich, meaningful personal life, but also in order to be intellectually prepared for professional membership.

Entrance Requirements

Certain standards must be met by those who seek entrance to a profession. In the case of the teaching profession, standards for entrance are, in the final phase, established by the state and embodied in certification laws. The state educational authority, however, works closely with leaders in the profession and with those in higher institutions responsible for administering teacher education programs.

The nation has had to learn that in order to provide the manpower necessary in certain professional fields, concerted efforts are required to maintain reasonable standards of admission as well as to make the conditions of work attractive to able personnel. Throughout the United States there is adequate and capable manpower to answer the national demand for teachers and, at the same time, to maintain high standards of admission. But the American public has not been sufficiently concerned to eliminate those conditions that disparage a teaching career in the eyes of capable men and women who can meet high professional qualifications.

HOW IS THE TEACHING PROFESSION DIFFERENT?

While all the professions have some features in common, they differ in the amounts and kinds of preparation required, in personnel, remuneration, security provisions, and the like. The teaching profession has certain unique characteristics related to function, control, support, size, and the sex of its membership. These differences necessitate a special approach by the profession to the attainment of a higher level of professionalization.

Function

The primary function of the teaching profession is stated in its name—teaching. The schools of the nation are structured to encourage good teaching. Teachers are selected in terms of their potential ability to perform well, school buildings are planned to encourage expert teaching, and citizens devote much time and spend much money to promote and encourage the best possible discharge of this function.

Control

The legal control of education lies *outside* the profession, in the hands of the public. What the teaching profession is, therefore, and what it develops into depend partly on what those in control want it to be or, perhaps, to put this a little more strongly, on what the public will permit it to be. That the American public firmly holds the reins is evidence that they have a deep and abiding concern for education. It also means, however, that teachers must continually strive to keep the public intelligently informed about their problems and needs. Public control over the schools is continuing and extensive. Hence teachers, as a group, must interact with the public in a more direct and vigorous manner than is necessary for other groups.

Support

Closely linked with control is the matter of financial support. He who holds the purse strings wields the power. Public education in the United States is financed through public taxes. Private education is privately financed, largely by fees and tuition. Those who establish the policies of school support determine the financial status of members of the teaching profession. Adequacy or inadequacy of support, for example, has a bearing on the number of applicants for entrance to the profession and thereby affects selection policies. It influences teachers' living conditions, affects the amount and kind of education that can be required, and raises or lowers prestige. A generation of citizens that places a low priority upon teaching, and that wishes to get good teaching but does not wish it strongly enough to pay well for it, is a generation that will impede the progress of the teaching profession toward desirable professional goals. Generally speaking, a narrow-minded community, whose support of its schools is niggardly, is likely also to be niggardly in granting the degree of freedom that is necessary to good teaching. The result is professional regression rather than progression.

Size

The teaching profession has far more members than any other profession. Its membership numbers well over 2,000,000. Size has a special bearing upon selection and, conversely, selective policies have an effect upon the size. Size dictates that standards for selection be moderate. In order for any selective policy to operate, there must be considerably more applicants than openings. Since the profession is large it is impossible to limit membership to a very select group. The teaching profession cannot adopt the selective procedures that can be followed by medicine, for instance—a profession that included 278,420 persons on January 6, 1964. Great reliance must therefore be placed on superior preservice and in-service training to obtain teachers of superior quality. Efforts to increase the attractiveness of the profession so that a measure of selection is possible are necessarily directed toward improving working conditions.

Ratio of the Sexes

Women outnumber men in the teaching profession. Among the classroom teachers in the nation's schools in 1962, approximately 70 percent were women. The preponderance of women seems to decrease as the grades ascend. According to an NEA research study of the American public school teachers for the school year 1960–1961, approximately 69 percent of public school teachers were women, of

FIG. 4.1   SIZE OF SELECTED OCCUPATIONAL GROUPS, 1964

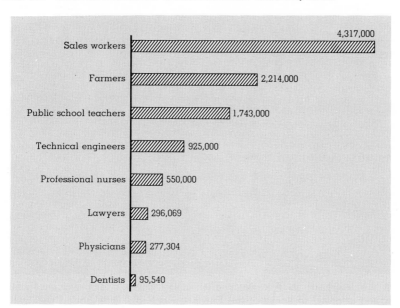

(Data from U.S. Bureau of Census, 1964, and from national organizations representing the professions)

which 73 percent were teaching in elementary schools. In the secondary schools, 57 percent of the teachers were men.

The majority of America's teachers are or have been married and maintain homes. Apparently, teachers who board and room are rarities.

The predominance of women differentiates the membership in the teaching profession from that in the other professions. This influences other characteristics of the profession too. Traditionally, in America, women have constituted the most important economic minority group. There has always been an unwritten policy in the United States to pay women less than men and to deny them those positions that are most lucrative. In the past, women elementary teachers typically received less salary than men elementary teachers. The effect of artificial barriers resulting from deeply imbedded social attitudes toward women in the professions is also significant. Restrictions on the entry of women to some fields, e.g., law and medicine, has led to a disproportionate representation of women in others, e.g., teaching and nursing.

Most of the teachers in America's elementary schools are women, which is in marked contrast to some of the European schools. It is hoped that better salaries will attract more men into elementary school teaching. (Ford Foundation)

In summary, then, the teaching profession differs from other professions in its primary function, in the nature of its control and support, in size, and in the ratio of men to women in its membership. Any program of improvement initiated by the public or by the profession must be planned with these differences in mind. They will have a bearing upon procedures used in the selection of members for the profession, upon the specialized training that is required, and upon other qualifications for admission.

TEACHER RECRUITMENT

It is important that an adequate supply of teachers come into the profession regularly. As we have said, selection occurs at the time of admission to teacher preparation in college and is continued at the time of admission to student teaching, at the time of employment, and again prior to granting tenure. With recent rapid growth of school population, the demand for teachers has been great, making selection very difficult. The problem of recruiting and retaining capable young people in teaching has become so acute as to demand the attention not only of the profession but also of numerous lay groups.

Recruitment is conducted through publicity, through direct personal conference, through opportunities for exploratory experiences, and through scholarships. The NEA has been actively engaged in teacher recruitment through all these channels. Every April the NEA conducts a "Teaching Career Month." During this time national broadcasting networks, the magazines, and the nation's press focus the spotlight of public attention on the American teacher—how he is recruited, prepared, and retained in the classroom, and the importance of his position in a free society. Special posters, leaflets, booklets, and films on such subjects as the current problem of teacher dropout, certification practices, and teacher education are channeled through the local branches of the NEA to students considering careers in teaching, to parents and citizens who can help recruit promising youngsters, and to the general public.

Since 1938 the NEA has sponsored the Future Teachers of

Some high schools encourage students who have an interest in teaching to observe and work directly with children. These students in Evanston Township High School are working with children as part of their assignment in the study of child development. (Evanston Photographic Service)

Career days and opportunities for individual discussions of careers are a part of the program of every progessive high school. This interested student discusses teaching as a career with a head counselor. (Audio-Visual Department, Berkeley Unified School District)

America, an organization with local clubs in every high school and junior high school in the country where there is sufficient interest and leadership. In addition there are "chapters" of the organization located on the campuses of teacher education institutions.

Teachers are encouraged to promote interest in teaching by providing exploratory experiences for their pupils. Children in the upper grades, for instance, may be allowed to read stories to younger children. High school pupils may be assigned as "aides" in the kindergarten. It is important that high school counselors have an appreciation of the great possibilities open in the teaching field and have an interest in pointing these out to capable young people.

Perhaps the vital key to teacher recruitment lies within the community. If the public pays teachers adequate salaries and provides for teacher security and teacher welfare, and if teachers are respected and have prestige, conditions are favorable for interesting the young people of the community to go into teaching. Many organizations of lay people, like the American Association of University Women and the Optimists Club, offer scholarships and conduct essay contests to promote teacher recruitment. Scholarships frequently are offered by local teachers' organizations, by the P.T.A., by state teacher organizations, and by state governments.

THE PRESTIGE FACTOR

When the individual assumes membership in the teaching profession, he accepts not only the obligation to render certain services and to play a certain role according to established rules but also the social status associated with people who fulfill that role. Prestige is the distinction or reputation that people attach to individuals or groups. It has a great deal to do with determining those who enter the profession and how long they stay. Once established, it is very difficult to improve.

How highly does the public regard teachers? How highly does it value intellectual endeavor? Do the positive and sympathetic features of the social climate in the United States assure the kind of prestige status to teachers that will encourage a desire to enter the profession? Effective teacher recruitment, then, will include efforts to improve teacher social status, teacher prestige.

The Scale of Social Prestige

Prestige is, to be sure, related to income and education. It is determined also by a combination of other factors including what the public thinks of the kind of service rendered to humanity; the special training, intelligence, and ability needed; and the morality of the group. In more than 30 studies of occupations made in the United States between 1925 and 1947, consistency in the way occupations were ranked was remarkable. Table 4.1 gives the ratings of 88 occupations made by 2,290 people in 1947. The study shows that a college professor outranks others in the teaching profession, that schoolteachers are above average in prestige in that they outrank members of such occupational groups as radio announcers, newspaper columnists, insurance agents, and traveling salesmen. But teachers are outranked by physicians, lawyers, airline pilots, state governors, and captains in the army.

Other studies show that teachers rank higher as credit risks than clergymen, lawyers, judges, musicians, and some others. Morally and ethically, schoolteachers rank high. College teachers

TABLE 4.1. THE RATINGS OF OCCUPATIONS[a]

Occupation	Score	Occupation	Score
U.S. Supreme Court Justice	96	Railroad engineer	77
Physician	93	Farm owner and operator	76
State governor	93	Official of an international	
Cabinet member in the federal		labor union	75
government	92	Radio announcer	75
Diplomat in the U.S. Foreign		Newspaper columnist	74
Service	92	Owner-operator of a printing	
Mayor of a large city	90	shop	74
College professor	89	Electrician	73
Scientist	89	Trained machinist	73
U.S. representative in Congress	89	Welfare worker for a city	
Banker	88	government	73
Government scientist	88	Undertaker	72
County judge	87	Reporter on a daily newspaper	71
Head of a department in a state		AVERAGE	69.8
government	87	Manager of a small store in	
Minister	87	a city	69
Architect	86	Bookkeeper	68
Chemist	86	Insurance agent	68
Dentist	86	Tenant farmer—one who owns	
Lawyer	86	livestock and machinery and	
Member of the board of direc-		manages the farm	68
tors of a large corporation	86	Traveling salesman for a	
Nuclear physicist	86	wholesale concern	68
Priest	86	Playground director	67
Psychologist	85	Policeman	67
Civil engineer	84	Railroad conductor	67
Airline pilot	83	Mail carrier	66
Artist who paints pictures that		Carpenter	65
are exhibited in galleries	83	Plumber	63
Owner of a factory that em-		Garage mechanic	62
ploys about 100 people	82	Local official of a labor union	62
Sociologist	82	Owner-operator of lunch stand	62
Accountant for a large		Corporal in the regular army	60
business	81	Machine operator in a factory	60
Biologist	81	Barber	59
Musician in a symphony		Clerk in a store	58
orchestra	81	Fisherman who owns his own	
Author of novels	80	boat	58
Captain in the regular army	80	Streetcar motorman	58
Building contractor	79	Milk route man	54
Economist	79	Restaurant cook	54
Public school teacher	78	Truck driver	54
County agricultural agent	77	Lumberjack	53

TABLE 4.1 (*Continued*)

Occupation	Score	Occupation	Score
Filling station attendant	52	Soda fountain clerk	45
Singer in a night club	52	Bartender	44
Farm hand	50	Janitor	44
Coal miner	49	Share cropper—one who owns	
Taxi driver	49	no livestock or equipment	
Railroad section hand	48	and does not manage farm	40
Restaurant worker	48	Garbage collector	35
Dock worker	47	Street sweeper	34
Night watchman	47	Shoe shiner	33
Clothes presser in a laundry	46		

a From *Opinion News*, Vol. IX (September 1, 1947). Reproduced by permission of the National Opinion Research Center, University of Chicago. Drs. Cecil North and Paul Hatt designed the study upon which these data are based.

and school administrators, predominantly men, as well as high school teachers, have a higher position on the prestige scale than teachers in the lower grades. That the teaching profession establishes levels of stratification within its own group will be discussed later.

Although a combination of factors determines prestige, when other factors are equal, higher income means higher prestige. Inasmuch as the public determines teacher income, what the public does in the matter adds to or detracts from the prestige status of the teacher. To the extent that members of the profession suffer financially in comparison with other groups, they also suffer in comparison on the social status scale. It must be remembered, though, that the amount of money spent for schools must be judged in terms of complete community spending. An economically poor community may pay low teacher salaries but show that it places high values on teaching by spending a relatively large proportion of its total funds for classroom teaching.

On the whole, prestige is determined outside the profession. Members of the profession may, however, exert some influence. If a teacher has an apologetic attitude about teaching, if he says, "I'm only a teacher," members of the community are going to think that if those within the profession think little of the social standing of the teachers it really is not very high. If teachers take a positive stand, if they attempt to refute ridicule, they help to raise prestige. Tradition, caricaturists, fiction, movies, folklore, catch phrases, and the like have tended to lower the prestige status of teachers by perpetuating false and derogatory pictures of them. Fortunately, during periods of teacher shortages when teacher recruitment is a vital social concern, lay persons, such as journalists, and certain lay organizations, such as the National Citizens Commission for the Public Schools, have contributed significantly to increasing the social status of teachers.

Effects of Ascribed Status

The status ascribed to teachers has a number of effects, negative and positive, upon the individual and upon the entire profession. One is to strengthen the teaching profession. The profession becomes increasingly conscious of the need for solidarity. This leads, in turn, to the building of stronger and more effective local, state, and national associations. In order to promote its welfare and, thereby ultimately, to raise its prestige, the profession must present a common front to the public. The factors that promote division and conflicts within the profession tend to impede progress toward the attainment of a higher degree of recognition, prestige, and social status.

Doc once said to me:

You don't know how it feels to grow up in a district like this. You go to the first grade—Miss O'Rourke. Second grade—Miss Casey. Third grade —Miss Chalmers. Fourth grade—Miss Mooney. And so on. At the fire station it is the same. None of them are Italians. The police lieutenant is an Italian, and there are a couple of Italian sergeants, but they never have made an Italian captain in Cornerville. In the settlement houses, none of the people with authority are Italians.

Now you must know that the old-timers here have a great respect for schoolteachers and anybody like that. When the Italian boy sees that none of his own people have the good jobs, why should he think he is as good as the Irish or the Yankees? It makes him feel inferior.

If I had my way, I would have half the schoolteachers Italians and three-quarters of the people in the settlement. Let the other quarter be there just to show that we're in America. . . .

From William Foote Whyte, *Street Corner Society* (Chicago: The University of Chicago Press, 1943), p. 276. Copyright 1943 by the University of Chicago and quoted by permission of The University of Chicago Press.

A nationwide sampling reveals that teachers, in general, rank relatively high on the social prestige scale. However, it does not follow that the prestige rank is the same in all communities. In those communities where education at all the grade levels enjoys high priority, a higher value is apt to be placed also upon the teachers. This acts as an incentive to better professional achievement. Conversely, in a community that gives low priority to education, the prestige of the teachers is likely to be lower, and consequently the efforts of teachers are likely to be less appreciated and the incentives to high achievement greatly lessened.

SECURITY PROVISIONS

Security Defined

Security is a basic personality need, a frame of mind, an attitude defined by psychologists as a persistent state of readiness to use the self for motive satisfaction. All attitudes have an emotional core. They are related to the affective aspects of our lives. A teacher with a sense of security feels protected, is free from fear of unfair dismissal or unjust and unwarranted treatment. But security does not imply complacency. Rather, it builds confidence. The teacher becomes more sure of his own personal and professional adequacy, is encouraged to improve, to become more proficient. Insecurity has the opposite effect. The teacher who is insecure tends to feel inadequate to meet his assignments, lacks confidence in his ability to achieve.

State and local school systems and the teaching profession strive to provide teachers with a suitable degree of security. Certain security features, like tenure, retirement, and salary scales, are illustrative of the provisions intended to avoid the ill effects of insecurity.

Associations

So numerous and so influential are associations that the United States is sometimes described as an "associational" society. Organizations of both private and public employees have been accepted as an important phase of American life. As many as 340 different kinds of local teachers' organizations have been identified. Some are entirely local, some are affiliated with a state-wide group, and some are units in an organization of national scope.

The fact that schoolteachers are prolific organizers may be an indication of their deep-seated desire for greater personal security.

Their numerous organizations indicate confidence in affiliation and association. The relationship between the individual teachers and the profession may be better understood by a brief look at some of these associations.

1. National Education Association

The National Education Association (NEA) is the largest professional organization in the United States. It celebrated its centennial birthday in 1957. Its membership exceeds 860,000 and continues to grow. As William G. Carr, the executive secretary, said in a centennial celebration speech, "Our Association represents an unwritten but powerful treaty of mutual assistance among its members."

This imposing structure in Washington, D.C., houses the national headquarters of the National Education Association. NEA's constantly growing membership exceeded 90,000 in 1964. Through its publication (*The NEA Journal*) and the numerous activities of its thirty-three influential departments, it renders incommensurable service to the profession. It has also contributed importantly to developing intelligent public understanding of the problems of education among the citizens of America.

NEA headquarters are located in an eight-story modern building in the nation's capital. The business of the national office absorbs the full time of over three hundred persons.

Among NEA objectives that bear directly upon the security of its members are better salaries, improved tenure, sick leave and retirement provisions, desirable working conditions, reasonable

In June, 1961, the Representative Assembly of the NEA passed the following resolution defining the policy it believes should be followed in teacher–school board relationships.

Teacher-Board of Education Relationships. Since boards of education and the teaching profession have the same ultimate aim of providing the best possible educational opportunity for children and youth, relationships must be established which are based upon this community of interest and the concept of education as both a public trust and a professional calling.

Recognizing both the legal authority of boards of education and the educational competencies of the teaching profession, the two groups should view the consideration of matters of mutual concern as a joint responsibility.

The National Education Association believes, therefore, that professional education associations should be accorded the right, through democratically selected representatives using appropriate professional channels, to participate in the determination of policies of common concern including salary and other conditions for professional service.

The seeking of consensus and mutual agreement on a professional basis should preclude the arbitrary exercise of unilateral authority by boards of education and the use of the strike by teachers as a means for enforcing economic demands.

When common consent cannot be reached, the Association recommends that a Board of Review consisting of members of professional and lay groups affiliated with education should be used as the means of resolving extreme differences.

From NEA Research Division Memo 1961–31, revised, August, 1961.

teaching loads, and increased social recognition. The organization strives to achieve wide dissemination of *accurate* information about the profession, both to the membership and to the public at large, to promote desirable legislation, and to conduct and report on research. The organization is pledged to aggressively promote educational campaigns for the improvement of education and the education profession in the United States.

2. State Teachers' Associations

The NEA has branches in each state. The state organizations, sometimes referred to as the state education associations, are among the most effective of all organized teachers' groups. They enroll a majority of the teachers in the state. Generally they have a well-paid executive secretary who is an able and experienced professional educator. Most state associations have well-equipped offices and able personnel. Many of them publish a monthly journal that compares well with the best professional magazines.

State teachers' organizations are generally effective in their relationships with the state education authority and with the state legislatures. It is through the state organization that local groups or individuals can make known the specific nature of the security provisions needed to improve education in a particular state. Teachers indicate confidence in this kind of association through their financial support and their participation.

Leaders in the profession, as pictured above, have been brought together by the NEA to discuss how to upgrade the profession by establishing prerequisites to membership based upon clearly defined standards of competence. (National Education Association)

Teachers in fields such as English or social studies, those working at a particular educational level such as nursery or elementary, and educators in special fields such as guidance or administration have their own associations. Typically these comprise local or regional units that are part of state organizations that, in turn, hold membership in a national unit more or less directly affiliated with the parent organization, the NEA.

3. Local or City-Wide Teachers' Organizations

Local teachers' organizations are the oldest, the most numerous, and the most varied of all teachers' organizations. Their number attests to general confidence in their worth. They provide most individual teachers with an opportunity for participation in the affairs of the profession that is not possible in the groups covering a broader geographical area. The individual teacher, through the local organization, has the opportunity to experience the satisfaction of actively helping to protect his and his profession's security. Local organizations also serve a significant social function in some communities by providing a common meeting place for teachers.

Local organizations have a variety of patterns. Some admit all the teachers in a system; some admit only those working in a given field or at a specific level or those discharging a common specialized function, like guidance or administration. The aims are always broader than that of providing security for the members, but security for the members is an implied complement to all the other stated aims. Local associations strengthen group loyalty and reinforce the members' efforts to protect the organization's and the profession's reputation for the benefit of the membership.

Local associations enable teachers to become better acquainted with each other, with their school systems, and with their more urgent local problems. Thus they can learn more directly what the community is like and what the attitudes of its citizens are toward the maintenance of good schools. Local organizations open paths of communication by functioning as liaison between teachers, teachers and the public, and teachers and school administrators.

Should a local teachers' organization have the same rights as organizations in private industry, the right to call a strike, for example? The American tradition is that the public interest should come first, that the servants of the people may not strike against the people. In some instances this principle has been recognized by the courts. Since teachers, in general, lack the right to strike, those who administer the schools have a responsibility to establish fair and positive personnel procedures and working conditions. Teachers in local organizations should have the right to organize for bargaining purposes, the right of free discussion, the right to appeal over the decisions of local administrations, and, ultimately, the right to take their case to the people.

One of the thorniest problems concerns the right of organized teachers to engage in political activity. While studies of the past voting records of all elementary and secondary public school teachers show that well above 90 percent of them have voted regularly, fewer than 7 percent of them participated actively as members of a political organization and only 2 percent had ever been candidates for elective public office.

Perhaps the future welfare of the profession will depend in large part upon how wisely teachers exercise their right to organize. It seems likely that in the future, local teacher groups will seek to advance the interests of the profession by increasing their activities through organizational channels. In other words, the teacher will act less as an individual and more as a member of an association. Questions of rights, privileges, and teacher welfare, for example, will be answered in terms of a mature, carefully planned policy presented to the public or its representatives by an organized education group. In order that these policies might be more expertly formulated and effectively presented to the public or its representatives, local teachers' organizations in larger school districts are employing specially qualified executive secretaries who spend full time in representing the interests of the local teaching group.

The more successful local teachers' associations seek to protect the standards of performance within the schools from unwarranted encroachments from outside interest groups that are unfavorable to the cause of good education. They seek to enforce upon the membership a reasonable regard for their own professional code. They disapprove of the individual who would advance his interest at the expense of the group. They seek to promote the welfare of the group through advocating carefully formulated policies regarding salary, retirement, sick leave, and the like. They seek to alter any community condition that is considered inimical to the cause of good education. Finally, while guarding the interests of individual teachers, they function to guard the interests of the professional organization itself by being alert to those influences that operate to weaken it.

Effective local teachers' organizations show a variety of organizational patterns, but in most of them, appropriate committees carry out self-assumed functions. Perhaps careful study of a problem basic to policy formulation is cared for by a research committee. Perhaps a welfare committee functions in the interest of any individual member; a public relations committee channels communication between teachers and the public; a legislative committee keeps the membership informed about impending state or federal legislation of interest to the profession. The local teachers' organization is instituted to meet the problems peculiar to the local system. It is through their organizations—local, state, and national—that the teachers claim their rights to professional autonomy like that granted by the American people to other professions.

4. American Federation of Teachers

The American Federation of Teachers is a federation of local teachers' unions. It is an affiliate of the AFL-CIO. The strongest locals are found in those cities where labor unions are strong. The membership is limited to teachers. The programs of teachers' unions are focused on such security provisions as salary, retirement, tenure, teaching load, pensions, sabbatical leaves, sick leaves, academic freedom, and the like. On December 15, 1961, the New York City local of the United Federation of Teachers won the right to represent the teachers in bargaining with the City Board of Education.

Although the membership of the AFT is tiny when compared to that of the NEA—82,000 to 860,000 in 1963—the contributions of AFT to teacher welfare have been considerable in several of the larger cities such as New York, Chicago, and Detroit. In many school districts, however, teachers have preferred to belong to the NEA and its branch organizations. Three reasons have been given for this. First, the labor movement, the AFL-CIO influence, has never successfully penetrated any of the leading professions. Education is in a group with law, medicine, or engineering when it takes the stand that its organizational needs can best be cared for by its own associations. Second, it is feared by many that the prestige of a profession would suffer if the profession were affiliated with labor and adopted the methods that labor unions use to obtain benefits for their members. Third, the effectiveness of the labor movement has been lessened by division and dissension within. Even the recent amalgamation of the AFL and the CIO has brought only a measure of unity.

5. National Congress of Parents and Teachers

The largest organization connected with education in the United States is the National Congress of Parents and Teachers. Membership surpasses eleven million. As the name implies, members are both lay and professional, with the lay membership far outnumbering the professional. This organization represents one of the greatest educational movements in history. It operates largely through state congresses which in turn reach down into the local community through local parent-teacher associations. It is influential and provides for active, direct participation at local, state, and national levels. The state and national congresses speak with authority to legislatures. The National Congress of Parents and Teachers, recognizing that security is linked with the other aims of the organization, has consistently and effectively advocated policies favorable to improving teacher security.

6. World Organization of the Teaching Profession

A constitution for the World Organization of the Teaching Profession (WOTP) was adopted when fifty-six delegates from thirty-eight national education associations and nine professional and intergovernmental organizations concerned with education met in Scotland in 1947. The purposes of the WOTP as stated in its constitution are:

To make the highest standards of full and free education available to all without discrimination;

To improve the professional status of the teachers of the world and to promote their intellectual, material, social and civic interests and rights;

To promote world-wide peace through the building of good will founded upon co-operation between nations in educational enterprises, based upon pertinent and accurate information;

To advise the appropriate organs of the United Nations and of other international bodies on educational and professional matters.[2]

The Teacher and Teacher Associations

Teacher associations reflect the collective judgment of schoolteachers as to the goals of education. The large number of unre-

[2] As listed in Walter S. Monroe (ed.), *Encyclopedia of Educational Research* (New York: The Macmillan Company, 1950), p. 1446.

lated organizations is one evidence that the teaching profession, nationally, is not fully unified to achieve these goals.

A well-informed profession is one safeguard to education. The individual teacher becomes informed about current educational needs through periodicals and yearbooks that are issued by most state, regional, and national organizations. Speakers and consultants are sent out from headquarters to local groups. Many of the organizations have regular state or regional and national conventions. Often teachers are excused from teaching in order to attend meetings, e.g., the annual convention of the National Council of Teachers of English. Frequently planning and executing a program for special days called "institute days" is delegated to a regional or state organization.

Through associations the teachers gain a reasonable degree of autonomy of action that would otherwise be denied them. This is essential to securing and maintaining a satisfactory degree of professional solidarity. Because control of the schools lies outside the profession this is especially important to schoolteachers. Teachers, unless well organized, are vulnerable to all kinds of external influences, some of them inimical to the cause of education and threats to the individual teacher. Influential groups exist throughout the United States that consistently oppose state and community efforts to improve education and to improve the welfare of teachers. For instance, an organized group may be dedicated to reducing taxes. Such an aim will usually lead to opposition to any teacher association program that requires tax money for the improvement of teacher welfare. Individual teachers cannot be alert to all such organizations and pressure groups in the community or in the state, but teacher association officers are trained to recognize and to recommend action to deal with such situations.

Security Policies in School Administration

Local policies of educational administration, especially those related to security provisions for teachers, vary strikingly throughout the United States. Not all state school authorities agree regarding what security provisions are appropriate. Policies toward contracts, promotion, tenure, retirement, pensions, and salary scales illustrate rather vividly some of the concrete problems in procuring reasonable security provisions.

1. Contracts

"Contract" is the legal term for a binding agreement between two parties. A teacher's contract is prepared by the local school district and is a statement of terms and conditions of employment. It generally stipulates that he shall receive a certain salary for his services for a period of time. Contracts vary all the way from a simple, oral agreement to extended technical statements of terms. What is said in the contract is a fairly good expression of the attitude of the school officers toward the individual teacher.

The present trend is greatly to simplify teachers' contracts. Frequently school policies, as they pertain to teachers, are worked out with the help of the teachers' associations. The school system may publish the policies, including specific statements relating to teacher welfare, in a handbook. When the teacher accepts a position he then knows precisely the commitments of the school system. Large school systems, and most smaller ones, make the community's commitments to its teachers unmistakably clear and binding on the community.

2. Tenure

Tenure refers specifically to the period of time a teacher is entitled to hold his position—the length of his term of appointment. A teacher beginning in a school system ordinarily serves a probationary period before receiving what are called continuing contracts, indefinite contracts, or permanent contracts. Tenure provisions, as they are stated in official pronouncements of school district policy, vary from community to community and from state to state, and there is some disagreement within the profession about what constitutes the best manner of stating the terms of tenure. In most states the circumstances under which teachers are entitled to permanent tenure are defined by law.

Tenure is an important security provision. Free from any fear of unfair dismissal, the teacher is relieved of a strain which might impair his teaching effectiveness. This means, however, that the three steps in the selection of teachers are especially important.

The initial selection comes when application is made for admission to teacher training. It is impossible to state definitely the qualifications for a successful teacher, much less to assess an individual's possession of potential powers for good teaching. It is possible, however, at the time of original application to eliminate some individuals who because of intellectual, physical, or social factors seem poor prospects for teaching. Some institutions select again when students apply for the privilege of student teaching.

After a student has completed the training requirements and has received his college degree, an employing official, perhaps a superintendent of schools, makes another evaluation of potential success. If the applicant is given a teaching position, the initial contract is typically for one year. Sometimes a teacher beginning in a system has three of these one-year contracts. During the period of the one-year contracts he is "on probation." At the end of each year, often in joint conference with an administrator, the teacher's work is reviewed and direction and advice given. At the end of any one year a teacher's contract may not be renewed.

The most important point of selection comes at the close of the probationary period. At this time the teacher is eligible for a permanent contract—for tenure. He also is eligible for an extension of the probationary period, or he may be dismissed. The employing official faces a significant responsibility. If only those of proven competence are allowed to have permanent contracts, the virtue of the tenure provisions for teachers will not be questioned and most future dissatisfaction with the tenure laws will be avoided.

When a teacher has permanent tenure, when he has passed the selection barriers, his tenure then is for *a* position in the school system—not for *the* position that he holds at any particular time. For instance, a principal might be shifted to a classroom teaching position without any violation of his tenure privileges.

The burden of the proof of incompetence or misbehavior rests with the school officials. A teacher who is "on tenure," who has permanent employment in a school district, cannot be dismissed because of the personal whim of an administrator, school board member, or political manipulator. The protection of tenure, however, as well as any of the other security provisions provided teachers, does not relieve the teacher of responsibility to fulfill his obligations to the school system to the best of his ability. He has been judged the kind of individual who has the qualifications for professional membership. He owes it to himself and to the profession to merit this confidence. The tenure laws are not intended to protect the incompetent.

3. Promotion

In joining the profession and in affiliating with a local school district it is important to know what lies ahead, what the avenues for advancement are. One may decide advancement lies in leaving classroom teaching and entering some specialized educational field. There are many such opportunities—e.g., special teaching, supervision, and school administration. Outside-the-classroom positions often offer such rewards that the individual decides early in his career to prepare for one of them. Unfortunately, a skillful teacher is all too frequently rewarded with an appointment to such a position rather than to a position that fully utilizes his teaching skill. This policy reflects a tendency in the profession itself to depreciate the importance of teaching, to attach greater significance to non-teaching functions. It would seem logical that an outstanding teacher who prefers to remain in the classroom should be given the same recognition and salary that would be his in an administrative or supervisory post. But practice within the profession itself does not encourage this.

Many excellent teachers who, with considerable sacrifice, have stayed with classroom teaching have been resourceful in supplementing their salaries with other employment. Part-time services of teachers have always been in great demand. The poorer the school district, the more likely it is that the more competent classroom teachers will be encouraged to move up to other positions or to seek other teaching positions which offer financial inducements. Partly as a result of policies of this kind, teaching is an excessively mobile profession. And for this, education in the United States pays an enormous price. Preparing prospective teachers and orienting new teachers are expensive operations. Too rapid personnel turnover results in diminished returns from this investment. This turnover is also educationally wasteful, not only from the viewpoint of the pupils who suffer from lack of educational continuity over a period of years, but also from the viewpoint of a personnel handicapped in its long-term plans and frustrated in carrying on activities designed to be built up over the years. Rapid turnover is costly in terms of group morale and is detrimental to teacher prestige because a transient group usually does not command the respect afforded a stable, continuing, professional group.

4. Retirement

Admission to the teaching profession assumes the candidate intends to serve the profession and devote his energies to improving it the remainder of his employed years. At the age of seventy, or thereabouts, he will be expected to retire from teaching. The problem of income for the remainder of his life must be solved. Because education is a state function each state has the responsibility to establish laws regarding public school teacher retirement policies. All the states have done this with characteristic variations consistent with differing points of view about educational policy.

In general, retirement provisions are developed in terms of three plans. The state may establish its own system—define its own policy toward retirement and retirement pay. When this plan is followed the teacher usually contributes a share toward retirement pay. By basing the plan upon actuarial predictions the system adopted tends to be sound. In some cases special provisions are made for those becoming disabled before retirement age and for those who for personal reasons desire to retire at an earlier age as well as for survivor's benefits to protect a teacher's dependents.

The second plan is for the state to join the federal government in providing for old-age benefits. It conforms to the current tendency to shift state and local financial burdens to the national government. Teachers' associations, however, are generally opposed to this. A pension plan set up within a state for teachers is usually also a savings plan. A teacher may withdraw funds invested at any time he leaves teaching, regardless of his age. The plan provides some flexibility in that the age of retirement is determined partly in terms of years of service and is not set at a chronological age point. Teachers' associations contend also that a pension fund worked out for them specifically is unifying for the teachers and is more within their own control. For a career teacher, the benefits of a state teacher retirement plan tend to be much more generous than those offered under a federal plan for old-age security.

The third general plan is for the local school district to gain state permission to administer its own pension program. A few larger cities continue to support local teacher retirement plans established years ago. New adoptions of the plan are rare.

Programs of retirement have some weaknesses. Differing state policies make it difficult for a teacher to transfer to another state without sacrificing some accrued pension benefits. The question of what percentage teachers should contribute to the costs is difficult to decide. What to do about disability insurance and what the age of retirement should be are points of disagreement. Survivor's benefits have not always been made clear. But improvements in retirement provisions are gradually being made. The NEA, state teachers' associations, local teachers' unions, and other organizations are working on the problem.

5. Leaves of Absence

Teachers who have some good reason for enforced absence, who are perhaps ill, are given further security through a policy providing sick leaves. It is usual for a school system to grant two weeks' leave a year for enforced absence, to permit these leaves of absence to be cumulative, and to inflict no loss of pay. Some systems grant extended leaves on full- or part-time pay, or without pay. These leaves may be for a semester or more to be devoted to study or travel or something else that will enhance a teacher's worth to the community.

6. Salary

Improvement of education depends upon adequately prepared, professionally competent classroom teachers. To get teachers of this caliber and training, the structure and level of teachers' salaries must be attractive to the right kind of men and women. Even though teaching has many appeals to young people, the profession will not attract its share of well-qualified college graduates, especially men, as long as it is associated in the minds of the public with low salaries.

The American public is currently aware of the critical financial needs of its schools, and almost every community is making extraordinary efforts to improve classroom teachers' salaries. The problem is complicated by rapidly growing school enrollments. Additional money for schools is continually needed to add teachers required by expanding enrollments. The U.S. Office of Education, for example, estimates that by 1968–1969 five classroom teachers will be needed where four were employed in 1961–1962. If the recommendations of the NEA Policies Commission were followed, the ratio would be increased in 1968–1969 to seven teachers compared with five in 1961–1962. One thing is plain: increasing teachers' salaries while at the same time adding to teachers' loads will not solve the problem of attracting and retaining capable young men and women in the profession.

Two aspects of the salary situation of special significance to beginning teachers—the variations among states in paying teachers, and the still greater variations among school districts in paying teachers—are illustrated in Figs. 4.2, 4.3, and, on page 309, Fig. 12.4. Other financial aspects of the American school system are analyzed in Unit Three.

The data show that some of the states making the greatest efforts are unable to pay good salaries. Variations in such factors as birth rate, personal income, and taxable wealth make the problem more difficult in some states than in others. Mississippi, for example, ranks fiftieth in average instructional salaries, first in the average salary increase over a ten-year period, and thirteenth in the percentage of personal income expended on education. Although Mississippi is making a great effort to improve its educational situation, it has been unable to reach a desirable salary level.

The salary situation among the more than 35,000 school districts in the United States is, perhaps, of more immediate personal importance to the individual seriously considering entering the profession. After all, the teacher will be employed by an independent school district, and the policy of that district toward paying teachers will have much to do with his future satisfactions in teaching.

Local salary policy is reflected in the salary structure and in the salary scale for a given year. Since the salary structure and salary scale are developed and formulated to attract and retain capable teachers, taken together they constitute a fairly reliable criterion for judging the value a given school district places upon good teaching.

The salary structure, usually printed or mimeographed, is a written statement of the policies that govern salaries in a given school district. The policies adopted by the board of education include salary differentials for preparation and experience—and sometimes for so-called "merit" differences—allowances for sick leave, for dependents, for health insurance, sabbaticals, pensions, extra pay for extra work like coaching, and other matters related to teacher welfare. The salary structure specifically states the principles upon which the plan for paying teachers is based. For example, in a 42-page booklet issued in 1961–1962 to teachers, the San Francisco Unified School District states:

FIG. 4.2 ESTIMATED AVERAGE SALARY OF INSTRUCTIONAL STAFF IN PUBLIC SCHOOLS, 1963-1964

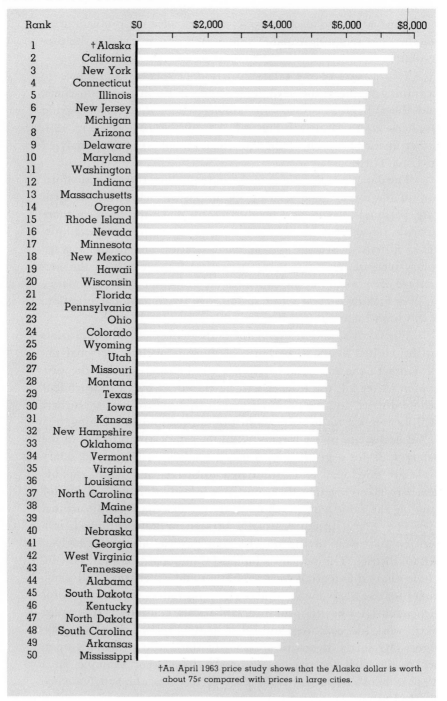

Rank		$0	$2,000	$4,000	$6,000	$8,000
1	† Alaska					
2	California					
3	New York					
4	Connecticut					
5	Illinois					
6	New Jersey					
7	Michigan					
8	Arizona					
9	Delaware					
10	Maryland					
11	Washington					
12	Indiana					
13	Massachusetts					
14	Oregon					
15	Rhode Island					
16	Nevada					
17	Minnesota					
18	New Mexico					
19	Hawaii					
20	Wisconsin					
21	Florida					
22	Pennsylvania					
23	Ohio					
24	Colorado					
25	Wyoming					
26	Utah					
27	Missouri					
28	Montana					
29	Texas					
30	Iowa					
31	Kansas					
32	New Hampshire					
33	Oklahoma					
34	Vermont					
35	Virginia					
36	Louisiana					
37	North Carolina					
38	Maine					
39	Idaho					
40	Nebraska					
41	Georgia					
42	West Virginia					
43	Tennessee					
44	Alabama					
45	South Dakota					
46	Kentucky					
47	North Dakota					
48	South Carolina					
49	Arkansas					
50	Mississippi					

†An April 1963 price study shows that the Alaska dollar is worth about 75¢ compared with prices in large cities.

(Data from NEA Research Division, Research Report 1964–R1)

Fig. 4.3 Percentage Increase in Estimated Salary of Instructional Staff, 1953-1954 to 1963-1964

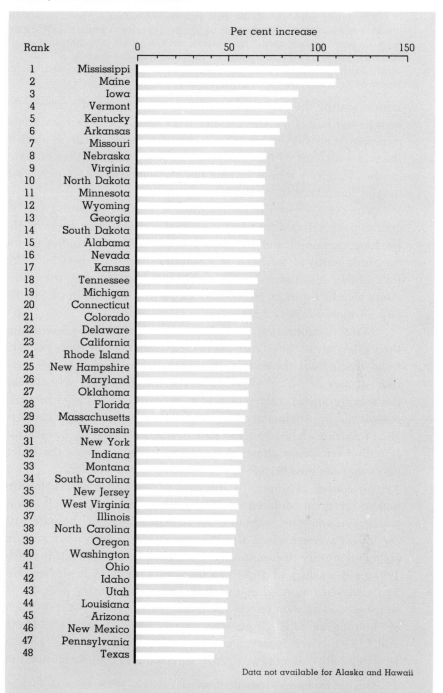

Data not available for Alaska and Hawaii

(Data from NEA Research Division, Research Report 1964–R1)

The salary schedule of the San Francisco Unified School District for teachers is a single salary schedule of the preparational type. Every teacher is in his proper place on the schedule according to his preparational qualifications, his years of experience in the San Francisco public schools and such additional outside teaching experience as has been approved by the Board of Education for salary increment credit.

Besides stating the policies that govern the payment of teachers, the booklet explains how the policies were formulated and states the minimum and maximum salaries for the current year as well as the salary increments for each year. Inasmuch as each school district in the American school system has considerable autonomy, each district formulates its own salary structure.

The NEA views the formulation of a salary structure (see vignette, page 85) as a matter for mutual consideration by both the teaching personnel and the school board. From its studies of the economic status of teachers[3] it concludes that, if teachers in America's schools are to attain a reasonable standard of living, the initial salary should begin at $6,000 and range to a maximum of $13,000 and, in some districts, higher.

Many communities are in continuous process of reexamining their salary structures. Over the decade 1953–1954 to 1963–1964 the trend throughout the country has been toward higher salaries, the rate of increase being 4.9 percent. For the 1963–1964 school year, the average annual salary of classroom teachers in the elementary schools was approximately $5,800, and of secondary school teachers, $6,214. Although elementary school teachers' salaries have traditionally been below those of secondary school teachers, the differences over the past decade appear to have grown smaller.

Of course, as shown by the data in the above charts, locality makes for great differences. The average salary paid classroom teachers in one state is about twice that paid them by the state with the lowest average salary. But the comparison is even more striking from community to community. For example, one suburb in 1963–1964 paid a salary of $6,400 to teachers with an A.B. degree who had achieved tenure after the three year probationary period, and in the second year on tenure the teachers received $7,000. For teachers holding an M.A. degree the salaries were, respectively, $7,000 and $7,600. After 14 years, teachers with an M.A. degree plus 30 semester hours of graduate work received $11,200. Remuneration

3 See, for example, "Economic Status of Teachers," NEA Research Division, Research Report 1961–R44 (March, 1961), p. 52.

for teaching may be expected to improve to a point where teaching will attract more of the abler college graduates and keep them in the profession. Salary structures and salary scales alone will not, of course, bring all this to pass. They are, however, important elements.

SUMMARY

Membership in a social group has striking effects upon the individual. Assuming membership in a professional group implies acceptance of standards of behavior adopted by the group. The standards not only protect the teachers but also guarantee children a satisfactory quality of education.

Opportunity to improve the profession is afforded teachers through membership in teacher associations that influence both local and state governments. The status of the profession will not rise perceptibly unless the profession itself exerts its energies to bring this about. The problem of improvement is different from other professions because of the differences in functions, control, support, and the ratio of the two sexes in the teaching profession, and also because teaching is a tax-supported profession.

The prestige status of teachers is well above the average. A measure of the value placed on education by a state or by a community is reflected in the security provisions made for teachers. Salary scales are especially important. Often teachers, through their associations, participate in determining their security provisions.

A 1963 NEA research publication shows that most teachers would enter the teaching profession again if they had to make the choice once more. The professional features of teaching help to make it very desirable work.

QUESTIONS

1. How can an individual teacher contribute to upgrading the teaching profession?
2. How do social attitudes toward the teaching profession affect the level of professionalization the membership of the profession is capable of achieving?
3. What are some of the sacrifices an individual must make when he becomes a member of the teaching profession?
4. How does social stratification within the teaching profession affect the prestige of the membership?

5. What evidence is there to support the contention that a reasonable degree of security is essential to the development of a healthful personality?

6. What do you consider legitimate pressure-group methods that a teachers' association is justified in using to obtain what it considers to be rightful ends?

7. What are some of the benefits a teacher may expect to receive from belonging to a local teachers' association?

8. What security provisions do you hope to find provided for the teachers by the community in which you begin your teaching?

9. How would your own obligations be affected by a liberal policy toward teachers?

10. Which policy do you prefer—including school administrators in the local teachers' association, or excluding them?

PROJECTS

1. Evaluate the features of a salary scale that has been adopted in some school system. If possible, compare this salary scale with that of another school system.

2. Describe the activities engaged in by the National Congress of Parents and Teachers. Evaluate its services.

3. Analyze the contents of a late issue of the NEA journal and evaluate the contribution the magazine makes to the membership of the NEA.

4. Analyze the contents of a current issue of the journal of the state education association in your home state and evaluate the contribution it makes to the membership.

5. Analyze the contents of the teachers' handbook issued by a local school district. List the kind of information it supplies.

6. To bring pressure on local school boards the NEA has worked out a policy with regard to "sanctions." Explain what sanctions are, how they are to be applied, where they have been used, and with what results.

CHAPTER 5

The teacher
and his philosophy

From this book, and from other books about education, and from teachers of education as well, the student receives advice on how to answer many of the perplexing questions he must face as a teacher. The advice is both abundant and diverse. Education, like parenthood, religion, and politics, is a subject on which every man thinks himself something of an authority and on which recognized experts seldom approach consensus.

Some of the questions that confront the teacher are the center of public debates about education: What are the goals of education? What should be included in the curriculum? How can the schools meet the challenge of Russian technology? Should federal aid to education be increased? The teacher is expected to have an intelligent point of view upon all such questions.

Other questions that the teacher faces are of more immediate and direct personal concern. The teacher asks himself: What kinds of rewards and positive incentives can I use in the classroom to encourage desirable forms of behavior? How shall I take into account the special problems of the pupils? Shall I judge the work of each pupil relative to the achievements of the rest of the class, or in terms of his individual efforts? How do I determine a reasonable standard to apply in judging the work of pupils? How much weight should I give to the differences in learning ability of my pupils?

There are also questions of another kind that the teacher must answer. These center around relationships of a teacher with the community, the parents of the pupils, fellow teachers, and administrators. A teacher must answer such questions as: What responsibility should I take in the total program of the school? What should my relationships be with my fellow teachers and with school administrators? If there is a teachers' union in my city, should I belong? In what ways should I participate in the administration of my school? In the programs of the P.T.A.?

The answers teachers give to these questions and to others like them are reflected in classroom teaching. Great variation in teaching methods and procedures stems from varying answers.

DIFFERENCES ON AN EDUCATIONAL ISSUE

The variations among answers given to questions revolving around an educational issue may be illustrated by analyzing the use of motivation in classroom teaching. Practices related to motivation are selected as illustrative because there are few subjects in the field of teaching that lead to more heated controversy than pupil motivation. From the following descriptions of the practices of three conscientious and intelligent teachers, it is apparent that each teacher has asked and answered in radically different ways such questions as: What teaching methods will motivate pupils to learn that which, as I see it, they should learn? What degree of coercion is appropriate to motivate children to learn? What kinds of coercion are most likely to lead to the best results? Are grades, examinations, credits, graduation requirements, and the like, the most promising tools for motivating learning? To move to a set of broader and, in the long run, more significant questions: How can I motivate children to be strong and self-respecting? To have wholesome relationships with their classmates? To resist exploitation? To avoid gullibility in the face of constant streams of propaganda? To put the questions in still more comprehensive terms: How can I so motivate my pupils that my whole educative influence will be oriented toward encouraging pupil growth—growth toward what the psychologists call self-actualization of the child?

Teacher A exacts strict obedience from his pupils. He tells the pupils all that they need to know and expects them to be able to repeat what he has told them. He makes daily assignments to be completed before the next class meeting. He gives frequent tests based upon the assignments; they are objective and rigorously graded. His methods of teaching are founded on the principle of authority. Pupils are trained to "behave" and to study "because the teacher says so." Teacher A relies heavily upon coercion, rewards for merit, definite assignments, and the like to motivate the pupils to learn what he expects them to learn.

In teacher B's class the pupils all study the same assignment. Learning is a contest. Pupils compete with one another, with the awards and approval consistently going to the winners. Pupils are graded on a curve of probability. The highest grade is awarded to the pupil at the top, with the lowest going to the pupil at the bottom. In the minds of the pupils, certain children are consistently "good," others are habitually "bad." The teacher believes that motivation stems from rivalry, and that the race for mastery is a fair one even though those who are required to compete are unequally endowed. He acts as a referee, making and enforcing the rules of the game. The strong survive. The weak fail—"as in life," teacher B observes. Success and failure, as measured against classmates' performances, are the primary sanctions.

Teacher C emphasizes group accomplishments and tries to build confidence in each pupil and goodwill among all of them. He encourages each pupil to contribute what he can to class projects. There is an exchange of ideas among pupils and between pupils and teacher, a sharing of responsibility. The theme of class work is cooperation. Grading is considered to be of minor importance. The teacher strives to encourage each pupil to develop along lines that are in accordance with his natural talents, to build confidence and self-respect, to develop a feeling of responsibility, and to be resistant to exploitation either of himself or of others. Sanctions lie in the success of the group and in the individual's acceptance by the group. Methods that motivate the pupils to learn allow the pupils considerable freedom of choice.

Let us assume that the three teachers are equally capable of

being good teachers. Why do they differ so markedly in their procedures? Fundamentally, they have different educational philosophies
that lead them to teach differently. They give different answers to the
question of what is good education. An analysis of their teaching
reveals several kinds of disagreement. There is, of course, the initial
disagreement about the most successful way of motivating pupils—
to put it briefly, whether authority, rivalry, or cooperation can best
stimulate pupils to achieve the desired ends. But there are also
disagreements about the ends themselves—whether, for example,
learning academic subjects is more worthwhile than learning to
compete with others, or learning to get along with others, and
whether all are desirable goals for the teacher in the classroom.
There are also disagreements about the justice of judging pupils according to a single standard. There are disagreements about the
relative value of directed and nondirected inquiry. Further, among
teachers who might agree that cooperation is the most desirable
basis for motivation, there will be innumerable differences about
what cooperation means in practice, and to what extent the restrictions of a classroom situation allow cooperation to be put into practice at all. There are just as many disagreements about the meaning
and practicability of authority and rivalry.

SOURCES OF DIFFERENCES

The kind of wide differences discerned in the examples illustrat-
ing questions related to motivation may be discovered in many
educational situations. Why are there such differences? What differences are typical? Where do differences originate?

We must not be led into the error of thinking that the differences that teachers have in answers to questions of an educational
nature can be explained in terms of differences in intelligence or
sincerity. Wide differences on many issues and problems may be
expected of teachers who are fully capable and deeply concerned for
the welfare of their pupils. If a teacher is not intelligent or interested, the decisions he makes may be wrong; but for a teacher to
make what others conclude is a wrong decision does not imply that
he is dull or insensitive.

That teachers cannot turn to a single unquestioned authority
for established answers to their questions explains in part the vari-

ation in their responses. If psychologists, for instance, knew a great deal more than they now know about the behavior of human beings, they might develop an authoritative theory that would be an accepted guide to teaching practice and thereby encourage uniformity.

Often the answers of the experts are in conflict. Teachers must choose among them. In answering questions related to motivation, for instance, it is generally agreed that the purposive activity a child engages in originates in his instincts and is expressed through learned incrustation of cultural derivation. Psychologists disagree as to what the instincts are and as to how they are molded by culture in determining the whole pattern of a child's behavior.

The answers to educational questions tend to be relative, not absolute. May a teacher use coercion? Perhaps the answer is a qualified *yes*. Coercion, yes, but coercion that is reasonable. What is reasonable coercion? Is there an ethical implication? Is the matter of good taste involved? Answers are also relative in terms of their setting. As new situations arise, not only do new questions arise, but the old ones take new forms. What was once considered a correct answer may, at another time, be thought incorrect.

Where, then, does the teacher turn for answers to his questions? What is the base that gives consistency to his educational practice? Our answer is, as the title of the chapter indicates, the teacher turns to a kind of thinking to which man has always turned throughout his historical existence—namely, philosophy. It is the principal purpose of this chapter to show the source of an educational philosophy and its place in helping the teacher to answer many questions he will have to answer, to resolve seemingly contradictory issues, and to give consistency to his educational practices.

WHAT IS PHILOSOPHY?

What is this base in terms of which educational questions are answered and educational practices patterned? This broad source which helps teachers answer questions? Where does it come from? A practical philosophy—which in contrast to a speculative philosophy is what we are concerned with here—is a thoughtful and critical view of the world that carries implications for action. This meaning of philosophy is in direct contrast with that which the term carries in popular usage, such as when any set of beliefs, unexamined and

The Peace Corps teacher above is teaching arithmetic to Bolivian children. These teaching experiences provide an important source of the educational philosophy she will evolve for herself. (Peace Corps, Washington, D.C.)

uncriticized, is spoken of as a philosophy—or as a philosophy of life —thus overextending a term that etymologically means a love of wisdom. Everyone holds a set of beliefs that guides his actions; not everyone has, by study and reflection, systematized those beliefs into a consistent philosophy.

A philosophy useful as a guide to the teacher in handling the problems that face him in his work is his philosophy of education.

SOURCES OF A TEACHER'S PHILOSOPHY

The more prominent sources from which philosophical truth has been derived are: personal experience, common sense, religion, science, and systematic philosophy. These terms, obviously, are not mutually exclusive. All of them, for example, include something of experience. We treat them separately because in common usage they are spoken of as though they were entities. In examining each of these sources we shall note that each has contributed to man's search for philosophical truth. We shall also discover that no one of these sources in itself is sufficient to serve as the sole base for an educational philosophy.

Experience

How does experience, one's self-conscious interaction with one's environment, contribute to an educational philosophy? A child's experiences, from the beginning, make impressions on him concerning the kind of world he lives in and the worth of people and things, including himself. He can develop a feeling, for instance, that he lives in a world that allows him to satisfy himself and to explore; or he can come to feel that he must constantly guard against threats to himself and his private belongings. Such feelings may remain as unformulated—sometimes unrecognized—attitudes, or they may be translated into conscious convictions. Some of the child's most lasting beliefs come from what people tell him. His parents, his teachers, and his peers make pronouncements with various degrees of authority. Some of their statements, to the extent that his experiences do not contradict them, are accepted by the child as fundamental truths. He develops deep-seated beliefs, too, based upon his emotional needs. If, for example, he has a strong need for rules to guide him in all his actions, he might invent such rules and come to regard them as moral laws. On the other hand, if he has an aversion for authority he might flagrantly disregard authority and rationalize his behavior. Some of his beliefs are based on his explorations of the world itself, still others on projecting analogies from what he has experienced to what is beyond his experience.

As his experience broadens, he comes in time to see that he cannot depend entirely upon his past experiences as a basis for his beliefs. He becomes conscious that beliefs based upon past experience are in need of constant critical examination and, perhaps, continual modification. He comes to realize that some of his beliefs, picked up haphazardly from so many random sources, conflict with one another. Stories he was told as a toddler are contradicted by what he is told in school. Earlier experiences are contradicted by newer experiences. New authorities may replace older ones. Reliance in the findings of the senses may grow stronger, and confidence in the discoveries of the imagination may weaken. When a person's beliefs conflict, he strives to resolve the dissonance. This attempt

The boys and girls in this mathematics class in a high school on a Navajo reservation are drawing up plans for new homes. Note the relaxed, friendly, cooperative atmosphere. (Ewing Galloway)

may lead him to drop or to ignore those beliefs that clash with more strongly held beliefs or to find ways of modifying the conflicting beliefs so that none needs to be completely relinquished. As experience and reflection add new data and new interpretations, new conflicts arise and some of the older beliefs fade into the background. In a continuous process, a person's system of beliefs ever evolves, becoming more and more complex.

Regardless of their range, an individual cannot depend solely upon his personal experiences to provide him with wholly reliable guides to action. If we look upon philosophy as a thoughtful and critical view of the world with implications for action, then our own experiences and the beliefs derived from them cannot be exempted from that critical view. A teacher's experiences, for example, do not provide him with answers to such educational questions as: What reason do I have for believing that a classroom with an atmosphere of democracy is to be preferred over one with an atmosphere of autocracy? One in which the teaching procedures are humane rather than harsh? How do I know that one kind of social arrangement in the classroom provides pupils with a more worthwhile experience than some other? What criteria shall I use to judge the educative values of certain kinds of classroom experiences? And where do I go to find those criteria? Although the student will raise many such questions as he proceeds with serious professional study, we shall not attempt to answer them here. We cite them to illustrate that beliefs derived from experience, while valuable, cannot answer every question that can legitimately be raised.

Common Sense

Aristotle is credited with having first used the term "common sense" to include the beliefs and knowledge people gain through their senses and reactions in the processes of ordinary day-by-day living. In America "common sense" is generally used to denote the fund of knowledge growing out of ordinary experience in solving practical questions. Common sense is frequently used carelessly to mean shrewdness and sharpness in practical matters. We use common sense to mean the accumulated body of knowledge that has been gained through common daily experience. Our generalizations from common experience include such patent rules as "food satisfies hunger," "fire burns," or "lightning strikes." The range of common sense beliefs in time becomes great, and such beliefs become important determinants in our day-to-day decisions.

It would be a mistake for teachers to place undue reliance upon common sense for wise solutions to educational problems, for dependable answers to questions about teaching. Knowledge that is shared by all must be based upon the most elementary kinds of human experience. In fact, no knowledge can be more elementary, no beliefs more simple, than those classified as common sense, because that is the knowledge and those are the beliefs that are derived from the simple, common experiences of daily living. Any educational belief that is said to be sanctioned by common sense, therefore, is a belief that is accepted at face value by a person who has received no training whatever, because no training was necessary to its formulation. Common sense cannot answer questions that call for specialized, technical knowledge.

Critical scrutiny is a preliminary requisite for most of the beliefs incorporated in an educational philosophy. The beliefs growing out of common sense tend to be accepted without critical scrutiny.

Excessive reliance upon common sense as the source of an educa-

A teacher's philosophy influences what the teacher thinks is important for children to learn. This teacher in a Hawaiian school is developing a social attitude by having the boys and girls participate in a community welfare project. (Penny Hunt, Department of Education, Honolulu)

tional philosophy may have unfortunate effects. It minimizes the importance of a methodical, cultivated philosophical foundation for educational beliefs. This means that the importance of extended training, thoughtful study, and serious pursuit of educational understandings are likewise minimized. If teaching problems could be solved by the application of common sense, then every citizen who believes he possesses common sense is justified in believing himself an educational expert. The opinions of the man on the street, the parents of the children, the popular journalist, the lecturer who talks on all subjects—opinions that may be expressions of biases and prejudices gained from simple experiences—would carry as much weight with the public as the opinions of the wisest educators.

What, then, is the contribution of common sense to the teacher's educational philosophy? How does it help him to answer educational questions, to make decisions related to his teaching practices? Common sense—good common sense—is essentially reliable. Danger lies in *undue* reliance on common sense. Common sense is one good source of beliefs, but it must be utilized in proper relationship to the other sources. It must not blind the teacher to the importance of seeking more training and experience, of going to the experts. The teacher must diligently seek help from sources that extend far beyond the sphere of common sense.

Religion

The universality and continuity of religion throughout history are evidence of its strength. Religious beliefs have had a pronounced influence upon all the major trends of human events.

A teacher's educational philosophy, being concerned with basic beliefs, has relevance in religion. Religion includes an unquestioned faith, indeed, an unshakeable conviction, about certain matters. In terms of these—man's highest values—man evaluates all else. Religious principles are not derived solely from experience past or current; they also originate in mystical insight. Religion is concerned with the ultimate end of man. It is also concerned with questions related to the good life. It is in this second of its concerns that it contributes most significantly to educational philosophy. Since

This is the Milwaukee in-migrant staff of specialists in a planning conference. Teachers who teach in culturally deprived areas are assisted in developing a workable philosophy by others who have made a study of the educational problems of deprived groups. (Arthur Leipzig, Ford Foundation)

both religion and education seek to promote the good life, religion contributes to the philosophy of education.

To say that one concern of religion is to promote the good life is not to say that every guide or signpost to the good life is furnished by religion. There may be several good answers to a particular problem, all of them acceptable from a religious standpoint. Another problem may have no religious implications at all. While the lessons of personal experience and common sense tend to help a teacher over familiar ground, the lessons of religion help him never to forget the ultimate goals of education and life.

Science

In our modern world of atomic energy and planetary satellites, science is probably the most highly respected source for educational beliefs and practices. Can science provide the answers to all our educational problems? Does an available fund of scientific knowledge obviate the need for a teacher to formulate an educational philosophy? Or does science serve as a ready reference in the development of a philosophy rather than as a substitute for a philosophy? In order that we may see clearly that science, undoubtedly, has an important relationship to philosophical thinking, but that science cannot provide answers to all of our educational problems, we shall briefly consider the nature of science, observing the subjects with which science deals.

From training in science in high school one gains an idea of what science is like. Perhaps one already knows, for instance, that science has customarily been subdivided into two categories—formal science and natural science; that mathematics is the classic example of formal science; that the natural sciences are those concerned with nature, such as biology, astronomy, and physics. Let us look more closely at each of the classifications.

Formal science, as the name indicates, is a science of form. It is an outcome of logical reasoning. Formal science begins with hypotheses or axioms that are taken to be true. Following the dictates of certain rules and definitions, the formal scientist reasons from these hypotheses and determines other truths that logically follow. If the hypothesis is true, the subsequent statements *have* to be true. The last statement in the sequence logically follows from the first. It is true, providing the first statement or hypothesis is true.

Euclidean geometry, more commonly called demonstrational geometry, is an example of a formal science. Algebra, too, is a formal science. It begins with a set of axioms thought to be true, that is, the truth is thought to be self-evident. Reasoning logically from these axioms leads to other truths.

A pure formal science is an exercise in logic in which the original statements are *assumed* to be true. The primary concern of the formal scientist is not with the truth of the original assumptions but with the logic followed while reasoning from the basic assumptions.

To what extent can we depend upon formal science to furnish answers to educational problems? We may be justified in answering, "Very little." Formal science is morally and ethically neutral toward all human issues. When, for instance, the mathematician proves a theorem, he accepts his proof as true because he rigorously followed certain rules and applied certain principles in arriving at that proof. He does not assume any responsibility for explaining to people how they should use the theorems he deduces and the formulas he accumulates. This he leaves to others.

The natural sciences are, in the order of their historical development, astronomy, physics, chemistry, biology, and sociology. This is a very broad classification that will serve the purpose of our discussion. For sake of simplification it omits such modern divisions as history, political science, psychology, and zoology, each of which may be considered a branch of one of the five basic classifications.

Can all our fundamental educational questions be answered from what is supplied by the natural sciences? Can we develop from the findings of the natural scientists a complete and harmonious educational philosophy? Note the kind of problems the natural sciences deal with and consider the principal characteristics of a field of knowledge that carries the distinction of qualifying as a science.

Alfred North Whitehead in his Lowell Lectures, given at Harvard University in 1925, expressed in very few words the underlying principle upon which the natural sciences are developed.

The faith in the order of nature which has made possible the growth of science is a particular example of a deeper faith. This faith cannot be justified by any inductive generalization. It springs from the direct inspection of the nature of things as disclosed in our own immediate present experience. There is no parting from our shadow.[1]

1 Alfred North Whitehead, *Science and the Modern World* (New York: The Macmillan Company, 1926), p. 27.

This inexpugnable faith of mankind that there is an order of nature defines the principal, if not the single, aim of natural science. The aim of the natural sciences is to discover the laws to which events in nature conform. It is this aim that motivates the natural scientists to strive so energetically to discover the pattern of natural events.

> The raw material of every science must always be an accumulation of facts. . . . But, as Poincaré remarked, an accumulation of facts is no more a science than a heap of stones is a house. When we set to work . . . to create a science we must first coordinate and synthesize the accumulated piles of facts. It is then usually found that a great number of separate facts can be summed up in a much smaller number of general laws. . . . These express the pattern of events for which we are searching.[2]

If we wish to discover the truth about nature . . . the only sound method is to go out into the world and question nature directly, and this is the long established and well-tried method of science. Questioning our own minds is of no use; just as questioning nature can tell us truths only about nature, so questioning our own minds will tell us truths only about our own minds.

The general recognition of this has brought philosophy in closer relations with science, and this approach has coincided with a change of view as to the proper aims of philosophy. The ancient philosophers pursued their studies in the hope of finding a lantern which should guide their feet along the best path in their journey through this life, the philosophers of the seventeenth and eighteenth centuries in a fixed determination to find evidence that this journey ended in a life to come. This humanistic tinge has taken a long time to disappear, but has almost done so in recent years; philosophy has become less concerned with ourselves and more concerned with the universe outside ourselves. . . .

This may seem to suggest that philosophy should have not only the same methods but also the same aims and also, broadly speaking, the same field of work as science. . . . The tools of science are observation and experiment; the tools of philosophy are discussion and contemplation. It is still for science to try to discover the pattern of events, and for philosophy to try to interpret it when found. . . .

From Sir James Jeans, *Physics and Philosophy* (New York: Cambridge University Press, 1943), pp. 80–81. Quoted by permission of Cambridge University Press.

It should be noted that the natural scientists make no claim to a discovery of the causes of natural events. They are content to learn,

[2] Sir James Jeans, *Physics and Philosophy* (New York: Cambridge University Press, 1943), p. 8.

with the limited tools at their disposal, what the pattern of events is and to describe the pattern as accurately as they can. Whatever discoveries they make seem to be in answer to man's insatiable curiosity to learn the pattern of the natural events that govern the world in which he must live. The primary aim of natural science, namely, to discover the pattern of natural events, leaves to the province of others the task of deciding what is to be done with their findings.

The development of science, of course, is inherently dynamic. Its findings have positive and immediate effects upon men's lives in untold ways. Particularly does science lead to a progressive modification of many of man's traditional beliefs. Education is not exempt from its tremendous influence. Sociology, mathematics, biology, political science, psychology, history—all make notable contributions. They do not, however, provide an authoritative base for educational decisions or serve as a substitute for educational philosophy.

The aims of both natural and formal science render them philosophically neutral and impersonal. Science endeavors to tell us what is. Science does not claim to tell us what should be. Educational philosophy utilizes the knowledge of formal and natural science, but its concern extends beyond the limitations of the sciences.

Philosophic Doctrine

In philosophic doctrine, in the particular principles advocated or taught by the various so-called "systems" of philosophy or "schools" of philosophy, we have another resource that is valuable in formulating an educational philosophy.

Professional philosophers over the years have thought about man's problems in the light of knowledge from various specialized fields and have developed solutions and drawn conclusions about how solutions can be derived. A philosopher may have selected a particular problem or a particular hypothesis regarding the solution of a particular problem. By studying the main lines of relationships among all the facts that have a bearing on the making of human decisions, the philosopher finally has arrived at a generalization, a particular world view, a potential guide in making such decisions. If the process of reasoning leads logically to a statement of a philosophy that advocates a particular viewpoint, one that is consistent in all its parts and in the relationships between the facts used, and if

William James, about 1885. (From Ralph Barton Perry, *The Thought and Character of William James*, Little, Brown and Company—Atlantic Monthly Press, Boston)

the principles derived and the bearing they have upon arriving at human decisions are set forth in logical order, the philosophy is said to be a systematic one, an expression of a philosophic doctrine.

Some of the better known philosophic doctrines have been classified in terms of their general characteristics and are known by such names as dualism, eclecticism, idealism, realism, rationalism, pragmatism, or existentialism. Sometimes a philosophic doctrine is identified with the name of the man who developed it. Taking the German philosophers, for example, we have doctrines identified with Kant, Fichte, Schelling, Hegel, Schopenhauer, Fechner, Lotze, Hartmann, Nietzsche, and Wundt. Sometimes a doctrine may relate to a single area of knowledge. A scholar may, for instance, develop a systematic philosophy of history. This has been done by such writers as Toynbee, Mannheim, Niebuhr, Frankel, and Maritain. One may find a philosophy of physics, of law, of religion, of biology, of government, of psychology, of education. Great thinkers are concerned with the development of philosophic doctrine. They do not bother with problems of little significance.

It is generally accepted that William James (1842–1910) has no peer among the philosophers of America. He received the M.D. degree at Harvard University in 1870 and taught at Harvard from 1872 until his death in 1910, first teaching anatomy and physiology, then psychology, and finally in the latter stages of his academic life, philosophy.

In 1891 James published a monumental work in two great volumes called *The Principles of Psychology*. The books were immediately recognized as innovating and definitive. They can still be read with enjoyment and profit. These works completed, James turned to that profoundest of subjects—philosophy—for which he now believed himself prepared. Subsequent to 1900 most of his writing was done in this field.

Like Peirce by whom he was influenced, James was trained as a scientist. It is not strange, therefore, that in harmony with Peirce's Principle, he constructed a philosophy that was a generalization of the scientific attitude toward the whole of life. James believed that philosophy, like science, should follow the method of finding the facts and of then harmonizing the facts to provide man with a basis for reasoning out answers to his perplexing problems, for solving his enigmas, and for making his distinctions, and to supply man with more or less valid principles to use as instruments with which to think. Using the descriptive term first used by Peirce, James referred to the method of pragmatism as "a new name for some old ways of thinking."

In December, 1906, and in January, 1907, James developed his understandings of the meaning of the pragmatic movement in a series of eight lectures given at Columbia University.

A number of tendencies that have always existed in philosophy have all at once become conscious of themselves collectively, and of their combined mission; and this has occurred in so many countries, and from so many different points of view, that much unconcerted statement has resulted. I have sought to unify the picture as it presents itself to my own eyes, dealing in broad strokes, and avoiding minute controversy.

James not only stated that he was not expounding a new philosophy; he even questioned the propriety of calling the method of pragmatism a philosophy. Subsequent to these lectures, however, throughout the English-speaking world, he became the leader, if not of a new philosophy, at least of a new philosophical viewpoint.

Although James died August 6, 1910, it is still too early to estimate the influence of his philosophy. It is, however, obvious that his high place among philosophers is secure. While he assiduously avoided erecting a new philosophy for others to repeat, he nevertheless supplied the seed and the soil that germinated new thought in all who considerately weighed what he said.

Charles S. Peirce (1839–1914) was a graduate of Harvard University and the Lawrence scientific school. As a member of the staff of the U.S. Coast Survey, his work on the problems of geodesy and his researches on the pendulum received wide recognition. In 1880 and 1881 he gave a series of lectures at Johns Hopkins University on philosophical logic, expanding upon the ideas he had advanced in his article in the January, 1878, issue of *Popular Science Monthly*. Although he had not used the word "pragmatism" in his article, he is credited with having formulated the idea which is generally referred to as Peirce's Principle and to have connected the name "pragmatism" with the idea. According to William James, the principle of pragmatism lay unnoticed for twenty years until he, in 1898, in a lecture at the University of California, reintroduced the term. Said James, "By that date [1898] the times seemed ripe for its reception. The word 'pragmatism' spread, and at present it fairly spots the pages of the philosophic journals."

Peirce was the first of the famous trio of American pragmatists—Peirce, James, and Dewey. The combined influence of the three upon education in America can scarcely be assessed.

As discussed in this chapter, the responsibility for developing one's philosophy lies within oneself. In developing a personal philosophy one often turns for help to the writings of the professional philosophers. Whether one accepts or rejects, in whole or in part, the philosophy from these writings, one will discover the professional philosopher's point of view, his line of reasoning that led to his beliefs about the solutions of various human problems.

As the teacher turns to science for scientific knowledge, he turns to philosophic doctrine for scholarly conclusions about philosophic matters. The philosophic doctrine expounded by a scholar like John Dewey, for example, is a helpful guide to a teacher in forming his own philosophy. How a specific doctrine affects a teacher will depend upon the teacher's understanding of and response to the philosophic doctrine. His response will be conditioned by his understanding and by his entire thoughtful, critical view of the world.

CHARACTERISTICS OF A TEACHER'S PHILOSOPHY

A teacher's philosophy reflects his experience, his common sense, his religion, science, and philosophic doctrine. Some characteristics are clear in the definition of an educational philosophy:

John Dewey.
(Courtesy Columbia University)

a thoughtful and critical view of the world that carries implications for educational action. Two important specific characteristics are, in a sense, an amplification of this definition. An educational philosophy is personal. An educational philosophy is socially conditioned.

Personal

A teacher's educational philosophy grows out of his own experiences and is modified by his own reexamination based upon the principles of criticism that he chooses to apply. His developed philosophy is a description, explanation, and evaluation of the world as seen from his unique perspective. He can turn for help to many sources, but no matter how many sources he may draw upon or how many authorities he may listen to, the decision is his to accept or reject the would-be truths presented to him. His decision is free; it is shaped by his attitudes and presuppositions.

Although a teacher may not get outside himself to develop a purely objective view of the world, he can broaden himself by expanding the area of his experience, by trying to understand other people's perspectives, and by developing the habit of analyzing problems from various perspectives. He can also cultivate the practice

John Dewey (1859–1952) developed the pragmatic philosophy with an educational and social focus. He was a native of Vermont and a graduate of the University of Vermont and later of Johns Hopkins University. After graduation from Johns Hopkins he went west to teach philosophy, first at the University of Minnesota (1888–1889), then Michigan (1889–1894), and then Chicago (1894–1904). As Director of the School of Education at the University of Chicago, he established an experimental school that carried out his ideas of the new pedagogy. It was through this work and his writings in connection with it that he won national fame. In 1904 he became Professor of Philosophy at Columbia University. It was here that his philosophy began to influence the social and philosophical thought of his time. His numerous writings have had a profound influence on the theory and practice of education in American schools. One of Dewey's students, William Heard Kilpatrick (1871–   ), speaks of Dewey's influence on education as follows:

Possibly no service of John Dewey to American education, in fact to American thinking in general, has been greater than his help in better methods of thinking. The America of his youth was on the whole content to think in terms of unexamined terms most of which meant entities where in fact there were no entities but processes. Will, consciousness, faculties as memory, reasoning and the like, instincts, intelligence, mind—these are but samples of processes masquerading as entities. James's pragmatism (following Peirce) and Dewey's experimentalism here joined hands with the rising army of scientific thinkers to question everything that could be questioned.

For teachers Dewey's *How We Think,* and particularly the seventh chapter (of the original edition) on "The Analysis of a Complete Act of Thought," has directly and indirectly brought great tonic effect. Through these, as stated earlier, American education discovered, so to speak, "the problem approach" as a teaching device. The effect has been very great. . . . It is . . . easy to assert that this one book has brought a wide emphasis on problems and the conscious use of problems in school work.

From Paul Schilpp (ed.), *The Philosophy of John Dewey* (2d ed.; New York: Tudor Publishing Company, 1955), pp. 469–470. Quoted by permission of The Library of Living Philosophers, Inc.

of subjecting his own cherished beliefs to a critical cross-examination. The quality of his educational philosophy rests on his willingness continuously to explore and criticize.

Take as example a teacher who, let us assume, comes from a middle-class background and who, during and prior to his teaching career, has had experience only with children of one fairly homogeneous ethnic, social, economic group. He will tend to apply generalizations based on his experiences with them to children generally. He may, for instance, believe that high-school boys develop interest in a subject only when its vocational possibilities are stressed. His belief may be justified in terms of his experience. But faced with a conflicting view from a reputable source, or, more important, faced with a different group of children, it is a grave mistake for this teacher blindly to maintain his existing beliefs.

Because his educational philosophy is personal, it will not be static as long as the teacher continues to grow. A broadening of experience and a critical evaluation of it will result in a constantly evolving and improving educational philosophy. We observed earlier that a person's collection of beliefs develops gradually with experience. Similarly, the critical examination of beliefs, called philosophizing, is not a temporally bounded event that should come to a final solution. It, too, is a continuing process. A person does not overhaul his entire set of beliefs at one time. Modifications are made under the impulses of observed conflict.

It is important for the teacher to regard his beliefs, and particularly his educational beliefs, as tentative, properly subject to reexamination whenever facts or other beliefs challenge them. To fail to recognize the imperfect foundations on which all beliefs are built is to endorse the delusions of dogmatism. Equally dangerous is the contrary fault, indecision, which is often an attempt to avoid commitment to a belief until irreproachable grounds for it are discovered. A measure of positive conviction is essential to prudent and courageous action even though objective certainty is not within human reach. Holding beliefs as tentative does not necessarily lead to a lack of conviction. A teacher can arrive at his conclusions on the best evidence available to him but can be prepared to change them when better evidence arises.

Socially Conditioned

The sources of a teacher's educational philosophy—the areas of experience and knowledge that are open to him—are contingent upon the society and the groups in which he lives. He speaks the language of his society and develops his ideas in its terms. He tends to adopt the customs of his society as his own habits and to value what his society approves. Even the methods of critical reflection by which he can reevaluate his beliefs are limited by what he learns from his environment. To the extent that a person is a creature of his society, so also is his philosophy.

Thus, in a society dominated by a single set of values, a teacher has little opportunity to make an independent choice of values. But where, as in America, ranges of values exist, the teacher, while not entirely free, is able to exercise much more leeway in his choice of values. This requires him to have greater responsibility for making his value choices intelligently. Value choice means, in simplest terms, the act of choosing between what is thought to be good education and what is believed to be bad. Education that is good is a value; so, likewise, is bad education.

Throughout discussions on educational practice we find almost continual reference made to terms implying values such as purposes, goals, preferences, interests, correctness, character, duties, ideals, freedom, truth, beauty, self-actualization—to list a few. Each of these terms implies that choice must be made. What purposes are most worthy? What goals are most desirable? What interests are the most wholesome? In American education, no one set of values can be considered dominant, as one will discover when he attempts to satisfy any group of educators with answers to the questions just raised. Different teachers make different value choices. Fortunately for the teaching profession in America, more than in most societies, there is both public and official toleration of diversity and dissent, as well as opportunities for varied experiences and frequent exposure to many value systems. This is perhaps because American society comprises many groups who have differing traditions, who live in greatly varied circumstances, and who cherish differing sets of values, many in transition and many displaying the internal conflicts that result from eclectic development. The multiple origins of the American people, the social mobility characteristic of a democracy, and the rapid changes of a technological age are responsible for diversity and flux both in basic beliefs and in value systems.

Among the conflicts that beset a socially conditioned educational philosophy is the conflict between traditional and emergent beliefs. Values on which the American society was once in substantial agreement—hard work, personal success, planning for the future, an emphasis on the good of the individual, a deep-seated respect for moral law—are being challenged by emerging value systems that stress sociability, sensitivity to others, present values in contrast to deferred values, group harmony, and a relativistic attitude toward morals. Other conflicts are caused by differences among ethnic groups and economic classes. Yet, with all the diversities in values and beliefs, there exists in America a pragmatic unity, especially in political life, and a willingness to compromise and cooperate. For example, democratic processes are uniformly held in deep respect. This unity in viewpoint stems in part from an orientation to action rather than to theory, and from a recognition that disagreement in philosophy does not preclude agreement in practice.

Over-all unity and internal diversity of value systems carry numerous implications for teaching. The unity tends to bring practical agreement on educational questions and to make persuasion effective where disagreement exists. Teachers strongly desire consensus before making final group decisions. Efforts are made to reason questions through to a point where consensus is reached. Teachers, for example, may agree that good citizenship is a worthy goal, but what good citizenship is when judged in terms of specific schoolroom situations may be a matter of some disagreement. Even so, the teaching staffs of individual schools can and do arrive at intelligent agreement about matters calling for practical action. This is partly because the individual school in American education is a subsociety in which the range of differences is normally smaller than in the whole society. The more intimate interaction among the teachers, strengthened, perhaps, by similar backgrounds, leads in time to a degree of homogeneity in basic beliefs. This core of common beliefs makes it easier for teachers in an individual school to communicate with one another, with pupils and parents, and to understand the problems of individual pupils. Thus teachers are able to develop a healthy degree of teamwork as they face educational situations.

Diversity, of course, makes communication and agreement somewhat more difficult. At the same time, however, it opens the way to an enriched education for pupils through teachers who have outgrown the provincialism of limited experience and unquestioning acceptance of early beliefs. Diversity entails a contrast among traditions that is necessary if pupils are to appreciate fully the worth of their own traditions and those of others. It also causes a conflict among ideas, a conflict that is necessary and desirable if ideas are to be judged on their merit rather than on their orthodoxy. But the actualization of the more valued of the possibilities requires a teacher with intellectual toleration.

A teacher, then, should always be aware that diversity leads to conflict, not only between groups, but within the growing individual who borrows beliefs from various groups and thereby internalizes intergroup conflict. Cultural diversity is thus responsible for some of the inconsistencies a person discovers on examining his own be-

Booker T. Washington (1859–1915) ranks among the most influential American educational leaders. He founded Tuskegee Institute at Tuskegee, Alabama, in 1881 and remained as its head until his death. Under his leadership the institute became an outstanding educational institution in the fields of teacher education, nurse and hospital education, industrial arts, and household arts. He excelled in the art of teaching, writing, and public speaking, through which avenues he influenced countless numbers of people. He propagated a definite educational philosophy. The education program at Tuskegee was built on the principle that education would be more meaningful "if it stuck close to the common and familiar things—things that concern the greater part of the people the greater part of the time." His emphasis was upon solving problems that arose in connection with the practical needs of those who were being educated. Thus he provided an outstanding example of how a philosophy of education could be incorporated in institutional practice.

liefs. A teacher may find, for example, that his belief in the importance of group harmony both as a principle and as a guide to classroom conduct conflicts with his belief in the importance of individual development. Conceivably he can find ways of eliminating or reducing such conflicts. The first step, of course, is to become aware of important conflicts and conscious of the major issues. Subsequently, as the teacher analyzes his problems and decides his course of action, he will use his personal yet socially conditioned educational philosophy to help resolve his problems and to decide his plans of action.

CONCLUSION

The task of developing his educational philosophy belongs to the individual teacher. As he develops his philosophy he will seek help from many sources, even though the philosophy will be his own. It will be consonant with him and with everything that has made him what he is. He will use his philosophy in choosing his ideals and in deciding on educational aims. His educational philosophy will be a practical help in answering questions related to the selection of subject matter, in choosing teaching procedures, and in determining relationships with associates in the school.

QUESTIONS

1. What, in your opinion, should be the relationship between philosophical thinking and educational practice?
2. Why is it that one's educational philosophy must, perforce, be one's own?
3. What is there about educational philosophy that makes it impossible for one to state one's educational philosophy once and for all? What kinds of experiences should a teacher seek in order to broaden his educational philosophy?
4. What is a value? How does one decide that one value is better than another?
5. What is the difference between the word "principle" used in the scientific sense, and the same word used in the ethical sense?
6. Referring to the three teachers described in this chapter, choose the one you think is best. What is the basis for your choice?
7. Why is it not possible for one to make his educational practice conform at all times to the dictates of the more recent findings of physiology and psychology?
8. Why have the educational philosophies that have evolved from past philosophical thinking differed so markedly from one another?

PROJECTS

1. Give an example that will illustrate how each of the following contributes to the formulation of one's educational philosophy: (a) personal experience, (b) common sense, (c) religion, (d) science, and (e) systematic philosophy.
2. (a) State an educational question the answer to which cannot be found in your past personal experience; (b) the answer to which cannot be supplied by common sense; (c) the answer to which is not supplied by science.
3. State an educational principle you believe to be true. Locate the sources that led you to believe in its validity.
4. Give a number of concrete examples that illustrate how one's educational philosophy is socially conditioned.
5. List a few of your cherished beliefs and comfortable patterns of living that have undergone modification in recent years. Explain what caused you to modify your beliefs.

CHAPTER **6**

The teacher
and the institution

W e have examined what a teacher does, how he qualifies, what
his relationships to the profession are, and why his philosophy
is important. It is also important to interpret what he does and
should do in terms of his reciprocal relations with the total personnel of a school or a school system. For an accurate picture of the
total work of the teacher we must take into account the institutional character of the school and recognize the impact of the
school as an institution on what the teacher does and how he does it.

SCHOOLS AS INSTITUTIONS

What an Institution Is

In order to understand how the institutionalization of education dictates to a considerable degree what education shall be and
conditions somewhat the work of teachers, we turn to the question
of what an institution is and then discuss some of its effects.

"Institution" is defined with slightly different emphasis by the social philosopher, the social psychologist, and the sociologist. We turn to the definitions of the latter because it is the sociologists who, more than the highly specialized social philosophers or social psychologists, deal with the fundamental laws of social relations and institutions and who concern themselves with basic social phenomena.

One sociologist writes:

More commonly the term *institution* is applied to those features of social life which outlast biological generations or survive drastic changes that might have been expected to bring them to an end. . . . Institutions are the established forms of procedure by which group activity is carried on.[1]

Another sociologist states:

Institutions . . . are patterns governing behavior in social relationships which have become interwoven with a system of common moral sentiments which in turn define what one has a "right to expect" of a person in a certain position.
. . . the essential aspect of social structure lies in a system of patterned expectations defining the *proper* behavior of persons playing certain roles, enforced both by the incumbent's own positive motives for conformity and by the sanctions of others. Such systems of patterns of patterned expectations, seen in the perspective of their place in a total social system and sufficiently thoroughly established in action to be taken for granted as legitimate, are conveniently called "institutions."[2]

Another sociologist gives still a slightly different emphasis in his definition of "institution."

The real component units of culture which have a considerable degree of permanence, universality and independence are the organized systems of human activities called institutions. Every institution centers around a fundamental need, permanently unites a group of people in a cooperative task and has its particular body of doctrine and its technique or craft. . . . But institutions show a pronounced amalgamation of functions and have a synthetic character. Each of them satisfies a variety of needs.[3]

From these general definitions it is not difficult to identify the characteristics of a school that qualify the school and various features of the school as American institutions. As society felt the need

[1] R. M. MacIver, *Society: A Textbook of Sociology* (New York: Holt, Rinehart and Winston, Inc., 1937), pp. 14, 15–16.
[2] Talcott Parsons, *Essays in Sociological Theory* (rev. ed.; New York: The Macmillan Company, 1954), pp. 143, 231. Quoted by permission of the publisher.
[3] Bronislaw Malinowski, "Culture," *Encyclopedia of the Social Sciences* (1931), p. 626.

for ordered, systematic fulfillment of the educational requirements of children, the school came into being. As it acquired the qualities of permanence, universality, and independence, the institution emerged.

We note that an institution possesses the characteristic of persistency. Even if some technical advance were invented that might achieve a desired end, the institution and its established practices of achieving the end tend to persist.

The definitions also stress continuity in conscious forms of group behavior. The history of the school is, in one sense, a history of a continuous form of collective behavior. When we think of the school, just as when we think of the family or the church, we immediately summon certain images of definite forms of collective behavior which are characteristic of the institution—forms of behavior continuous from generation to generation. An individual within the school realizes that the institution is older than he and is expected to outlive him. He fits into the stream of continuity. He expects to behave, within limits, as have his predecessors.

Another idea carried by the definitions is that the institution exercises a degree of restraint upon the individual. Participants are subjected to a degree of control. The school, for instance, furnishes the pupils, personnel, and, to an extent, also the parents with a routine of life, with patterns of expected behavior by which they will be judged, and with objectives and ambitions toward which they may strive. The school encompasses recognized rules, formal procedures for their application, and a structure consisting of persons acting officially. The school and all other institutions are subject in some measure to the common mores. In addition, the school is a vehicle of conscious and formal control over the years when children are compelled or are voluntarily enrolled. School personnel often attempt to bring to explicit formulation matters that have been subject to the mores, and to apply to them the formal procedures of the school. Insofar as teachers and other school personnel successfully set themselves up as the proper persons to define and enforce the mores, these take on the qualities of the law. Identification with the established rights and duties growing out of society's deliberate organization of knowledge and techniques to fulfill the need for education is part of the process by which a teacher becomes a person with a social identity.

Institutionalization embraces the concept that human relation-

The school serves the community in many ways. Here it serves as a center for the administering of polio vaccine to the citizens. (Monkmeyer)

ships within its organization are structured, that they are consistent with a fairly well-defined pattern. A school—an institution—has a basic structure, and he who functions within the school fulfills a fairly definite role—a role that fits into the total pattern of roles played by all the participants. As Parsons expresses it, "His role is defined by the normative expectations of the members of the group as formulated in its social traditions."[4]

On a wider perspective we see the school as a social institution playing its part in a total pattern of institutions and contributing to a total system of social integration of which it is a part. Along with other institutions the school contributes to uniting human beings in a stable system. It shares in regulating and establishing the rules that determine the relations of individuals to one another. Also, in common with the other social institutions, the schools make such adaptations to the environment and such internal adjustments as seem necessary to advance a well-ordered social life.

The school shares in the fulfillment of unique and significant functions. It is vitally responsible for teaching children the techniques and rules of society, the particular ways of doing all the things society cherishes. The school is interrelated with other institutions, for example, the family. It is also interrelated with informal parts of our culture such as community attitudes. The school's functions are to be understood only in relation to the total social system. The same is true of any institution.

[4] *Op. cit.,* p. 230.

Schools in all parts of the country serve as voting centers. (Shelton from Monkmeyer)

Why Education Is Institutionalized

The education of the young in any country can, conceivably, be carried on without the establishment of schools. It may be left, for example, to the family or to the church or to industry, or it may be shared by all these. Why have various societies chosen to institutionalize education? Why do the schools in the United States have a kind of organization, rules, regulations, customs, traditions, and practices that are now associated with them? How do these common understandings among many people about the functions of the schools influence the work of the teachers in the schools?

Basically the reason for the institutionalization of education is the same as the reason for the institutionalization of other large group interests. There has been first of all a felt need. Driving on the right side of the street became an institution in the United States because of a widely recognized need for traffic order. Institutionalization was the solution to a perplexing social problem. When people felt the need for children to be educated in a deliberate fashion, their common response was the organized school, eventually with the rules, organization, and customs that are attached to it.

The school was established for a particular purpose—as an answer to a felt need. This does not mean, however, that originally there was unanimity as to how, specifically, this need should be met. Eventually a pattern, conforming in general to the broad outlines of what most people desired, was evolved. In time the pattern became standardized and ultimately the word "school" meant approximately the same to everyone. The school had become an institution as the result of a degree of unity of beliefs about what it should be and should do. Once established, the school served to further the degree of unanimity of belief.

Effects of Institutionalization

The institutionalization of education brings many benefits to the individual pupil and to the individual teacher. It preserves cultural values in customs and traditions. As an institution the school has qualities of endurance and stability. It benefits from being uni-

Usually public schools are centers for adult evening classes. These mothers are learning how to decorate a whole cold ham for buffet serving. Adult education is generally based wholly upon the needs and interests of the students. In large cities the adult day and evening programs are attended by large numbers. The offerings are extensive and expertly taught. (Shelton from Monkmeyer)

versally accepted. Conformity to and continuance of accepted practices result in universal familiarity and encourage understanding and sharing.

On the other hand, the characteristics of continuity may have some adverse effects. Accepted practices, customs, and traditions may exert undue pressure on an individual to conform. Originality may be curbed and wholesome freedom for creativeness restricted. Likewise, change within the institution may be retarded. Because the school is an institution, it is based on cultural values and is related to the preservation of social values. This means that, in some measure, the schools resist change.

Institutions are viewed in their educative effect:—with reference to the type of individuals they foster. The interest in individual moral improvement and the social interest in objective reform of economic and political conditions are identified. And inquiry into the meaning of social arrangements gets definite point and direction. We are led to ask what the specific stimulating, fostering, and nurturing power of each specific social arrangement may be. . . . Just what response does *this* social arrangement, political or economic, evoke, and what effect does it have upon the disposition of those who engage in it? Does it release capacity? If so, how widely? Among a few, with a corresponding depression in others, or in an extensive and equitable way? Is the capacity which is set free also directed in some coherent way, so that it becomes a power, or is its manifestation spasmodic and capricious?

Since responses are of an indefinite diversity of kind, these inquiries have to be detailed and specific. Are man's senses rendered more delicately sensitive and appreciative, or are they blunted and dulled by this and that form of social organization? Are their minds trained so that the hands are more deft and cunning? Is curiosity awakened or blunted? What is its quality: is it merely aesthetic, dwelling on the forms and surfaces of things, or is it also an intellectual searching into their meaning? Such questions as these . . . become the starting-points of inquiries about every institution of the community when it is recognized that individuality is not originally given but is created under the influences of associated life.

From John Dewey, *Reconstruction in Philosophy* (New York: Holt, Rinehart and Winston, Inc., 1920), pp. 196–198. Quoted by permission of the publisher.

As the story of education in the United States unfolds, we become conscious that so-called "cultural lag" and "institutional lag" apply to education. For example, technological advances may indicate the desirability of changing techniques in teaching science and mathematics. Certain well-established traditions, however, may be a bulwark sufficiently strong to perpetuate techniques inconsistent with the contemporary life picture or inadequate in terms of current social demands. Sometimes practices in the schools lag behind those in other institutions or do not keep pace with the needs of pupils. There is a tendency for the school, since it is a social institution with the characteristics of permanence and continuity, to lag behind the point of advancement indicated by social understanding and professional theory. The lag varies with communities, with states, and with sections of the country.

It is important that a teacher be conscious that he is part of an institution. He makes decisions and acts in terms of a superstructure that has both a regulatory and a protective effect upon everything he does. The institution is embedded in customs and traditions that have origins historically remote. However, it is also currently dynamic, an organization that contributes to the teacher and to which the teacher contributes.

Ideas and the Institution

The current pattern of American schools and school systems and the contemporary traditions in educational practices have resulted from a recombination of ideas and from institutional accommodations to the ideas that have been influencing social institutions for countless thousands of years. Because this topic justifies a more extended discussion, a study of the impact of some of the ideas and their influence on present-day institutional patterns of education in the United States is pursued in Unit Two. Obviously, no adequate interpretation of education is fully explored if regulations, rules, customs, and typical practices are considered apart from the ideas and social values upon which these institutional characteristics have their foundation.

THE TEACHER AS A GROUP MEMBER

Variety of Memberships

In studying the work of the teacher we indicated certain duties and responsibilities which were added because the teacher is a mem-

One could not even begin to count all the ways in which the citizens of America make use of their schools. These children are viewing pictures and sculpture at an annual art auction. Prominent artists contribute their work. Proceeds defray some school expenses not covered in the budget. (Courtesy Downtown Community School, New York City)

ber of an organized group that shares certain common tasks and whose work has to be coordinated with the work of others. Besides being associated in an institution established for the education of the young, a teacher is part of a variety of other groups also, by virtue of his employment in the school.

The over-all, organized group is, of course, the faculty group which may be a district-wide group or a school-wide group. Whether the group is an intra-school or extra-school group, membership is implied with employment and the duties assigned the teacher always include certain tasks that are related to coordinating work within both kinds of groups. Often the meetings of the district-wide group are annual or semiannual, coming perhaps before the opening of school in the fall and at some designated time during the year when the pupils are dismissed. Frequently, the district-wide meeting is enlarged to include a number of school districts in some geographical unit determined by county limits or by the sections of the state organization of the NEA. Often the local teacher groups cooperate with school administrators in planning and executing the meetings.

In the local school the number and kind of professional groups to which the teacher belongs will be determined somewhat by the size of the school and somewhat by the philosophy of the school. If the school is large and the policy is to encourage cooperation and participation, the teacher may belong to several professional groups, in addition to the general faculty group. These might include, for instance, all the social studies teachers, all the freshman homeroom teachers, or a group made up of the teachers new to the system.

In addition to the groups to which the teacher is probably required to belong and that are directly related to his professional work, the teacher belongs to numerous groups which may be quite nebulous in their purpose and indefinite in their membership boundaries but which usually, nevertheless, have a significant bearing upon the teacher's satisfactions and happiness in his job.

When a number of people are together for any considerable length of time, they tend to form small groups based upon some shared purpose, common interest, or other factor which draws individuals together. For instance, a teacher may be a member of a married teachers' group. The group probably will not be related to

The oft-repeated statement that the school is a social institution calls for liberal interpretation. Here the lunch room serves as a center for the annual senior mother-daughter party. Social events like dances, teas, and dinners are often held in the schools. (Bloom from Monkmeyer)

any school activities; it may get together only after school hours. But the fact remains that it *is* a group and members talk things over and present a more or less common front on many matters, often matters pertaining to the school. The group may be comprised of those interested in a particular hobby. The golfers, for instance, may get together for dinner and golf or for week-end outings. Perhaps the teachers who live in a particular region have a car pool and discuss and develop a measure of unity as they share time spent in transportation. Perhaps a difference of opinion over some school policy divides the teachers into opposing groups. Those in an elementary school who believe, for instance, in traditional report cards and letter-grading oppose those who advocate written messages and parent conferences. They may form a group, a kind of clique, and sit together at faculty meetings and vote alike even on issues entirely unrelated to the report card matter.

The possibilities of group membership for the teacher, even in his school associations, are many and exceedingly varied. A point to remember is that such memberships may be a powerful factor in the teacher's satisfaction with his work. A teacher's pleasure in helping Johnny advance to sixth-grade reading level may be mitigated by the knowledge that some other teachers have a weekly card game to which he has not been invited.

A teacher, and especially a new teacher, should be conscious that it is possible to make errors of lasting effect by hastily affiliating with some social group or other. Groups cannot usually be judged at their face value; they often are in conflict with one another; potent feelings of security and respect may be involved. Social groups within the faculty, as social groups within any other group, represent a challenge to human relations, a problem requiring tact and consideration.

Evaluating a Teacher Membership Group

In evaluating the effectiveness of a school as an institution contributing to the requirements of its personnel for group membership, what criteria should be used? What should participation in a school group contribute to the members? For, just as each individual is expected to contribute to the institution so, likewise, should the institution be expected to contribute to the individual.

First, participation in the school group should entail fulfilling a clearly designated role which, when successfully and efficiently performed, brings to the individual a feeling that he is respected and considered to be important by all those with whom he has institutional connections. It is particularly important for him to know that his superior officers respect him and feel that he is important.

An individual's work in the institution should net a financial reward high enough to ensure physical health and the fulfillment of reasonable desires with respect to food, clothes, housing, travel, automobile, and hobbies.

The school should not unduly inhibit the desire of an individual teacher to make his own decisions, shape the course of his own life, and direct the course of his own actions.

It is important also that the institution make it possible for each of its members to contribute to the full extent of his abilities. In a school where, because of the narrowness of an assigned role, only a portion of a teacher's capabilities are permitted to function, both the school and the teacher suffer a loss.

The individual's desire for and achievement of a well-integrated personality and group morale can be encouraged or hindered by the institution. A school in which the efforts of the personnel are carefully and skillfully coordinated contributes to these ends.

Adjustments Within the Group

What adjustments must teachers make because they are guided in their actions by the goals of an institution and are thus subject to institutional restraints?

Institutional behavior is, to a considerable degree, regulated behavior. The school legislates this behavior through a social superstructure consisting of traditions, rules, regulations, school laws, and the like. In addition, a complex pattern of school administration is set up in every community to guarantee that the laws, rules, and regulations will all operate effectively. The individual in this structural pattern, then, must make certain accommodations or adjustments. For example, the school has its institutional goals which, in certain instances, may be at variance with those of the individual teacher. Since the individual cannot very well change the institutional goals, he must adjust to them. Occasionally, the goals of the individual may be so completely out of harmony with the institutional goals that the adjustment required is especially difficult and is accompanied with heightened tension. Likewise, an individual teacher may be out of harmony with certain administrative policies in the school and this also may necessitate a serious problem of adjustment.

The most desirable and fortunate situation is, of course, one in which the individual finds his personal goals in complete harmony with institutional goals and administrative policies. Since, however, complete harmony is not usually possible, how may the tensions of personal adjustment be reduced? Some social psychologists suggest that participatory action should be the basis of institutional patterns of behavior that are determined by rules, regulations, laws, and other structurized elements in the institution. For example, a school policy toward teacher promotion should be the product of the thinking of all the personnel. It should be noted that those who advocate participation in making school policy are not arguing that the resulting rules and regulations will be wiser because of the participatory procedure, or that group judgment will be any wiser than the judgment of a single expert. What they argue is that participation in and of itself is valuable wherever action within a group must be uniform or patterned. It should be fostered in every institutional situation because it contributes to better adjusted personalities and is an essential element in the maintenance and improvement of a satisfactory level of group morale. Although participation does not provide the entire solution to the problem of tension in individual adjustment, it nevertheless is a significant factor.

Through his various group memberships the individual seeks to promote his security and insure his respect. How can the individual make his adjustment to the group and within the group? How may *he* attempt to influence the adaptation of the group?

Each group—faculty group, departmental group, or even a bridge-playing or golf-playing group—has more or less definite goals. In the case of the organized, professional group, goals may be stated, perhaps broadly and generally, or may not be expressly stated. There may be long-term or short-term goals.

In addition to the goals of his group, each member also has his own short- and long-term goals. Individual and group goals may not always be in harmony. The individual may belong to a number of groups whose goals are in conflict. The teacher's problem, then, is to establish a proper relationship between his goals and the goals of the groups in which he holds membership.

1. Interaction

Interaction within the group provides members with the opportunity to influence others and to be influenced by them. Two teachers may begin with conflicting goals, disparate views, or divergent opinions. In their direct relationships, afforded by the school, they have the opportunity for interaction. Each has the chance to learn about and to evaluate the other's views, an opportunity to exert mutual influence for mutual change. Interaction may not result in unanimous agreement, but it may lead to a modification of views which will result in substantial agreement either in terms of one view or another, or in terms of a compromise that includes something and eliminates something of each. The agreement, on the other hand, may be something new and different. Through the process of group interaction, not only is agreement reached but, through the process itself, enrichment of personal satisfactions accrues.

2. Discussion

Discussion is the basic procedure of group action, the tool of interaction which leads to integration. Discussion is the method of group deliberation. It is an observable manifestation of a group studying and learning together, a group thinking out loud, a group interacting within itself. The success of discussion in any school group in promoting interaction and achieving integration depends somewhat upon the discussion leaders.

Discussion may degenerate into a kind of "bull session." Sometimes individuals turn a faculty meeting into an unproductive kind of parliamentary debate. Or it may be a meeting of listeners receiving decisions and directions from a school authority. To insure faculty-wide participation in a discussion, it is usually necessary to have the topics well selected, pertinent to the interests of the members of the group, and appropriate to the time available. Usually they should be announced in advance so that the members are prepared. The discussion leader—the school administrator, the teacher chairman—at the faculty meeting, like any other discussion leader, has the responsibility of keeping discussion "on the track," encouraging effective participation, summarizing the main points, and directing the group toward sound conclusions.

In all group relationships, but especially in a faculty group and particularly during discussion, tact is of great importance. Tact does not imply weakness or lack of standards. It means, rather, treating other people in such a way that their self-respect as well as your own is preserved. The desire for prestige and importance is universal. In using tact in discussion, one is consciously sparing pride, developing confidence, and assuring the other person a sense of importance. Ridicule and sarcasm are an anathema to effective discussion.

The new teacher who is intolerant of experienced faculty members must realize that anything different from what he anticipated is not necessarily bad. It is only after one has acquired intimate personal acquaintance with a specific school situation that one is in a position to evaluate policies and practices. What might at first seem undesirable may, after careful examination in the light of a specific situation, be very desirable. A new teacher from another school should not be tactless in references made to his previous employment. Both the experienced and the inexperienced teacher in group discussion, in personal conversations, and in other school relationships should be alert to the danger of seeming to feel superior, seeming to believe that it is his business to enlighten and to point the way. By failing to understand the merits of the institution in which he works and to recognize the importance of respect for the staff members' achievements, a teacher retards his own integration and cannot achieve the climate most favorable for his maximum success.

3. Integration

The goal of group action is integration. Integration is achieved when all members of the group are completely identified with the group, when individual pleasures and satisfactions accrue from the successes and achievements of the group as a whole. An integrated faculty group exhibits *esprit de corps,* has good morale.

Integration is particularly desirable in a school faculty group because a teacher's role is interlocking, never individual and independent. It is especially important for a teacher to be completely identified with the institution. The goals of the school and his own goals should be harmonious and to some extent identical. If a teacher has been a participant in discussion which led to the agreement on matters related to these goals, he will probably have a sense of personal responsibility for his contribution. This will facilitate his acceptance of the goals and his identification with them. A new teacher who joins a faculty group whose goals are in conflict with his, whose ways of doing things are different, will make a temporary acceptance and, eventually, through processes of group discussion and interaction, achieve personal or group adaptations which will promote his identification with the faculty and his integration within the group.

It is essential that integration be achieved because even a teacher with superior teaching skill cannot make his best contribution to the institution's program unless he sees his job always in reference to the services of other staff members. The success of the school is determined by its total performance. A teacher who is integrated within the group will perform as a member of the group. He will not seek exclusive limelight apart from his achievements as a contributor to the institution's goals.

In many schools an effort is made to acquaint the entire faculty with what is being done throughout the school and within the system. This is done not only to increase understanding and cooperation but also to promote mutual respect among all staff members. Such acquaintance leads to an appreciation that many diverse tasks are performed by members of the school group and that the tasks are coordinate in importance. It also may contribute to the individual's confidence in his ability to contribute successfully to the school's program.

INDUCTION OF NEW TEACHERS

How is the new teacher to be directed and aided in fulfilling his role in the school personnel group? What steps are taken to "induct" him into a school system, a school group, a classroom group? This is a problem that has been gaining more and more attention from school administrators. When there is a shortage of teachers it is particularly important to assist teachers in their initial adjustments, to avoid having teachers drop out of the profession or change their positions because of unhappy initial experiences.

Handbooks

In many school systems, particularly the larger school systems, handbooks are issued to new teachers. This is an effective way of eliminating indiscretions and uncertainties and disappointments that grow out of ignorance about what is expected of the new teacher, what is available, and what the teacher can expect to receive. The handbook speaks for the institution. It usually tells something about the community, its location, transportation facilities, resources, and so forth. It tells about the history and location of the schools and the policies concerning salary, tenure, and sick leave. It gives the calendar of events and holidays. Usually the handbook is very helpful. In some cases, however, it is so detailed that the teacher tends to be overwhelmed. Ideally, it is not considered the final word but rather the basis for personal discussions with the new teacher. It gives the teacher some idea of what to expect.

Presession Workshops

Sometimes a new teacher attends a presession workshop, an orientation week, a get-acquainted period in advance of the regular opening of the school session. Often the teacher receives extra compensation for this work, especially in those cases where it takes as much as a week's time. Customarily, the principals, supervisors, and certain others of the regular staff work with the new teachers during this period. The activities include tours of the community and discussions of school policies. The teacher is given an opportunity to become acquainted with his classroom, with the resources of the school—audio-visual aids, library, art facilities, and so forth—and also with community resources. He is given an opportunity to ask questions which would be inappropriate in a larger faculty meeting scheduled after the opening of school. Such minor questions as "Does the teacher lead her children in line to the lunchroom?" "With whom should I communicate when I am forced to be absent from school?" "Are children allowed to go to their lockers at any time?" would be a waste of time in a faculty meeting and would seem so petty in that setting that they would never be raised. Knowing the right answers to such seemingly insignificant questions might, however, be quite important to the teacher's initial adjustment.

Faculty Adviser

It is common practice for one experienced teacher to be assigned to advise each incoming teacher. This is an arrangement that continues throughout the school year. The incoming teacher knows where to go for directions and information, and the experienced teacher feels a responsibility for giving the newcomer hints, suggestions, and directions that he feels may be helpful.

Other Plans for Induction

Perhaps fortified with a handbook of information, the experience of a presession workshop, and the name of a faculty member to whom he is expected to turn for advice, the new teacher arrives at school on the opening day. Typically the session opens with meetings—district-wide and school-wide, and then perhaps at the department or grade level. The new teacher is introduced to the groups. He meets most of his colleagues for the first time. He is informed of the plans for the opening of school and is supplied with the details of his assignment, with his textbooks, and with information about his pupils. At once, the duties of checking, organizing, reporting, and accounting begin.

Usually an effort is made to have a tea or some other social gathering where the new teachers can meet the other teachers informally. Typically the older teachers tend to get together and the new teachers usually find the tea of little value in furthering acquaintance with the group. Perhaps if the function of such teas were more clearly understood this shortcoming would be alleviated.

SUMMARY

The institutional aspects of a school have a bearing on what the teacher does and how he does it. The opportunities provided for participation in a group have an influence on the total adjustment of an individual teacher. The program of induction is important to a new teacher. His feelings of security and pleasure in his work may be directly related to his knowledge about what is expected of him and what traditions he should respect. There are important, continuing relationships that he will have with other members of the personnel on a social and professional basis which are exceedingly important to his success in teaching.

A teacher is likely to work more efficiently, discharge his duties with greater satisfaction if, at all times, he is conscious that the nature of the institution is an influence both upon him and upon his work. The institution contributes to him while he is contributing to the institution.

The school must be viewed as a group enterprise. The teacher's attitude toward his own role in relation to all other roles has a direct bearing on group morale, on personal satisfaction, and even on the school's educational achievement. Although the teacher has an assignment that is largely individual and a great deal depends upon his individual initiative, he also must perform as a member of a group. This means that he sees his own achievement in the light of the total achievements of the group and recognizes that the group has contributed to his achievements, that he is part of a system characterized by interlocking roles, and that he has group-wide, institutional responsibilities.

The group, in order to perform in the desirable climate of wholesome group relations, must be characterized by a high degree of mutual respect on the part of all staff members. The teacher must appreciate that all tasks contribute to the whole and that each contribution is different and must be so because functions and needs are different and also because individuals cannot follow stereotyped patterns in carrying out any educational assignment.

Being a member of a teaching group implies the responsibility of adaptation leading to general understanding and a common acceptance of satisfactory goals. Adaptation depends upon interaction within the group. Discussion is the important group method of communication leading to integration. Developing skill in discussion is a sure path to effective performance in one's institutional relationships.

QUESTIONS

1. How are American schools affected by the attitudes of the people?
2. What are some of the principal effects upon the individual teacher that result from the institutionalization of education?
3. What are the principal ways in which institutionalization influences educational progress?
4. When may a school be said to be progressive? conservative? reactionary? stereotyped?
5. Assuming that institutional changes should be made, how may the direction for desirable change be discovered?

PROJECTS

1. Explain the ways a school represents the common response of the people of a community.
2. Describe some of the adjustments that an individual member of the teaching profession must make by virtue of his membership in a group.

Ideas Influential in

Merrim from Monkmeyer

American Education

7

Ideas from European
social movements

Ideas that become incorporated in institutions do not come into the world spontaneously. They have originated at some time in history, from a combination of sources, and they have been propagated. Ideas are somewhat like large streams of water. They are in constant motion, are constantly being swelled by tributaries whose identity is more or less lost in the main stream. The ideas that contribute to the main stream of thought, however, do not entirely lose their identity in the way the waters of tributaries are lost in the main stream. Their identity and the degree of their influence wax and wane.

Institutions like the school result when certain ideas eventually crystallize, are widely accepted, and are incorporated into practice. It is from a confluence of ideas in motion that the fabric of modern educational thought has been created. An educator does not create or invent current ideas any more than an economist invents the ideas of inflation, devaluation, price supports, or social security. Some recognized need gradually brought the ideas into being.

TWO SOURCES OF IDEAS

Where did our ideas about education originate? What was their genesis? Educational thought can be traced to a flow of ideas from two general sources—from social movements and from educational leaders. When a series of ideas is adopted by a mass of people and leads to widespread action toward some socially significant end, we have a social movement. When the ideas and resultant actions affect large masses of people so significantly that the course of history is influenced, we have what we call a historical movement, such as the Renaissance or the Christian movement. In the wake of historical movements, through the impetus of social thought, all institutions, all marks of the culture are swept along. Out of such movements many influential ideas, in education and other fields, emerge.

Concurrent with historical movements, and sometimes in advance of them, learned men, thinkers and writers, have formulated more or less generally accepted ideas into a system of thought. We can trace certain current educational thought back to these individuals. They saw more clearly than others of their time what the ideas were that answered the needs felt by the people. They were more skilled than others in organizing the thought and in putting it into a form that made the ideas clear. Because of their superior intelligence and shrewder insights, they discovered new underlying principles or enhanced the attractiveness of old ones.

What educational ideas have come to us from these two sources? In this chapter, a brief examination of the ideas and the propelling forces of three great European movements will make clear that some social thought of the past is related to educational ideas that have survived and continue, to some extent, to exert an influence. In the succeeding chapter, by turning attention to the other source of educational thought, to certain representative thinkers and writers, it will become evident that what they produced also has been, and is, related, to a considerable degree, to current educational thought.

In examining the historical movements two limitations are imposed. First, we must be brief. A description of any one of the large-scale social movements, giving an adequate picture of its background, its unfolding, its ramifications, its consequences, its sweeping historical effects, would take the efforts of a specialized historian and involve many pages of material. Obviously, that is not necessary.

Our purpose can be achieved by focusing, not upon details pertaining to events, causes, and results, but by focusing directly upon certain ideas that are part of the movement—ideas that have been most vitally related to modern educational thought.

The second limitation is in the choice of movements. Only those movements that are mainly European are included. This seems to be a logical selection inasmuch as it is the historical movements of Europe which have led to the emergence of ideas that have had the greatest impact upon education in the United States. The great movements selected, and discussed briefly, are the Athenian movement, the Christian movement, the Renaissance, particularly the Italian Renaissance, and the American frontier movement. The first three are studied as European movements and are included in this chapter. The American frontier movement is explored in a separate chapter because of its importance to American education.

THE ATHENIAN MOVEMENT AND
CRITICAL THINKING

The Athenian movement, characterized by some historians as an episodic and somewhat fleeting event in history, grows in its appeal and takes on added significance with the perspective provided by passing years. The important point to remember here is that an idea emerged—an idea that eventually was accepted by Western civilization, an idea that has been an influence in shaping American educational institutions. The idea is *that habits of critical thinking are dynamic elements in personal and social progress.*

The city of Athens was a center of early cultural and intellectual development. The number of persons who participated in the intellectual movement was, perhaps, never above thirty thousand. At the peak of intellectual development, the Golden Age of Pericles (500–400 B.C.), the population of Athens was only slightly over a hundred thousand including slaves and women who were denied citizenship.

Prior to the Athenian movement, before the advent of the method of critical thought, criticism of a deep-seated, widespread tradition was considered offensive. If an institution was well established, no one dared to question its favored practices or even to inquire about the premises upon which the institution had been built.

To question a religion, for example, was thought to invite the wrath of the gods. It definitely brought down the wrath of all the citizens who believed in the particular religion. To question a religion was to classify oneself as a heretic and to lay oneself open to persecution. To think critically was dangerous. To differ from existing popular beliefs, to do something in a way which differed from custom, resulted in extreme unpopularity, perhaps even in being publicly designated an unworthy citizen. Such were the social attitudes that characterized civilizations preceding the Athenian era.

Since, in these earlier civilizations, only the tried ways were right ways, since there were no alternatives to the ways considered right, all that education could do was to justify and intrench the existing ways of thinking and of doing. The pupils were told how to act. Schools extolled the virtues of the past. Schools never, intentionally, attempted to show how the ways of living could be improved. The task of the pre-Athenian school was to protect the way of life, to serve as a brake upon any attempt to change it.

Critical Thinking in the Education of a Citizen

Life among the people of Athens was changed when a new type of teacher, a Sophist, came among them. Sophists were teachers of superior skill and enlarged vision. They claimed that they were not attempting to prepare pupils for any particular profession or field of study but were teaching definitely and specifically to develop their pupils into intelligent citizens. They stressed liberal education as a supplement to the customary instruction in reading, writing, music, and gymnastics.

The Sophists—such as Protagoras (481–411 B.C.), the first of the Sophists, and Isocrates (436–388 B.C.), perhaps the greatest of them —were, above everything else, teachers. They contributed an education of positive merit. Because they were also orators, they taught their pupils and other listeners to place high value upon literary and oratorical excellence. It was the Sophists who helped Plato, author of *The Republic,* and Demosthenes, who delivered the Philippics, develop their consummate powers of expression.

With the advent of the Sophists, the citizens of Athens, for the first time in history, were taught to think critically. Teachers encouraged the boys, the future citizens, to be critical. The premise was that each social custom, each social belief was only one step toward a still higher form of social custom, toward a more mature development in social belief. Each custom and each belief, therefore, should be subjected to continuous, critical scrutiny and to thorough, constant reconsideration. Critical thinking, in other words, should precede social reconstruction.

The Athenians developed the point of view that man's nature permits him, when properly educated, to attain an indefinite degree of perfectibility because man possesses an almost limitless capacity to improve. They believed that the only instrument that man can use to achieve the higher life is *trained intelligence*. Critical thinking is an essential method for developing trained intelligence. They succeeded, through a highly skilled application of the method of critical thinking, in developing intelligence among their Athenian students to a degree unknown to any prior civilization.

Through the use of their opportunities to educate and train the citizens in the method of critical thinking, the Sophists truly wrought a revolution in the intellectual life of the Athenian people. They spread knowledge, but they also spread a new way of thinking through the use of knowledge. Books assumed an important place in the lives of the Athenians. The shelves of the citizens' libraries were filled with row upon row of cylindrically shaped baskets which held the books. Higher education became an accepted feature of civilization, and learning with the aid of professional teachers became the accepted mode of educating citizens.

Critical Thinking as Method in Education

Among the educational leaders of Athens is one whose name has always been associated in history with unsurpassed teaching. He was not a Sophist but he built upon much that the Sophists developed. He personifies the teaching spirit of his age. Socrates (469–399 B.C.) started with a basic principle of the Sophists—"Man is the measure of all things." He taught that, since this is so, the first and highest obligation of man is to know himself, that knowledge is the basis of all virtuous action, and that the best method for an individual to obtain knowledge is by use of the dialectical method, or logical disputation.

Socrates entered into conversation with other Athenian citizens and adroitly questioned them. He made it appear that he accepted the answers given him and then developed his subsequent questions

Socrates (469?–399 B.C.) was born in Athens. His parents were too poor to give him the education of a gentleman—training in music and dancing—but he learned to read and write. At an early age he took up sculpture as a vocation, following in his father's footsteps. We do not know when or under what circumstances he left sculpture for teaching, but he declared that he knew he was divinely commissioned to teach.

Socrates' teaching was not conventional instruction or formal lecturing. Instead he went about Athens—to the marketplace, the gymnasia, or some other place where men gathered in numbers—and sought out some individual whose ideas needed modifying or whose technique or conduct called for expert guidance. When he discovered such an individual he plied him with question after question, often leading him to contradiction and confusion. Socrates did this to develop powers of reflection and self-criticism, to foster the ability to think consistently and comprehensively, and to grow in skill in reaching clear conceptions. He believed these powers and abilities were antecedents of a virtuous life.

For thirty years or more Socrates followed this way of life. He consistently sought to develop the excellence of man as a universal being rather than as a mere citizen of Athens. His most notable disciples, therefore, were dangerously lacking in old-fashioned patriotism which many of his contemporaries believed was essential to the survival of Athens. When he was confronted with the alternative of quitting or changing his teaching or being condemned to death, he chose to be a martyr to his ideas.

Socrates wrote nothing. It is his conversational method as recorded by Plato, his most distinguished pupil, that assures his immortality as a great teacher.

in terms of the answers given, until the person being instructed was brought face to face with the follies and absurdities of his own superficially formulated answers. The first aim of Socrates' method was to bring recognition of error. The second aim was, through critical questioning, to develop the whole of the truth, of which the original opinion might have been a fragment. So representative of this method of inquiry was Socrates that the method came to be called the Socratic method of teaching.

Skilled use of the method of inquiry which Socrates developed is still considered a mark of a great mind. It takes understanding and intelligence to formulate a wise question. It takes serious study and reflection to arrive at an intelligent answer. It is clear that Socrates did not believe that a teacher should merely impart knowledge to the pupil, which had been one of the methods used by the

Socrates engages his friends in discussion. This mural, painted by John La Farge, is in the Supreme Court Chambers of the Capitol Building in St. Paul. (Courtesy Department of Administration, State of Minnesota)

Sophists. The pupil should *use* knowledge. He showed by his example that proper methods of teaching could generate powers of *thinking* in the learners. Critical inquiry was appropriate to every subject, be it the operation of natural laws, principles of economics, moral principles, or politics. Nothing should be exempt from the arena of public discussion. In numerous respects the method of Socrates is still a considerable influence in current educational thought.

The State and the Cultivation of Critical Thinking

The Sophists, who expanded the functions of education and developed the field of higher education in Athens, and Socrates, the great teacher, had a marked influence on the renowned writer and thinker of the period, Plato. One educational aim that emerged during the Athenian movement, one that is associated with Plato and contributed to the fundamental idea that habits of critical thinking are related to personal and social progress, is that education should lead the child to yearn to be a good citizen. This was not just the aim of teachers. It was the central aim of government, and the entire life of the State was organized to enable boys to live richly the life of the free citizen. The philosophy of government was that government should be used as a means for developing the individual, that the State existed to serve Man. This was a marked departure from the philosophy that Man existed to serve the State.

To carry out this aim, teachers taught that which was desirable for good citizenship. Only boys were included in the program; women were not citizens. Boys lived with adult men and shared in all civic activities. They mingled with the men in the market place, at the theater, and at the games. At every turn a boy was encouraged to ask questions, to raise and discuss vital issues, to pursue knowledge for the purpose of living a freer, a richer, a more morally satisfying life. And of all his intellectual pursuits, the most highly respected was the search for truth. To discover truth he was encouraged to think critically.

As a result of expert, professional instruction and firsthand experiences that young men had in the conduct of public affairs, including freedom to raise questions, for the first time in history a considerable body of people representative of those qualified as citizens took part in governing the State. The community life of the Athenians unfolded at an unprecedented rate. The results, as James Henry Breasted has described them, were indeed impressive.

> Here had grown up a whole community of intelligent men, who were the product of the most active interest in the life and the government of the community, constantly sharing in its tasks and problems, in daily contact with the greatest works of art in literature, drama, painting, architecture, and sculpture—such a wonderful community indeed as the ancient world, Greek or oriental, had never seen before.[1]

Critical Thinking in Modern Education

From the standpoint of modern education, the most notable contribution of the Athenians was their method of critical thinking. It has been widely accepted and adopted by the Western world, and the effects upon Western civilization and Western education are of incalculable magnitude. Leading historians believe that the Greek emphasis upon the method of critical thinking was responsible for the greatest intellectual revolution of all times.

What do we have in our present educational situation that bears witness to the Athenian pattern? How has the method of critical thinking influenced current educational thought?

With us, as with the Athenians, the habit of critical thinking is considered something that must be nurtured in realistic, community surroundings. The community, as such, is an educative agency. The

[1] James Henry Breasted, *The Conquest of Civilization* (New York: Harper & Row, Publishers, Inc., 1926), p. 383.

problems of the educational theorist then and now are: What kind of education will make citizens intelligent and willing participants in the sphere of everyday social action? How can the schools realize this ideal and at the same time develop to the fullest extent the personality of the individuals?

We follow in the footsteps of the Athenians when we adopt as one of our principal objectives the development in the pupils of the power to think with knowledge, not just to absorb it, when we utilize conversational methods for helping pupils to obtain knowledge, and when we stimulate pupils to ponder and classify their own experiences. We reflect the influence of the Athenian movement when we say that that knowledge is of most value which in some way affects the course of human conduct.

THE CHRISTIAN MOVEMENT

Emphasis on Ethical Behavior

The Christian religious movement followed in historical sequence the Periclean Athenian period just discussed. About this time many people in the Mediterranean area were turning from their traditional religions. The Oriental religions, especially, were becoming influential. The center of political power was shifting to Rome where the people were susceptible to new religious doctrines. The old Roman faith did not stress higher forms of human conduct, nor did it give its followers any promise of a future life. The trials of the populace were heavy. The common people longed for some assurance of blessedness beyond the grave. They turned in increasing numbers to a new faith which gave them an enlarged vision of the brotherhood of man and the fatherhood of God. A Jewish tentmaker from Tarsus, named Paul, preached the new doctrine far and wide and left a train of converted cities stretching from Palestine to Rome. This new religion placed strong emphasis upon ethical behavior in the conduct of human affairs. An ethical strain became influential in the determination of goals of education. Again, an idea was set in motion—an idea that subsequently affected intellectual thought throughout the Western world.

The central personality in the Christian movement, Jesus, a Hebrew, was born in Palestine in the days of Augustus. Like the

Jesus was a master teacher. The ethical emphasis of Christian teaching is reflected in present-day education. (Courtesy Parke-Bernet Galleries, New York City)

Sophists, he was a teacher. Like Socrates, he was one of the greatest of teachers. His teaching incurred the hatred of the Roman rulers, and he was accused of political conspiracy. Jesus was put to death as was Socrates before him. So strong was the appeal of his religion to men in all walks of life that within two hundred years the new religion outstripped all others throughout the whole of the Roman Empire. The influence of Christianity upon subsequent formal education in Western civilization can scarcely be assessed. In the United States, teaching has at all times reflected certain of the ethical emphases placed on education by the religious leaders of the Christian church.

Jesus developed the sublime art of addressing the imagination by appealing alike to the emotions and reason. The parables are examples of his method. The language used is both colorful and dramatic. His subject matter was derived from the common incidents of life and from the ordinary objects of nature. He so directed these simple tales that they became vehicles for conveying the profoundest of lessons.

Professional Education

In time the leaders of the Christian church became the spokes-men of the people. When the common man was denied the privi-lege of playing a part in the control of public affairs, large numbers of them turned to the leaders of the Christian church for spiritual and political guidance.

The educational methods used by the Christian church to de-velop leaders were those of teaching, debate, and discussion. History saw the rise of educated religious leaders, the Christian clergy, who built a powerful religious organization. By A.D. 311, Christianity had been legalized by the Romans. It continued to spread through Europe. Its spectacular growth in influence was supposedly due to its stress upon education and to its creation of a specialized clergy for the purpose of advancing education.

Throughout its history and continuing to the present time, the Christian church has depended upon education. This is evident, for instance, in the creation of parochial elementary and secondary

Library of Pope Sixtus IV (1470-1484). It was in libraries like this that priests studied to prepare to Christianize schools already established in Western Europe. Teaching as a profession and modern elementary education are generally dated from the fifteenth century. (Courtesy Pio Istituto di S. Spirito, Rome)

schools, in the establishment of many colleges for training leaders in the Christian faith, and in the evangelistic campaigns to build a Christian community across the breadth of the United States. Many of these educational institutions rank among the top of their kind in the United States.

The Ethical Strain in Secular Education

The Athenian philosophers advanced the idea that the key to the solutions of the problems of life was to be found in the intellectual nature of man. Because the level of intellectual attainment expected by them was very high, the aim of education could not be attained by the masses. They sought an aristocracy of brains. The Christian educators, on the other hand, offered a goal that was within the power of everyone's attainment. They argued that man's moral nature is common to every man and that, given proper instruction, it is within the power of every man to develop his moral nature. They offered a universally applicable solution. Stress was on ethics and morality rather than on intellectuality.

The ethical strain introduced by the earlier Christian leaders into educational thought and practice has persisted in educational philosophy to the present day. Education is to build better behavior, to improve conduct, to advance the cause of human relations, to emphasize the higher traits of character. This kind of aim for education receives, perhaps, a greater emphasis in modern educational theory than at any time in history. As will be pointed out in the chapter on aims, ethical character has been one of the principal aims stressed in various official statements of the aims of American education. Secular education, in the theories that guide it at least, has stressed the ethical factor, and there is no indication that the emphasis upon ethical outcomes will not be stressed in the future as much as in the past.

Many different kinds of Christian groups settled in the United States. Each sect had its own notions about how children should be educated. Partly because of dividedness, public education in the United States became secularized, that is, it became an education that was conducted without reference to any particular religion. It was public education, free from religious control. The teachers, however, were convinced of the importance of stressing ethical behavior. Many who taught in public schools stressed ethical conduct as consistently as teachers in church schools. It is possible, according to a secular philosophy of education, for every man to develop his moral nature, and it is held that one of the first duties of teachers is to help individuals develop personalities that are permeated with those ethical characteristics, such as love and charity, that have been emphasized throughout the history of the Christian movement.

THE RENAISSANCE: A NEW METHOD OF INQUIRY

The Renaissance Period

One of the most interesting periods in European history is that which culminated in the Renaissance at the close of the Middle Ages. The story of the revival of classical learning has been told many times. It is the story of the achievements of great artists like Da Vinci, Raphael, and Michelangelo, of the rebellion against the authority of the Christian church, of the mathematicians who infused new life into an old subject, of the astronomers who gazed at the heavens and discovered new explanations for the universe, and of the physicists who abandoned the method of speculative theory in the study of nature for study through the techniques of controlled experimentation.

Actually the Renaissance encompasses an indefinite period of time. No year marks its onset. The middle of the fifteenth century is sometimes mentioned as being near the beginning of the break away from the older intellectual patterns, principally because by 1440 printing was developed. No date can be assigned to the ending of the new movement, for the spirit of the Renaissance is a vital force today.

When the Renaissance originated, Italy consisted of city states like Venice, Florence, Genoa, Milan, and Pisa. In his novel *The Romance of Leonardo da Vinci,* the great Russian novelist Dmitri Merejkowski (1865–1941) gives us what historians say is a fairly realistic picture of the times. He paints a vivid canvas of a great genius living in a civilization filled with stupendous contrasts, with extremes of extravagance and magnificence, with foibles of sensuality and of human frailty.

The flow of thought that stemmed from the Renaissance must be interpreted against a background of social organization as well as disorganization. In this Italian civilization, with its intense rivalries, political betrayals, and lust and licentiousness on the one hand, and on the other, a growing sensitiveness to the values of scholarship, of the arts and sciences, and of critical thinking and education, modern ideas found their greatest propagating force. The sea of inquiry was widened. Men were both tied to and cut adrift from their ancient intellectual moorings.

The movement was of such great breadth that its results made the modern world modern. But ideas that were set into motion and that have since affected thought in the United States were not altogether harmonious in character. There were cross-currents of thought and variations in practice. There were classicists; there were naturalists; there were scholastics. One thread of events and thought did emerge, however, and resulted in the development and propagation of a new method of inquiry. In addition to the old method of inquiry, the deductive method, a new pattern of thinking, the inductive method, gained prominence. In order to understand better its present ramifications in educational thought and practice, we must consider what brought the idea of the inductive method of inquiry into being, what it involves, and where it has led.

Influence of Classical Language upon Modes of Thought

1. Created a Class

All books and legal documents in Italy at the time of the Renaissance were written in classical Latin although the common people spoke regional Italian dialects. The learned teachers delivered their lectures in Latin. In time, skill in the use of classical Latin became the badge of the educated man. It separated him from the uneducated, gave him membership in a distinguished prestige group.

2. Made the Past Authoritative

Because of his mastery of classical Latin, the educated man was able to study the great works produced before the Renaissance. Many an educated man also mastered classical Greek. Through his command of Greek he had access to the works of the Athenian scholars—to their drama, their philosophy, oratory, poetry, and the great literature of the perfectionists. To the Italian scholars of this period there was no source of learning so rich in quality, so universal in application as that handed down by the Greeks.

The effects of this emphasis on Latin and veneration for the works of the Greek scholars have been far reaching and long lasting. The Italian scholars believed that the works that the Athenian scholars had produced were unsurpassable, well-nigh perfect, sufficient for exclusive study, and applicable to every aspect of human conduct. The knowledge of the ancients became the authoritative guide for man's every endeavor. In the books of the ancients were found all the answers to man's aesthetic, ethical, and political problems. Thus a knowledge of Latin and Greek was the key to all the answers. The man with the key was in a position of intellectual power and consequently had social prestige.

3. Perpetuated a Pattern

Naturally, classical Latin became the core of the educational curriculum. Methods of teaching it were developed into highly refined techniques which had the psychological advantages of being both logical and definite.

The effects of these methods upon teaching in general seem fairly clear. A definiteness was given to teaching methods. The selection and management of subject matter were made more logical. The effects were felt long after the classical languages ceased to serve as the official language of communication. Latin continued to hold the central place in the curriculum. Methods of teaching Latin were deemed suitable for teaching the subjects in most other fields.

The predominance of Latin also served to perpetuate the separation of scholars into a class apart from the practical affairs of life. Even after newer subjects came into the curriculum, teachers of the older subjects retained special prestige, were considered to be more erudite, and were ascribed higher social status.

A Changed Emphasis

With time, veneration of the past and viewing writers of the past as authorities waned. Fewer and fewer of the Italian scholars followed the classical pattern. They increasingly focused education upon current problems. Eventually the fundamental premise of the scholastics—namely, that the present could not be much different from the past—was no longer widely accepted. Scholars did not cease to study the past, however. Simultaneously with an effort to achieve understanding and appreciation of the past, teachers strove to achieve understanding and appreciation of current problems. Sometimes older ideas became gradually blended with newer ones. Sometimes they flowed separately. Sometimes they were antagonistic.

The new emphasis and its consequences resemble, in some respects, the curriculum situation in modern education where social studies have been viewed in a somewhat unfriendly fashion by those who believe pupils should study historical episodes and not waste much time trying to acquire an intimate acquaintance with problems of modern life. The blending and reconciliation of old and new, a problem that dates back to the Renaissance, continues to be a sharply debated educational issue.

Emergence of the Inductive Method of Inquiry

The inductive method of inquiry emerged during the Renaissance. This method and its application permeates the whole of modern educational philosophy.

1. What the Inductive Method Is

The inductive method involves reasoning logically and methodically from a part to a whole, from particulars to generals, from the individual to the universal. Making generalizations is probably as old as human thought but, prior to this time, the method used to arrive at generalizations had received little attention. In order to make the generalizations of mankind more authentic, more valid, and more likely to be true, the leaders in the Renaissance popularized the inductive method as a mode of study, as a manner of reasoning.

The inductive method is a model of simplicity. It involves two steps: first, observation, and then, generalization. Johann Kepler (1571–1630), reasoning inductively, proved mathematically that the orbit of Mars is elliptical. Subsequent observations proved his "laws" to be true. He first collected all the available facts about planetary motion. This fulfilled the first step in inductive reasoning. Through careful study and application of mathematics he arrived at a generalization that he believed was true and that would either refute or fortify the generalizations previously reached. In other words, he subjected the generalizations made by others about the orbit of Mars to the proof furnished by his own observations and by further application of his knowledge of mathematics. The kind of orbit that was consistent with his observations, with the observations of others, and with mathematical proof was elliptical. Kepler's success helped "popularize" the inductive method and encouraged others to study and employ it.

2. Why the Inductive Method Emerged

The intellectual powers of the most learned men of the Renaissance had been challenged by one novel, basic question to which the older sources afforded no satisfactory answer. The question involved two parts: What is man's relationship to nature? and What is nature? A modern way of seeking an answer to educational implications of the problem would be to ask, "What should be the relation between the education a child receives in school and the nature of that child?" The scholastics had given little recognition to the problem, and the best the later scholars of the early Renaissance could do was to raise the question. They could not find a satisfactory answer in that which was already known to them.

So tenacious was the hold of tradition upon methods of inquiry that even as late as 1400, despite the use of critical thinking by the Athenians which was a near approach to the method, it was actually dangerous to arrive at any generalizations about nature through an application of the inductive form of logic. So impelling was the question, however, and so strong was the intellectual interest in it that, despite the danger involved, the newly discovered method was used in certain quarters. Copernicus (1473–1543) was one thinker who proceeded to employ inductive logic despite personal danger. He questioned the validity of the generally held beliefs about the motions of the heavenly bodies—beliefs that had been popularly accepted as part of the so-called Ptolemaic system. Copernicus, reasoning inductively, concluded that the earth is spherical, rotates on its axis, and revolves around the sun. He explained for the first time the phenomenon of the seasons. He gave permission for his work to be published, and he escaped certain persecution only because he died before the work was published.

This new method that was leading to discoveries about nature, as startling then as the present-day launching of earth satellites, appealed increasingly to men of trained intelligence. The pace of discoveries, especially discoveries about nature, was greatly accelerated. Advanced thinkers, through the use of the method, became more proficient, and their ranks swelled.

Later on, physical scientists developed the inductive method to its highest point of refinement, and the method now is often referred to as the scientific method. Seemingly the physical scientists now find it an almost ideal answer to their quest for a method which, when used in conjunction with the mathematical sciences, will lead to valid answers to perplexing questions about the nature and behavior of the physical world. The social scientists, however, have not found it equally suitable in the study of human behavior, principally because of wide-spread public opposition to engaging in any social experimentation that is carried out under conditions of deliberate control.

3. Conflict Aroused

While the inductive method rapidly became acceptable among scientific thinkers, differences arose about its application and implications. Is the method applicable to the study of every kind of problem? If not, then to what kinds of problems may it properly be applied?

The use of the inductive method of inquiry gained increased attention when Galileo (1564–1642) dropped two bodies of un-

The development of the method of inductive verification of hypotheses by observation and experimentation, and the use of the new mathematics were accelerated by such men as Copernicus, Galileo, and Kepler. Unquestioned dependence upon Greek authority began to falter.

equal weight but of equal densities from the top of the leaning tower of Pisa and based his generalizations about falling bodies upon what he observed. Despite the fact that Galileo afforded all the professors and students at the local university ocular demonstration that bodies of different weights fall with the same velocities and showed that the path of a projectile is a parabola, his theories were reviled. He was forced to resign his professorship at the University of Pisa and to withdraw from teaching. His later discoveries, made through the same inductive method, were termed heresies because there was a seeming discrepancy between his new view of the solar system and certain passages in the Bible. He was subsequently subjected to extreme ecclesiastical censure.

The first experiments, which Galileo made while he was a young professor at Pisa, were decidedly dramatic. At that time the doctrine that the rate at which a body falls depends upon its weight was generally accepted as true, merely on the authority of Aristotle. It was even held that the acceleration varies as the weight. Prior to Galileo it did not occur to any actually to try the experiment. The young professor's tests went contrary to the doctrine held for two thousand years. Allowing for the resistance of the air, he found that all bodies fell at the same rate, and that the distance passed over varied as the square of the time. With all the enthusiasm, courage, and imprudence of youth, the experimenter proclaimed that Aristotle, at that time believed by nearly everyone to be verbally inspired, was wrong. Galileo met with opposition, but he decided to give his opponents ocular proof. It seems almost as if nature had resorted to an extraordinary freak to furnish Galileo at this critical moment in the history of science, with an unusual convenience for his public demonstration. Yonder tower of Pisa had bent over to facilitate experimentation, from its top, on falling bodies. One morning, before the assembled university, he ascended the leaning tower, and allowed a one pound shot and a one hundred pound shot to drop together. The multitude saw the balls start together, fall together, and heard them strike the ground together. Some were convinced, others returned to their rooms, consulted Aristotle, and, distrusting the evidences of their senses, declared continued allegiance to his doctrine.

From Florian Cajori, *A History of Physics* (New York: The Macmillan Company, 1924), pp. 32–33. Quoted by permission of Florian A. Cajori.

The inquisition to which Galileo was subjected resulted from a conflict between two methods of thinking—the deductive, older method of arriving at generalizations, used by the classicists, and the inductive, newer, and perhaps more dependable method of arriving at valid generalizations. The conflict was an intellectual one. No one was expected to examine or question the laws of courts and the principles of government, politics, education, and ethics. The underlying premises upon which conclusions in most areas of social endeavor were based were not to be discussed or investigated. Many people feared that if the new method were applied to revered social traditions, to cherished educational patterns, society would be undermined, man made insecure. Galileo, however, had taken an important pioneer step, the imprint of which could not subsequently be erased. He has been called the father of our modern times partly because of his scientific discoveries but mainly because he reinforced confidence in the inductive method of reasoning which has become a distinguishing characteristic of our modern age. This idea from the central stream of Renaissance thought has had a deep and lasting effect upon all subsequent intellectual thought.

SUMMARY: EFFECTS OF THE IDEAS FROM SOCIAL MOVEMENTS

We have said that the ideas that led to the forming of social institutions, for example the school, emerged from a broad stream of ever moving thought. Many of the most influential of our modern ideas originated in the sweeping changes caused by social movements. From the Athenian movement we gained a belief in the value of critical thinking; from the Christian movement an ethical strain became part of our educational philosophy; and from the Italian Renaissance we inherited the method of inductive reasoning.

American schools stress education for citizenship. Teachers emphasize the importance of making critical judgments and personal evaluations. Information and knowledge are acquired for use in thinking and reasoning. Did these practices and beliefs come to us from the Athenians? We cannot say that the connection is direct and unbroken. We can say that the Athenians originated a belief in critical thinking, that the belief has survived throughout history, and that it is a characteristic of our present-day educational thought.

Christianity stressed the ethical aspect of living. The individual became the pivot of the universe. Teaching became the great conditioner of lives. There is little question that the emphasis in present-day educational philosophy on the importance of relating education to desirable conduct, of attempting to design all phases of our educational scheme in terms of the best interests of the individual child, was nourished by the Christian influence. Philosophy, for example, stresses accommodations to individual differences because it is the individual and not the mass of children on which we attempt to focus. Education is not only to serve all; it is to serve each.

Perhaps when we come to the ideas that emerged from the Italian Renaissance we recognize the ideas that unmistakably mark our schools as modern. Our modern schools do not limit themselves to the methods and the tools of the classicists. They go beyond. Many teachers in America's schools who teach subjects other than the classics are tremendously influenced by the inductive method of reasoning. They are influenced by it in the way they guide children and youth. They encourage pupils to raise questions, to investigate, to confirm, to generalize. What the expert educator supports as sound educational practice is based on research that follows the inductive method. Much that is known about the nature and development of children has resulted from an application of the inductive method.

The importance of the ideas that grew out of the three great European social movements is so vast that it cannot be pinpointed. We know that certain ideas originated in great social movements. We know that these movements affected the thinking of great masses of people in the Western world and that all the succeeding generations of Western people have been influenced by their heritage from such movements. But great social movements are instituted by men and propagated through men, and it is only through the thoughts of men that the ideas behind the movements are made clear to succeeding generations. As we move into the next chapter, we shall see that certain individuals—thinkers and educators—have been essential in propagating the ideas, in clarifying and expanding them, and in bridging the gap between the results of the Athenian movement, the Christian movement, the Renaissance, and other great movements and modern practices in the schools of the United States.

QUESTIONS

1. Why was it that most of the social movements that affected early American education were European in origin?

2. What evidence may be offered to justify the belief that critical thinking is essential to social progress?

3. What have been the principal positive and negative effects upon American education of the Christian religious movement?

4. What are the deductive and inductive methods of thinking?

5. How did the exclusive study of the classics affect the educational viewpoints of the classical scholars?

6. What, in your opinion, might be the educational effects of an overemphasis upon some given field, say, science or mathematics?

7. What were the forces in the Renaissance that led to widening the sea of inquiry?

8. Why have the physical scientists employed the scientific method more than the social scientists?

9. How do you account for the fact than when study in the schools was confined almost exclusively to a study of the classics, the area of investigation was being widened?

PROJECTS

1. Consult some standard treatise, such as an encyclopedia, on the nature of deduction. Cite several examples of legitimate uses to be made of the method.

2. Consult a standard treatise dealing with the nature of induction. Cite examples of legitimate uses made of the method.

3. Explain why the Athenian citizens developed a critical attitude toward their own civilization.

4. List a number of common practices in present-day education that are suitable for critical analysis.

5. Explain what is implied by the assertion that building character is a major responsibility of classroom teaching.

CHAPTER 8

Ideas from European leaders

New, propulsive ideas were the mainsprings of the three great social movements referred to in the previous chapter. And the distinctive philosophies of life that emerged from each underlaid the social fabric of the Europe of the time.

History records that individuals—thinkers, writer, orators—are inevitably associated with the dissemination and implementation of new ideas. Eminent leaders have shown the ability to see more clearly than most of their contemporaries, to distinguish the more significant trends, and to extract from these the most vital ideas. They have, perhaps, felt no more strongly than many others the social significance of some idea, but they have had the power to be articulate, have not been discouraged by timidity, and have not succumbed to the pressure for conformity. Such leaders are the life-blood of social movements. They are also the ideological pioneers who are in the forefront, preparing the way for new advances, removing obstacles, and setting up markers to give directions.

European leaders who have fulfilled this kind of role in relation to thought that has had an influence on our present school program are numerous. Many sensed the essence of educational problems and indicated promising solutions.

We have selected six representative leaders of European thought whose influence we experience today. John Amos Comenius (1592–1670), Jean Jacques Rousseau (1712–1778), Johann Heinrich Pestalozzi (1746–1827), Friedrich Wilhelm Froebel (1782–1852), Johann Friedrich Herbart (1776–1841), and Herbert Spencer (1820–1903) were conspicuous as contributors to and disseminators of ideas that have become part of the main current of educational thought in the United States. Their ideas have had a striking influence upon modern educational theory and a lesser but important effect upon current educational practice.

What type of person has pioneered in educational thought? What do the six leaders selected have in common? Are the thinkers in the field always educators? Actually, they come from all walks of life and have different interests and vocations. Comenius was a Moravian priest, Rousseau a writer on political theory, and Pestalozzi a practicing schoolteacher as was his follower, Froebel. Herbart was a professor of psychology, Spencer an English philosopher. Their lives spanned approximately three centuries. They differ in their point of focus on social problems, but they share an intensive interest in social advancement. All have contributed ideas that have proved helpful in conducting our modern schools—ideas which, if we but grasp them, will lead us to a better understanding of our schools today.

COMENIUS: APPLICATION OF THE TECHNIQUE OF INDUCTION TO TEACHING

In the sketch of historical movements we noted that the inductive method was developed during the sweep of the Italian Renaissance. It was Comenius who advanced the idea of applying this inductive technique to teaching.

In the time of Comenius, school leaders generally agreed with his definition of the primary aim of education—"The ultimate end of man is eternal happiness with God." It followed, then, that the methods of teaching in the schools should be such as to enable man to attain this end. Education was to help pupils learn moral and mental discipline. The method used completely ignored pupil interest, emotion, natural desires, specialized abilities, and back-

Comenius is generally considered the greatest educational theorist and practical reformer of the seventeenth century. Notice in the picture evidence of his three great interests: religion, the encyclopedic organization of all knowledge, and education. (Slavonic Division, New York Public Library)

ground of learning. In fact, some of the pupils' most active interests were entirely suppressed.

Comenius' Ideas

Comenius became director of a school where he observed the ostentatious display of knowledge by teachers, the lethargic if not contemptuous response of the pupils to what was taught, and the stress on memorization of information without reference to its application. He set about to devise improvement and, in time, published among other books *The Great Didactic* which, even as late as 1907, was described by Paul Monroe, a careful student of educational history, in this way:

> . . . so sane and far-seeing are the precepts of this work that it may now be read with greater immediate profit to the teacher, sufficiently intelligent to avoid many minor errors, than the majority of contemporary writings.[1]

Comenius proposed changes that, for the most part, were consistent with the application of the principle of induction to classroom teaching. He did not disagree with the accepted religious aim of education, but he differed in the approach. He argued that moral control over oneself and consequently control of all things would grow out of the acquisition of knowledge, virtue, and piety, in this order. To knowledge, the one element relating directly to the school, Comenius gave a new and vastly different interpretation.

He started with the organization and selection of subject matter, which he decided must progress step by step from the familiar to the less familiar. He wrote textbooks in which, as he said, he aimed to give "an accurate anatomy of the universe, dissecting the veins and limbs of all things in such a way that there shall be nothing that is not seen and that each part shall appear in its proper place and without confusion."[2] The textbooks, instead of presenting a collection of facts, presented material arranged so that study could proceed by slow degrees from what is best known to what is less familiar. Each chapter and each paragraph led to the next. Comenius stressed the soundness of connecting words with the objects for which they stand, of learning a language the natural way—that is, by topical

[1] Paul Monroe, *A Brief Course in the History of Education* (New York: The Macmillan Company, 1907), p. 247.
[2] *Ibid.*, p. 240.

The Great Didactic, or *Didactic Magna,* was a theoretical treatise on education that contained all the views of Comenius upon education. It laid the foundation for educational development for all the succeeding centuries. Examples from the Table of Contents illustrate the nature of the educational topics he discussed:

6. If man is to be produced, it is necessary that he be formed by education.
7. A man can be most easily formed in early youth, and cannot be formed properly except at this age.
8. The young must be educated in common, and for this schools are necessary.
9. All the young of both sexes should be sent to school.
10. The instruction given in schools should be universal.
11. Hitherto there have been no perfect schools.
12. It is possible to reform schools.
13. The basis of school reform must be exact order in all things.
14. The exact order of instruction must be borrowed from nature.
16. The universal requirements of teaching and of learning; that is to say, a method of teaching and of learning with such certainty that the desired result must of necessity follow.
17. The principles of facility in teaching and in learning.
18. The principles of thoroughness in teaching and in learning.
19. The principles of conciseness and rapidity in teaching.
20. The method of the sciences, specifically.
21. The method of the arts.
22. The method of languages.
23. The method of morals.
26. Of school discipline.
27. Of the fourfold division of schools, based on age and requirements.

As given in Paul Monroe, *A Brief Course in the History of Education* (New York: The Macmillan Company, 1907), pp. 247–248. Quoted by permission of The Macmillan Company.

conversation—of making generous use of pictures and natural objects as classroom aids to instruction, and of including singing, economics, world history, geography, science, politics, art, and handicrafts as everyday parts of the subject matter of classroom instruction.

The most remarkable and most successful of all the Comenian textbooks for children was *Orbis sensualium pictus* ("The World of Sensible Things Pictured"). Its method of dealing with things was that of leading by inductive process to a generalized knowledge. It was also the first textbook for children that utilized illustrations.

A New Method

Comenius considered subject matter and method as inseparable aspects of teaching. The nine principles of teaching method that Comenius stated reflect his devotion to the inductive method, his long experience as a teacher, and his sensitiveness to logical and psychological relationships:

1. Whatever is to be known must be taught by presenting the object or the idea directly to the child, not merely through its form or symbol.
2. Whatever is taught should be taught as being of practical application in everyday life and of some definite use.
3. Whatever is taught should be taught straightforwardly, and not in a complicated manner.
4. Whatever is taught must be taught with reference to its true nature and its origin; that is to say, through its causes.
5. If anything is to be learned, its general principles must first be explained. Its details may then be considered, and not till then.
6. All parts of an object (or subject), even the smallest, without a single exception, must be learned with reference to their order, their position, and their connection with one another.
7. All things must be taught in due succession, and not more than one thing should be taught at one time.
8. We should not leave any subject until it is thoroughly understood.
9. Stress should be laid on the differences which exist between things, in order that what knowledge of them is acquired may be clear and distinct.[3]

Besides improvements in subject matter and method, Comenius proposed improvements in the organization of the schools so that they might also be more consistent with his basic philosophy. He proposed an organization of schools providing four levels of education based on the growth and development of children. Each level was to be a different kind of school, and each school was to be six years in length. This is basically the pattern of organization that we follow today. The system proposed a single program applying to all classes. He rejected the idea of one school system for upper-class children and another, poorer one for the children of the lower classes. The first level, for infancy, should be at the mother's knee; the second, for children at the vernacular school; the third, for boyhood at the Latin school or gymnasium; and the fourth, for youth at the university or in travel.

Other educators who were the contemporaries of Comenius

[3] *Ibid.*, p. 242. Quoted by permission of The Macmillan Company.

seem to have been unaffected by his practices and by his educational philosophy. He was, however, without doubt the greatest educator of his century. Many of his ideas are incorporated in our present educational system. All of his ideals have not as yet been attained in the countries where he lived and worked. The ideas of Comenius, especially his application of the technique of induction to teaching, are important because of their profound effects upon the formulation of subsequent educational theory.

Over three hundred years ago Comenius helped to lay the foundations of what we now think of as modern education. He was a teacher of teachers. He stressed methods of instruction that have since been embodied in the thinking of the education profession. He was a writer of textbooks that encouraged the use of improved methods of teaching. His were the first illustrated textbooks. He first described a ladder system of schools, organized to harmonize with the developmental stages of learners. Although his ladder system was unlike the European pattern of organization at his time it is fundamentally akin to the present ladder system in vogue in the United States.

Comenius believed in universal peace, and he believed that proper education of the young was an avenue to the advancement of peace and the elevation of society. Like some other advanced social thinkers, Comenius underwent severe persecution. He suffered greatly in the religious persecutions that were inflicted upon him and his fellow Moravians during the Thirty Years' War. His wife and children were murdered. His home was twice plundered, and his books and manuscripts were burned. He was exiled from his native land and worked as an educational reformer, successively in Poland, Sweden, England, Sweden a second time, Hungary, and Poland again, where he underwent severe persecution and was again exiled. He finally found refuge and support in Amsterdam where he spent the later years of his life.

ROUSSEAU: EDUCATION IN ACCORDANCE WITH NATURE

The question of the relationship of man with nature, which came to the forefront near the end of the Renaissance, continued to be of growing interest. Eventually those who devoted themselves to the subject developed a belief that their answer should be translated into social practices in various areas. In terms of their understanding of nature, they advocated certain revolutionary social reforms. The movement became known as the "naturalistic movement." It marked a reaction against formalism in education, but it was much wider than an educational movement. The naturalistic tendency in education was part of a vehement and revolutionary reaction to the dominance of arbitrary authority as exercised in all institutional life, including the family, the church, and the government. The naturalistic movement has been as revolutionary in its effects on broad and general intellectual conditions and on specific educational thought and practice as the Renaissance.

In education the naturalistic movement contributed to undermining the deep-seated, widely entrenched conception that education consisted chiefly of the mastery of books. The highly formalized kind of teaching that fostered this conception was adapted to the clergy and teachers who constituted an aristocracy of special privilege. The naturalistic movement, on the other hand, since it was opposed to all kinds of artificial conventionality and formalism, tended to conform to the tenets of the doctrine of the rights of common man. The leaders of the movement directed most of their criticism toward political and social practices which they expected to reform. It is not at all strange, therefore, that it was a political theorist interested in interpreting the naturalistic idea as it applied to social and political life who also devoted a fair proportion of his thought toward influencing education, which he believed to be an avenue for bringing about the social reform he so earnestly desired.

Jean Jacques Rousseau was born 120 years after Comenius. By that time the inductive method was much more popular. Reform in the method of arriving at generalizations had been great, at least in the field of scientific investigation. Progress in social reform, however, had not been impressive. The lot of the common man had changed but little. Rousseau revolted violently against the social absurdities and glaring social inequalities of his time. He was a man who had the unusual gift of clearly comprehending great ideas and of embodying these ideas in noble words. The great ideas that flowed along with the naturalistic movement were not originated by him, but he was their most forceful proponent. He had a unique ability to select the principal idea and to express it more clearly than others could. It was this ability that made him one of the most powerful figures not only in education but in all intellectual thought.

The life Rousseau lived and the life he envisaged in his writings seem strangely and unexplainedly paradoxical. He possessed an acute intellect and his powers of expression were unsurpassed. He was not an originator of ideas, but he could size up the importance of an idea and, as a proponent, develop it in a way that greatly furthered its influence. He was not wholly sane in the last ten or fifteen years of his life, during which time he wrote his *Confessions*, an undependable although, perhaps, partly true story of a sordid and not-to-be-admired kind of personal life.

His personal life aside, Rousseau holds a place in literary history which is unrivaled. His emphasis upon the doctrine that all education must be in accord with nature brought forth a new emphasis in education which up to his time had been almost totally disregarded. Subsequent developments in the fields of physiology, psychology, and biology have reinforced the doctrine he so forcefully set forth. He did not minimize the great significance of nurture. What he did was to emphasize that the inherent capacities of the child constitute the foundations for all human development.

An Idea with a Lasting Effect

Rousseau set forth his educational theory in his well-known semifictional exposition which he called *Émile*. According to the preface, *Émile* was written primarily as a book on child study to describe and analyze children's characteristics. Rousseau's fundamental thesis is clear-cut: "Everything is good as it comes from the hand of the author of nature; but everything degenerates in the hand of man." Education, he held, is natural. It is development from within. It comes from the natural workings of instincts and interests. It is an expansion of one's natural powers. It is life itself, not a preparation for life. Deliberate, formal education must, therefore, be in accordance with nature. So clearly and so forcefully did Rousseau express his idea that his words can scarcely be improved upon. They will repay careful study.

Education we receive from three sources—Nature, men and things. The spontaneous development of our organs and capacities constitutes the education of Nature. The use to which we are taught to put this development constitutes that education given us by men. The acquirement of personal experience from surrounding objects constitutes that of things. Only when these three kinds of education are consonant and make for the same end does a man tend toward his true goal. . . . If we are asked what is this end, the answer is that of Nature. For since the concurrence of the three kinds of education is necessary to their completeness, the kind which is entirely independent of our control must necessarily regulate us in determining the other two.[4]

Rousseau believed that education must be based upon recognition of the rightful place of nature, men, and things in learning. His ideas, as expressed in the above quotation, when properly interpreted would be accepted as sound by the most critical of our educational thinkers today.

Rousseau advocated that the education of a child should follow four principles.

1. The physical activity of children is important for the development of physical strength and of intelligence.
2. Sense perception connected with motor activity and with experimental investigation is fundamental in elementary education.
3. Children reason about matters related to their immediate experience and interests, and hence the reasoned solution of small scientific problems should be part of their education.
4. The premature memorizing of words spoils the child's judgment.[5]

The fundamental point in the psychology of children, according to Rousseau, is that they exhibit characteristic differences at different stages of maturing, and that appropriate activities should be provided for each stage; the child should be treated as a child and not as a miniature adult.

The Idea Interpreted

Rousseau accepted as fundamental to teaching the naturalistic principle that "the spontaneous development of our organs and capacities constitutes the education of Nature." Consider how a child develops his ability to talk and how, as he attends school, he improves in his ability to express himself intelligently. The larynx, a valve guarding the entrance to the trachea, is the organ of the voice. It contains the vocal chords which are necessary to developing the power of speech. Sounds are formed by directing expiratory blasts of air across these chords. The physiological structure and the activities which it is capable of performing condition all of the teaching that one can do toward influencing the child to use the organ of speech properly. The degree to which development takes place, even under the most expert pedagogical direction, is limited in the very beginning by that which nature has provided.

---

[4] As quoted in John Dewey, *Democracy and Education* (New York: The Macmillan Company, 1916), pp. 131–132.

[5] As quoted in Samuel Chester Parker, *A Textbook in the History of Modern Elementary Education* (New York: Ginn and Company, 1912), p. 181.

"Take the reverse of the accepted practice, and you will almost always do right," advised Rousseau. In Rousseau one finds the negation of the conception of education that developed during the Renaissance. Some of his criticisms are considered pertinent to modern educational practices. (Prints Division, New York Public Library)

When Rousseau said that "the use to which we are taught to put this development constitutes that education given us by men," he wished to make clear that man determines the ends toward which all the natural forces shall be directed. The kind of language the child learns to speak and the kinds of thought he expresses are man-directed.

When he said that the acquirement of personal experience from surrounding physical objects constitutes the education of things, he was explaining that the child interacts with his physical environment as well as with his social environment, and from these interactions he derives a considerable amount of learning. Providing a child with a suitable physical environment is as important to the promotion of optimum learning as providing him with trained teachers to direct his learning.

When Rousseau wrote that "Only when these three kinds of education are consonant and make for the same end" and that "the kind which is entirely independent of our control necessarily regulates us in determining the other two," he was emphasizing the necessity of consonance and cooperation between natural endowment, social environment, and physical environment in desirable education. Rousseau's emphasis, which led educators to a consciousness of the interrelationship of the three factors, changed the whole direction of teaching method. It made clear that the conception of education consisting almost entirely of the mastery of books was to die a slow death. The attention of schoolteachers was directed to the need for recognizing, as they taught, the innate differences in the inherent abilities of the children, their differences in temperaments, and the wide variance among the pupils in their social and experiential backgrounds.

Educating in accordance with nature requires full recognition of the importance of attitudes, preferences, interests, likes, dislikes, and habits, because these become as much a part of nature as do the intellectual factors. For the first time in education the affective factors were acknowledged as important influences in learning. Schoolteachers of young children realized as never before the need for building bodily tone and vigor, saw the relationship of their teaching to a child's health, and recognized the need for manipulative experiences and the necessity for a reasonable degree of physical mobility among children if they were to be properly taught in accordance with nature.

Some Effects upon Modern Education

In a social field like education it is always hazardous to attempt to trace cause and effect. The influence of an idea cannot be accurately estimated. It can be said that the implications of the belief presented by Rousseau—the belief that education should be in accord with nature, should take full cognizance of the child's instincts and capacities—did have a marked effect on some schools of the time of Rousseau and has had a part in the thinking of subsequent educators, especially the theorists. We are perhaps justified in saying that although the systematic study of the nature of children and of the variations in their patterns of development is still in its infancy, it is being encouraged and is progressing as a result, partly at least, of Rousseau's pioneer writing.

It can also be said, with considerable assurance, that teachers generally accept the principle that nature certainly must be taken into account if teaching is to be good, not only in terms of child welfare, but also in terms of social effectiveness. A wide discrepancy often exists between a principle and the incorporation of that principle into practice. The road to good teaching which Rousseau outlined so eloquently has not even yet broadened into a wide highway that teachers, by and large, attempt to follow.

PESTALOZZI: EXPERIMENTING TO DISCOVER EFFECTIVE METHODS OF TEACHING

The Experimental Movement

To state the principle that education should be in accordance with nature gives no indication of how to incorporate that principle into classroom teaching. How that principle can be connected with concrete teaching realities and made a part of teaching in a specific school setting with a whole set of customs and traditions remained a problem.

Following Rousseau's enunciation and elaboration of his principle, experiments in teaching were undertaken to discover the most promising methods for interpreting the principle through practice. Rousseau's ideas appealed to numerous European teachers, but it was Pestalozzi who established the first of the European experimental schools. Pestalozzi was a Swiss schoolteacher, the ablest of the advocates of Rousseau's ideas. Because his experiments with Rousseau's ideas set a pattern and his conclusions and theories had a wide circulation, the educational trend became known as the Pestalozzian movement.

The experimental schools that Pestalozzi conducted in Switzerland between 1799 and 1825 were visited by educational leaders from many countries. Through these schools, through his writings and the teachers he trained he exerted great influence over early educational reforms in America's elementary schools. (Swiss National Tourist Office, New York City)

The First Experimental School

Pestalozzi's first experimental school—he conducted several—was at Neuhof, near Zurich, Switzerland. He moved to a farm and combined the teaching of children of poor parents with work at agriculture. He failed financially and was thereby forced to discontinue his experiment. He had, however, made a beginning which strengthened his faith in experimentation in education. He had gained some insights into educational method appropriate for implementing the naturalistic principle. He began to publish his educational ideas, and his influence spread. The conclusions Pestalozzi arrived at as a result of these first experiments in teaching were consistent with Rousseau's principles. In *The Evening Hour of an Hermit* he wrote:

> Man driven by his needs can find the road to truth nowhere but in his own nature. . . . Man, if you seek the truth in this way of Nature, you will find it as you need it according to your station and your career. . . . Whoever departs from this natural order and lays artificial emphasis on class and vocational education, or training for rule or for service, leads men aside from the enjoyment of the most natural blessings to a sea of hidden dangers.[6]

He also said:

> Man can, at best, do no more than assist the child's nature in the effort which it makes for its own development; and to do this, so that the impressions made upon the child may always be commensurate, and in harmony, with the measure and character of the powers already unfolded in him, is the great secret of education.[7]

Basic Theory and Later Experimentation

Pestalozzi and his followers continued with their experiments to discover better methods of teaching and to work out practical applications of the naturalistic educational principle. Pestalozzi, teaching without pay, experimented with various school subjects. His most productive period was from 1799 to 1804 when government and private financial assistance enabled him to conduct an experimental school in Burgdorf, Switzerland, an industrial community near Berne. The experimental school enrolled 72 pupils and employed 10 teachers. Here he participated also in a program for the training of teachers. In 1802 he had 102 teachers studying in his institute, among them a number of foreigners who were studying in order to take ideas about teaching methods back to their homelands. Thus experimentation in methods of teaching and the training of teachers were related through a single program.

The Pestalozzian movement was a direct continuation of the

[6] As quoted in Robert Ulich, *History of Educational Thought* (New York: American Book Company, 1945), pp. 259, 261. Translation is by Ulich.

[7] As quoted in H. Holman, *Pestalozzi, His Life and Work* (New York: David McKay Company, Inc., 1908), p. 172.

Pestalozzi was a Swiss educational reformer whose principles of teaching found manifold application in the United States. The principles of teaching that he developed in his experimental schools were especially influential in teaching elementary school subjects like language, science, domestic geography, and primary arithmetic. In part as a result of Pestalozzi's influence, the methods of instruction that were developed in America in these subjects represented an enormous improvement over the methods that had been prevalent in the schools before 1800—methods that were highly routinized, mechanical, and flagrantly wasteful.

Following the French invasion of Switzerland in 1798, Pestalozzi collected in a deserted convent a number of children made homeless by the invasion and spent his energies reclaiming them. In 1781, he had written his educational masterpiece, *Leonard and Gertrude,* and his acquirement of the indigent and forsaken children now gave him an opportunity to test his educational theories.

In his later years he was visited and consulted by many political and educational leaders who recognized him as one who had demonstrated the worth of his educational ideas.

Around 1860, Edward A. Sheldon of the Oswego, New York, Normal School introduced the new Pestalozzian procedures to American teachers. The school was visited by leading educators from all parts of the United States, and it has been said that within twenty years the "Oswego movement" had completely reshaped instruction in the better elementary schools throughout America.

strivings for social reforms stimulated by Rousseau's revolutionary books. At first Pestalozzi's endeavors were directed toward an improvement of the social condition of the lower classes through industrial education. It was in later experiments that he attempted to determine the psychologically soundest methods of teaching subjects in the elementary school. He protested vigorously against teaching children words and phrases that they did not understand, and insisted upon the substitution of firsthand experience with natural objects as the fundamental starting point of instruction. He believed that the primary purpose in teaching through observation and concrete experience was to have the children get real and clear ideas instead of mere words and hazy notions. The teacher became an active instructor of groups of children instead of a hearer of individual recitations. Children were freed from the dominance of textbooks and given training in oral expression. In all subjects— geography, science, arithmetic—emphasis on training in oral expression was prominent.

The Experimental Idea in Modern Education

The Pestalozzian movement was an attempt to translate an acceptable principle of teaching into actual practice. Pestalozzi's own book, *How Gertrude Teaches Her Children,* based on his experiences at Burgdorf, popularized some of the ideas and stimulated further experimentation. Slowly, but with certainty, the Pestalozzian emphases in teaching and in the training of teachers gained a firm and lasting foothold upon educational practice. Experimentation in education eventually led to a new philosophy of education known as the philosophy of experimentalism. This philosophy has been, and remains, a considerable influence in present-day education in the United States. Universities and colleges that educate teachers conduct experimental schools and combine the education of teachers with direct study of the methods used by the teachers in the experimental schools.

FROEBEL: EMPHASIS ON SOCIAL PARTICIPATION AND SELF-ACTIVITY

Importance of Early Beginning

Concern that education begin in early childhood followed directly Rousseau's principle that education should be in accord with the child's natural design. Froebel, who had studied Pestalozzi's experiments carefully and who was convinced of the soundness of both the principle upon which they were based and of the conclusions drawn by the Pestalozzians, considered as most precious the waxing and waning of children's interests and the irregularities in the growth patterns in the development of the very young. Froebel believed it important that later education should never have to undo the evil effects of earlier, inferior education. He believed that, in order to avoid this, deliberate education should begin earlier than had been the custom. To test his theory he, like Pestalozzi, established an experimental school in which he experimented with programs for children too young for the ordinary elementary school. The chief feature of this new school to which Froebel gave the name *kindergarten* was organized play. Little children were given instructive diversions and healthful games. Froebel's experiences led to a deep conviction that the kindergarten age is the appropriate time to begin deliberate education. Realizing that teachers, in gen-

Pestalozzian methods were popularized by Reverend Charles Mayo (1792–1846) who spent three years in Yverdon teaching under the direction of Pestalozzi. Returning to England in 1822, he opened a private school for children of the upper classes that proved highly successful. In several subjects he used Pestalozzi's methods—definitely organizing object teaching. Mayo's sister, Elizabeth, wrote a manual for teachers outlining methods of object teaching. The manual was published in 1830, passed through twenty-six editions, and was influential in the widespread adoption in England and America of formalized object teaching. The formalization of object teaching eventually became so exaggerated that it was ludicrous. Literary satires dissecting the educational practices of the times were numerous. Perhaps the most biting was written by Charles Dickens in his novel *Hard Times* (1854). The following excerpt describes how Mr. Gradgrind, school patron, demonstrates model teaching for the schoolteacher.

"Now what I want is Facts. Teach these boys and girls nothing but Facts. Facts alone are wanted in life. Plant nothing else, and root out everything else. You can only form the minds of reasoning animals upon Facts: nothing else will ever be of any service to them. This is the principle on which I bring up my own children, and this is the principle on which I bring up these children. Stick to Facts, Sir!"

. . .

"Girl number twenty," said Mr. Gradgrind, squarely pointing with his square forefinger, "I don't know that girl. Who is that girl?"

"Sissy Jupe, Sir," explained number twenty, blushing, standing up, and curtseying.

"Sissy is not a name," said Mr. Gradgrind. "Don't call yourself Sissy. Call yourself Cecilia."

"It's father as calls me Sissy, Sir," returned the young girl in

eral, had meager knowledge about early education to guide them into sound practices, he decided to devote his later life to studying the needs of very young children, to providing an educational program suitable to their age, and to propagating the ideas that seemed justified by his studies.

Although many ideas about method accrue from Froebel's experiences and studies, two principles which he developed have had great effect upon modern education. These are, even today, of interest to the student of education in the United States where the idea of kindergarten education has become so common that no one questions that it is essential in a good education program. These two

a trembling voice, and with another curtsey.

"Then he has no business to do it," said Mr. Gradgrind. "Tell him he mustn't. Cecilia Jupe. Let me see. What is your father?"

"He belongs to the horse-riding, if you please, Sir."

Mr. Gradgrind frowned, and waved off the objectionable calling with his hand.

"We don't want to know anything about that, here. You mustn't tell us about that, here. Your father breaks horses, don't he?"

"If you please, Sir, when they can get any to break, they do break horses in the ring, Sir."

"You mustn't tell us about the ring, here. Very well, then. Describe your father as a horsebreaker. He doctors sick horses, I dare say?"

"Oh yes, Sir."

"Very well, then. He is a veterinary surgeon, a farrier, and a horsebreaker. Give me your definition of a horse."

(Sissy Jupe thrown into the greatest alarm by this demand.)

"Girl number twenty unable to define a horse!" said Mr. Gradgrind, for the general behoof of all the little pitchers. "Girl number twenty possessed of no facts, in reference to one of the commonest of animals! Some boy's definition of a horse. Bitzer, yours."

. . . "Quadruped. Graminivorous. Forty teeth, namely twenty-four grinders, four eye-teeth, and twelve incisive. Sheds coat in the spring; in marshy countries, sheds hoofs, too. Hoofs hard, but requiring to be shod with iron. Age known by marks in mouth." Thus (and much more) Bitzer.

"Now girl number twenty," said Mr. Gradgrind. "You know what a horse is."

From Charles Dickens, *Hard Times* (New York: E. P. Dutton & Co. [Everyman's Library]), pp. 1, 2, 3.

ideas are called the principle of self-activity and the principle of social participation. The two were inextricably interrelated in Froebel's theory of teaching.

Self-Activity as a Starting Point

As Froebel emphasized in his teaching of the very young, the principle of self-activity, or motor expression, followed the logic that self-activity is *the* process through which one realizes his own nature. It is natural for a child to be active. Self-activity, however, is not just any kind of activity. It is that kind of activity that is strongly influenced by one's motives, the kind that arises out of one's own

Although Froebel is popularly associated with the kindergarten, his doctrines of development and self-activity are considered to be applicable to all levels of education. (Prints Division, New York Public Library)

interests. In a word, it is the kind of activity that is compelled by one's own nature. It is the individual's response to forces within him, rather than to forces without him. It is this kind of activity which is of the highest educative value to the growing child.

Froebel first made these ideas concrete and meaningful in his experimental kindergarten. The children were permitted to use all those forms of self-expression that would further their development. Self-activity provided the starting point. What was learned was a result of this self-activity.

Froebel was a German educational reformer. As a boy he attended the village school in his native town, Oberweissbach, Thuringia, where he was classified by his teachers as a dunce. When fifteen years of age he was apprenticed to a forester, and it was through his experiences in the forests that he gained his profound insight into the laws of nature. Throughout the remainder of his life he was dominated by the thought that his greatest and most propelling aim was to advance the good of humanity through education. Like Pestalozzi, by whom he was greatly influenced, he conducted experimental schools. He was much concerned about the education of the younger children, those under seven years of age whose education he thought had traditionally been greatly neglected.

Froebel's greatest work, *The Education of Man*, deals chiefly with the education of children in their early years. Although the principle he emphasized—that self-activity is the surest road to sound education—found its greatest acceptance among those who taught younger children, it was Froebel's belief that the principle applied to the education of all ages.

Froebel stressed that the tendencies of early childhood become fixed fundamental dispositions according to the ways the young are taught in their early years. This teaching in the early years also affects deeply the turn taken by the powers that develop later. Froebel's insistence that the education of children in their earliest years is critically important has had a lasting influence upon all serious-minded educators since his time.

As his idea developed, Froebel learned progressively better ways of applying the principle. Some of the activities which he, along with his followers, found that children liked and which seemed to bring the best learning results were rhythms, music, singing, creative dramatics, handicraft, drawing, painting, modeling with clay, collecting art specimens or objects of nature, growing plants, bringing animals into the school, and playing on a suitably equipped playground. All the activities required the supervision of a teacher trained to teach and understand children of that particular age. The principle of having children learn *through* activities suited to their age became an accepted principle of education for children in their earlier years.

It was never Froebel's belief that the principle of self-activity applied to younger children only. He believed it was also applicable to education at later levels. In order for later education to be most effective it must be built upon sound earlier education. But it must also continue to apply the principle of self-activity.

The emphasis Froebel gave to social participation followed his belief that cooperation is a fundamental social necessity, that it should be one of the goals of all education and must be cultivated very early in a child's life. He made considerable use of play activities to achieve this end, but in all other activities as well, cooperativeness among the children was one of the outcomes for which he continually strove.

Influence upon Modern Education

Froebel's recognition that children have natural cravings for activity and that this desire for activity can be utilized by teachers to promote the development of children in a natural way has been reinforced by all subsequent educational experience. When education was narrowly conceived to be a mastery of books, teachers practiced a deadening kind of pedagogical pedantry which resulted in sterile schooling, uninteresting to the child and lacking in challenge to those teachers who possessed fertile minds. Teaching then was largely a matter of enforcing restraints. Froebel's experimentation not only led to the establishment of kindergartens, but it added an element to educational theory that has never been questioned.

It is not easy to appraise the effects of his emphasis upon cooperativeness as an aim of education. One can still find in modern educational practice the manifestation of the opposite belief, namely, that teaching should stress competition, that competition is the principal motivating force in encouraging pupils to learn. This tendency seemingly runs counter to the one that Froebel indicated was worthy of developing.

HERBART: EDUCATION IN HOW TO THINK

Teaching and the Recitation

From the time of the earliest schools, children met with their teachers in some designated place and a definite period of time was set aside for certain kinds of learning. The word "recitation" became a common term in the vocabulary of every school child. As the term implies, the period was used for the "re-citation" of lessons learned. Usually learning came from a book. The pupils recited back to the teacher what they had learned out of the book. Sometimes the recitation was almost a verbatim reproduction of the

Herbart is considered the forerunner of educational experimentation and organized instruction in education in American universities. As a Professor at the University of Köenigsberg he established a pedagogical seminar with a practice school attached. Much of his life was devoted to lecturing, writing, and investigating.

thought expressed in the book. The nearer the pupil came to an actual reproduction, the more likely it was that he would be judged a good learner.

Memorizing was much emphasized and methods for effective memorization were often explained to the pupils. Of course, children improvised all kinds of methods of study in the preparation of their lessons. Some studied at home where they could read aloud. Sometimes they read a few sentences and then tried to repeat them aloud.

The organization of the school day and the equipment of the schoolroom were planned to be suitable for a full exploitation of this method of teaching. The seats were in rows and firmly anchored to the wooden floors. Children were seated one behind the other as though they were never to talk to one another but were always to address their remarks only to the teacher. The textbooks were learned. Pupils were often rated in terms of their ability to recite faithfully the materials of the book.

Many leading scholars of the Middle Ages practiced learning by memorizing. Some of them could recite the entire works of Aeneas or Ovid. Their writings were replete with verbatim quotations from memory from their favorite authors. The biographers of some of the great scholars of earlier times demonstrated that power of memorization was considered almost synonymous with great genius by pointing out with pride that the biographee had memorized the whole of some classical treatise. This was the picture of formal education when Johann Friedrich Herbart advocated a change in the prevailing method of conducting the recitation.

Herbart was a philosopher-educationist of scholarly bent. He studied under Johann Gotlieb Fichte, the noted German philosopher. In 1809, he was called to a professorship at Königsberg and occupied the chair formerly held by Immanuel Kant, the great German philosopher. From the standpoint of his exactness in analysis and his penetration of thought, he ranks in importance as the equal of any of the great German philosophers with the possible exception of his contemporary, George Wilhelm Friedrich Hegel (1770–1831).

Speaking of one of Herbart's contributions to methods of teaching, John Dewey says:

But few attempts have been made to formulate a method, resting on general principles, of conducting a recitation. One of these is of great importance and has probably had more and better influence upon the hearing of lessons than all others put together; namely, the analysis by Herbart of a recitation into five successive steps.

Herbart placed strong emphasis upon the importance of instruction and instructional techniques in the classroom. In his own words, we indicate the nature of his influence: "Instruction will form the circle of thought, and education the character. The last is nothing without the first. Herein is contained the whole sum of my pedagogy."

Emphasis on How to Think

Herbart was a professor of philosophy and psychology at universities in Germany from 1802 to 1841. He is sometimes referred to as the first of the educational psychologists. He advocated a method for the recitation period that would train pupils to develop habits of thought. It is not difficult to imagine how little a teacher had to know, how shallow his thinking could be, when all he had to do was to hear pupils faithfully recite their assigned lessons. It is also not difficult to imagine the kind of social attitudes people developed toward such teachers.

Herbart did not hold memorization in low esteem. He was concerned because the memorizing method was used almost exclusively. He believed that other activities should be introduced into the formal recitation—activities that would be planned for the express purpose of encouraging pupils to think. He made clear that the method of reproducing that which had been learned from textbooks overlooked certain significant educational values that come from studying with a purpose in mind, supplementing thought from one's own experiences, arriving at definite conclusions, and organizing one's own ideas. As an educational psychologist, he saw great need for broadening the then current narrow concept of the function of a recitation period.

Herbart recommended the employment of a wider range of activities during the recitation period. Pupils should react to the ideas and judge their worth, not only in terms of their soundness, but also in terms of their relative worth to the individual pupil. Pupils should be encouraged to make applications of what they learned and to relate the applications to their own experiences. Instead of the learning in the recitation being a passive affair devoted wholly to the absorption of material, Herbart advocated that it be an active-reactive period in which the pupils gave consideration to what was being studied, supplemented what they were studying, and ultimately assimilated what they had been studying.

The time seemed ripe for a change, and Herbart's ideas were received with immediate enthusiasm. Nowhere were they more cordially accepted than among the educational theorists in the United States. The interest continued and around the year 1890, close to half a century after Herbart's death, educators were giving expression to educational theories which today are still being considered and elaborated. These ideas of the American educators will be discusssed later.

Herbart's Principle

In contrast to the other educators discussed, whose ideas applied to the whole of the educative process, Herbart made his greatest contribution by concentrating on a single aspect of the educative process, namely, the recitation. He advocated making the recitation methodical by conducting it in four steps: preparation, presentation, comparison, and generalization or conclusion. Later, a fifth step was added by his followers: application. These became known as the five formal steps in the recitation.

Herbart attempted to deliver classroom teaching method from the routine and accidental habits it had become heir to by setting forth a formula which, if followed, would lead to far more wholesome results. It would be just as ill-advised, however, to follow the five formal steps in Herbart's principle slavishly as it would to embrace unquestioningly the principle of learning by memorization.

The Principle Interpreted

Herbart recognized that the period set aside for recitation brought the teacher into close and intimate contact with the learner. It was a period that gave the teacher his greatest opportunity to influence the pupils in what they learned from their textbooks, in their ways of thinking and the habits of language they would develop, in the observations they would make, and in the generalizations and conclusions at which they would arrive. Therefore, the recitation period should be a period for *reflection,* for stimulating and directing thought, rather than a period for rehearsing in detail all of what the pupils had learned.

1. Preparation

The first logical step in the recitation is that of preparation. In preparing the pupils the teacher asked questions to help them recall familiar experiences related to the new topic that they were starting to study. This topic was always to be related to what the pupils already knew. At the end, a statement of the purpose of the new material was formulated with the class.

2. Presentation

Presentation is the next step toward learning something new. Herbartians often took the pupils on excursions to see firsthand what they were studying. The pupils would then give vivid oral descriptions of what they had seen. Presentation was a period for challenging interchange of experience and for discussion.

3. Comparison

The third logical step is comparison. Comparison was used to establish important thought connections. Each new connection, Herbart believed, not only insured more lasting impressions of what was being presented for the first time, but it also established new and closer associations among the ideas that had previously been studied. This comparison was for the main purpose of making the one central object of the lesson clearer. Every comparison was made *deliberately* to clear up some obscure aspect of the central problem or object of the recitation.

4. Conclusion

Finally, one conclusion or generalization or definition was reached. The conclusion then served as a basis for the next logical step in the further adventure in learning.

5. Application

The step added by Herbart's followers is application. In this step the child applied or utilized his general conclusion growing out of the study. By making a sufficient number of applications, the conclusion or definition or generalization would remain indelible in the minds of the learners.

One additional point about the five formal steps of the recitation should be emphasized. The steps applied to the teacher's preparatory work as well as to the actual manner in which he would conduct the recitation. He had not only previously gained a mastery of his subject matter but he had also, through careful advance work, arranged an approach that would enable him to conduct the recitation in a manner best suited to cultivating thought. He would carefully prepare himself by thinking through what might be done in each of the five steps. He would need to review: What do my pupils already know? What questions shall I ask in order to bring out what they know and think? What aids shall I use? What incidents shall I relate? What are the difficulties some of the pupils may have? What conclusions should be reached?

Through preparation the teacher freed himself from any necessity of further study during the recitation and was able to focus his entire attention upon skillfully conducting the recitation. The teacher could be flexible, teach as the occasion demanded, and still end with some order and organization in what had been learned by the pupils. He did not intend to blindly formalize the recitation into a pattern of five steps. Rather, it could be modified as needed by a teacher alert to the opportunities for stimulating pupil thought. In interpreting Herbart's principle this point should always be kept in mind.

Herbart's efforts have had a great and wholesome influence. For the first time, trained schoolteachers generally realized the importance of turning periods for reciting into periods for stimulating and directing reflection. In fact, in the modern school, perhaps because of Herbart's emphasis on thinking as an important part of teaching, recitation periods are no longer called by that name.

SPENCER: EDUCATION AS PREPARATION

Establishment of a Pattern

By 1850, education was receiving considerable attention from leading philosophers. Educational theory was perceptibly changing. The English philosopher Herbert Spencer added still another emphasis. In 1859 Spencer published "What Knowledge Is Most Worth," an essay on education. In it he proposed that an analysis of life's activities be used to determine what subject matter should be included in the school curriculum. He advocated classifying adult life activities into five categories and then selecting subject matter that would prepare the young to engage successfully in all those activities. The five classifications, which would constitute the objectives of all education, were related to preserving life and health, earning a living, family duties and the care of children, social and political responsibilities, and leisure time activities.

Many educators in the United States seized Spencer's idea as a suitable pattern for the statement of educational objectives in American schools. A pattern for building the school curriculum, in time, became established. It followed rather closely that proposed by Spencer.

Effects upon Modern Education

The pattern set by Spencer fastened upon modern education the principle that education should be carried on mainly to prepare the

Spencer is usually not thought of as an educational philosopher. His contribution to education was somewhat incidental although what he wrote about education has had far-reaching subsequent effect. He was a self-taught philosopher of the scientific movement of the latter half of the nineteenth century. He was influenced in his thinking by his friends Charles Darwin (1809–1882), the British naturalist, Thomas Henry Huxley (1825–1895), the British biologist and writer, and George Henry Lewes (1817–1878), the British philosophical writer and critic.

Inquiring what knowledge is of most worth, Spencer contended that all considerations lead to the conclusion that scientific knowledge is the most valuable. He spoke for all those who believed that the chief purpose of education in the schools should be to give a practical preparation for life. To use his own words: ". . . To prepare us for complete living is the function which education has to discharge; and the only rational mode of judging of any educational course is to judge in what degree it discharges such function."

pupil for adult life. Although there have been dissenters, the principle has had a conspicuous effect on the character of present-day American secondary education. It has also, but to a lesser degree, had a marked influence upon teaching at the elementary level. Seemingly, there has been little question about the use of the activity analysis method in selecting the subject matter that prepares for the vocations. There seems now, however, to be a growing sentiment among educational theorists that the method is used too generously when it is applied to the whole of education and at all levels, that it is not applicable to teaching when growth is made the one important over-all objective of all education.

INTERMINGLING OF IDEAS

The six ideas—applying the technique of induction to teaching, educating in accordance with nature, experimenting to discover effective methods, emphasizing self-activity and social participation, considering education in how to think as of primary importance, and seeing education as preparation—have been potent in shaping the character of formal education in the United States. The eminent European scholars who propagated these ideas were all productive thinkers and prolific writers. Each covered other aspects of education in addition to those discussed. The ideas selected are those that seem to have had greatest influence upon modern education in the United States.

As these six broad educational ideas were carried westward, they took root and became intermingled with other ideas. Maintaining more or less their individual identities, they became part of the great stream of thought that continues to flow and make modern educational theory what it is.

How the ideas intermingled when transplanted to a wholly new cultural soil is one of the exciting stories of social history. It is one, however, that cannot be even remotely understood without first taking a careful look at what that new soil was like. To develop a true picture we must turn to a discussion of the American frontier movement—a movement that has had lasting effects upon American education.

QUESTIONS

1. What is your explanation of how Comenius became skilled in applying the inductive method to teaching?
2. What were the features of Comenius' textbooks that gave them their long-lasting quality?
3. Why has Rousseau's influence on education been so great?
4. Why did the schools of Rousseau's time place such great emphasis upon the use of artificial effort? Do the schools show any such tendencies today?
5. How does it happen that it was a political scientist instead of a leading educator who called the attention of educators to the need to recognize the nature of the child when directing his learning?
6. What are some of the obstacles to conducting worthwhile experiments in modern American schools?
7. Assuming the conclusions drawn from research studies in education are valid, to what degree should a teacher permit himself to be guided by these findings?
8. In what ways were the teachings of Pestalozzi a logical sequence to the social reforms initiated or stimulated by Rousseau's books?
9. Which changes introduced into American education can be traced to the influence of Froebel?
10. Why was the influence of Herbart upon American education around 1890 of such magnitude? How far has modern teaching practice advanced beyond what he advocated?
11. Why were Spencer's ideas so enthusiastically adopted in American education by those working at the secondary level?

PROJECTS

1. Contrast the ideas of the six educational theorists whose ideas have been discussed in this chapter.
2. Explain why it was so long before an idea that was accepted became incorporated into educational practice.
3. Estimate the influence upon modern American education of Spencer's contention that the teaching of the classics in the elementary and secondary schools should largely give way to the teaching of science.

CHAPTER 9

The frontier heritage

The present educational system in the United States had its origin in the streams of thought that grew out of the great social movements of history and the theories expounded by European leaders. Both were adapted to frontier conditions and altered by pioneer thinking. Understanding the nature of those earlier European influences is crucial to any evaluation of education in the United States. It is equally impossible to make a sound assessment without first recognizing and appreciating the significance of features that were molded by the frontier movement. The broad outlines of the movement are known to most students, but its specific direct impact upon modern American education is not always fully understood. It is important to focus attention upon the effects of the movement, upon the character of what is, perhaps, America's largest social undertaking, its educational program.

The migration to America was only one of the numerous migrations of Europeans to many new, sparsely populated lands. Behind this European "invasion" lay one simple assumption, the assumption that the lands lying immediately ahead were free for the taking. This assumption was applied to the whole vast expanse of the American continent. It was the backbone of a philosophy of

In America the word [frontier] is hardly used at all to indicate the nation's limits. No American would refer to the line separating the United States from Canada or that from Mexico as the frontier, and to apply it to them in this sense would lead to misunderstanding. The American thinks of the frontier as lying *within*, and not at the edge of the country. It is not a line to stop at, but an area inviting entrance. Instead of having one dimension, length, as in Europe, the American frontier has two dimensions, length and breadth. In Europe the frontier is stationary and presumably permanent; in America it *was* transient and temporal.

The concept of a moving frontier is applicable where a civilized people are advancing into a wilderness, an unsettled area, or one sparsely populated by primitive people. It was the sort of land into which the Boers moved in South Africa, the English in Australia, and the Americans and Canadians in their progress westward across North America. The frontier movement is the invasion of a land assumed to be vacant as distinguished from an invasion of an occupied or civilized country, an advance against nature rather than against men. On a frontier the invaders often have immediate and exclusive possession whereas in a nonfrontier the invaders have to contend with the original inhabitants whom they always find troublesome and frequently too much for them. Inherent in the American concept of a moving frontier is the idea of a body of free land which can be had for the taking.

From Walter Prescott Webb, *The Great Frontier* (Boston: Houghton Mifflin Company, 1952), pp. 2–3. Quoted by permission of Houghton Mifflin Company.

the people. It resulted in one of the most dramatic population movements in all history, and its effects on educational policy in the United States are incalculable.

As the frontier continually moved westward from the first settlements on the Atlantic coast, it was marked not only by the development of new areas but also by a return to primitive conditions for the settlers. American social development was continually beginning over again on the frontier. American life achieved a fluidity which was marked by a steady movement away from the influence of Europe, a steady growth in independence, a reliance on American strenuous endeavor, a remolding of the older ways of life.

The movement lasted nearly two hundred and fifty years. Free land is not inexhaustible in a rapidly expanding population, and all exoduses end somewhere and at some time. Historians generally record 1890 as the year when almost all free lands in the United States had been settled. Thus the movement ended. However, the values established in the frontier period continue to be cherished, continue to influence the thinking and determine the action of modern Americans who are part of the postfrontier period. The philosophy of the frontier was adaptable to rapidly changing conditions. That kind of adaptation is still in process. Educational institutions, and especially American educational philosophy, today reflect clearly the continuing impact of the philosophy of the frontier.

THE PHILOSOPHY OF THE FRONTIER

Love for Freedom

The frontier brought about changed relationships between individual man and his neighbor. In crowded Europe the density of the population in 1500 was about 27 persons per square mile or something like 24 acres of land, good and bad, for each person. On the frontier in America there was plenty of room and all the land one might wish to occupy. This meant release for the individual. His way of living began to reflect a hitherto unknown independence built upon the challenge of opportunities, the privilege of choice. He had freedom. His biggest responsibility was to learn how to make the most intelligent use of the freedom he more or less by accident had become heir to. We do not pretend that he always used his newly discovered inheritance wisely. His ideas of democratic government, his sometimes extravagant exploitation of natural resources, the unconventional forms of behavior he sometimes engaged in, his rude manners, his raw language, and the like attest to the fact that he did not always use his freedom wisely. The point is that the new frontier conditions granted him a degree of freedom that he had never known before, and his knowledge that he had this freedom changed both his ideals and his fundamental social beliefs. In time, this ideal of freedom of the individual became strong, and, as the meaning was made clearer, it became a cherished guide to action.

The frontiersman's esteem for freedom resulted in a reliance on his individual intelligence. He did not want someone to tell him what to do. He believed that the application of his own intelligence, whether trained or not, was the best method of arriving at conclusions. He did not have to appeal to the judgment of someone higher

His supreme generalization [Frederick Jackson] Turner presented in an address delivered in Chicago in 1893, entitled "The Frontier in American History." Within a few years his generalization became the most influential single interpretation of American history. Hundreds of disciples, inspired by Turner, diffused it in every section of the continent; and in time Turner was called to Harvard, under the presidency of Charles W. Eliot.

What had Turner said at Chicago? He had declared that the frontier and free land accounted for the characteristics that differentiated the evolution of society in the United States from the evolution of society in the Old World: "The existence of an area of free land, its continuous recession, and the advance of American settlement westward, explain American development." The statement, in its unqualified simplicity, was categorical and sweeping. Apparently Turner believed that if it had not been for the advancing frontier, for the free land on the frontier, if the English colonists had been hemmed in on the Atlantic seaboard, American development would have followed European patterns. If this was his belief, then American civilization, without the advancing frontier, would have duplicated the European process of civilization, at least in its main stream. . . .

This, however, had not been the main course of American history: "American development has exhibited not merely advance along a single line, but a return to primitive conditions on a continually advancing frontier line, and a new development for that area. American social development has been continually beginning over again on the frontier. This perennial rebirth, this fluidity of American life, this expansion westward with its new opportunities, its continuous touch with the simplicity of primitive society, furnish the forces dominating American character. . . . The frontier is the line of most rapid and effective Americanization. . . . The advance of the frontier has meant a steady movement away from the influence of Europe, a steady growth of independence on American lines. And to study this advance, the men who grew up under these conditions, and the political, economic, and social results of it, is to study the really American part of our history."

From Charles A. Beard and Mary R. Beard, The American Spirit (The Rise of American Civilization, Vol. IV [New York: The Macmillan Company, 1942]), pp. 360–361. Quoted by permission of The Macmillan Company.

up in seeking a solution to his problems. His intelligence was sharpened by constant application to numerous everyday practical problems, some of which involved his very survival.

Freedom to arrive at his own conclusions and to use his own solutions led the frontiersman to place a high value upon the opportunity to develop his intelligence, to use it in solving the problems of his life and in advancing his own material welfare. Freedom was a gift which, to him, became a right. Only through the development of his intelligence could he learn to use his freedom wisely.

Freedom of intelligence became a kind of religion. As the Christian minister and essayist Ralph Waldo Emerson (1803–1882) said in his essay on self-reliance, "Who would be a man, must be a non-conformist. He who would gather immortal palms must not be hindered by the name of goodness, but must explore if it be goodness. Nothing is at last sacred but the integrity of your own mind. Absolve you to yourself, and you shall have the suffrage of the world."

What kind of school would such freedom-loving people build? What happened to the freedom philosophy as the frontier moved westward and the civilization advanced? As schools become systematized in a developing civilization, must a degree of freedom be correspondingly relinquished? How much freedom must Mr. Average Citizen surrender, and what methods should be used to achieve the surrender as the educational system develops and as smaller educational units are integrated into larger units? The frontier American cherished freedom and he established a halo of inviolability about it. How are those highly cherished, lasting, and theoretically desirable attitudes to be acknowledged as a new type of education develops under changed and still rapidly changing social conditions?

Regard for the Individual

The picture of the frontiersman as a lonely, isolated individual is largely a myth. He was a man with a family and a man in a group. The pioneer was just as interested in having standing with the other members of his group as he would have been in a European setting. The difference was that on the frontier his standing depended on different factors, not so much on his ancestors, his education, or even the money he had available, as on his success in adjusting to his environment and in triumphing over current vicissitudes, and on his effectiveness in helping the group to do likewise. The frontiersman was not satisfied with a new culture that would barely meet his biogenic needs. He also strove for the satisfaction of his biosocial needs including that for prestige. He was a highly sensitive, social creature with natural concern for what others thought of him.

The frontiersman expected the respect of other individuals; he also expected to accord respect to other individuals. This was a natural corollary to his love for freedom. Freedom of the individual must include freedom to attain prestige and standing which, in turn, depend upon respect for individual personality. What did the frontiersman's respect for the individual imply? It implied first a recognition that each individual is unique. It implied also an appreciation that each must be allowed to develop his pattern of living in a way that gives full recognition to the need for individuality and for individual expression.

Rousseau would have felt at home in this kind of philosophical surrounding. The social soil that nourished the individual afforded limitless opportunity for self-development. It was thought that there was something incommensurable about every man and that every man should have the opportunity to develop all his natural endowments.

The whole idea of forcing the individual to conform to a norm, of reducing everything to an average, of emphasizing the mediocre as a reasonable standard for all was discarded as an untenable educational theory. It was argued, instead, that each individual should be encouraged to develop to the limit of his capacities. People were, by nature, constituted differently. One person should be as highly respected as another. Since each was different from every other, then each should be educated differently from all the others.

On the frontier there were always more jobs to be done than there was help available. All individuals, regardless of natural design, had the opportunity to be of worth. The frontiersmen developed a philosophy toward the individual which recognized that worth. Everyone should and did respect the inherent worth of the individual.

Belief in Equality

Égalité is the French word for "equality." Under the influence of Thomas Paine and Thomas Jefferson, egalitarianism became a highly favored philosophy in the new land. Paine was a clever journalist, usually remembered as the author of an essay written in France in 1791 called "The Rights of Man." Jefferson, too, could write with impelling force. He was the author of the Declaration of Independence.

The attitude of the frontiersman was expressed in the Declaration of Independence and reiterated in the Bill of Rights. In essence, the American spirit was pledged to an extension of equality. Equality, it was held, was essential to the maintenance of the general welfare of the people and to raising the level of well-being of every American citizen.

Regard for the individual—with its implied appreciation of individual differences and recognition of individual needs for social standing—was woven into a philosophy broadly based on the principle of equality. On the frontier all men were important; each had a significant job to do; the worth of each was taken for granted. As the frontier moved westward, the frontiersman expressed his belief in equality by insisting on universal suffrage. Property restrictions on voting were removed. Frontiersmen gave women their first chance to vote. The common man, the man of the people, was elected to the highest offices.

As the nation developed, educators were constantly faced with the question, What does egalitarianism mean when incorporated into educational practice? What does it mean in terms of educational opportunity and in terms of teaching in the classroom? In the lands from which pioneers had come, it was held that people were unequal and that they should be educated as unequals. It called for thought and courageous action to build new schools and to follow new practices consistent with a philosophical position almost the reverse of that assumed by most leaders in the other lands.

Faith in Oneself

The pioneer's love for freedom, his respect for the personality of others, his recognition of individual worth, and his devotion to egalitarianism had certain correlative values. One of these was a deep and abiding faith in his own power and ability to meet whatever problems he, in the course of common events, might happen to encounter. The frontiersman possessed an almost unlimited and unbounded optimism, whether he was considering his own future or that of the nation whose destinies he was helping to shape. This is an attitude in sharp contrast to the pessimism that prevailed around 1700 among the individuals of Europe and that is reflected in the literature of such writers as Dryden, Swift, and Montaigne. Faith in oneself and one's future was a lasting characteristic of the frontiersman.

Faith in Common Man

Life on the frontier also deepened the pioneer's faith in the common or average man. Once the door of opportunity was opened, common people proceeded to build a new nation. So great was their success that the European critics of the new American civilization, the European aristocratic leaders who had expressed misgivings about the ability of common men to build a great civilization, were confounded. To the frontiersman who believed that the worth and welfare of every citizen was important, the achievements of the common man forcefully verified his confidence. The frontiersman simply assumed that the common man could achieve a stable government, develop and diffuse the material necessities of a civilized life, create literature, art, and music, develop education, recreation, and health—in short, do whatever he deemed important for making life worthwhile. He had a boundless faith in the possibilities of himself and every normal man if adequately encouraged and wisely influenced. This faith in the intelligence of the common man has often been expressed by liberal philosophers who have advanced the principle that individual man may, if he strives to do so, make an almost limitless advance toward perfectibility. This is true because man possesses individually and collectively an almost infinite capacity for making new discoveries and for adapting his knowledge to improving the quality of living. Like the frontiersmen, liberal philosophers today believe man possesses the intelligence to achieve in an almost unlimited degree. He needs most to learn how to use that intelligence wisely. It is an important responsibility of education to develop that intelligence.

Belief in the Value of Work

Out of the experiences of the frontier a high regard for the disciplinary value of work developed in America. To the frontiersman the value of actual work in educating the boy or girl was equal or superior to the training he received in formal education. Somewhat like the Athenians, the boy and girl on the frontier were educated most by living and working with others. The future of a boy or girl who would not work was in jeopardy. It was work that brought a measure of unity into life and was considered the source of all of man's enduring satisfactions. Not to *earn* one's living was like being a traitor to one's country. It followed, then, that a proper education of the young called for opportunities for the young to work, which they were given. Enforcing or allowing the young to be idle was tantamount to leading them into paths of wickedness. From this came the fully accepted principle of education that an individual develops more rapidly and more wholesomely when he is faced with and assumes responsibility. The frontiersman believed that education should be essentially practical, that it should have a direct relation to building character. He rejected the idea of education for ornament, for superficial polish, as appropriate only to a leisure class.

Faith in the Common School

As schools became a necessity in the frontier, the ideas about education that the settlers brought with them were modified and incorporated into new practices. It cannot be said that the early frontiersman believed strongly in formal education, but it is clear that some of the leaders did. Many expressed a conviction that the common school was the hope of our country.

Settlers in the earliest New England frontier communities unknowingly established a lasting pattern for educational organization in the United States. The unit of educational organization, the local school, was controlled and supported by the community. The one-room school that eventually led to one of America's most lasting, sentimentalized pictures—the "Little Red Schoolhouse"—was established in almost every community. It displayed inevitable and flagrant weaknesses, but it symbolized, nevertheless, the pioneer's acceptance of a plan to give his children the benefits of a formal education. It was a manifestation of most of the frontier leaders' faith that a school was necessary to raise the level of American civilization.

This small school, meager in outlook and thwarted by the inadequacy of available teachers, was, nevertheless, the kind of educational institution that fitted admirably with the conditions and spirit of the time. It was a *little* school, close to the people it served. It was controlled locally by those who had complete confidence in their own vision and their own skill in management. It was supported locally. It truly belonged to the people it served. The influence of the traditions built up around this little school, the idea of neighborhood schools, local control of the school, and local support took a firm hold upon the hearts and minds of all early Americans.

With characteristic attention to detail, Currier and Ives depict a school house in a frontier community. (The New-York Historical Society, New York City)

In studying the manner in which education is now conducted in the United States and in evaluating the paths being advocated for its future progress, it is important always to be conscious of the persistent philosophies of life and of education that were a natural and unquestioned part of the beliefs and attitudes of the frontier. The frontiersman's faith in the common man, his regard for the worth of the individual, his belief in equality and freedom, and his confidence in the common school are a significant heritage directly related to the qualities that make our present school unique and culturally characteristic.

EDUCATION ON THE FRONTIER

It is well known that the American frontier movement was one part of a series of events—the conquest of a new continent, the planting of colonies, the conflicts between the incoming Europeans

The Sod School. From the pictures of such one-room frontier schools one may conclude that education in a frontier environment was somewhat cheerless and barren. What was learned, however, was often a useful supplement to the practical education received at home. (Courtesy Nebraska State Historical Society)

and the American red man, the fighting among Europeans for control of the new continent, the fight of new settlers for their independence, and the establishment of a new nation. From the very first arrival of settlers, civilization moved steadily westward. As the nation expanded, sectionalism—the identification of the people of one section of the country with that section rather than with the nation as a whole—nurtured competition for control of the West. New lands were exploited.

As the frontiersmen adjusted to the conditions of westward expansion, what were their educational plans like? By examining briefly some details of the educational experiences of the Puritans and the Massachusetts colony we can see, in some measure, how the frontier philosophy, in its early form, was put into action.

Puritan Education

When, owing to a caprice in the weather or because of geographical convenience, the Pilgrims came to anchor on the shores of the Bay of Cape Cod on November 11, 1620, they immediately drew up articles of government ". . . which shall be thought most

Seven year old Abe walked four miles a day going to the Knob Creek School to learn to read and write. Zacharia Piney and Caleb Hazel were the teachers who brought him along from ABC to where he could write the name "A-b-r-a-h-a-m L-i-n-c-o-l-n" and count numbers beginning with one, two, three, and so on. He heard twice two is four.

The school house was built of logs, with a dirt floor, no window, one door. The scholars learned their lessons by saying them to themselves out loud till it was time to recite; alphabets, multiplication tables, and the letters of spelled words were all in the air at once. It was a "blab school"; so they called it.

.   .   .

A few days of this year in which the cabin was building, Nancy told Abe to wash his face and hands extra clean; she combed his hair, held his face between her two hands, smacked him a kiss on the mouth, and sent him to school—nine miles and back—Abe and Sally hand in hand hiking eighteen miles a day. Tom Lincoln used to say Abe was going to have "a real eddication," explaining, "You are a-goin' to larn readin', writin', and cipherin'."

He learned to spell words he didn't know the meaning of, spelling the words before he used them in sentences. In a list of "words of eight syllables accented upon the sixth," was the word "incomprehensibility." He learned that first, and then such sentences as "Is he to go in?" and "Ann can spin flax."

Some neighbors said, "It's a pore make-out of a school," and Tom complained it was a waste of time to send the children nine miles just to sit with a lot of other children and read out loud all day in a "blab" school. But Nancy, as she cleaned Abe's ears in corners where he forgot to clean them, and as she combed out the tangles in his coarse, sandy black hair, used to say, "Abe, you go to school now, and larn all you kin." And he kissed her and said, "Yes, Mammy," and started with his sister on the nine-mile walk through timberland where bear, deer, coon, and wildcats ran wild.

From Carl Sandburg, *Abraham Lincoln: The Prairie Years* (New York: Harcourt, Brace & World, 1926), pp. 19–20, 38–39. Quoted by permission of Harcourt, Brace and Company.

meet and convenient for the general good of the colony; unto which we promise all due submission and obedience." The new frontier colony was rapidly settled by middle-class businessmen and country gentlemen, many of whom belonged to a religious group known as Puritans. The Puritans believed that the principal reason education was necessary was because one should learn to read the Bible. Of the many effects the earlier attitudes of the Puritan lead-

As visits and pleasure were interspersed with hard work for Robert, he developed rapidly in physique and in character, and by the time he was thirteen he had learned all that could be conveniently taught him at home and at Eastern View [a private elementary school]. Accordingly, by 1820, possibly before that year, Robert entered the Alexandria Academy. This had been established about 1785, and had been privileged to list Washington as one of its trustees. Occupying a one-story brick house on the east side of Washington Street, between Duke and Wolfe, the school was made free to all Alexandria boys after January, 1821. Here Robert met at their desks the boys with whom he had played in the fields, and here he came under the tutelage of William B. Leary, an Irishman for whom young Lee acquired enduring respect.

For approximately three years Robert studied the rudiments of a classical education under Mr. Leary. He read Homer and Longinus in Greek. From Tacitus and Cicero he became so well grounded in Latin that he never quite forgot the language, though he did not study it after he was seventeen. Later in life, he expressed deep regret that he had not pursued his classical course further. In mathematics he shone, for his mind was already of the type that delighted in the precise reasoning of algebra and geometry.

From Douglas Southall Freeman, *R. E. Lee* (New York: Charles Scribner's Sons, 1934), pp. 36–37. Quoted by permission of Charles Scribner's Sons.

ers had upon educational practice, perhaps the most enduring effect was upon classroom methods of teaching.

From our present perspective we conclude that Puritanism led to a way of life narrow and petty in its formalism. Hard work, approaching slavishness, became a moral virtue. The arts were discouraged as needless and useless frills. Nurtured in such a soil, edu-

At that time [1830] there were no free schools in Ohio, but Georgetown, like many other communities, had a subscription school—so called because the parents of the scholars subscribed various sums for the support of the teacher. In this school a Professor John D. White, for three months in a year, scattered knowledge to his pupils as one scatters crumbs to sparrows. The crumbs were poor in quality and few in number, but this meant nothing to Ulysses, whose intellectual hunger was easily satisfied. The simple curriculum consisted of reading, writing, arithmetic, and nothing else.

From *Meet General Grant* by W. E. Woodward. Permission of Helen Woodward and Liveright Publishing Corporation, Copyright: R 1955, by Helen Woodward.

cation sank to a low level. Traditional education was condemned as being associated with an aristocratic, leisure, lazy type of citizenship. The Puritans felt that education, as it had been conducted up to that time, resulted in the creation of a class more ready to exploit than to serve, that it had acted as an alley of escape from the rigors of work, and that it did not adequately educate the pupil to meet conscientiously the requirements of a responsible and participant citizenship which the times demanded. It would be better for him to receive most of his education in the home under the guidance of watchful parents than to receive it in schools that divorced him from the values so highly respected in the home.

The Puritans practiced what they thought were educational theories clearly dictated by the Scriptures. They modeled their laws to conform with these. Their educational philosophies harmonized completely with their religious convictions. In such an atmosphere, superstition and ignorance thrived and opposition to learning in the schools flourished. They limited formal education to the study of reading, writing, and arithmetic at an elementary level. The principal textbook was a religious text for lay people known as *The New England Primer*. Teaching methods were primitive and grossly inefficient. Equipment was limited and neglected. At least two-thirds of the pupils' time was wasted or worse than wasted. At this distance the picture is, at best, dreary and discouraging. But the Puritan strain survived, and although some of the lasting effects upon subsequent philosophies have been harmful, some of them have been sound and helpful.

The emphasis of the Puritans that every future citizen should be a person who could read and write and cipher was antecedent to the acceptance of the principle in the United States that education should be compulsory. By 1918 all 48 states had enacted a compulsory attendance law.

The insistence of the Puritans on shaping elementary education so that it would contribute to the building of character gave an ethical emphasis to classroom teaching that still permeates both the theory and practice of teaching in the elementary schools. Behavior is one of the uppermost concerns of every present-day elementary classroom teacher.

The emphasis the Puritans gave to reading, and especially to the reading of the Bible, and their insistence that the reader be given freedom to interpret what he read according to his personal

FIG. 9.1   AVERAGE LENGTH OF SCHOOL TERM

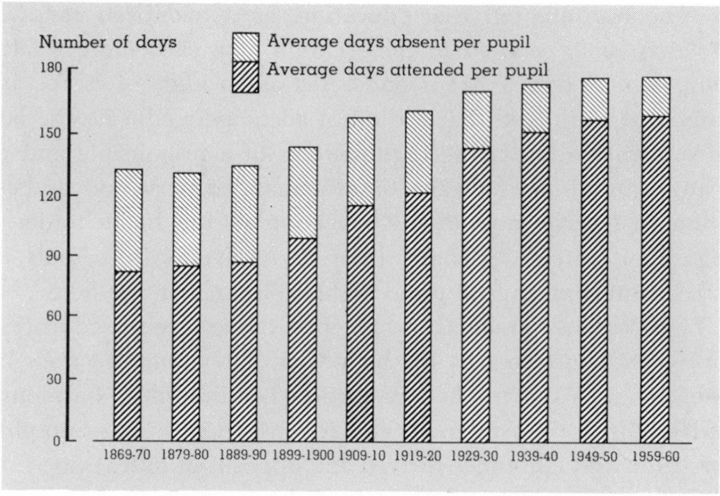

(Data from U.S. Office of Education, updated from *Biennial Survey of Education in the United States, 1954–1956*, Chap. 2, "Statistics of State School Systems: 1955–1956")

values paved the way for the belief that a similar freedom should be granted in the whole world of thought. Freedom to think and to act in terms of one's own thinking led to an emphasis in education on granting freedom and on teaching pupils to use this privilege wisely. Building habits of self-direction and achieving self-control became the abiding aims of the elementary schools. Such values are still cherished. In current professional literature we read that every citizen should be an enlightened citizen, that education in the schools should stress the building of good character, and that those of stronger character are those who have learned the lessons of self-direction and self-control and have learned to act in the light of a progressively more insightful intelligence that has been trained to think and to act. These effects of the Puritan doctrine have been deemed good and they have been lasting.

There were some effects of the Puritan influence that were also potent and lasting but that are now considered to be negative and unfortunate when viewed from the perspective of modern educational theory. The Puritans had a deep-seated belief in the efficacy of coercion and punishment to promote healthful learning. It was assumed that children could never learn anything on their own volition. Their own interests were considered worthless. Teachers were to force the child to learn, using severe and vindictive methods of punishment as the chief instrument of motivation. As history so vividly shows, this philosophy was not only the philosophy of the teachers in the schools, it was the philosophy of the whole of the Puritan society. Punishment, whether administered in school or out, was an ethical social instrument admirably suited to building the kind of society the Puritans desired. Believing that coercion is the most effective method of promoting learning is not surprisingly backward in a society that as late as the seventeenth century put 32 persons to death, some by torture, because they were accused of practicing witchcraft.

The nature of subject matter, its arrangement, the equipment of the classroom—all reflected the same severe, authoritarian atmosphere. All subject matter was laid out in advance, and all pupils were to master precisely the same material. The teacher's desk was in front. Pupils faced the teacher, never one another. The whole process of education was harsh, sometimes inhumane. Pupils, generally, developed a dislike for the teachers—a dislike often kept through adulthood. Everything done conformed to narrow interpretations placed upon the meaning of the Scriptures, with the approval of the most learned men of the times. On August 9, 1681, Cotton Mather wrote in his diary:

> This day I took my second degree, proceeding Master of Arts. My Father was president, so that from his hand I received my degree. Tis when I am Gott almost half a year beyond eighteen, in my age. And all the circumstances of my commencement were ordered by a very sensibly inclined Providence of God. My Thesis was *Puncta Hebraica sunt Originis Divinae.* ["Hebrew vowels are of divine origin."]

The attitudes toward education were not only deep-seated but because Puritan Massachusetts was a colony of great influence, its attitudes and practices prevailed rather generally throughout the rest of the New England colonies. The Puritans left enduring traditions, some of which still can be identified, sometimes in most unexpected places.

Education in Massachusetts

Some features of the educational experiences of the Massachusetts colony are particularly significant because it was Massachusetts that, early in American history, initiated certain educational legal principles that have endured.

A brief twenty-two years after the 102 passengers disembarked from the Mayflower at Plymouth, the central legislative authority, the General Court, meeting in Boston, enacted what is probably the first school law to be passed in what afterwards became the United States. Officers chosen in the local town were empowered to find out whether parents and schoolmasters were teaching the children "to read and understand the principles of religion and the capital laws of the country" and to levy a fine on those who failed to report on these matters when required. This was in 1642. As it worked out, a new legal principle toward education was established by the law, namely, *the education of children is a proper subject for legal control.* Thus a first step was taken toward building a legal system of education in the United States. In a law passed in 1647, the General Court strengthened this principle. The student will profit from reading this law as it contains a clear expression of both the Puritan theory and an early frontier attitude toward education.

The principle established by the two Massachusetts laws was generally accepted throughout the colonies. The Massachusetts plan of leaving control and support of the schools to the citizens was inefficient when local interest in maintaining good schools declined. The frontier practice of having small school districts had become established, however. As we shall discuss later, largely because of deep-seated tradition, no problem in education has, through the years, been more difficult to cope with than the problem of organizing school districts logically. It is only in the twentieth century that earnest thought has been given to the problem, that any real progress has been made.

Gradually, the small, local school districts in Massachusetts became centers of selfish political activity. Election of school committeemen, location of school sites, and the payment of teachers' salaries became intense local political issues. Poor districts remained poor. The richer districts fought any action that would give them a part in alleviating the weaknesses of the poorer districts. Poor districts, settled by poor people, were expected to have poor schools. Since poor districts greatly outnumbered wealthy districts, the typical school of the day was a poor one. It was only after poor schools in Massachusetts became so numerous as to constitute a disgrace that a reform movement set in.

In 1826, the state of Massachusetts passed a law that required every town to choose a school committee that would have general

Many older buildings like this one in Chicago are still in use. They reflect somewhat the severities of earlier times. Note the cramped grounds even though land values were relatively low when the building was constructed. (Chicago Public Schools)

charge of *all* the schools within the town. The authority of this school committee extended to the selection of the textbooks, the examination and certification of teachers, and other matters that hitherto had been left to the jurisdiction of the local school committee, which had authority over only one school in a town. The first significant step in regeneration of the schools had taken place. Control of and supervision over all the schools in a town had become centralized under a single authority. Thus was begun the policy of organizing school units into a school system. The reform movement had commenced too late to change greatly the educational practices that by then had become fixed and had spread as the frontier moved westward to other colonies and to other states. The evil had mounted, and it would take a long time to eradicate its effects.

It is well to note, at this point, that efforts to regenerate education have, at times, been significantly influenced by laymen as distinguished from professional educators. The law of 1826 was a result of a vigorous, personally waged campaign conducted by James G. Carter (1795–1849), a skilled parliamentarian who had become deeply concerned over the flagrant evils that he, and many others, recognized were sucking whatever lifeblood had been left in the degenerate public school system. Once Carter got the reform movement started, regeneration of the schools continued. Instances of lay leadership to improve public education in the United States have been common in most of the states and throughout the history of American education. Lay leadership was, and still is, one of the sources of strength of American public education.

In 1837, the Massachusetts legislature created the first state board of education. The board had eight members appointed by the governor. Its function was to gather information about education in the state and to make recommendations to the legislature. The board employed a secretary to study the needs of the schools, point out these needs to the public, diffuse other information about the schools, and help the board formulate its recommendations to the state legislature. The first secretary was a lawyer, Horace Mann (1796–1859), whose achievements have captured the admiration of all succeeding generations interested in education.

In the law of 1837, Massachusetts had contributed another principle to the building of an educational system in the United States: *School administration is a branch of public administration.* The state is the unit of school administration and organization. It is the supreme authority. It can determine the conditions under which local schools operate. The implications of this principle, now accepted throughout the nation, are very wide and are not even today fully realized. Some of the implications will be discussed more fully in a later chapter. Once Massachusetts accepted the principle and created a state authority over its schools, the process of regeneration spread rapidly, and it has continued and persisted to the present time.

The Massachusetts story is but one example of how the social processes that built our national system of education during the frontier period and made a school district a corporate entity in social organization tended to operate. In any other state the story would be just as exciting and would illustrate, more or less, the same points. As would be expected, however, in each state the story would be different in many respects from all the others. For instance, New York furnishes an excellent example of how education in America came to be secularized; Texas, an example of how free lands have influenced education; and California, an example of how nonmineral underground resources like oil have contributed to the building of a great system.

Education in the South

Despite hardships and failures at its onset, Jamestown, Virginia, the first permanent English settlement in America, grew steadily. Within thirteen years its population numbered 4,000 and by 1700 as many as 100,000 people lived in Virginia. In 1693 William and Mary College, second college founded in America, was established at Williamsburg, a short distance from Jamestown. Many citizens of Virginia were men of culture, wealth, and refinement. From their ranks came some of America's greatest earlier political statesmen.

In Virginia and subsequently in other southern states, the development of education followed a distinctive pattern. This pattern was considerably different from that of the middle colonies, such as Pennsylvania, or of the northern range of colonies like New York and Massachusetts. Perhaps the views of the earlier Virginia settlers were somewhat like those Governor Berkeley reflected in his reply to the authorities in 1671. He thanked God that there were no free schools and no printing presses in the Province of Virginia, and expressed the hope that there would be none for a hundred years. "Learning," he said, "has brought disobedience, and heresy, and sects into the world, and printing has divulged them, and libels against the best government. God keep us from both." It was in 1779 that Thomas Jefferson showed that he had an extremely different view when he suggested his educational plan "for a more general diffusion of knowledge" among the people of Virginia.

The southern colonies, it seems, were not markedly influenced by the educational viewpoints of either Berkeley or Jefferson. Instead they developed plans for education along lines dictated by economic and social conditions. Children in the southern colonies did not attend school as we think of school today. Large plantations, located far apart and supported by a system of slave labor, led to a distinctive pattern of living and a special kind of educational or-

One can imagine some of the difficulties to be faced in teaching in a building like this rural school that was built as late as 1880 in Winneshiek County. (Courtesy Luther College, Decorah, Iowa)

ganization. The more affluent plantation owners employed private tutors to teach their children. Sometimes planters cooperated to build a small schoolhouse in which the children from several plantation families received instruction. Plantation owners, in general, believed that schools should not be provided at public expense for all children but only for the children of indigent or near-indigent families. The Church also separated those who could afford to pay for their education from those who could not by providing education for the poor and underprivileged. Those who were able to pay for the education of their children were expected to do so or suffer a decline in social prestige. In the southern colonies public education was definitely to meet the needs of the poor. In other sections of the country this came to be known as the charity conception of education.

As the American frontier moved westward, people in the newer sections were not strongly influenced by education traditions and practices of the South. Instead they tended to be influenced by the policies that had been developed in states like New York and Massachusetts.

THE EDUCATIONAL HERITAGE

Doctrine of Free Schools

To assess all the contributions of the frontier to American education would be infeasible because it would require study of how the frontier affected the entire scope of American life, including not only its institutions but also the philosophy that guided the nation in establishing those institutions. It is practicable, however, to focus on public policy toward economic support of schools extending from the kindergarten through the university. This seems especially appropriate and fruitful because economic support of an institution is one of the major factors in shaping the character of the institution. Economic support not only marks certain boundaries and to an extent limits what can be accomplished, but it is also a reliable reflection of the philosophy of the rank and file of the citizens. One may learn a great deal about a man, and a nation, by observing what they spend their money for.

The frontier philosophy toward human beings made the doctrine of free education inevitable and easy to accept. Jefferson, at this time the foremost political philosopher, forcefully expressed the doctrine of free education as early as 1779 in his "Bill for the More General Diffusion of Knowledge" as follows:

. . . And whereas it is generally true that the people will be happiest whose laws are best and are best administered, and that laws will be wisely formed and honestly administered, in proportion as those who form and administer them are wise and honest; whence it becomes expedient for promoting the publick happiness, that those persons whom nature has endowed with genius and virtue should be rendered by liberal education worthy to receive and able to guard the sacred deposit of the rights and liberties of their fellow-citizens, and that they should be called to that charge without regard to wealth, birth, or other accidental condition or circumstance; but the indigence of the greater number disabling them from so educating, at their own expence, those of their children whom nature hath fitly formed and disposed to become useful instruments for the publick, it is better that such should be sought for and educated at the common expence of all, than that the happiness of all should be confined to the weak or wicked.[1]

Jefferson's words constitute a liberal statesman's understanding of democracy as it is interpreted and applied to education. The sentiments he expressed were subsequently voiced by political leaders in almost every section of the nation.

Free schools, however, must be paid for, and it is the contribution of the frontier to a policy of economic support that we are primarily concerned with at this point. How were free schools paid for?

Not all schools of earlier times were of like quality. This school known as the Filers Corner School, named after the family that donated the site, was built in New York State in 1810. School buildings then as now reflected the resources of the community and the willingness of the community to support the schools. (Courtesy New York Historical Association, Cooperstown, New York)

Free Lands for a Free Education

Democracy seemed to demand free education. Theoretically, free education seemed ideal. Those who were unable to pay for education themselves, of course, favored it. Many of the richer people,

[1] As quoted in Paul Leicester Ford, *The Writings of Thomas Jefferson* (New York: G. P. Putnam's Sons, 1893), II, 220–221.

however, objected to paying for the education of the children of other families. To them free education at public expense was a startling if not radical step toward national or state socialism.

The frontiersmen resolved the problem of school support by granting subsidies of land to finance education. The income from the land would largely, if not entirely, remove the burden of support for education from the backs of the American taxpayer. Since all thirteen of the colonies prior to the American Revolution had granted land at one time or another for the support of schools, the citizens of the new nation were accustomed to the subsidy idea. When the Revolution ended, all of the lands owned by the Crown, and the extent of them was astounding, became the property of the states. Income from these lands relieved taxpayers of some of their responsibility for financing free public schools. How land subsidy for the support of public education operated in just one section of the nation, in what has been called the Northwest Territory, illustrates a principle of school support that has been made permanent.

When the colonies finally won their independence in 1781, the western boundary of the United States was the Mississippi River. The great expanse of land known as the Northwest Territory—land that has since been made into the states of Ohio, Michigan, Indiana, Illinois, Wisconsin, and into a part of Minnesota—became the property of the federal government. The federal government, forced to plan for the administration of this vast territory, expressed its policy in the well-known Land Ordinance of 1785 and the Northwest Ordinance of 1787. The Northwest Ordinance was to the frontier settlers of the territory what, later, the Constitution was to the states. It was the framework of their government. The statement of policy concerning school support was forthright and unequivocal. A precedent was established.

The Land Ordinance of 1785 provided that after the land was surveyed, one section (one square mile) of every township (36 square miles) was given to the people to help support the schools. During the last days of the Congress of the Confederation the Northwest Ordinance of 1787 was passed. This ordinance contained, in Article 3, the sentence that is accepted as the charter of public education in the United States: "Religion, morality, and knowledge, being necessary to good government and the happiness of mankind, schools and the means of education shall forever be encouraged."[2] In a second ordinance passed later in the same year, provision was made for the sale of the lands. This repeated the 1785 provisions reserving lands for public education. Any income received from the school lands, whether by sale or from rent, was earmarked for support of the schools. Thus, even before the Constitution was adopted, a policy of federal support of schools was established. The federal government has never since withdrawn from the practice of participating in subsidizing schools.

As states were formed in the new territory, the lands of the Northwest Territory became the property of the individual states under agreements with the federal government. Since the lands then belonged to the central territorial government, or to the state, the schools, too, were viewed as belonging to the established central government. The subsequent story of education in the United States is largely a picture of how states have operated the schools under their authority. It is now an accepted principle of American education that the state, not the local government, is the unit of school administration. This principle, however, does not rule out certain of the interests of the federal government. The entire problem of organization of schools is described in detail in the next unit.

Higher Education

Frontier thinking about school support for free public education did not end with the elementary and secondary schools. The federal land-grant policy also provided for the building of colleges. In 1862, President Lincoln signed a bill known as the Morrill Act which made generous gifts of federal lands to states for the purpose of establishing what has since become known as land-grant colleges. The act provided that each state was to receive from the public domain 30,000 acres of land for each member it had in Congress. The proceeds from the lands were to be used in establishing agricultural and mechanical arts colleges. Free frontier land was a wedge sufficient to influence state legislatures to establish colleges that have since blossomed into some of the best and largest of America's universities. Subsequent acts have further fortified the principle that federal support should also be extended to institutions of college level.

2 As quoted in Henry S. Commager, *Documents of American History* (New York: F. S. Crofts & Co., 1934), I, 131.

SUMMARY

The frontier movement was a vast social movement that nurtured some of America's lasting educational traditions. Traditions brought from Europe were changed or abandoned as frontiersmen accommodated to a new civilization, a new way of life. Free schools, first supported through land grants and later through taxation, are important among the elements of our modern heritage from the frontier period.

As we proceed, it will become increasingly evident that the frontier has had a striking effect on present education. Contemporary problems of education still revolve largely around how best to modify traditions so that they may be appropriate to modern social conditions. We must understand our educational heritage and make no attempt to divorce ourselves from the past. We must recognize that the past lives in the present and that the wisest plan is to recognize and strive to build upon the past.

QUESTIONS

1. In what ways were the effects of the American frontier movement upon both America and Europe of a reciprocal nature?
2. How did the fact that the frontier movement in America was continuous affect the development of education?
3. What are the social ideas currently esteemed by the American people that are associated with frontier development? In your opinion, how should these ideals be modified in the light of modern conditions?
4. Which had the greater influence upon the character of education developed by the Puritans, religion or social conditions?
5. Why did the influence of the legal principles adopted in Massachusetts have such wide influence throughout the United States?
6. What were some of the lasting effects upon education in the United States that can be traced to the fact that the frontier moved rapidly?
7. What are some of the difficulties that confront modern educators in their attempts to formulate a postfrontier educational philosophy?

PROJECTS

1. Consult some standard work, such as an encyclopedia, for information on the meaning of Puritanism. Note the ways subsequent generations have tended to interpret the Puritan and what he advocated. Point out inaccuracies in popular interpretations.
2. Trace the main events in the history of education in some typical state, such as New York. Note the nature of the issues that arose and how they were settled.

3. Cite several examples to show that the use of free lands operated to shape the course of American education.

4. Trace the historical steps in the origin of the Northwest Territory. Show why it became a great influence upon subsequent education.

5. Trace the principal historical events in the westward advance of the frontier subsequent to the establishment of the Northwest Territory. Indicate the possible effects of each of the events upon the development of education throughout the United States.

6. Compare Jefferson's plan of education with the plans advocated today by those who favor complete state control of public education.

CHAPTER **10**

Impact of the contemporary social scene

Present-day education cannot be explained entirely in terms of the ideas connected with European social movements and the ideas of individual thinkers described in the preceding chapters. Nor can it be explained by what developed during the frontier period of American history. Contemporary life in the United States is different from life on the frontier; so education, also, is necessarily greatly different.

The education function is always related to time, place, and circumstance. The desire, the need, the opportunities, and the facilities for education at one time and place in the history of a nation are not the same as they are at another time and place. Demands may fluctuate even in a short period of time. Educational activities certainly must be appropriate to the place in which they are carried on. Education in a school on the lower east side of Manhattan Island will be different from education in a school on the plains of Texas. Also, education is related to circumstance. A serious war, a period of depression or marked economic inflation, or a lengthened period of peace and stability makes demands and leaves lasting impressions upon education. A social crisis will include an educational crisis. Ordered and peaceful social development will encompass ordered and constructive educational progress.

For the purposes of this study, we shall note some of the more significant contemporary social tendencies and, in broad outline, indicate their relation to education. Focusing on social influences or forces or analyzing the changes in some social institution to discover what effects contemporary ideas behind current changes have had is made especially difficult by the complex intermingling and blending of social forces. Although we shall look separately at technological changes and changes in the population and family pattern, for instance, they actually are all mutually interdependent social manifestations. All are part of an indivisible, constantly evolving whole.

THE INTERNATIONAL PICTURE

International relations grow increasingly complex. On the one hand, they are characterized by ruthless conflicts among and within nations, stemming from differences in socio-political and religious ideologies, by bitter struggles for dominance, and by intense competition for trade, for oil, for military advantages, for survival. On the other hand, the scope of interaction is expanding. Greatly improved transportation and communication have, in a physical sense, diminished the distances between the peoples of the world. An ideal of world cooperation struggles for survival in the United Nations. Branches of the United Nations, such as the World Health Organization, are dedicated to improving the welfare of mankind throughout the globe. Even the principal "cold war" protagonists, the United States and the U.S.S.R., encourage cultural exchange programs, hoping that increased contact will engender greater understanding and perhaps contribute to a relaxation of international tensions.

Is our relative emphasis on, say, the teaching of foreign languages, and especially on teaching a particular foreign language, influenced by the international picture? Is it our feeling of urgency to exceed the achievements of Russia that leads us to examine her educational system and to increase our own emphasis on teaching science, foreign languages, and mathematics? Is our acceptance of travel abroad as fulfilling a requirement in teacher education a reflection of our hope that increased understanding may serve to diminish the social distances between nations just as communication and transportation have decreased physical distances?

Obviously, what we seek to achieve in our schools is related to the broader picture of what we seek to achieve in the world picture and how we think we should go about doing it. As our ideas about how best to get along in the company of nations change, educational ideas are swept along in the same current of social forces. The international picture is complicated and fluid. One may find it discouraging and develop a feeling of futility. One may also find hope even in meager progress. Regardless of the net effect of the international picture, the fact that its impact on our schools is direct and striking cannot be questioned.

THE SOCIAL PICTURE

Though social forces and effects are always more or less international in their scope, for purposes of brevity and clarity, we shall look mainly at the forces that have an impact on education as they are seen in our own national setting.

Influence of Technology

Technological developments have accentuated social change. Living conditions and industrial endeavor, in particular, have felt their impact. The assembly line, prefabricated housing, standardization of parts in industry, automation, and selective personnel techniques in management are only a few examples of developments each of which introduces a revolutionary element into modern living.

What are some of the conspicuous effects of technology upon education? Technology determines, to a considerable degree, the background of experience the child brings to school and continues to influence what he learns throughout his school career. Television, movies, radio, the jukebox—these are among the monuments to American technology.

Technology influences where large masses of people shall be located, when and where they are moved, and the quality and con-

First of all, there is the role that technology plays in our lives. In no other age have men lived with so dizzying a sense of change, or seen their basic material and social environment being made over, and made over again, so steadily. Technology, plainly, is the fundamental dynamic element in modern society. It affects everything from the size, shape, look, and smell of our cities and suburbs to the mobility of populations, the character of social classes, the stability of the family, the standards of workmanship that prevail, and the direction and level of moral aesthetic sensibilities. The decision as to when, where, and how to introduce a technological change is a *social* decision, affecting an extraordinary variety of values. And yet these decisions are made in something very close to a social vacuum. Technological innovations are regularly introduced for the sake of technological convenience, and without established mechanisms for appraising or controlling or even cushioning their consequences.

A current example is the impact of television. It has affected education and home life, changed the patterns of congressional behavior and political discussion, and fundamentally altered, for better or worse, the operating conditions and purposes of traditional political institutions like legislative investigations and political conventions. But the decisions on how to use television, and how not to use it, have been made almost entirely by men whose area of responsibility is very narrow, and who have to think about only a very few, selected values. . . . The engineers and industrialists who make decisions concerning technological changes have enormous power to affect the quality and conditions of our lives even though they do not know they have this power and have no interest in exercising it. This does not change the fact that their decisions are often decisions about basic social policy, and that the traditional liberal mechanisms of public consultation and consent, on which the authority for such basic decisions has been supposed to rest, have next to no influence here. From the point of view of most of us these decisions just seem to happen; and it is one reason why so many ordinary men and women have come to feel that they are being manipulated by invisible persons whom they do not know and cannot control.

From Charles Frankel, *The Case for Modern Man* (New York: Harper & Row, Publishers, Inc., 1956), pp. 197–199. Quoted by permission of the publisher.

ditions of life that surround them. It determines where the schools shall be located. It influences the standards of workmanship children will be taught to respect and, to an extent, shapes their standard of life values.

The social changes caused by technology lead to a need for (1) longer periods of schooling, (2) specific vocational training, (3) greater emphasis upon learning how to take advantage of greatly lengthened periods of leisure, (4) more attention to providing useful and productive work for younger adults, and perhaps (5) an intensification of effort to keep the American public vitally interested in the affairs of public and private education.

Certain technological activities have added directly to present-day stress. Children, especially, have been frightened by atomic and hydrogen bomb tests, by press and radio descriptions of the destructive capacities of guided missiles, and by descriptions of other inventions whose main purpose is human destruction. The first atomic bomb, dropped on August 6, 1945, upon the Japanese city of Hiroshima, killed 66,000 of its 343,000 people and wounded many more. On August 9, 1945, the United States dropped an atomic bomb on the Japanese city of Nagasaki, killing 39,000 people and wounding many more. Many bombs several times more destructive than these have since been tested. So powerful are some of the hydrogen bombs that an explosion of one will imperil the life of every living thing within an area of 7,000 square miles. Some loss of life would occur as many as 20 miles away from the center of the explosion. The psychological effects upon school children of frequent exposure to the vivid descriptions of such destructive devices is pronounced. The fire of fear and the fear of fire are kindled weekly in community after community by wailing sirens and occasional drills for self-defense. It may be said that on August 6, 1945, a new instrument for personal disorganization as well as for human destruction was released, the effects of which can only be fully assessed several generations in the future.

Technology brings with it some perplexing educational problems. What should the schools do about the strain attendant on testing war materials and defense practices? When should specialization begin in the schools? Should the gifted pupils receive more attention and be educated less generally and more in a specialized manner? In view of the personnel demands made by automation, should the high schools utilize their best teachers exclusively to select and train only those who give promise of developing into high-grade specialists in technology? What is the optimum class size for efficient teaching in an elementary or a high school? To what degree should standardization, mechanical aids, and mass methods be introduced into classroom management and at what grades? These are but a few of the urgent but as yet unanswered questions

Mechanical aids assume an increasingly important place in directing the education of children and youth. Here we see a class in stenography taking dictation from a tape recorder. The teacher has full control of the speed of dictation and the volume of the sound. Note that the mechanical aid enables the teacher to make careful advance preparation of what is to be taught and that it frees her to observe the reactions of the pupils as they practice. The tape recorder is a flexible teaching aid which affords many opportunities for creative teaching. (City School District, Rochester)

posed by a rapidly changing and highly technologically minded society.

Automation

This period in history is often referred to as the age of automation. Automation, an important angle of technology, is a symbol that stands for a large class of mechanical processes in which machines feed machines. Automation refers to mechanical processes in which the operation or control of a process is accomplished by automatic means. A simple illustration is the thermostat turning on the gas in the furnace when the heat of the room reaches a certain level. The word aptly expresses this meaning since it is an abbreviation of two words, auto(matic) and (oper)ation.

The trend toward expanding automation has been accelerated because of some pronounced improvements it has brought to modern living. In America, for example, the standard of living has been markedly raised because automation has led to more efficient manufacturing with lowered costs to consumers. It has also brought benefits to labor—made work less taxing, made the worker's environment more pleasant and healthful, increased the worker's income while extending his leisure. Automation has been extended into every principal field of human endeavor—housekeeping, banking, office procedures, medicine, dentistry, merchandising, communication, transportation, teaching, and many other fields.

With its many benefits, however, the expansion of automation has been accompanied with very significant and baffling problems. It has, for example, eliminated the need for many of the older manipulative skills, rendering them obsolete. Many workers, both trained and untrained, have been displaced and a serious imbalance in the labor market has resulted. More and more it is demanded that those who maintain their employment must first become technically skilled to a degree that requires an extended, highly technical education. For those who can attain the skills required, the rewards are considerable, both in enhanced social recognition and from a monetary standpoint. But the upgrading of this relatively small group leads to the downgrading of those who cannot qualify. They are demoted and occupy what has come to be called the economic underclass.

It is clear that automation leads to societal change, that it introduces new and perplexing problems. It is not clear, however, what the changes and problems imply about adjustments required in the schools, although America's schools have made some modifications that seem indicated. More emphasis is placed upon earlier specialization. Efforts are made to identify the more gifted pupils early and to provide them with opportunities to make the most of their unusual talents. By the time they reach high school many of them are placed in advanced placement courses equivalent to courses given in the early years of college. Special emphasis is placed upon improving the college preparatory curriculums, especially upon providing better opportunities in the study of mathematics, physical science, and foreign languages. An effort is made to identify slow learners, the physically handicapped, the mentally retarded, the emotionally disturbed, and to give them specialized service. Also, an effort is made to improve textbooks, supplementary materials, and teaching aids, and to experiment with and improve various methods of teaching.

The problem of training high-school youth for the age of automation, of decreasing high-school dropouts, and of retraining those who have dropped out of high school and are unemployable are receiving serious attention at all levels, including the national level.

The following proposals for action to meet some of the demands made upon education by automation illustrate the trend of current thinking. It is considered essential that the tax policies for support of education be radically amended, that the tax base be changed from that of an outmoded system of taxing property—the principal source of support in the past—to a base more consistent with the economics of the changing times. As the expertly prepared Rockefeller Report on Education stated, "There seems to be only one alternative, a thorough, painful, politically courageous overhaul of state and local tax systems."

A much greater share of the national income must be allotted to education. As President Eisenhower's Committee on Education pointed out, "America's teachers at all levels of education, in view of the low salaries they have received, have actually been subsidizing education at considerable sacrifice to their families."

Communities must adjust to changes in school policy and support that will permit a greater efficiency in the operation of schools. For example, the schools should operate more hours in the school day and for 48 weeks in the year. School plants are too expensive to be allowed to lie idle so much of the time. Youth problems would be lessened were all youth not released to idleness at the same time. A four-year high-school course could be greatly enriched and, for some, more advanced study could be available.

Such proposals, and a number of others, currently discussed among better informed citizens and professional educators, are urgently in need of attention. They are so sweeping that they demand a nationwide effort to achieve worthwhile progress.

Effect of Economic Cycles

Economic conditions in the United States fluctuate. The economy rises and falls as production, employment, and national income rise and fall. Like the waves on the ocean, the ups and downs follow one after another but in a somewhat erratic, unpredictable manner. Economic cycles are not easy to explain or to control. Seemingly, the transition of the American economy from the self-sufficiency typical of the frontier to a money economy which charac-

But what should concern us much more is how the passion for popularity translates itself into an almost universal tendency to conformity among our younger generation. It runs through all social classes. American teenagers show substantial class differences in many aspects of their behavior, problems and aspirations, but in their desire for popularity and their conformist attitude they are as one: low-income or high-income, their highest concern is to be liked.

This is the most striking and most consistent fact that has emerged from our polls through the 17 years. Poll after poll among our youngsters has given statistical confirmation of the phenomenon of American Life which David Riesman, in his book *The Lonely Crowd*, named "other-direction"—extreme sensitivity to the opinions of others, with a concomitant conformity. As a nation we seem to have a syndrome characterized by atrophy of the will, hypertrophy of the ego and dystrophy of the intellectual musculature.

This rather unpleasant portrait is an inescapable conclusion from the mass of data on the attitudes of the younger generation.

From H. H. Remmers and D. H. Radler, "Teenage Attitudes," *Scientific American*, Vol. CXCVIII, No. 6 (June, 1958), pp. 25–26. Quoted by permission of *Scientific American*, H. H. Remmers, and D. H. Radler.

terizes present-day industrialized society has accentuated the magnitude of the economic cycles. The more extreme the economic fluctuations, the more profound their social effects.

During the great depression of the thirties, to take an illustration, the birth rate dropped precipitately. So did school enrollments. Subsequently, high-school enrollments declined for as many as fourteen years, and college enrollments continued to decline for as many as eighteen years. Deviation in enrollment that results from an economic cycle poses serious problems in school adjustment. In one large city during the thirties, the high-school enrollment within a period of less than ten years dropped from a high of 155,000 to a low of 83,000. This amounts to as many as 36 high schools, each with an enrollment of 2,000 pupils, closing their doors. What to do with the surplus of high school teachers was just one among many serious problems!

The psychology of the people in general is in tune with the economic cycle. During periods of economic depression the schools, as well as other social institutions, reflecting the general pessimism, caution, lack of confidence, and feelings of futility and despair characteristic of the people, hesitate to move forward or to experi-

FIG. 10.1   1963 COSTS OF PUBLIC EDUCATION AND SELECTED EXPENDITURES
(IN BILLIONS OF DOLLARS)

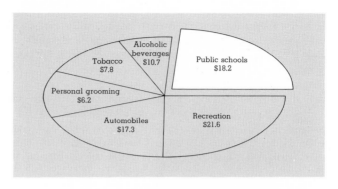

(Data from NEA Research Division, Research Memo, September, 1963)

ment or to make changes. On the other hand, during these periods
of economic depression there is a desire to find some kind of security,
a disposition to cling to the tried and the true, even when the forces
of reason are all on the other side. To this is added the desire to
economize. Extracurricular activities, music, art—frequently called
the frills of the curriculum—come under fire.

In addition to adverse psychological effects of an economic depression, teachers suffered financial losses during the thirties. Payment of teachers' salaries was suspended in many public schools. In
others the payment was in scrip, a certificate promising to pay at a
later date. Many teachers had to cash the scrip at a discount and
suffer a considerable loss of money.

The effect on education of a dip in the economic cycle is, at best,
whether viewed from the personal or the institutional angle, one
of serious disorganization.

During the upward sweep of the economic cycle, schools tend
to share with the people a feeling of confidence and optimism. In
1960 gains in teachers' salaries were slightly greater than propor-
tional gains in the wages and salaries of all employed persons. Their
average annual salary, however, was still 2.3 per cent below the
earnings of manufacturing employees. Costs of school buildings
and equipment soar, taxes must be increased, the public feels the
pinch, and schools hear complaints. Inflation, like deflation, also
has an impact upon the schools, and not all of the effects are wholesome.

The Corporate Trend

In business and in other areas of American life, there is a growing trend to act through corporations. A corporation is an association of persons that is viewed in many respects as though it were one person. It has legal rights and duties that are not the rights and duties of the individual members of the corporation. Furthermore, the rights and duties of the corporation descend to successive members of the corporation. A corporation, then, has the capacity of perpetual succession. There are government corporations and private corporations. A school district is a government corporation although usually it is referred to as a quasi-corporation, that is, an organization that operates like a corporation but is not incorporated by the state.

The standard organizational features of a corporation include a policy-forming board of directors, an executive chairman of the board, and a general manager. These persons may not own the company. Other stockholders may own it in whole or in part. In general, the corporation may go into debt—and it generally does—may sue and be sued, and may make changes in the structure of its organization, all without any authorization other than that contained in the original articles of incorporation. These corporate features apply also to school districts.

The courts have held that school districts may function as municipal corporations, and, consistent with the corporate trend, school districts have become larger. Individual schools have increased their enrollments. It is just as difficult to assess the total effects of the corporate trend upon school life as upon American life in general. There are advantages in increased size. Economy and efficiency can be improved. A broader curriculum, more specialization, and a greater variety of physical facilities are practical. On the other hand, greatly increased size may be accompanied by an undesirable degree of impersonalization, by submergence of the needs of the individual pupil. Will schools be removed further from the people who support them? Will the goals related directly to instruction be relegated to an inferior position? In general, will the important values of traditional education in America be sacrificed in the wake of the corporate trend? These questions remain to be answered.

Dominance of Pressure Groups

A majority of pressure groups—groups that seek to influence state or national governments or other public bodies—are devoted to economic ends. The National Association of Manufacturers is one example; the Chamber of Commerce of the United States, organized in 1912, is another. The largest and most important of the farm pressure group organizations is the American Farm Bureau Federation. Labor is represented in part by the powerful AFL-CIO. Professional groups lobby through such organizations as the American Medical Association, the American Bar Association, the American Dental Association, and the National Education Association. The number of pressure groups is legion although no one knows precisely how many exist in the United States or understands fully the aims of many of them.

Each group seeks to promote special benefits for its members. Obviously, the schools open a fertile field for pressure group practices. Educators themselves are, of course, a pressure group. Many pressure groups have made definite statements about what they would like to have included in the curriculum. Others make their wishes felt more subtly. Some pressure groups desire to slant the material of the social studies in a particular direction. Some want increased opportunities for children to prepare for particular vocations such as chemistry or agriculture. Teachers and administrators must look carefully at free material offered by pressure groups before presenting it to children. Assembly programs, movies, and bulletin board displays, though often acceptable for school use, must always be evaluated in advance of their use.

Some pressure group influence is directed toward proposed school legislation. Great effort is also devoted to influencing public opinion about education. Some pressure groups support the improvements that the education profession advocates. Others, however, are openly antagonistic and carry on their activities in a subtle, sinister manner or publicize inaccurate or untrue accusations against the activities and achievements of the schools. Everyone is part of the "school public," either as pupil, parent of a pupil, former pupil, or school taxpayer. Thus the audience that the pressure groups work on—those who feel they know a great deal about the school and have a stake in its future—is wide. Unfortunately, sometimes its knowledge is so meager it is carried away by false but clever propaganda.

Perhaps even the efforts of groups that seem opposed to school progress are not entirely bad. They do challenge those who have other views to organize a sound and effective defense. At certain times the pressures and activities of some organized groups become very annoying. The answer is vigilance by the teaching profession and by all others who are concerned with building strong schools. An effective program of public relations, information, and understanding, spread throughout the community, may serve to minimize the effects of antischool pressure groups and, ideally, will lead to an opportunity for interaction and a change in point of view.

FAMILY LIFE

Improved Standard of Living

Some of the changes in contemporary family life are due to a greatly improved standard of living. More comforts in everyday life, distributed more generally among the people, are a mark of modern times. The average person is better fed, better clothed, and has better medical care and more luxuries than ever before. His life expectancy continues to climb. Children come to school with this background of material benefits.

Compared to earlier times there is an abundance of leisure time. Work itself is less physically exhausting. Illiteracy has been largely eliminated. A greater degree of equality is in evidence among people. Personal incomes have reached an all-time high. The conditions and opportunities for employment for women have been greatly improved.

In their facilities the schools reflect the rise in standard of living. The crude, unattractive, uncomfortable school of the frontier period compares so unfavorably with facilities to which modern children are accustomed that, even if other factors had not rendered it obsolete, it could have no place in the contemporary setting. People who are used to a certain standard are generally unwilling to accept an inferior standard of living for their children at school. The trend is toward more beautiful, comfortable, and healthful buildings and equipment. Textbooks are more attractive, pleasanter to read, and more durable. Children receive medical and dental attention. As the standard of living has improved, schools have also improved in their physical provisions for children's welfare.

Changed Functions of the Family

Progress has been marked in the physical welfare of children in the home and in the school. What about other features of their welfare? Is the contemporary picture one that also shows improved social and psychological conditions for children? Have we made some changes in our concept of the function and structure of the family, perhaps inevitable changes, the results of which are not entirely wholesome?

Note how the learning environment may be improved through the generous use of space, as in this modern schoolroom. (Fein from Monkmeyer)

The isolation of the family on the frontier and its ability to provide the necessities for its own living rendered the family an almost self-sufficient social unit. Many of the earlier activities and purposes of the home were primarily economic. The social status of the families in any given community was relatively equal. The neighborhood was stable and provided many opportunities for intimate and lasting personal relationships.

With the close of the frontier period, the advance of industrialization, and the progress of technology, marked changes occurred in the function of the family. In modern times the purposes of the home are no longer largely economic. Outside employment for wages is the typical pattern. Children no longer have work responsibilities essential to the survival of the home. Services and needed goods can be bought. The work that women used to do in the home has been diminished; more and more women are employed. Not all these changes necessarily weaken the effectiveness of the home. For instance, release from household drudgery may mean that mothers can give more time to supervising and guiding their children.

Urban living may separate a commuting husband from his family during the day and thus bring a new status to the wife and mother who has to make many of the family decisions. The community no longer provides insurance against destitution and loneliness in old age. The neighborhood has become less stable, less the kind of environment that provides satisfying interpersonal relationships. It is less likely that urban dwellers can find business associates, neighbors, or personal friends to whom it would be safe or proper to express deepest hopes and fears. The family has become increasingly important as the avenue for the satisfaction of affective, intimate, intense, and exclusive types of relationships. The degree to which the family satisfies this need is in dispute.

Family Disorganization

Changes in social conditions and in the structure and function of the family have, in a measure, contributed to family disorganization. The divorce rate in the United States gradually increased over the first half of the century, reaching an all-time high in 1946. The explanation is not readily evident. Although marriages increased after 1945, the year of the end of World War II, a decline in the divorce rate set in.

Divorces always have a serious effect upon children. The disorganization of a family has roots in a conflict of attitudes. The lack of unity and mounting tensions in a disorganized home do serious psychological damage to the children. When final dissolution of a family is reached, the child usually finds himself the cause of argument over custody, a bewildering and perhaps devastating experience. At school the child may encounter jibes of classmates. In the case of a remarriage of father or mother, further adjustments must be made.

Into our schoolrooms come some children who are worried and distracted by persistent tensions at home. Does the school have a responsibility to provide a measure of security for such children? Should school experiences be planned to lead to improved ability to achieve a happy marriage and wholesome family life when adulthood is reached? Does the high school have an obligation as well as an opportunity to offer training that will promote good family living?

> The erratic behavior of the adolescent, then, which proves so irritating to his elders, represents his clumsy attempt to balance between the pressure of his growth and the constraint of his codes. It is not at all surprising that he wobbles occasionally from the even poise of strict conformity. But to think that he is making no effort or that he has no codes, is an assumption that is not justified. Not that this anxiety about the behavior of youth is limited to our particular part of the world. An anthropologist friend tells me that he has never visited any tribe of primitive people where the elders of the village did not tell him that the young people were going to the dogs.
>
> In looking at the conflict between nature and nurture, we see succeeding generations of young people driven on by the inherent forces of their growth, the most vital of which are restrained and opposed by the solicitous efforts of generations of adults who, ironically enough, have just gone through the same struggle. Considered dispassionately, one might wonder why we humans have to be so hard on ourselves.
>
> From C. Anderson Aldrich and Mary M. Aldrich, *Babies Are Human Beings* (2d ed.; New York: The Macmillan Company, 1954), pp. 117–118. Quoted by permission of The Macmillan Company.

Community Relationships

Sometimes a process of disorganization, not unlike that which dissolves families, goes on in communities. A good community is a unified community. The attitudes of the people regarding the over-all interests of the community in the development and maintenance of its institutions, in the support of good schools, and toward the welfare of all its citizens are similar. This unanimity in attitudes necessary for effective community action may be destroyed by conflicts over politics, control, or taxation. Sometimes conflicts between the older and younger generations cause serious problems. Teen-agers may get entirely out of hand and engage in bizarre forms of rebellion against the social restraints. Since the young adults are of school age, they may engage in deviate forms of behavior in school as well as out. Where a community possesses the characteristics of disorganization, institutions, including the school, are always adversely affected.

What should be the effect of this kind of contemporary experience on educational thought? American educators are devoting considerable attention to the problem. Recommendations for alleviating the problem usually include some type of educational program or adaptation. Should the curriculum be changed? Should work experiences be substituted for compulsory school attendance? Should the military take a larger part in the education of youth? The problem remains unsolved. There has been so little agreement that the general direction of possible solutions cannot, with confidence, be predicted.

POPULATION CHANGES

Our population has increased markedly. The percentage of people in the youngest and in the oldest age groups has likewise increased. There has been a shift in population toward suburban areas and a marked growth in the Pacific states.

Factors in Growth

The chief factor of population growth in the United States has been the excess of births over deaths throughout the world. We add "throughout the world" because without an excess of births elsewhere the second principal factor, immigration, would not have existed. There has also been a great reduction in the rate of infant and early childhood mortality. In 1955, more than 4,076,000 children were born in the United States. Practically all of these children were eligible to enter kindergarten in 1960 because the mortality rate of children and youth between the ages of 5 and 19—the principal ages for school attendance—dropped 40 percent between 1945 and 1951. In 1955, the death rate per 1,000 among children ages 1 to 24 was 0.6. The rate was uniform for each of the age intervals. It did not reach 1 per 1,000 until after age 34. The death rate among adults has also been reduced. Now the life expectancy of the newborn is more than 70 years.

Absolute and Relative Growth

Absolute figures of the population in the country or in a single community give a realistic picture of the number of people who must be afforded the means of living. Ten-year comprehensive census surveys give the absolute figures with respect to population. One can compare the different periodic census surveys or any other of the many population surveys and arrive at relative rates of growth and population change. In studying the growth in total population or growth in any segment of the total population, such as the number of children who may be eligible to enter a given grade at a given time, one must consider both the absolute figures and the relative ratios. Taken together, they make possible a more helpful and accurate understanding of the trends.

Growth Trends

Benjamin Franklin noted that the population of the thirteen colonies doubled about every twenty years. From its beginning, the United States has been a constantly expanding nation, in population, in economics, in education, and in government. So used to expansion has the nation become, and so great has been the influence upon the outlook of the people, that any aspect of life that is not expanding is viewed with some suspicion. The nature of the overall trend in population may be seen from the following data.

United States Population Totals

1880	50,000,000
1890	63,000,000
1900	76,000,000
1910	92,000,000
1920	106,000,000
1930	123,000,000
1940	132,000,000
1950	151,000,000
1960	179,000,000
1970	214,000,000—estimated
1980	260,000,000—estimated

Gross increase in population, while it has a bearing upon the expansion and support of education, does not give a full description of what has taken place. There are trends within these trends, such as shifts in age ratios. Fig. 10.2 shows the increase of school-age population as compared with the total population.

Clearly, the age composition of the population has been changing. Since 1950, the two groups that have increased most, proportionately, have been the oldest and the youngest age groups. It is estimated that the burden of education resting upon the American people in 1960 was 35 percent heavier than it was in 1950. Following World War I and the depression of the thirties, the birth rate dropped precipitately in the United States. Following World War II, the pattern of fertility among the population of child-bearing age steadily climbed until new heights in fertility were reached. Trends before these years in net reproductive rates had been steadily falling. During the fifties, this trend was reversed, and as a result the United States faced an acute problem of how to establish and main-

FIG. 10.2   SCHOOL-AGE POPULATION AS A PERCENTAGE
OF TOTAL POPULATION

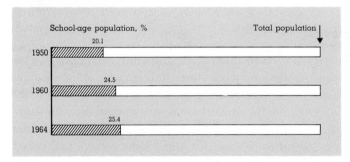

(National Industrial Conference Board, *Road Maps of Industry*, No. 1245)

Over one-fourth of the total resident population of the United States in 1964 was of school age (five through seventeen years) as compared with only one-fifth in 1950. More than 49 million children and youth entered school in the fall of 1964, taxing the nation's classrooms. All the states did not share alike in the rise as earlier estimates such as shown in Fig. 10.3 predicted. It is hazardous to make long-term predictions regarding the school-age population of any specific area or state because of current population mobility which seems to be increasing. Most school systems, in fact, make continuous studies of their school population. On the basis of these they make predictions for only a few years ahead.

The Bureau of the Census tells us that in 1960 there were 20,364,000 children under five years of age in the United States. It predicts that in 1985 there will be 33,048,000 children under five years of age in the United States. The chances are that this prediction is reliable. How these children will be distributed throughout the United States is impossible to predict.

tain schools that were equal to the task of caring for the increase in school population. It is relatively easy to determine what is needed by way of current expansion, because the children who are born each year will become the pupils in the kindergartens of the various schools five years later and will then ascend to the grades above in fairly predictable numbers.

Population Prediction

Since population trends fluctuate because of a variety of human factors, short-term predictions tend to be more accurate than long-term ones. For example, most of the 4,076,000 children born in the United States in 1955 were eligible for the kindergarten in 1960. But no one can accurately predict how many children will be born, say, in 1965, and a prediction as to how many will be born in 1975 would be still more open to inaccuracy. Changes in economic conditions, shifts in social attitudes, governmental policy toward immigration, and attitudes toward education, to mention a few factors, render a population prediction less valid as the term of the prediction is extended. Even the minor depression of 1958 was characterized by a drop in the marriage rate and a decline in number of births.

Differentials

There are marked differences in birth rates among the communities within a state, between states, and between different regions of the nation. These differences have been great enough to create considerable inequality in education. No one can predict how long these regional and state differences in fertility will continue; however, it does seem logical to believe that there must come a time when they will level off. That time, however, seems to be in the somewhat unpredictable future. In the past, fertility rates have been lowest in our regions of highest income, thus accentuating the degree of educational inequality. Obviously, if future economic policies toward educational support tend to mitigate the effects of differentials in income in different regions, the regional and state differentials in birth rates will no longer present so great a problem for education. Currently, the problem is a serious one. Where standards of living are the lowest, fertility rates are the highest; and where education should be strong, it is sometimes pathetically weak.

FIG. 10.3 SCHOOL-AGE POPULATION

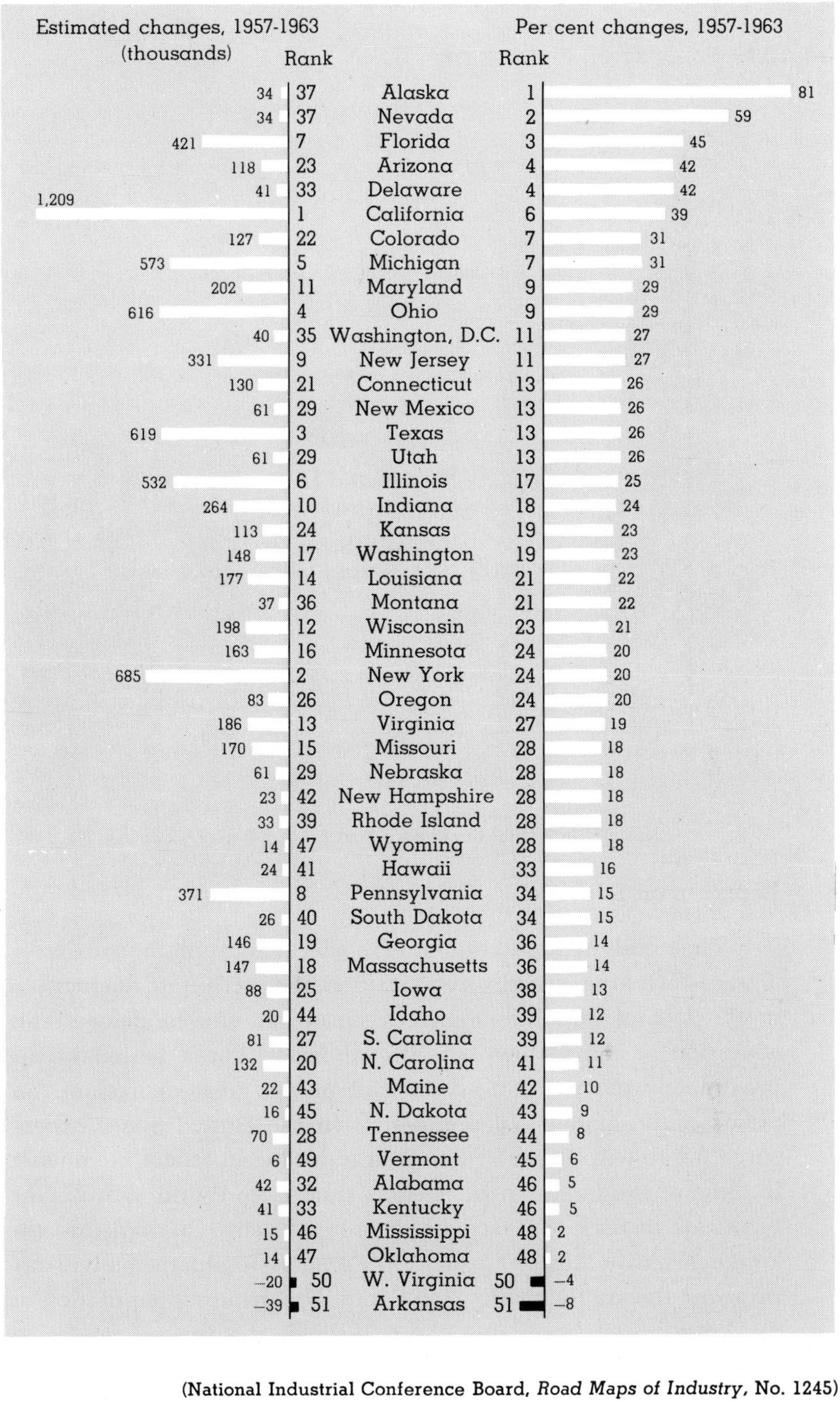

Estimated changes, 1957-1963 (thousands)	Rank	State	Rank	Per cent changes, 1957-1963
34	37	Alaska	1	81
34	37	Nevada	2	59
421	7	Florida	3	45
118	23	Arizona	4	42
41	33	Delaware	4	42
1,209	1	California	6	39
127	22	Colorado	7	31
573	5	Michigan	7	31
202	11	Maryland	9	29
616	4	Ohio	9	29
40	35	Washington, D.C.	11	27
331	9	New Jersey	11	27
130	21	Connecticut	13	26
61	29	New Mexico	13	26
619	3	Texas	13	26
61	29	Utah	13	26
532	6	Illinois	17	25
264	10	Indiana	18	24
113	24	Kansas	19	23
148	17	Washington	19	23
177	14	Louisiana	21	22
37	36	Montana	21	22
198	12	Wisconsin	23	21
163	16	Minnesota	24	20
685	2	New York	24	20
83	26	Oregon	24	20
186	13	Virginia	27	19
170	15	Missouri	28	18
61	29	Nebraska	28	18
23	42	New Hampshire	28	18
33	39	Rhode Island	28	18
14	47	Wyoming	28	18
24	41	Hawaii	33	16
371	8	Pennsylvania	34	15
26	40	South Dakota	34	15
146	19	Georgia	36	14
147	18	Massachusetts	36	14
88	25	Iowa	38	13
20	44	Idaho	39	12
81	27	S. Carolina	39	12
132	20	N. Carolina	41	11
22	43	Maine	42	10
16	45	N. Dakota	43	9
70	28	Tennessee	44	8
6	49	Vermont	45	6
42	32	Alabama	46	5
41	33	Kentucky	46	5
15	46	Mississippi	48	2
14	47	Oklahoma	48	2
−20	50	W. Virginia	50	−4
−39	51	Arkansas	51	−8

(National Industrial Conference Board, Road Maps of Industry, No. 1245)

FIG. 10.4 POPULATION PROJECTIONS, U.S.A.

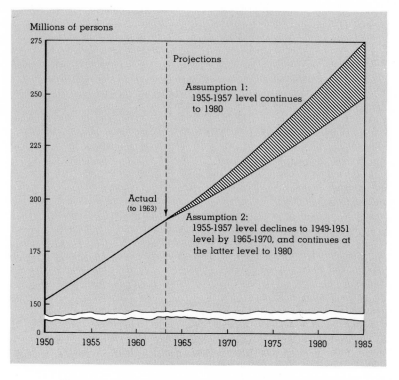

(National Industrial Conference Board, *Road Maps of Industry*, No. 1472)

Impact upon Education

The trends in population growth affect education in many ways. Three effects are especially notable. First, the precipitate fluctuations in the rate of population growth create an uneven demand for education at the various educational levels. For a period of approximately ten years, near the end of the great depression, for example, the high-school population in the United States experienced no growth. Instead, there was a decline in school attendance in some of the larger cities. A short time after World War II, the birth rate increased markedly and brought many children into the kindergarten by 1950. The nation's schools found themselves unprepared to care for them. As the rapidly expanding population at the kindergarten level moved up through the various grades, it caused more crowding at the higher grade levels.

Second, a rapid expansion in the school population leads to a rapid expansion in the material needs for education, such as buildings, equipment, and well-prepared teachers. Since most educational expansions seem never to be planned far in advance, the result usually is that schools become overcrowded and undermanned.

Third, costs suddenly increase. In most states the tax system, mainly designed to meet frontier conditions, is inadequate to meet the kindergarten level moved up through the various grades, it in a short time, impairment in educational efficiency is usually the result. A tax system, for example, that in the school year 1954–1955 was already under strain to furnish adequate school support for the elementary and high schools could anticipate serious difficulty in meeting the expanded responsibility of educating an estimated 12,000,000 more pupils in the school year 1964–1965.

Future generations will be made up of educated people sensitive to the nation's educational needs. There are many indications

FIG. 10.5   EDUCATIONAL STATUS, U.S.A.

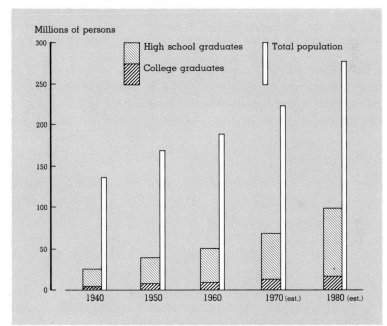

(National Industrial Conference Board, *Road Maps of Industry*, No. 1205)
High school graduates include all persons who have completed four years of high school or beyond, and consequently include college graduates shown separately above.

Unfortunately the education of children in some urban areas is hampered by overcrowded conditions as shown in the above picture. Many school systems are inadequately prepared for the population explosion. (Wide World)

that the schools in the United States during the second half of the twentieth century will hold a prominent position in America's social plans. Expanding school attendance, lengthening the school term, upgrading teaching, redistricting, building new schools, and increasing school support all indicate forces at work that encourage, even make mandatory, the future expansion and reshaping of education in the United States.

CONTEMPORARY FRONTIERS

Our brief examination of the contemporary social scene shows the dynamic nature of the social picture but leaves us with a somewhat uneasy feeling. Where will the trends lead?

In one sense the trends are facts. They are the bases upon which action must be built. They are factors that should be taken duly into account but that are nonetheless ignored or slighted. We know in advance, for instance, that the children who are two years of age are destined to go to school three years hence. We know, too, that the chances are that when they go to school, the schools will not be ready for them. It is true that societal change is somewhat unpredictable, but that is no excuse for a complete lack of preparation for probable changes.

Contemporary frontiers are not in the form of free lands and abundant natural resources. They are not the border lines between settled and unsettled regions of a country. Instead they are the unexplored regions of knowledge, the untried institutional practices. Just as physical frontiers were pushed back, so likewise will new educational frontiers in America be explored and developed.

Education in America faces a new and somewhat uncharted frontier. The physiologists have strengthened Rousseau's contention that efficient education is in accordance with the child's nature. In the face of antagonistic traditions, can the schools modify to conform with this now almost two-century-old dictum? Are the principles of education for social living set down by Froebel accepted by current educators? What the Americans of today and of the future

Audiovisual aids are exceedingly numerous and varied, and sometimes are too complex for teachers to use without help. Many school systems have audiovisual aid centers in charge of a specially trained specialist. He renders many services such as recommending material, selecting equipment, and scheduling. Sometimes, as in the picture above, the director of the audiovisual aid center trains pupils in efficient operation of equipment. (Audio-Visual Section, Los Angeles City School Districts)

make of education may be as surprising as were the achievements of the earlier frontiersmen.

EMERGING FRONTIERS

Since education always has adjusted to social changes, it seems sound to assume that such adaptations will continue in the future. What are some of the foreseeable future events that will lead to

> Telstar, the first communications satellite raised hopes for the future. One may watch live television every day from around the world; see the rest of the world at work and play; see news as it happens around the world; see people all over the world—how they frown, how they smile.
>
> They'll see us—and we'll all know each other a little better—which we critically need to do in these days when mass destruction has become possible.
>
> Television by satellite will be everybody's window on the world—and bring us all closer together.
>
> . . . let's look ahead for a minute to the day when our ventures into space will lead us to interplanetary traffic—when we'll be able to make round trips to far distant planets—you do hear some questions raised about *what* might make such travel worthwhile.
>
> What commerce might profitably flow over such awesome distances?
>
> There is one commodity, a very special kind, well-suited to interplanetary commerce.
>
> It weighs nothing. It travels cheaply at the speed of light. That commodity is *communication*.
>
> To be of value, information requires communication.
>
> From a television presentation by the Bell Telephone Company written on September 1, 1962, entitled "Telstar and Tomorrow."

social change and necessitate educational adaptations? Coming events are said to cast their shadows before them. What are the events forecast by the shadows we see today?

First, consider the rapidity with which space exploration is developing. The earth has now been orbited a number of times. Plans are being made to place explorers on the moon. From this, it is expected that much will be learned about the age and origin of the earth. With modern 200-inch telescopes man can see into space a distance of 200 million light years. Radio telescopes enable him to see much farther. From the moon his vision will be even clearer. Space exploration, now in its infancy, will bring much new knowledge. Can we anticipate, from what we now know, what kind of new knowledge we shall attain? What changes in thinking and learning by children will result? Will children need to learn more in less time? If new knowledges are brought into the curriculum, some of the older subject matters will have to be dropped. How will these new knowledges affect the preparation of teachers? Will the present classifications of subject matter remain unchanged? Will new names be used to identify the new subject matters?

Think of some of the developments man has made in the realm of energy. The energy famine that threatened mankind for many years is past. Man no longer must depend wholly upon the resources nature stored beneath the surface of the earth millions of years ago—resources man has lavishly wasted, largely in waging wars. The potential effect of nuclear power on man's future can only be con-

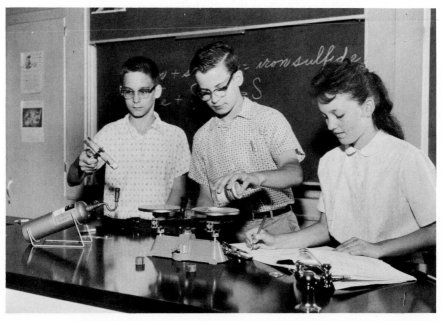

Well-equipped laboratories are essential for every junior and senior high school. The success that teachers of science have had in utilizing laboratories and laboratory methods has influenced methods in other fields. Teachers of social studies, for instance, may look upon the community as a laboratory. (Chicago Public Schools)

jectured. In addition to nuclear energy there remains for man creatively to appropriate the energy of the sun and of the ocean waves.

How about travel in the foreseeable future? Will new means of transportation affect man's relations throughout the world? His educational requirements? Speed is now the key emphasis in travel. The jet plane has diminished physical distance in earth travel. As the wheel and axle eliminated the skid some thousands of years ago, so are modern developments in modes of travel eliminating the wheel. The so-called VTOP (vertical take-off plane) presages still further changes in travel.

We have noted that the home is a changed and changing place. Mechanization and the availability of processed foods have eliminated much of the drudgery of housekeeping. Short wave, hi-fi, and television have made the home a center for entertainment. It is said, perhaps with some degree of truth, that American people spend as much time watching television as they spend on their jobs. Will the future find families with more leisure becoming more closely knit as family units centered in the home?

What does the future promise in the area of human relations?

In 1921 James Harvey Robinson, a historian, discussed how far the human race has advanced in applying the method of critical thinking to human affairs.

Human affairs are in themselves far more intricate and perplexing than molecules and chromosomes. But this is only the more reason for bringing to bear on human affairs that critical type of thought and calculation for which the remunerative thought about molecules and chromosomes has prepared the way.

I do not for a moment suggest that we can use precisely the same kind of thinking in dealing with the quandaries of mankind that we use in problems of mechanical reaction and mechanical adjustment. Exact scientific results are, of course, out of the question. It would be unscientific to expect to apply them. I am not advocating any particular method of treating human affairs, but rather such a *general frame of mind, such a critical open-minded attitude,* as has hitherto been but sparsely developed among those who aspire to be men's guides. . . .

From James Harvey Robinson, *The Mind in the Making* (New York: Harper & Row, Publishers, Inc., 1921), p. 12. Quoted by permission of Harper & Brothers.

We see the "Dark Continent" emerging to a place of prominence. We see nations becoming increasingly aware of the necessity of working together on tasks to achieve modernization, to formulate joint policies for economic and social progress, to open wide the doors for education of the masses, to develop a climate of peace, and to create a new and brighter picture of international cooperation for the elevation of mankind. Will the efforts be fruitful in raising the level of human relations among all the people of the world? How will the schools fit into the picture?

How will new knowledge and understandings accruing from areas like those mentioned affect education? New knowledge so tested that it merits the appellation "scientific knowledge" is rapidly accumulating in all fields of learning. Much knowledge that now exists was not included in the textbooks studied by many of today's adults. Much that today's adults have learned has been learned after they left school. The expansion of knowledge promises to continue. What will this mean for education in the future? Note the characteristics of new knowledge as described by a renowned scientist.

> To sum up the characteristics of scientific knowledge today, then, I would say that it is mostly new; it has not been digested; it is not part of man's common knowledge; it has become the property of specialized communities who may on occasion help one another but who, by and large, pursue their own way with growing intensity further and further from their roots in ordinary life.[1]

In one's own picture of the foreseeable future one may include such details as travel beneath the ocean waters by nuclear propelled submarine, communities transforming the waters of the ocean into usable fresh water, a nation of people with leisure time so increased by the development of automation that citizens are largely free to engage in self-chosen occupations. Regardless of how one looks at the future, however, of how one predicts man's ascendancy over his physical environment, it is inevitable that the problem of what happens to the individual will be a major concern of education. As invention and discovery force man to reorganize his way of life, how will he use his time? Will he learn to be creative? to rise to new heights in science, in the arts, in the humanities? In short, will new

[1] Robert Oppenheimer, "Tree of Knowledge," *Harper's Magazine,* CCXVII (October, 1958), 57.

knowledge lead to enrichment, or will it lead to frustration, impoverishment, and conflict? The responsibility for providing guidance and doing the very best possible to develop insights and understandings to equip future generations to meet new challenges and cope with new problems rests with education.

QUESTIONS

1. How are the two social phenomena, mobility and technology, related?
2. How have the two current social trends, uniformity and standardization, seemingly affected educational practice?
3. In your opinion, how far should education go toward contributing to the solution of a contemporary social problem?
4. In what respects does education contribute to increased social mobility?
5. To what degree and in what ways should teachers give social direction to the achievements of pupils?
6. What are some present-day mental hazards of American youth? What are some of the problems these mental hazards introduce into the high schools?
7. Why is it difficult for a state to change its system of taxation to meet new educational demands?
8. What are the implications for education of the travel times made possible by faster planes as predicted by the chart below?

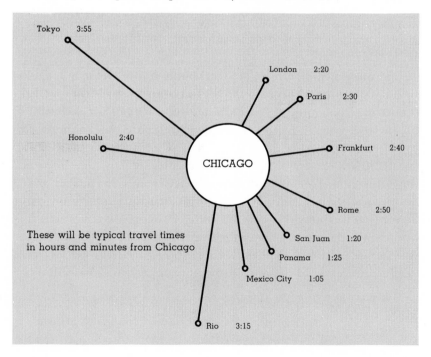

Tokyo   3:55
London   2:20
Paris   2:30
Honolulu   2:40
Frankfurt   2:40
CHICAGO
Rome   2:50
These will be typical travel times in hours and minutes from Chicago
San Juan   1:20
Panama   1:25
Mexico City   1:05
Rio   3:15

PROJECTS

1. List eight major social trends and show some effects of each upon education in America's schools.

2. Explain how the later discoveries about hydrogen in the universe influence the education of the young.

3. Give an illustration of automation and explain how this kind of development may affect education in the future.

4. Explain what steps need to be taken to make the education of children in the economically depressed areas of America's larger cities socially and educationally effective.

UNIT THREE

The American

Hays from Monkmeyer

School System

CHAPTER 11

Local aspects of
public school organization
and administration

American tradition, our heritage of frontier days, serves to perpetuate esteem for the local school, the school of the neighborhood. All the states legislate in a way that gives local citizens a voice
in determining how their schools shall operate, how much money
shall be spent on the schools, and the kind of education the children
shall receive. What are the legal avenues for the exercise of local
power in operating the schools? We hear about school districts.
What is a school district? How is it established? We are acquainted
with a board of education. What is a board of education? Why do
we have boards of education? What do they do? From whence do
they derive their power? How are their members selected? What is
the organization of a school district like? What is its structure of
authority and responsibility?

PUBLIC SCHOOL DISTRICTS

What a District Is

When the earliest schools were established, a political boundary line was set around the school, designating the area from which the children were to come and inside of which the residents who were to support and control the school were to live. This geographical area, or territorial political division, was called a school district. Essentially this is still what a school district is. Over the years, of course, the states have seen fit to modify the character of school districts—enlarge the area, include more schools, redefine the functions, add to or take away some of the powers of control.

The National Commission on School District Reorganization defines a school district thus: "A basic unit of local school administration is an area in which a single board or officer has the immediate responsibility for the direct administration of all the schools located therein. Its distinguishing feature is that it is a quasi-corporation with a board or chief school officer that has the responsi-

Although the one-room school is rapidly disappearing, it can still be found in some rural areas. Here at recess time pupils enjoy outdoor play. (Lanks from Monkmeyer)

bility for, and either complete or partial autonomy in, the administration of all public schools within its boundaries." As is true of most definitions of complex social undertakings, the definition needs analysis.

What do we mean when we say that a school district is a quasi-corporation? It operates like a corporation. Its powers and liabilities cannot extend beyond those prescribed by state legislatures for school districts. Unlike the municipal corporation, however, it is purely a political or civil division of the state. As an instrumentality of the state, it is created in order to facilitate the administration of the state government. A municipal corporation, on the other hand, is created, in the main, to enable the locality to regulate and administer its own local concerns. The school district's powers are not essentially local. Its function is the execution of state policy. Unlike the municipality, it is not a corporation, therefore, but a quasi-corporation.

Patterns of School Districts

There are several general patterns for basic school districts. Any attempt at classification is complicated by overlapping districts and by exceptions in districting practices. For instance, in California and in Illinois the independent high school districts are sometimes superimposed upon a series of independent elementary school districts. Within a plan for county districts we find separate districts, such as a small city, excluded from county jurisdiction. The details of organization vary among the states and even within some of the states. The following general descriptions will be helpful in understanding the various kinds of school districts, but one must be conscious that the descriptions do not attempt to cover all the variations and exceptions.

1. Common-School Districts

The term "common school" is sometimes used to designate lower schools as opposed to higher schools, but it is more properly applied to such schools as are supported by general taxation and open on a common basis to all. It is practically synonymous with the term "public school." The common-school district has its own geographical boundaries, which may or may not be coterminous with the boundaries of another unit of local government—city, village, town, or township. As the districts were originally established, their boundaries often followed the boundary lines of an existing political unit. Nonetheless, they are autonomous local subdivisions created separately only for school purposes, and operated by a board or school official. As originally established, most had one-room schools covering four to eight grades.

Thirty states, mostly in the West and Middle West, have some form of common-school district system. Most of these states have, in addition, independent urban districts and also one other type of district—a township district, or, as in some parts of Illinois, a township district for the high schools. The earlier common-school districts were much smaller than those under either a county or township plan. They averaged slightly more than 20 square miles with five teachers to the unit. This type is now considered to be the least efficient and the most expensive of all the forms of administrative organization.

In 1959–1960 there were 40,286 school districts in the nation. Of these, 25,803 were in the twelve Great Lakes and Plain states, states which also had more than half of the nation's one-teacher schools. Since then there has been a marked trend in most of the states toward a reduction in the number of school districts and one-teacher schools. The greatest changes have occurred in the Great Lakes and Plain states. Illinois, for example, had 1,685 school districts and 237 one-teacher schools in 1960–1961. By 1962–1963 this number had been reduced to 1508 school districts and 29 one-teacher schools, and two years later, by June 30, 1963, the number had been further reduced to 1480 school districts and to fewer than 17 one-teacher schools. Similar sharp reductions are taking place in other midwestern states. It is clear from the data in Figs. 11.2 and 11.3 that the traditional school district is rapidly being replaced by the larger, more logically bounded school district, with larger and more desirably located schools.

2. Town and Township Districts

Nine states organize the administration of their public schools around town or township districts. Three other states permit organization on the township plan under certain conditions. Under this plan the boundaries of the school districts are coterminous with the boundaries of a town or township. This plan is particularly ap-

FIG. 11.1 A TYPICAL ORGANIZATION OF A LOCAL SCHOOL SYSTEM

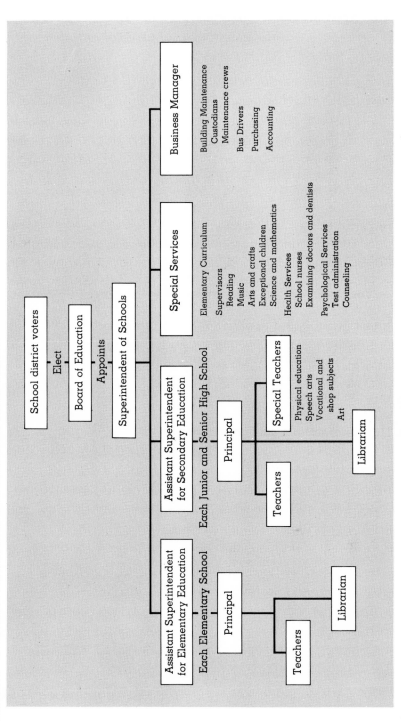

While each school system is organized somewhat differently, the pattern shown here is fairly typical. Size and location of the system lead to differences. In all of them, however, there is quite a similarity in the functions to be performed and in the manner in which these functions are allocated and performed.

FIG. 11.2 NUMBER OF SCHOOL DISTRICTS

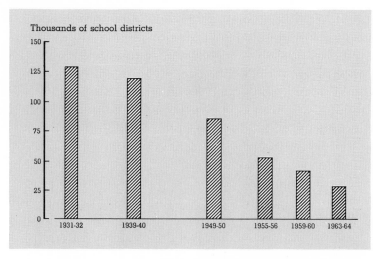

(Data from NEA Division, Research Memo 1959–61, and Research Report 1963–R12)

propriate in New England where the New England town—actually a combination of urban and rural territory—embraces an area of naturally related interests, logical for a school district. In the Middle West, township boundaries are not so appropriate to use as school district boundaries because they depend upon arbitrary

FIG. 11.3 NUMBER OF ONE-TEACHER SCHOOLS

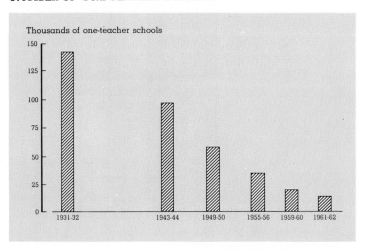

(Data from U.S. Office of Education)

and artificial land measurements instead of groupings of community interests.

3. City Districts

School districts that include cities frequently are organized with boundaries coterminous with the municipality. Under this plan the interests of both are interrelated. Sometimes the cities enjoy great wealth. Sometimes, however, they are handicapped by the pressure of powerful political machines. Then the schools are too frequently forced into the political arena. In some American cities, for instance, mayors select school board members. Aldermen may view the schools within their precincts as a fair field for political patronage. The selection of building sites and letting of contracts may invite local political interest.

4. County Districts

In 13 states the school district and county boundaries coincide. Perhaps the county district developed earliest in the South because there the states were not interested in investing in the common-school district so highly prized by the people of the more affluent states. In all but three of the states that have county districts, the organization is only partially based on the county system. There are one or more independent, usually urban, districts within the county that retain some separate educational function. Not all the schools within the county are under the county system. Sometimes the county district is just the high-school district. In this case there are numerous subsidiary common-school districts within the same geographical territory. Usually the administration of a genuine county district is very similar to that of a city district.

5. Intermediate or Supervisory Districts

In an intermediate district, a number of small school districts cooperate in organizing to provide specialized educational services such as supervision, guidance, and health. These are services that would be beyond the ability of any one district to furnish alone. Sometimes the intermediate system includes all the schools in a county. Although effective intermediate districts have not been developed widely, it is one of the really promising means of providing an adequate educational program for rural areas.

6. State-Centered Districts

Delaware, Alaska, and Hawaii have state-centered districts. The schools are highly centralized on a state-wide pattern.

Trends in School Districting

1. Consolidation

The organization of school districts is more varied within most states than would appear from the foregoing description because state legislatures are often disposed to make changes asked by local districts. Originally the common-school district was a small neighborhood district taking care of an eight-grade elementary school. Eventually, one school district might finance and care for several eight-grade elementary schools. With the increase in population and the improvement of roads and motor travel, consolidation of small rural school districts was advocated and the separate elementary school district with its own board of control and independent taxing power became typical. Where a plan for consolidation was carried out, buses transported children from various points within the geographically large area of the school district. Education in the district was more economically conducted, plans for financing were

Earlier transportation of pupils was by horse-drawn vehicles. As early as 1869 the city of Quincy, Massachusetts, transported pupils to the public schools. The appropriation for this service was $521.12! (National Safety Council, Chicago)

Just how extensive the travel system is that transports children daily throughout our country no one knows, although it has been estimated that more than eight million children go to and return from school in the school bus every day. This makes the school bus transportation system one of the most extensive travel enterprises in our country. Safety records attest to the fact that it is one of the safest.

Although the school bus is so common as to be taken for granted on our highways, it is a relative newcomer. With the school bus have come numerous and extensive improvements in the education available to many boys and girls. Good roads and school buses have been a necessary preliminary to consolidation of smaller school districts. Consolidation has meant an expansion of the geographical area and an increase in the school population of the unit school district. Perhaps one up-to-date and complete school for all the children in an area offers a broad program and complete services. The children come by bus from greater distances instead of attending a nearby one-teacher rural school. Economy and efficiency are achieved.

One community high school in Kansas enrolls seven hundred pupils who come from an area of six hundred square miles. Sixteen buses are used to transport the pupils to and from school. In this rural area the boys and girls have access to an educational program as diversified as the program available in the metropolitan areas.

Most states have passed laws requiring the school districts to furnish free transportation to pupils who may live farther than one and a half or two miles from the school, and to stop for all the children who may be waiting on the bus route regardless of how close they live to school. Other laws permit cities to transport pupils to schools operated for such special purposes as educating the physically handicapped.

The school bus has been an important factor in diminishing the distinctions between urban schools and rural schools. The school bus has made much progress possible toward the American ideal of equal educational opportunity for all children.

more efficient because of the broader taxing base, the curriculum was broadened, services were expanded, and the available equipment was improved.

Unification under a central administration and taxing authority that accompanied enlarging the districts in the agricultural areas made it possible for agricultural areas to support education similar to that offered by the city district. Ordinarily, the consolidated school district was able to build a larger and more up-to-date system of elementary schools and one or two large and conveniently located up-to-date secondary schools. It should be noted that these

School buses are used in many cities for transportation of pupils. The buses may transport the physically handicapped, or they may transport children from crowded schools to distant schools or from rural areas to urban areas. For special events like field trips, athletic contests, or musical events, the buses are usually used. (Crown Coach Corporation, Los Angeles)

schools are *not* "consolidated" schools. They are schools in a consolidated public school district. Each school is part of a system of schools. Technically, there are no consolidated schools although there is a popular tendency to refer to them as such.

In the earlier stages of the school redistricting movement, local traditions associated with the small school district were strong deterrents to change. Social conditions following World War II and continuing to the present, however, have accelerated redistricting. By 1948 Maryland, West Virginia, and Utah had reduced the number of their school districts to 24, 55, and 40, respectively. Hawaii has but one school district for the entire state. In Indiana the General Assembly on July 20, 1959, passed a law known as the School Reorganization Act. The act has already led to a considerable reorganization in a state that had previously made little change in its school districts. Between the school years 1962–1963 and 1963–1964, for example, the number of districts was reduced from 779 to 669.

Perhaps it would be only an idle guess to attempt to predict the future of school district reorganization in the United States. How far will the present trend proceed? In 1926 there were 40,286 independent school administrative units in the United States. In 1963–1964 there were still 31,319. As late as 1959–1960 there were still 20,263 one-teacher schools in the nation. These had been reduced to 13,300 by 1963–1964. Thus is seems that as the nation moves forward to improve its education, further reorganization of its school districts and the abolishment of many of its one-teacher schools will be one important part of the nation's program.

2. Setting Up Intermediate Districts

A number of states have experimented with various kinds of intermediate districts. Overlapping and divided authority between each separate district and the county, or other kind of intermediate authority, has been a very difficult problem to solve. Removing power from local hands and vesting it in a kind of superstructure is

This plan for a high school building is representative of the trend toward organizing large high schools into several smaller administrative units while, at the same time, making maximum use of certain special provisions such as gymnasiums, shops, and home economics and other laboratories. In the wings on the right are these shared facilities. The common auditorium is in the rear. The three unit high schools on the left use these facilities. (Bellflower Unified School District, Bellflower, California)

FIG. 11.4   HOW THE FORMATION OF UNIT DISTRICT NUMBER 10,
PITTSFIELD AND PIKE COUNTY, ILLINOIS, EFFECTED A REDUCTION IN THE
NUMBER OF SCHOOL UNITS

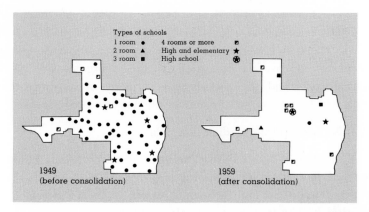

(Data from Pittsfield Community Unit School District No. 10)

looked upon with misgivings in some communities. As they now
operate, the intermediate districts function to promote cooperation
between autonomous districts by providing consultative, advisory,
and statistical services, and by performing certain regulatory and
inspectional duties. The independent district, whatever the voluntary arrangements made, remains the legal operating unit for all
elementary and secondary public schools.

3. Establishing Community School Districts

The New England plan of making a town and its surrounding
area the school district provides a pattern for the so-called community school district plan. Under this proposed plan, interrelated
and interdependent land would form the district. This would comprise an urban core with its suburban surroundings and the rural
area with which it has close economic and sociological ties. The
plan does not envision eliminating the one-room neighborhood
school and transporting all the pupils to some larger central school.
Instead, it proposes reducing the one-room schools to use for primary or preprimary classes, for which they would be excellently
suited. It is felt that broader administrative control over the several
schools is much more desirable than complete centralization within
each school.

This classroom in Lincoln, Nebraska, reflects the various interests of the local community. (Lincoln Public Schools)

Reorganization of School Districts

1. Disadvantages

Some critics feel that the power over local budgets, over local taxation, and over educational policy has slipped further and further from the hands of the local people with the ever-increasing tendency to consolidate. One of the foremost problems is how to preserve the many advantages of fostering local interest in education and, at the same time, to enjoy the benefits that accrue to local school systems as a result of expansion of the public school district. A balance between a reasonable degree of consolidation and desirable local control is sought. If the power over education is moved from the home neighborhood when public school districts are reorganized, local interest is endangered.

2. Part of Broad Social Trend

As pointed out before, the trend toward consolidation of assets and resources into larger and more powerful organizations is typical of modern life. In the movement to centralize school control and to consolidate school districts into larger units, school policy is consistent with the general social trends. This is not proof, of course, that every effort to enlarge school districts is necessarily wise.

Characteristics of Satisfactory School Districts

1. Number of Pupils

A satisfactory district has at least 1,200 pupils between ages 6 and 18. If it has a much smaller number, it can offer a good program only at a great cost per pupil. The more pupils it has up to 10,000, the broader the program it can offer at reasonable cost. If its enrollment is much below 10,000, it teams up with other basic units in a larger intermediate district in order to supplement its services.

2. Size and Qualifications of Staff

A satisfactory district has a corps of teachers, each one qualified to do a particular job well. It can provide one or more teachers for each grade or subject. It can employ specialists to give help in reading difficulties, health education, music, art, vocational education, attendance problems, and pupil guidance. It can assemble a competent staff of administrators, supervisors, and clerks to help teachers and to set up good conditions for learning. A satisfactory district is either big enough to provide all needed educational staff and services or it supplements its efforts by being part of a large intermediate district. It may look to the intermediate district for such services as supervision, transportation, guidance, and programs at the junior college level.

3. Number and Location of Schools

A satisfactory district has one or more elementary schools, at least one high school, and where possible, a junior college. The location of schools and the area that each serves are determined by three basic factors: (1) the number of pupils and teachers needed for a good program, (2) the travel time required of pupils, and (3) the natural community groupings.

FIG. 11.5   NUMBER OF SCHOOL DISTRICTS, STATE BY STATE, 1963-1964

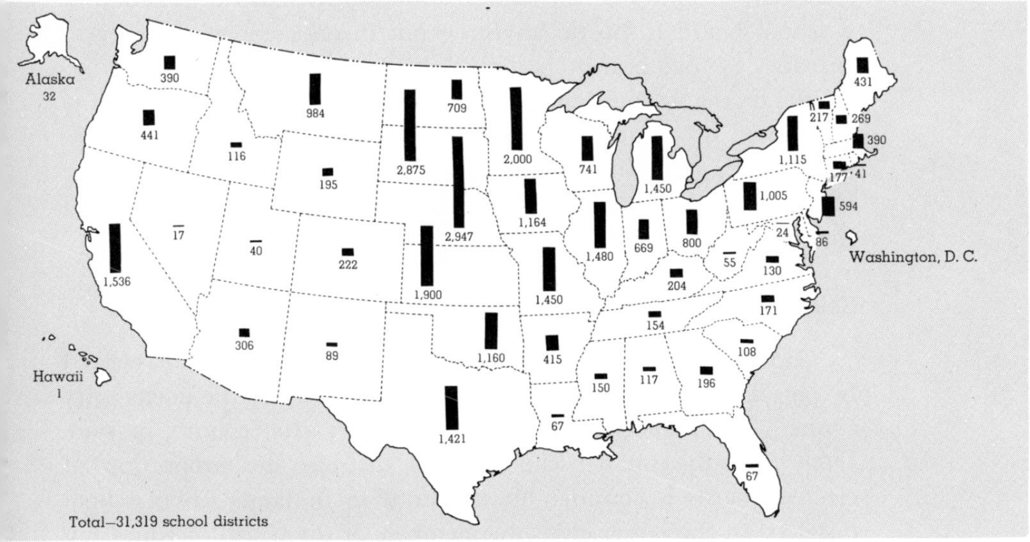

(Data from NEA Research Division, Research Report 1963–R12)

4. Administration and Finance

A satisfactory basic school district has its own board of education responsible to the people of the district. The superintendent is the chief executive officer responsible to the board. The board has ample resources from district and state funds to provide essential services on a sound basis.

THE BOARD OF EDUCATION

Nearly every school district in the United States is governed by a group of individuals known as a board of education, school board, board of trustees, the school committee, the township board of education, the county board of education, or some similar designation. In 1962, 166,571 American citizens served as members of local boards of education. A board of education is the legal agent specified by the legislature to be responsible for the conduct of education in the local district. By court decision such a board has been held to be a state agency rather than an adjunct of local government.

From the viewpoint of the state, the board's primary responsibility is to put into effect state and community plans of education. The general power in the statute which states that the function of a school board is "to do anything not inconsistent with this act" provides a broad basis for action. School boards engage in many activities on the assumption that it is proper to do so unless specifically prohibited by statute, and since many of these activities go unquestioned, they gradually become a part of routine practice. Flexibility in action and opportunity for experimentation in new areas are thereby made possible.

Selection

Boards are chosen in varying ways. About 85 percent are elected by popular vote. The rest are appointed, usually by the mayor, city council, city manager, judge, or some other city, county, or state agency. In the smaller-school school districts the proportion of elected boards is considerably higher than in larger-school school districts. In the larger cities the members of the board of education are usually appointed by the mayor. In smaller communities the members are elected. In some districts selection, whether by appointment or election, is preceded by some kind of screening participated in by representative groups of citizens. These groups are chosen in a variety of ways. The procedures for screening vary considerably.

The people have carried the nonpartisan concept of public education into practice by choosing their board members on a nonpartisan basis and at large rather than by wards or districts. Sometimes representatives of civic groups meet in a district caucus to prepare the slate of nominees presented to the voters on election day. Board members may be nominated by petition, primary election, individual announcements, mass meetings, or school district meetings. Unfortunately there is, on the whole, public apathy toward the business of electing school board members.

Term of Office

The current trend is to increase the length of the term served by school board members and also to make it more difficult to change the majority membership within too short a period of time. In general, terms for board members are from three to five years. By staggering the terms, continuity is assured and upheavals based on strong feelings or political considerations are avoided. In the 1963–

1964 school year, 47 percent of the members had been in office five or more years.

Size

The typical size for school boards is 5 members, although the range is from 1 to 21 members. The trend in recent years has been toward boards composed of not more than 9 elected members. There should be enough members on the board to represent the different points of view in the community so that a few close friends cannot dictate a board's actions. The one-member board, still found in some of the smaller districts, is probably too small to fulfill these requirements.

Compensation

Membership on a school board has traditionally been considered as unselfish service to state, community, and children, and the chief reward has been the satisfaction of doing good work. It is generally agreed within the profession that when compensation is provided, school board members tend to become executive in character in order to justify their pay. The result frequently is a strange mixture of spoils, politics, and constant interference with the professional personnel in the actual operation of the schools.

Qualifications of Board Members

Usually the law specifies only that the candidate for board membership shall be over 21 years of age, a qualified voter, and a resident in the school district. Obviously, meeting only these minimum legal qualifications provides no guarantee that an individual can be an effective school board member, that the board will be broadly representative of popular interest in the public schools. Other factors that should be weighed in the selection of members include:

1. Whether the individual enjoys community-wide respect and is able to discuss educational problems intelligently and convincingly. Board members must cooperate with the community as well as with each other.
2. Whether the individual will be able to understand and direct the financial—business—affairs of the school system.
3. Whether the individual is willing and able to devote sufficient time and energy to the office.

4. Whether the individual is likely to minister to the educational needs of all the children in the district. The school board should be representative of and serve all the people in the district. It cannot fulfill its responsibilities if it is faction-ridden, comprised of individuals each concerned only with promoting the interests of one socio-economic, racial, or religious group.
5. Whether the individual has children or grandchildren attending school or is active in youth work. An individual with such a background is more likely to be interested in and understanding of educational problems than, for instance, a middle-aged bachelor whose concern for children didn't survive his own childhood.

Generally, the educational qualifications of board members have been much higher than the educational attainment in the total population. In the school year 1963–1964, almost half were college graduates. School board members are typically chosen from those occupational groups called "successful men of business and professional affairs." These constitute 60 percent of board membership. Labor tends to be underrepresented. Surprisingly, women constitute only 10 percent of the board members. We say "surprisingly" because women seem to have a particular interest in education, have special insights, especially at the elementary level, have time and energy available, and meet the other qualifications.

Functions and Powers

The board is a policy-making body with broad prerogatives, but its powers and duties are limited by state law. School board members are, legally, *state* officers—locally elected representatives of the *state* school authority. They have practically every power and duty pertaining to the administration of the schools. Most school boards hold meetings open to the public and at least 60 percent of them issue printed or mimeographed statements of policy. Usually a board will delegate all of its executive functions to superintendents, principals, business managers, teachers, and other school employees. These employees possess only those powers explicitly or implicitly delegated to them by the board of education. The board will usually reserve to itself such functions as formulating policies and inspecting and appraising the work of the school system. On the basis of this inspection and appraisal, policies will be amended or new policies substituted for the old ones.

In general, the board will map out the overall education program, appoint the school personnel, fix salaries, draw up budgets, keep account of the money raised locally, fix the length of the school year, enforce compulsory attendance laws, determine when and where buildings shall be erected, make rules and regulations for the management of the schools, purchase materials, provide transportation, and do what is ordinarily deemed necessary to keep the schools in operation. By studying and understanding what the schools of the community are supposed to accomplish, how well the schools are succeeding, and what improvements and advances are to be desired, school board members contribute significantly to desirable public relations.

The school boards in city districts act as equalizers between the interests of the public and the interests of the professional staff which is employed by the public. They act also as a counterinfluence to excessive state-centered authority over the local public schools.

CITY SUPERINTENDENT OF SCHOOLS

The school board consists of laymen who do not profess expertness in school management. It is their responsibility to see that the work of the school is properly performed by professional personnel. It is essential that they employ a well-qualified professional educator to superintend the work of the schools. He is the chief executive. As superintendent of the school district, he occupies a central position in the overall structure of authority. The city boards of education delegate many of their own legal powers to him.

Since the superintendent's powers are broad, his duties are many and varied. As head of the district, he is professional adviser to the board of education as well as supervisor, employer, and organizer of the professional personnel and supervisor and employer of the nonteaching personnel, e.g. engineers and janitors. He is the expert in relations between the schools and the community and formulator of the policies that rule the selection, placement, and transportation of pupils. In other words, the city superintendent of schools is charged with the final responsibility for the efficient management and effective organization and administration of all the public schools in the school district. His position is important, calling for a high level of administrative ability and professional leadership. The position has become so important in city school administration that considerable study is devoted to defining the nature of the superintendent's work and to providing training programs.

In a smoothly running school organization only the chief executive is legally responsible to the board. In all but the smallest systems, however, he has administrative and supervisory assistants to whom he delegates responsibility and authority.

There is a growing tendency to recognize the need for including the teachers and, in some cases, the public in defining school policy. In earlier years the superintendent was considered to be more sympathetic to the board than to the teachers. Today he is considered not only the agent of the board but also the representative of the teachers. He tends to include teachers when he is formulating plans and policies and to encourage them to participate in making decisions.

COUNTY SUPERINTENDENT OF SCHOOLS

The professional staff of the school district in agricultural areas is often headed by a county superintendent of schools. From the title "superintendent," one might assume that his position is analogous to that of city superintendent of schools. Such, however, is not generally the case. In states where the school district in the agricultural areas is organized on the town or township basis, the county superintendent's functions are mainly of a clerical nature. Only a few executive responsibilities are delegated to him. For example, in Illinois the county school superintendent, who is elected on a partisan political ticket, visits the rural schools periodically. State monies are channeled through his office. As the legal representative of the state, he sanctions those who teach in county schools. He is the interpreter of school law when the need arises. As a rule, steps in the reorganization of school districts are cleared through his office. In the 12 states in which the school districts coincide with the county boundaries, however, the position is somewhat, but not wholly, like that of the superintendent in a city district.

County and district school boards look upon the county school superintendent as their professional adviser and leader. Whether he is appointed to be the chief executive officer for county boards of education, or whether he is elected on a political ticket and possesses only remote executive authority over individual school units within the county district, or whether he is selected by the elected trustees of the townships in the county, he is an important person in the direction and improvement of public education in the agricultural areas of the United States.

The trend toward the reorganization of school districts and the reduction or abolishment of one-teacher schools tends to change the functions of the county superintendent of schools. Perhaps the future of the office cannot be predicted at this writing. In some cases, where, say, the county is made the organizational and administrative unit, the powers and functions of the office might be expanded. In other instances, the opposite effect might even lead to making the office relatively obsolete. Different policies of reorganization in different states will almost certainly affect the office differently.

ABIDING TRADITIONS

The great variety in types of organization and administration results from (1) the unplanned development of education from semiprivate, short-term, low-cost schooling for the few to the huge public enterprise it is today and (2) the persistent emphasis on local initiative in educational planning. Despite this variety, however, traditions have persisted that cause schools to remain very much alike.

Self-Government

An insistence on locally administered school systems is a manifestation of the deep-rooted American belief in the doctrine of popular sovereignty. The people elect school boards, vote bond issues, employ and live close to educational personnel, and in many other ways participate in school management.

Local Interest

A Gallup survey of readership interest (1957) showed the two greatest interests of the American public to be health first and education second. Throughout the nation, citizens express pardonable pride in their local systems of free public schools. One way—the most effective way—educators can insure that the public's interest will be an enlightened one is to take advantage of this interest and to encourage wide, representative involvement in public education. Furthermore, every proposal to shift responsibility and power from the local system to, for example, a state-wide system should be examined closely to determine whether it may not weaken the system by diminishing the extent of local control and stifling the local public's interest in schools that they have come to regard as "theirs."

Dispersion of Power over Education

Most Americans realize that power over education "equals" power over the nation's future. They know also that if this power were concentrated in a few "wrong" hands, education might be used to change the next generation's whole social outlook. Traditionally, we have rejected such concentration of power over education and, instead, have distributed control among many agencies and among many people. Of all traditions in American education, this, perhaps, is the one most likely to persist.

In 1956 there were 54,802 elementary school districts in the United States, and all of these were controlled by the local citizens. Some of these districts had boards with as many as eleven members. The number of Americans who serve the schools on a voluntary basis is large indeed. Generally these people are capable and well intentioned. Only rarely has control fallen into incompetent, corrupt, or selfish hands.

When schools are under the general control of local boards, teachers are seldom under any pressure to court favor, as might be the case with a highly centralized governing body. Teachers are free to devote their energies to teaching and often are encouraged to contribute to the formulation of school policies. Local school boards —which because they are local are accessible—are becoming more and more aware of the value of direct communication with teachers, of the value of consulting with teachers before defining policies. Teachers' relations with a nonlocal governing body would probably be too impersonal to permit such cooperation.

The public, of course, does not want the professional staff to conduct schools only as they, the staff, desire. On the other hand, the public does not want to dominate the schools. What they seek is partnership. Partnership recognizes that the interests of staff and public are mutual. The public and the staff are closely related in the same venture, the success of which depends upon how each accepts and cares for the interests of the other.

Neighborliness

Neighborliness is a cherished characteristic of the typical American community. The school is highly suitable for the promotion of

FIG. 11.6 TOTAL EXPENDITURES ON PUBLIC EDUCATION, ELEMENTARY
AND SECONDARY

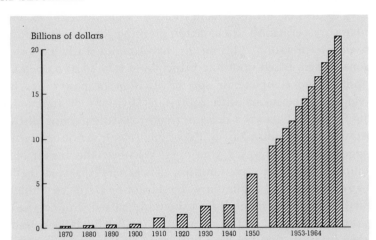

(Data from U.S. Office of Education and NEA Research Division, Research Report 1963–R12)

neighborliness because it is the one community institution that can cut across lines of class, religion, race, or political affiliation.

Only in a few communities is the school still the center of recreation and social life. But the same spirit of neighborliness is cultivated by such events as P.T.A. activities, parents' night at school, after-school teas for teachers, athletic events, parades, concerts, exhibits, and so forth. To the extent that the school is used to strengthen the tradition of neighborliness, it too is strengthened.

Free Choice

Parents are free to decide whether their children shall attend public or nonpublic schools. This is in accord with one of our democracy's central tenets: the individual has the right to believe in whatever he chooses. The individual's beliefs direct his choice among political parties, churches, clubs—or the school that his children will attend.

SUMMARY

We find great variation among school systems in the public school districts, even within the same state. Differences among the states and differences within districts in the same state are due in part to the fact that many state legislatures grant considerable authority to district boards of education. In some cases, for example, the laws are permissive in character, granting the boards wide latitude in interpretation. This means that America really has an educational system based upon the principle of state-local cooperation. At present no complete or specific division of power has been developed. Experiment with local-state divisions of functions is going forward. There is a definite trend toward enlarging districts, especially in agricultural areas. Experiments with various patterns of enlarged districts, however, continues. Whatever the answer to the question of local-state relationships, it is generally agreed that the self-governing school community should not be sacrificed. Problems related to the local school district should be solved without weakening the local interest of the community in its schools. Lay leaders, as they function through boards of education, are vested with authority over the schools. Fundamental changes in education are dependent upon aggressive lay leadership and an intelligently informed citizenry.

Under widespread control, no single agency, it is believed, can ever gain control of the public schools, nor can any one kind of selfish propaganda agency influence education throughout all the nation's public schools.

From the start it was believed that by leaving education in the hands of those who were most closely touched by it, the cause of education would be better cared for than it would be were it in the hands of those far removed from the community. A local school system is one that is more likely to respond quickly and sympathetically to a community's needs. Whatever the weaknesses of localism may be, it appears that the local school district, in some form, is likely to dominate the American educational scheme for years to come. There seems to be no strong desire on the part of the American people to discard the plan.

QUESTIONS

1. What are the principal advantages in the American policy of operating the schools largely through home rule? What are some disadvantages?
2. What have been the principal advantages and disadvantages to education of the district type of organization as it has functioned in the past?

3. What is a local board of education? What are its principal functions?

4. In what ways has local school management become more difficult in recent years? What may school boards do to compensate for the increase in their responsibilities?

5. How is the superintendent of a local school district appointed? What, ideally, are his principal functions?

6. How is a county superintendent of schools selected? What are his principal functions?

7. In your opinion, should the functions of county superintendents rightfully parallel those of the city superintendent of schools?

8. What are the principal differences between a local municipal government and a local school district government?

PROJECTS

1. Survey the pattern of school districting that prevails in your state. Point out where and how improvement has been brought about.

2. Draw up a list of standards for local school boards that should apply to such matters as selection, term of office, size, representation, qualifications, and compensation.

3. List the powers and duties of a local school board. Indicate how a community may guard against misuse of powers.

4. State the pros and cons of keeping school government separate from municipal government.

CHAPTER **12**

State public school systems

The Constitution of the United States separates the powers of the federal and state governments. The tenth amendment to the Constitution reads: "The powers not delegated to the United States by the Constitution, nor prohibited by it to the States, are reserved to the States, respectively, or to the people." The power of education is not delegated by the Constitution to the Congress, nor is it prohibited by the Constitution to the states. It therefore remains legally the right of the state legislatures to organize and administer education within the respective states.

Each state legislature has developed an individual plan for taking care of education. This has inevitably resulted in a variety of state patterns. In addition, there are federally administered school systems in the territories and in Washington, D.C.; these function somewhat as the state systems function. There is, therefore, no inclusive system of education in the United States as there is in England, France, and other European countries.

LEGAL STRUCTURE

As each state made provisions in its own constitution and passed laws for carrying out the function of public education, a legal structure was developed. This legal structure includes the basic law in the Constitution, subsequent legislation, school codes, and the decisions and precedents established by judicial review.

State Constitutions

Each state has a written constitution which follows, in general, the pattern set by the federal government. It provides for the popular election of a legislature and an executive—a governor—and for a system of state courts. Theoretically, the governor is free from the dominance of legislators because he is elected directly by the people. He is the titular head of his political party in the state. What the executive head favors with regard to public education, therefore, will be influential in determining how public education will fare under his executive and his party leadership. Thus a state's educational system is tied in with the leadership of a political party.

All the state constitutions contain provisions for public education. Some of our current attitudes and prevailing traditions can be traced to statements about education found in some of the original state constitutions. Section 44 of the Constitution for Pennsylvania, adopted in 1776, says:

A school or schools shall be established in every county by the legislature, for the convenient instruction of youth, with such salaries to the masters, paid by the public, as may enable them to instruct youth at low prices; and all useful learning shall be duly encouraged and promoted in one or more universities.

The constitutions of North Carolina of 1776 and 1835 contained an almost identical provision. The emphasis on low costs to the public occurs in the constitutions of several other states. The Vermont Constitution of 1787, for instance, provided:

Section XL. A school or schools shall be established in every town, by the legislature, for the convenient instruction of youth, with such salaries to the masters, paid by each town; making proper use of school lands in each town, thereby enabling them to instruct youth at low prices.

A different pattern is found in the constitutions of states admitted to the Union later. Section 2 of the Indiana Constitution, adopted in 1816, reads:

It shall be the duty of the general assembly, as soon as circumstances will permit, to provide by law for a general system of education, ascending in regular gradation from township schools to a State university, wherein tuition shall be gratis, and equally open to all.

Although it is evident that the states borrowed from one another in their constitutional provisions for public education, the systems of education that evolved from the interpretations of the legislators show great variation. One secures, therefore, only a partial view of the policies of a state toward public education from reading its constitution.

State Legislatures

It is in state laws for education that the essence of the differences among the states is evident. These laws, passed by state legislatures, determine what education shall be, how it shall be conducted, how it shall be financed, and who shall be responsible for its various aspects. At each legislative session there is apt to be some redefining, some modifying of the laws.

The school laws may be mandatory or they may be permissive. Laws that are permissive give a broad interpretation of policy, leaving the specific interpretation or implementation to local judgment. The local authorities, however, are required to conform to the general requirements made by the state law. Mandatory laws are uniform throughout the state and allow no local deviation.

State School Codes

Typically there is a difference of opinion among citizens over how to solve some specific problem of public education, for instance, the transportation of pupils. The legislators weigh various suggestions and then pass a law defining the policy which must be adopted. Local communities will then transport pupils in a way that conforms with the state law.

In time, school laws amass and are brought together. The systematic collection of all the laws in force, together with judicial opinion and court decisions, make up the state school code. Usually the state school code is published in a sizable volume of detailed, technical reading. For example, there will be an accumulation of many laws regarding such matters as compulsory school attendance, maximum liabilities of school districts, standards for teacher certification, charters for private schools, consolidation of school districts, the building and maintenance of school buildings, taxation for the maintenance of the schools, and policies toward pupil transportation—to name but a few.

The attitude toward education characteristic of the times is reflected in a law passed in 1647 in Massachusetts which has often been called the "Old Deluder Satan Act." It is quoted with original spelling.

It being one chiefe project of that ould deluder, Sathan, to keepe men from the knowledge of the Scriptures, as in former times by keeping them in an unknowne tongue, so in these latter times by perswading from the use of tongues that so at least the true sence and meaning of the original might be clouded by false glosses of saint seeming deceivers, that learning may not be buried in the grave of our fathers in the church and commonwealth, the Lord assisting our endeavors.

It is therefore ordered, that every township in this jurisdiction, after the Lord hath increased it to the number of fifty householders, shall then forthwith appoint one within their towne to teach all such children as shall resort to him to write and reade, whose wages shall be paid either by the parents or masters of such children, or by the inhabitants in generall, by way of supply, as the major part of those that order the prudentials of the towne shall appoint; provided, those that send their children be not oppressed by paying much more than they can have them taught for in other townes; and it is further ordered, that where any towne shall increase to the number of one hundred families or householders they shall set up a grammer schoole, the master thereof being able to instruct youth so farr as they may be fited for the university; provided, that if any towne neglect the performance hereof above one yeare, that every such towne shall pay to the next schoole till they shall perform this order.

The relation of the American public school to American society and to the individual pupil in the school is defined in the state school codes. Nowhere else is so complete and so dependable a source of information about public and private schools in America available. Teachers can profit by spending some time discovering precisely what legal principles their state legislators have decided should govern education. A copy of the published state school code will serve often as a handy book of reference within the school.

Judicial Review

The policy of an individual state toward public education is, then, expressed in the constitution and in the specific laws passed by legislatures. The state constitution is the fundamental law. State legislatures are subject to restrictions placed upon them by the constitutions. Those who challenge the constitutionality of a state law must refer to the state courts. The final authority to declare a state law unconstitutional belongs to the state court of highest appeal, usually called the "supreme" court. The supreme courts also may invalidate an action of a state board or department of education.

As we shall see in the next chapter, the United States Supreme Court sometimes gets into the picture. A conflict over the way in which some state legislature or some state supreme court judge has decided a matter may, under certain circumstances, be carried to the United States Supreme Court where the judges render what is expected to be, at least for some years to come, a final decision. The word "final" is a relative term and should not be too strictly interpreted. This is especially true when applied to court decisions concerning public education. Even supreme courts have been known to reverse themselves.

THE TREND TOWARD STATE STANDARDS AND STATE CONTROL

Despite their variety, state systems do manifest one common trend—that toward increased state centralization of control over local education. The tendency has progressed much further in some states than in others. The increased powers of many of the states have been extended to such matters as: licensing teachers, accrediting institutions of higher learning, collecting and distributing tax monies, reorganizing local school districts, limiting local authority over school taxation, defining standards for school building construction, requiring the transportation of pupils, requiring that local school budgets be approved by the state school authority, requiring that pupils shall study United States history, defining teacher tenure. So widespread is the influence of the state in education that a listing of all the manifestations in even a single state would be impractical. With each meeting of each state legislature the list grows longer. The end of the trail is not yet in sight.

While the trend toward state control over schools is general throughout the nation, the crucial question of the proper kind and degree of state control remains debatable. In some states the question is currently a heated political issue. The opinions range from making the state a single unit of school administration to having the public schools operate completely as local community units with a minimum of control from the state. Perhaps the most important consideration has been to strengthen public education while at the same time attempting to preserve the strengths of local school districts that have been built upon the idea of using local resources, both human and material, as much as possible.

THE STATE EDUCATIONAL AUTHORITY

State legislatures allocate specific authority over education to some person or office in the state government. They indicate the office to which authority shall be delegated and define its functions. Characteristically, states differ in the manner in which the state educational authority is organized.

State Boards of Education

In 42 states a state board of education has been established to supervise education. These boards of education, or their equivalent, such as the Board of Regents in New York State, constitute the highest educational authority in the state. There is great variation with regard to membership, methods of selection, and delegated functions.

1. Membership

The number of members on state boards ranges from 21 in Texas to 3 in Mississippi. Ten states have 7 members. Nineteen states have from 8 to 11 members. Seven states have fewer than 7 members. The trend is toward having smaller boards.

Most of the states prescribe no special qualifications for membership. The assumption seems to be that if the method of selection is sound, only men and women who are fully competent will be selected. A few of the states require that the education profession be represented on the board. Some indicate that the membership must come from representative parts of the state. On the whole, the question of what constitutes the best size and type of membership for a state board of education remains unsettled.

Fig. 12.1 A TYPICAL STATE EDUCATIONAL ORGANIZATION

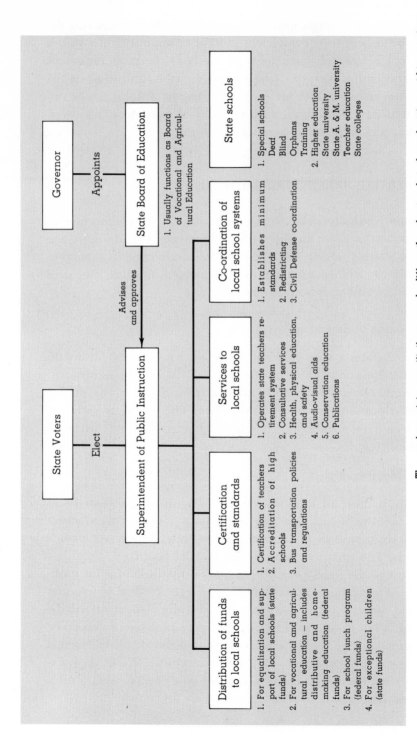

The various state constitutions speak differently about what the education within a given state shall be. Also, state legislatures do not pass identical laws nor do they organize the state educational authority along even approximately the same lines. There are trends, however, in the direction of a greater degree of state participation and state control of the local educational function. This chart shows one of the more common ways of organizing state authority. The student may

2. Selection

In some states, members are elected. Varying elective procedures are followed. In Utah, for example, members of the state school board are elected by the school boards of local school districts. In Texas, one board member is elected from each of the congressional districts.

Some of the state boards have members who are designated as ex officio members. They are members of the board because of some official position they hold in the state government. In 9 states the governor is an ex officio member. In 18 states the superintendent of public instruction is an ex officio member.

State school board members may be appointed by the governor, by the legislature, or by the chief state school officer. There are combinations of methods such as having a certain number appointed and the balance ex officio. Again, the best method of selection has not been settled.

3. Functions

The functions and duties assigned to state boards of education are analogous to those granted by boards of local school districts. The state board assumes the responsibility for those aspects of public education that are considered the legal responsibility of the state. Like the boards of local districts, the state body is a policy-making board with general supervisory control over all the educational enterprises of the state. This statement is more of an ideal, however, than a description of practice. Actually, the details of functions of no two state boards are the same. For example, in only 13 states are the state boards vested with all the general control of elementary and secondary education. In some states separate boards of education, sometimes called boards of trustees, are vested with power over public institutions of higher education. There may be several such boards. Occasionally each institution of higher education within the state has its own board of control. In some states there are a number of state boards of education, each with a separate function—perhaps one for the administration of vocational education, another to control institutions for the education of the deaf, and so on. The pattern for allocation of functions is both diffused and confused.

Chief State School Officers

All the states have an individual who is designated the chief state school officer. The trend of the past few decades has been to enhance the importance of this position. The titles of the state school officer generally are either "superintendent of public instruction" or "state commissioner of education." The chief state school officer usually operates either as executive officer of the state board of education, secretary to the state board of education, or supreme officer of education within the state. Duties and functions, usually delegated by the state boards, vary widely from state to state.

State Departments of Education

In all the states the chief educational officer uses the services of a professional staff. He, with his staff, constitutes the state department of education. It discharges manifold responsibilities in connection with such matters as certificating all teachers of the state, distributing state aid to local school districts, reorganizing school districts, enforcing various school codes, reporting the status of educational affairs to the public, and distributing large sums of money allocated to the state by the federal government for vocational education or some other designated purpose. Responsibilities such as these call for much careful, concentrated attention.

As is true with other practices of state education, there is variation in the importance of the state department of education. As an example, in 1955–1956 the number of staff members ranged from 19 in Connecticut to 537 in New York to 829 in California. The ratio of staff to teachers was approximately 1 to 780 in Connecticut, 1 to 175 in New York, and 1 to 100 in California. It may be assumed that where the number of staff members is large the duties are more numerous and the powers greater.

The areas of service covered by these staffs are many. In terms of staff time spent in all the states, the more important areas are vocational rehabilitation (on which one staff spent as much as 61 percent of its time), vocational education, instructional services, handicapped children, veterans' education, adult education, finance, teacher certification, research, statistical services, school lunch programs. Even though each state has its own ideas about the importance of the functions of the state department, none fails to

Chief among the central government agencies of every state is the State Department of Education. Such departments perform many important functions, including the enforcement of mandates of the state as defined by state law, computation of state aid, examination of the credentials of teachers, operation and maintenance of certain institutions. An efficient department requires a large staff. The impressive façade of the headquarters pictured above shows the importance the State of New Jersey attaches to its Department of Education. (State of New Jersey, Department of Education)

recognize it as an essential part of the educational organization of the state.

STATE PROGRAMS OF PUBLIC EDUCATION

All the states are making efforts to solve their state-wide educational problems. Some are struggling with more acute problems than others, and some have made far more significant progress than others. What are some of the problems more or less common to the states? Decentralization is a state as well as a local problem. Other problems concern minimum standards, foundation programs, an adequate financial policy in a decentralized system, and sources of public school revenue. The discussion that follows is meant to be illustrative of the problems that confront the state. It is not intended to be either comprehensive or to provide solutions.

Policy of Decentralization

As pointed out in the preceding chapter, Delaware is an example of a state that has its program of public education administered from a central state office. Regardless, however, of how far a state has proceeded toward centralization, all states continue, in varying ways, to keep education a responsibility of local citizens. All have some form of local school district that conserves localism as a reigning tradition. Centralization is a matter of degree. In all the states, the central state government delegates some measure of control over schools to local district authorities. The local authorities, of course, act in accord with the powers vested in them by the state legislatures.

While a decentralized administration of schools is common to all the states in greater or lesser degree, local responsibility does not relieve the state of important educational responsibilities. In one sense, the greater the degree of decentralization, the larger the responsibility of the state government. Local administration requires that state help and service be supplied to local school districts whenever they are not self-sufficient. All states are working at the state level to strengthen public education throughout the state. In the broadest sense, the problem each state faces is how to aid its local school units without displacing the authority of the local units to administer school matters, thereby causing the people to abdicate their concern and responsible interest.

Just as no state can function without having authority delegated to it by the federal government, so also, and to a much greater extent, are local school governments dependent on the central government of the state. Conversely, it is the local school governments, collectively, that administer the state's education program.

Minimum Standards

The state departments of education establish minimum standards which local schools must meet or else suffer such penalties as may be stated in the law—cutting down on state financial aid, for instance. As an example, a school may be required to employ only those teachers who possess minimum qualifications of training for state certification. Schools may be required to have pupils in attendance a minimum number of days each year. Some states require that certain subjects, like United States history or health education, be taught. Some states have established a minimum salary for beginning teachers. If a teacher, under contract, should perform services for a local school board and receive less compensation than the minimum prescribed by law, he is entitled to recover the deficiency.

When the state establishes minimum standards, it guarantees the individual pupil a basic standard of education regardless of where he lives within the state or which school he attends. All the states do not, of course, provide equal minimum standards.

Foundation Program

Despite the establishment of certain minimum standards, studies show that inequalities in educational opportunity characterize the schools in all the states. The discrepancy in educational opportunities available in the poorest schools and in the best schools in a state is, in some cases, so great as to constitute a social threat. The discrepancies in some states are greater than in others, but they are wide in all states. It might appear that poor schools are in communities of substandard wealth and that the discrepancy can be explained by lack of money. When we consider, however, that the entire state is an educational unit, it seems clear that it is not the substandard wealth of a community that is responsible. It is the policy of the state toward raising and distributing revenue for public school purposes that perpetuates the discrepancies. The state creates school districts. If a school district has low taxing ability and insufficient income to support the schools, the state has the responsibility for equalizing the educational opportunities. This can be done, if the state desires, by establishing first a foundation program for every district and then a policy of school support to insure that each district is able to maintain the foundation program.

To do this the state must begin by defining its foundation program—the minimum program of education to be available to each child in the state. Every state now prescribes some kind of foundation program for its schools, but many of these programs have been developed haphazardly, almost without plan. In many states, they have grown out of a long list of separate legislative actions. A legislature may decree, for instance, that every school in the state shall be open for a minimum of 180 days, that United States history shall be taught in all the secondary schools, and that examinations shall be passed by all eighth grade pupils showing knowledge of the federal and state constitutions. Sometimes such minimum programs do very little to reduce educational inequalities in a state. They may be legislated mainly to satisfy the passing fancy of legislators or to placate the persistent pressures of some highly vocal, organized group.

The foundation program that will reduce educational discrepancies and equalize opportunities must be expertly planned and broadly acceptable to the school public. The state can act in two general directions. It can pass legislation defining in detail the standards each school district must meet. These standards might prescribe a school session of 180 days, a specified minimum salary for beginning teachers, and buildings and equipment which must meet definite quantitative and qualitative standards. The maximum size of a class might be established and the maximum teaching load stipulated. Many details of the state program are thus settled. They are defined by state fiat.

A simpler way, and one that is more in line with American local school tradition, is to set a minimum expenditure per pupil as the standard for all school districts. This leaves the planning of the details to the local district with a minimum of state intervention. The expenditure standard may be changed from time to time as the occasion requires and as the state feels it is warranted.

Once the state requires that each public school district shall maintain a foundation program for all the children in the school district, it must collect and distribute school revenues so that the financial burden for this foundation program is no heavier in the districts of low taxing ability than in the districts with higher taxing ability. The cost factor must be equalized.

Financial Policy

What policy should the states follow in attempting to achieve a minimum program and at the same time to equalize the cost? It will require, initially, that each district in the state will make an effort to support the foundation program equal to the effort of every other district. The local tax rate for the foundation program in a poor district will be exactly the same as the local tax rate in a wealthier district. Obviously the returns from taxes will be much greater in the wealthier than in the poorer districts. The wealthier districts will be able to support the minimum program with considerable ease. They probably will pay for the entire foundation

Perhaps teachers and pupils, even in a well-taught junior high school class in social studies such as this, are not conscious that their school has a direct relationship to state educational policies. (Shelton from Monkmeyer)

program and will go as far beyond the program as they wish and further tax themselves accordingly. No limit is set on how much they spend on their schools or how good they make them.

The poorer districts, when taxed uniformly with the rest of the state, may find that they have collected insufficient funds to meet the cost of the foundation program. Funds from the state, called state aid, make up the difference. The poorer district will receive larger sums from the state than districts with more taxable wealth. All districts make an equal effort to pay, but some must receive more state aid than others.

State aid equalizes the cost of education for the foundation program but leaves the control of schools in local hands. The state remains the unit for providing some school revenue. The words "state aid" are appropriate since they imply that the state will assist local school districts but will not dominate them.

Sources of State School Revenue

Where does a state get the money for its education program, including state aid? Locally, as we have said, the school districts impose their own taxes. Traditionally these have been property taxes

—taxes primarily on real estate, land, and buildings—levied regardless of whether the property produces income. Sometimes levies are also made on personal property such as furniture, jewelry, automobiles, and the like. Each local community sets a local property tax rate within the limits permitted by state law.

The property tax is considered to be rather inflexible. Rates and assessments tend to rise slowly when school costs are rising rapidly but to fall precipitately in hard times. Tax burdens during depressions tend to become heavy, and business bankruptcies and forced sales create a climate of pessimism. Since many school costs are fixed, such as interest on debts and cost of maintenance, supplies, and equipment, and since fixed costs cannot be cut quickly, the local community typically turns to the heaviest of all school expenditures—the salaries of schoolteachers—for prompt cost-cutting.

Under the policy of decentralization typical of most states, some local school districts are at a disadvantage unless the state takes adequate steps to overcome financial handicaps. The substandard school pictured above would not be substandard if the state assumed the responsibility of assuring the children of all its communities the right to equal education. Equalization of educational opportunity, as of now, is more a slogan than a reality in most of our fifty states and territories. (National Education Association)

When raising the money to provide adequate school facilities is beyond the capacity of local communities, the state helps.

Besides its inflexibility, the property tax tends to be inadequate also because property is not income-producing to the degree that it used to be. Civic groups have for many years advocated diversifying the taxes used for school funds. The property tax remains, however, the principal base for local school support in many states.

Where does the state go for its revenue to distribute to the local school districts? There is variety in the state plans. Revenue from almost any state tax source may be used for school purposes if the state legislature desires. There is more and more dependence on general sales taxes. Sometimes excise taxes are levied on special products like alcohol or tobacco. The objection to the general sales tax is that it imposes a greater burden on the lower-income group which spends a larger proportion of its income on necessary items for daily living and thereby pays proportionately more of the tax. Theoretically, the income tax is considered most equitable. State constitutions and public opinion, however, sometimes make it difficult for a state to impose a state income tax.

Though the whole problem of state revenue, and especially of public school funds, is a difficult one, it should receive immediate attention in many states. That education should be equalized throughout a state seems an essential democratic principle. How to raise the money to accomplish this, however, remains an open question.

Policies of State Aid

All the states have programs of state aid, but the amount of state aid and the policy of distribution to the local public school districts differ vastly with the states.

It is evident from Fig. 12.2 (p. 307) that some states have moved further toward equalizing the cost of education than have others. In all probability, the state that has a lower level of state aid has had to reduce its minimum education program in order not to put an impossible tax burden on some of the poorer local school districts.

It is not difficult to reason logically that the state aid fund in any particular state should be larger, that improved foundation programs should be required, or that the brunt of the burden for local and state school support should not be concentrated on property taxes. Methods for making such changes, however, are not so readily apparent. Should the local school districts be modified? Should the kind of taxes levied be changed? Should the methods of assessing, levying, collecting, and distributing tax money be improved, and if so, how? Should the authority and functions of the divisions of the state school system be clarified, simplified, and made generally more effective? Where should we look for intelligent and dynamic leadership for necessary reorganization of a state school system? These are, as yet, unanswered questions.

The state is the educational unit. What may be done locally depends upon what the state constitution permits and what the state legislators feel inclined to do. The variations among the states regarding all details of state public school systems are imposing. Some states have advanced in their reorganization efforts, usually by gradual and continuous means. Some states have set up a permanent group, such as a commission on the reorganization of public school districts, to work on the problem.

From 1955 to 1964, the percentage of public school revenue from local, state, and federal sources remained fairly constant—

Fig. 12.2   Percentage of Public School Revenue from Local, State, and Federal Sources 1930-1964

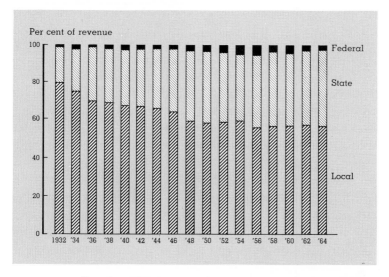

(Data from NEA Research Division, Research Reports 1959–R13, 1963–R12)

about 4 percent from federal, 40 percent from state, and 56 percent from local sources. Pressure on Congress to authorize federal aid for public school construction and teachers' salaries has increased. It seems likely that that the amount of federal aid to the lower schools will increase as has been the case with the higher schools.

QUESTIONS

1. What, in your opinion, is the responsibility of a state when it establishes a public school district that does not have the resources to provide the foundation program prescribed by the state?
2. What is meant by equalizing educational opportunity within a state?
3. What logical steps may a state take to equalize educational opportunities within its borders?
4. Is it possible for a state to equalize educational opportunity without violating the principle of local control over education?
5. Why were the powers to certificate teachers taken over by the state?
6. What provisions for public education are made in the constitution of your home state?
7. When should a state school law be mandatory? When should it be permissive?
8. When do you consider it right and appropriate for a state teachers' association to attempt to influence legislatures?

Fig. 12.3 Federal Aid Per Pupil in Average Daily Attendance, 1963-1964

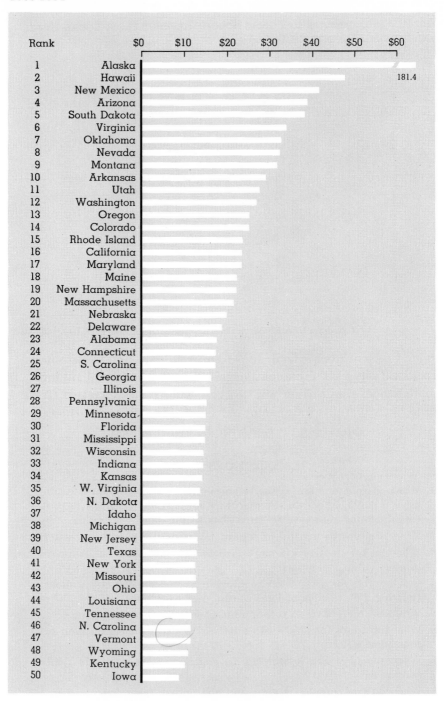

(Data computed from NEA Research Division, Research Report 1963–R12)

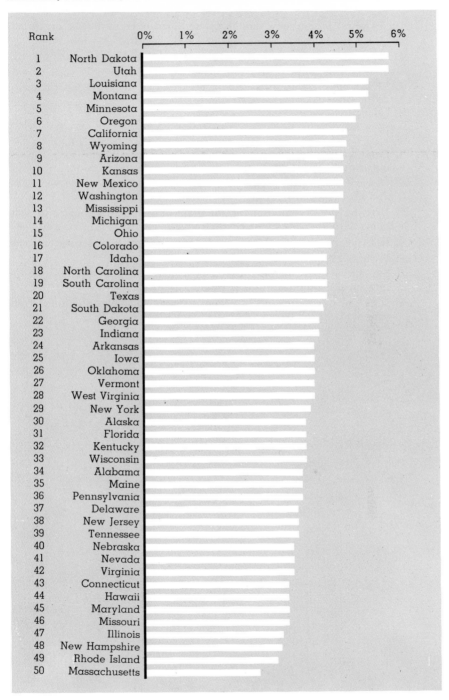

Rank		0%	1%	2%	3%	4%	5%	6%
1	North Dakota
2	Utah
3	Louisiana
4	Montana
5	Minnesota
6	Oregon
7	California
8	Wyoming
9	Arizona
10	Kansas
11	New Mexico
12	Washington
13	Mississippi
14	Michigan
15	Ohio
16	Colorado
17	Idaho
18	North Carolina
19	South Carolina
20	Texas
21	South Dakota
22	Georgia
23	Indiana
24	Arkansas
25	Iowa
26	Oklahoma
27	Vermont
28	West Virginia
29	New York
30	Alaska
31	Florida
32	Kentucky
33	Wisconsin
34	Alabama
35	Maine
36	Pennsylvania
37	Delaware
38	New Jersey
39	Tennessee
40	Nebraska
41	Nevada
42	Virginia
43	Connecticut
44	Hawaii
45	Maryland
46	Missouri
47	Illinois
48	New Hampshire
49	Rhode Island
50	Massachusetts

(Data from NEA Research Division, Research Report 1963–R12)

9. In your opinion, how should a state board of education be organized?

10. What should be the functions of a state board of education?

11. How should the state commissioner of education, or state superintendent of public instruction, be selected?

12. What powers and duties should be vested in the state department of education?

PROJECTS

1. From a study of the state school code for your home state, list the major problems to which the legislature has given attention.

2. Describe the organization of the state board of education in your state and list suggested reforms.

3. Describe the organization of the state educational authority in your home state. Indicate the strengths and weaknesses.

4. Describe and evaluate the foundation program as prescribed in your state.

5. Explain, perhaps by using a table or a chart, why the state must be the unit for the administration of public education.

6. State the conclusions about school support you believe justified from your study of the data in Figs. 12.3 and 12.4.

CHAPTER   13
Federal activity in education

While control of education traditionally is considered a matter for local prerogative and while the state is the unit for the administration of education, the federal government, nevertheless, plays a significant part in influencing and financing education and directly engages in education in a number of ways. How has the federal government secured authority to participate in education inasmuch as the words "education" and "school" are found nowhere in the Constitution? What are the limitations on federal participation in education?

CONSTITUTIONAL PROVISIONS FOR EDUCATION

Why did members of the Constitutional Convention omit any mention of education from the Constitution? For one thing, they were faced at that time with several other and more serious problems that had to be solved to preserve national unity. In the face of such emergencies it is not surprising that they should put less pressing matters in the background. We must remember, also, that at the time little thought had as yet been given to public education. The ideas and the theories developed by Pestalozzi, Herbart, and Froebel had not yet been born. Education in early America was largely a matter of interest only to those who could afford to pay for it.

In the preamble of the Constitution, however, the obligation to advance the cause of education is implied in the statement that it is the purpose of the Constitution to provide for the common defense and general welfare. The section of the Constitution that empowers Congress to levy and collect taxes, likewise, states that taxes shall provide for the common defense and general welfare of the United States. Although the founding fathers did not specifically mention education, they made statements that unquestionably obligate the federal government to advance public education.

On the other hand, the Constitution, by implication, also makes clear that the power over education is to be delegated to the states. Since power over education was not specifically delegated to the United States nor prohibited to the states, it was, according to the Tenth Amendment, definitely to be left to the individual states. That has consistently been the construction placed upon the wording of the Tenth Amendment.

A National Advisory Committee on Education appointed by President Herbert Hoover to study, among other things, the distribution of control over public education reported that there are six fields of educational activity that are clearly outside the jurisdiction of the states and are, therefore, fields for federal control. These six fields are:

1. The education of residents of special federal areas, such as government reservations and federal districts lying outside the legal jurisdiction of a state and other regional governments.
2. The education of the American Indians and other indigenous peoples within the national jurisdiction.
3. The education of the peoples of the Territories and outlying possessions.
4. The training of persons in the service of the national government.
5. Scientific research and the collection and diffusion of information regarding education.
6. The intellectual and educational cooperation of the United States with other nations.[1]

[1] National Advisory Committee on Education, *Federal Relations to Education* (Washington, D.C.: National Capital Press, Inc., 1931), pp. 9-10.

FEDERAL GRANTS TO EDUCATION

Unconditional Land Grants

Federal interest and participation in education go back beyond the adoption of the Constitution. In 1785 and in 1787, the Continental Congress passed two ordinances which provided for surveying the Northwest Territory and planning the administration of the territory (see p. 314). The first one of these ordinances established the policy of reserving every sixteenth section out of each township (one square mile out of 36) for the benefit of public schools. The precedent for this action was the reserving of land for school purposes by several of the former colonies.

The federal government did not put the land-grant policy into operation until 1802, when Ohio was admitted as a state. Vermont, Kentucky, and Tennessee, which were admitted to the Union as new states within a few years after the inauguration of the Constitution, did not receive any land for common school purposes.

The provisions of the Ohio Act were extended in 1803 to the national domain south of Tennessee and in 1821 to the Louisiana territory. Only three states admitted since 1802 have never received some kind of federal land grant for public schools: Maine, where the federal government had no title to any territory because Maine had been part of Massachusetts; Texas, which was a sovereign state when annexed; and West Virginia, which seceded from Virginia during the Civil War. Since 1850, when California was admitted, two sections of each township have been given for schools in all new states except Utah, Arizona, and New Mexico, which were allowed four sections because of the low value of the lands.

It is evident that the early federal legislators did appreciate the importance of public education and were interested in helping the states establish public schools. However, fostering education was secondary to other desired achievements. Their first interest was in selling and settling western lands. They believed that making school land available would promote the sale of real estate.

The land grants to education, considered an acceptable and essential federal aid policy, were to be out-and-out grants to the states, with no strings attached. After the state received the land, the federal government did not interfere with its use or management. This is an example of an early and prevailing attitude of the federal

The policy of setting aside a portion of the public lands for school purposes, rather than selling all the land or homesteading it, was first established in the Land Ordinance of 1785, enacted by the Congress under the Articles of Confederation on May 20, 1785.

AN ORDINANCE FOR ASCERTAINING THE MODE OF DISPOSING OF LANDS IN THE WESTERN TERRITORY

Be it ordained by the United States in Congress assembled, that the territory ceded by individual States to the United States, which has been purchased of the Indian inhabitants, shall be disposed of in the following manner:

A surveyor from each state shall be appointed by Congress. . . .

The Surveyors . . . shall proceed to divide the said territory into townships of six miles square, by lines running due north and south, and others crossing these at right angles, as near as may be. . . .

The plats of the townships respectively, shall be marked by subdivisions into lots of one mile square, or 640 acres, in the same direction as the external lines, and numbered from 1 to 36. . . .

. . . There shall be reserved the lot No. 16, of every township, for the maintenance of public schools within the said township; also one-third part of all gold, silver, lead and copper mines, to be sold, or otherwise disposed of as Congress shall hereafter direct. . . .

government—the principle of federal support without federal control.

In the states admitted early to the Union the plan generally was to sell the land and to place the proceeds in a permanent fund, using the interest for school purposes. This principle of permanent school funds has had a great influence on both public and nonpublic education and seems to have been widely accepted even in the earliest period of American history. Unfortunately, the sale and transfer of land was sometimes unwisely handled; much of the inheritance has been squandered. Selfish individuals and corporate interests were permitted to exploit the federal grant. However, in 1940, one-third of the land granted was still owned by the states. It is to the credit of the newer states that they have administered their share of public land for school purposes quite wisely. The value of their land grants is still growing.

The provisions of the early ordinances stimulated sentiment for public schools and may have suggested to the older states the idea of permanent public funds for school purposes at a time when taxation for schools was not yet popularly looked upon as legitimate.

Federal Grants for a Specific Purpose

1. The Morrill Acts

The policy of no restrictions on management or uses made of the income from land grants was not followed in some of the later federal programs, notably in the Morrill Act of 1862. In part this was because the earlier grants had been squandered in some states and in part because the earlier universities had remained almost entirely academic.

A proposal to establish a national agricultural college, analogous to West Point in the military field, had been defeated. The Morrill Act was intended to encourage the establishment "of at least one college where the leading object shall be, without excluding other scientific and classical studies, and including military tactics, to teach such branches of learning as are related to agriculture and the mechanic arts, in such manner as the legislatures of the states may respectively prescribe, in order to promote the liberal and practical education of the industrial classes in the several pursuits and the professions in life."

This act, signed by President Lincoln, granted to each state "an amount of public land . . . equal to thirty thousand acres for each senator and representative in Congress to which the States are respectively entitled by the apportionment under the census of eighteen hundred and sixty: Provided: That no mineral lands shall be selected or purchased under the provisions of this act." The act further stipulated that each state claiming the benefits of the act should make an annual report "regarding the progress of each college, recording any improvements and experiments made, with their costs and results. . . ."

This act and the Morrill Act of 1890 led to the establishment of 69 land-grant colleges, some of which evolved into some of America's largest and most influential state universities. At least one such college was established in each state. In some states, e.g. Illinois, Wisconsin, and Minnesota, the colleges were combined with the state universities. In others, the federally aided colleges were established as separate colleges, e.g. Iowa State University, Michigan State University, and Purdue University.

The principles of federal aid to higher education and of the legitimacy of permanent school funds, sometimes referred to as endowments, are recognized in the Morrill Act of 1862. The wording merits careful reading.

AN ACT DONATING PUBLIC LANDS TO THE SEVERAL STATES AND TERRITORIES WHICH MAY PROVIDE COLLEGES FOR THE BENEFIT OF AGRICULTURE AND MECHANIC ARTS

Be it enacted by the Senate and House of Representatives of the United States of America in Congress assembled, That there be granted to the several States, for the purpose herinafter mentioned, an amount of public land, to be aportioned to each State a quantity equal to thirty thousand acres for each senator and representative in Congress to which the States are respectively entitled by the apportionment under the census of eighteen hundred and sixty: Provided: That no mineral lands shall be selected or purchased under the provisions of this act.

Section 4. And be it further enacted, That all moneys derived from the sale of the lands aforesaid by the States to which the lands are apportioned, and from the sales of land scrip hereinbefore provided for, shall be invested in stocks of the United States, or of the States, or some other safe stocks, yielding not less than five per centum upon the par value of said stocks; and that the moneys so invested shall constitute a perpetual fund, the capital of which shall remain forever undiminished, (except so far as may be provided in section fifth of this act) and the interest of which shall be inviolably appropriated, by each State which may take and claim the benefit of this act, to the endowment, support, and maintenance of at least one college where the leading object shall be, without excluding other scientific and classical studies, and including military tactics, to teach such branches of learning as are related to agriculture and the mechanic arts, in such manner as the legislatures of the States may respectively prescribe, in order to promote the liberal and practical education of the industrial classes in the several pursuits and professions in life.

Federal policy enunciated in the Morrill acts was to give land grants to *higher* institutions, to state the principal objectives of the education for which the grants were to be used, and to require an accounting of the money spent. "Unconditional" grants as the *only* policy were considered insufficient to cover all needs.

2. Smith-Hughes Act

A number of Congressional acts have authorized federal grants-in-aid to vocational education. The grants, in all cases, have been

> The term "land grant" is significant, implying that land was the foundation on which the present structure of agricultural and mechanical and also military colleges has been erected. It would be more accurate, however, to call them "land bait" colleges, because the grants were relatively small moneywise. They were large enough, however, to induce the states to set up a system of colleges which are supported partly by state taxation and partly by federal funds. . . .
>
> The purpose is to show how a relatively small gift of frontier land was used to establish a system of education that is nationwide, closely integrated, and now supported almost entirely by taxation, both state and federal. And it was created and raised by a little wedge of frontier land.
>
> From Walter Prescott Webb, *The Great Frontier* (Boston: Houghton Mifflin Company, 1952), pp. 402, 404. Quoted by permission of Houghton Mifflin Company.

large and the effects upon public education have been far-reaching. The Smith-Hughes Act of 1917 was one of the first, and also one of the most influential, of a series of acts that gave aid to vocational education offered in the public high schools. It is a fairly typical example of how the federal government engages in educational activity.

Under the Smith-Hughes Act the federal government subsidizes high-school vocational education in agriculture, home economics, and industrial education. The act also makes provisions for the preparation of teachers of those subjects. Money is apportioned to the states on the basis of total population, and in order to receive it "the state or local community, or both, shall spend an equal amount" for this work. Each state and local community is required also to meet certain other standards. Congress has never failed to make the appropriation for these purposes but it could, of course, refuse at any time.

Certainly many favorable effects have accrued from the Smith-Hughes Act and from similar legislation. High schools have become more conscious of the great need for expansion in the vocational field. New instructional materials and methods have been developed. Shops and laboratories in the high schools have, for the first time, been well built and adequately equipped. Education and salaries of the high school teachers of vocational subjects have been greatly improved. Improving salaries for those who participate in the vocational education program at the state level also improves the personnel serving at that level.

Vocational education requires extensive and costly equipment. The pupils in the Aviation High School, Long Island City, are studying SNJ aircraft. (Board of Education, New York City)

Some believe that the principle of a federal-state or federal-local matching of school funds leads to unwholesome effects including federal domination. The power of a federal bureaucracy over the state programs—vocational or other—is considered a threat to the old principle of state-administered, locally controlled high schools.

Since the teaching profession has now become reconciled to federal controls over vocational education, it may, in the future, more easily adjust to federal control in some other areas of education. Whatever the future trend may be, the Smith-Hughes Act has afforded one example, among several, of the operation of federal control over certain parts of a program offered in the American secondary schools. The rapid industrialization of the nation since 1900 and the earlier neglect of vocational education by the high schools have been given as justification for the new policy. The arguments have been of sufficient weight to assure that the Smith-Hughes Act and kindred vocational acts will continue to operate.

The federal government has not, as yet, formulated a single policy with reference to granting aid to education. Earlier, it followed the policy of "unconditional" grants-in-aid. Later, notably in the Morrill Act of 1862 and the Smith-Hughes Act of 1917, the federal government stipulated certain conditions that the states, or some other unit of school administration, had to meet before aid would be available. Some believe that the federal government should define an overall, general policy as a guide in making future grants-in-aid to education.

Recent Federal Money Grants

1. Measures Passed During the Depression

During the depression of the thirties, grants to education were mostly outright, with no requirement of matching funds. Laws set forth conditions under which funds must be used but did not exert control over the programs.

Vocational education is provided in this fine machine shop. Federal aid is available to schools offering such training. (Board of Education, St. Louis)

The National Youth Administration was organized during the depression to provide aid for needy high school, college, and university students so that they might continue their education. The funds were administered and the work was assigned by the individual school in which the services were used. The federal grants-in-aid went directly to the high school or college students through institutional channels.

The Civilian Conservation Corps also was an emergency depression measure. Its purpose was "relief of unemployment through performance of useful public work." Camps were organized for young men, and an education program was made an integral part of the plan. The camps were under the administrative control of the army. So was the education program.

The school lunch program was an emergency relief program also started during the depression. With the passage of the National School Lunch Act of 1946, however, it became a regular part of federal participation in education. This act was designed "to safeguard the health and well-being of the Nation's children and to encourage the domestic consumption of nutritious agricultural commodities and other foods." Under this act, the federal government provides the local schools, through the states, both direct grants of surplus commodities for use in school lunchrooms and money to facilitate the distribution and use of these food products. This enables local public schools to provide federally subsidized, low-cost lunches to their pupils. Although this is a direct form of federal aid to education, it was, in the beginning, designed primarily to help the farmers rather than the school children. Its value has been such as to assure its continuance as an accepted federal policy.

There were numerous other federal programs of education initiated during the period of the depression, including the establishment of nursery schools, classes in avocational and leisure-time activities, special programs, and lectures. Funds for school buildings were also provided under the Works Progress Administration.

2. Measures Passed Preceding and During World War II

In the period immediately preceding World War II and during the war, disruptions growing out of such emergencies as the demand for many people with certain highly specialized training, the 're-location of masses of people, and the large-scale employment of mothers led the federal government to conduct some emergency

This school provides pupils with well-balanced lunches at nominal cost. In some localities the federal government subsidizes lunch programs through the use of surplus food, when such aid is requested by the school. (Board of Education, Columbus, Ohio)

education programs and to make grants for the administration of others. For example, the Lanham Act, passed in 1941, provided general appropriations for training war plant workers under the direction of the United States Office of Education, for constructing school plants in areas that were overburdened because of federal activity, and for maintaining child-care centers to take care of the children of employed parents.

3. GI Bill of Rights

In terms of influence and cost, perhaps the greatest federal participation in education is contained in laws collectively and popularly known as the "GI Bill of Rights." The program began with the Vocational Rehabilitation Act and the Servicemen's Readjustment Act signed by President Roosevelt in 1944. Since then other laws have been added. In the peak year, 1948, nearly three billion dollars were spent in subsidizing programs of education for veterans. Incidentally, only very rarely was any charge raised of "government interference" in the educational programs of high schools and colleges that were involved in this GI schooling. The GI Bill of Rights guarantees to veterans payment of tuition as well as payment for board and room for a specified number of months, based on length of military service rendered. The GI Bill has enabled millions of young men and women to attend high schools, colleges, universities, specialized schools, and adult education classes throughout the land. Several hundred also have studied abroad under the GI Bill. In addition to increasing the numbers enrolled in our schools, the GI Bill tended to change the character of our school population. It became commonplace for married men and men with families to be full-time students. Temporary housing for young families mushroomed on college campuses. The GI's were older and more serious. Their presence raised the age level of those in school and gave an impetus to adult education. The full impact of the GI program of the federal government is incalculable.

4. Federal Aid to Higher Education

Millions of dollars are now flowing annually from agencies of the federal government into educational agencies and institutions of higher learning. The National Defense Education Act, signed into law on September 2, 1958, is designed to strengthen American education at all levels. Under this law, up to September 2, 1963, the federal government had already expended $800 million to assist educational institutions of higher education, both public and nonpublic, and to aid state agencies with programs believed important to the nation's security. This included, for example, $330 million assigned to a Student Loan Program, 70 percent of which was lent to students of superior ability who intended to teach in the elementary and secondary schools. Another $65 million was spent on the education of school counselors. Over the five-year period, 1958–1963, $181 million was paid to the states and territories to strengthen instruction in science, mathematics, and modern languages in the public elementary and high schools. The number of language laboratories in public high schools rose from 46 in 1958 to approximately 6,000 in 1963. Equally large amounts were spent in improving other services. Periodically the U.S. Department of Health, Education, and Welfare issues a report on the National Defense

Education Act, a report that describes in detail the many purposes
for which federal funds are allocated. The report gives a vivid picture of the extensive scale of this federal excursion into a strengthening of American education.

Public Reaction to Federal Grants to Education

The practice of making federal grants is well established, widespread, and diversified. It seems, then, that there can be no argument
about whether we should have federal aid to education. Controversy is over such issues as how much shall we have, how shall it be
administered, what shall be the policy regarding to whom grants
should be made, and should the federal government pay all the
costs or should the costs be shared with other governmental units.

Some people oppose further increasing federal funds for public
education on the ground that federal control will inevitably follow.
They feel that even though federal funds are seriously needed, it is
better to go without them than to run the danger of the loss of local
freedom in the conduct of education.

Other people point out that federal funds are needed but add
that some measure of control is also needed because the funds must
be protected from waste by the unwise and the unscrupulous. They
point out that state funds allocated to local school districts have not
appreciably curtailed local control of education. Curtailment need
not follow as an inevitable consequence.

On the other hand, there are people who believe that federal
funds are seriously needed and the funds can and should be supplied with a reasonable degree of federal control. They believe that
by allocating the funds for a broad, general purpose which the individual states can interpret without interference, by deciding the
amount a state should receive on some kind of objective basis, and
by requiring an audit, the interests of the children could be served
without any damaging federal control.

In 1957, a Roper survey of public opinion on federal aid to
schools reported that 16 percent of those surveyed favored local
financing entirely, 30 percent favored federal aid for school buildings but for nothing more, and 43 percent favored federal aid for
school buildings and teachers' salaries. Roper's conclusion was, "If
the federal government were to take its courage in both hands and
decide tomorrow morning that our crippling educational shortages

were something for which it must now take a heavy responsibility for the first time in the history of our Republic, the heavens would not fall. More people favor such a course than favor any other single one."[2]

EDUCATIONAL ACTIVITY AT THE FEDERAL LEVEL

Education for National Defense

The United States Military Academy at West Point, New York, the United States Naval Academy at Annapolis, Maryland, the United States Merchant Marine Academy at Kings Point, Long Island, New York, and the United States Air Force Academy at Colorado Springs, Colorado, are all supported entirely by the federal government, and each is operated by an appropriate branch of the federal government. These are a few examples of federal education conducted for reasons of defense. The total program for such education is extensive.

Education under Special Federal Jurisdictions

Inasmuch as the District of Columbia is not part of any state, the operation of its education program is left to the federal government. Congress makes all the laws that govern the District of Columbia, including those that apply to the schools, makes all the appropriations, and provides the means for raising revenues, which are collected by a combination of direct taxes and direct appropriations from the federal treasury.

The citizens have the right to vote only in national elections for the president of the United States, and, therefore, those who are placed in control of the schools are not responsible to the community to the same degree as in public schools that are part of a state system. The public schools in Washington, D.C., according to an act of Congress, operate under the authority of a board of education that is comprised of nine members, of which three are women and, customarily, three are Negroes. The members are appointed for a term

[2] The findings of this survey appeared on May 12, 1957, in a syndicated newspaper column, "The Public Pulse," syndicated by the National Newspaper Syndicate in Chicago.

FIG. 13.1   1959 PUBLIC SCHOOL INCOME AND EXPENSES

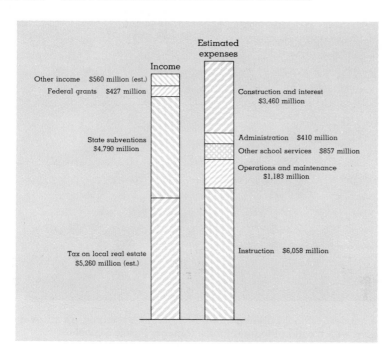

of three years by the justices of the District Court of the United States. The board appoints a superintendent of schools who performs the functions usually assigned such an officer.

Where the federal government has complete control, it shows its skill and reveals its attitudes toward public education. Generalizing from the Washington, D.C., school system, we may say that federally controlled systems operate about as efficiently and in much the same manner as do public schools in the rest of the country. None of the federally operated schools has ever been thought of as providing a model or pattern to follow.

The federal government also assists in promotion of education in the federal reservations, territories, outlying possessions, and United States trusteeship territories. It aids other countries through the United States Point Four Program, the Foreign Operations Administration, the United Nations Technical Assistance Program, and the Peace Corps. The widely varying educational problems involved testify to the extensive range of federal activity in education.

Handsome, modern school buildings like this one are springing up all over the country, often with the aid of federal funds. (Lincoln Public Schools)

Individual Schools

All of the executive departments of the federal government engage in some kind of educational activity. Some of them operate schools to train government personnel and to help improve the personnel once they are in the employ of the federal government. The Department of State, for example, gives instruction to all newly appointed diplomatic and consular officers. The Treasury Department maintains a training school for the Coast Guard service, one for stenographers, a correspondence school for the employees in the Bureau of Internal Revenue, and a number of others which the department considers essential to the proper performance of its functions. The Department of Justice's school to train its personnel and the schools maintained by the Social Security Board are other examples of the numerous individual schools set up and administered by various departments of the federal government. Their educational activities are of great magnitude, affecting in some form well over a million civilians.

Howard University, in Washington, D.C., is a private university, although it is supported almost entirely by federal appropriations. It has the second largest enrollment of foreign students among American universities. Founders Library is shown above. (Howard University, Washington, D.C.)

THE UNITED STATES OFFICE OF EDUCATION

The chief educational agency of the federal government is the United States Office of Education. In addition, there are numerous other federal agencies that render service to education. In fact, every department of the federal government may be said to exist partly for purposes of giving service to the public—service that includes providing educational information to any citizen who may request it.

The legal foundation for the United States Office of Education was laid in 1867:

> Be it enacted by the Senate and the House of Representatives of the United States of America, in Congress assembled, That there shall be established at the city of Washington, a department of education, for the purpose of collecting such statistics and facts as shall show the condition and progress of education in the several states and territories, and of diffusing such information respecting the organization and management of schools and school systems and methods of teaching as shall aid the people of the United States in the establishment and maintenance of efficient school systems, and otherwise promote the cause of education throughout the country.

39th Congress, 2nd Session:
Approved by President Andrew Johnson March 2, 1867.

Two years later the department was reduced to an "Office of Education" in the Department of the Interior. In 1870, the office was renamed the Bureau of Education and that title was retained until 1929, when the title of Office of Education was restored. In 1939, the Office of Education was transferred from the Department of the Interior to the newly created Federal Security Agency. In 1953, the Office of Education became a part of the newly created Department of Health, Education, and Welfare, with a secretary in the President's Cabinet. In its present setting it receives greater recognition than previously.

Since 1918, bills for the establishment of a separate federal department of education and a secretary of education in the President's Cabinet have been proposed again and again. Those who favor these proposals believe that, at present, public education does not have sufficient prestige in the federal government and that a separate department could more effectively articulate the achievements and outstanding problems of public education. Opponents point out that placing a secretary of education in the President's Cabinet would move education into the arena of "politics" on a national scale and perhaps increase the danger of federal control over state and local education.

The main responsibilities of the Office of Education at present, as enumerated in the law, are collecting statistics and facts, diffusing information about schools, and otherwise promoting the cause of education. As one of the commissioners has said, "The U.S. Office of Education is not an operating agency. Our main task is to gather facts and interpret them for the people." The Office diffuses information through a number of publications including reports of special studies, *A Biennial Survey of Education,* and the magazine, *School Life.* Many of its publications are available free or at a nominal cost from the Superintendent of Documents, Government Printing Office in Washington. Despite the fact that the Office of Education does not have the legal power to require state and local school officials to provide the information on which its reports are based, its statistical reports are widely recognized as among the best available.

For the use of its staff and of any citizen, the Office of Education maintains the most complete library on education in the world. Among its numerous services, the library staff has prepared bibliographies on many educational topics and will, upon request, and as far as its time and its other resources permit, prepare other bibliographies. In addition, diffusion of information is achieved through conferences of educational and lay leaders, exhibits, addresses by staff members, radio and television broadcasts, exchange of books, letters answering inquiries, and loans of audio-visual materials.

The third major duty of the Office—"and otherwise promote the cause of education throughout the country"—is almost limitless. The Office administers numerous programs dealing with special phases of education—education for the blind, vocational education, and vocational rehabilitation, for instance. Funds appropriated by Congress for special activities, such as land-grant colleges and vocational education, are administered through the Office of Education. Through its exchange program of students and teachers, the Office actively promotes international education.

The regular full-time staff of the Office of Education has increased from five workers in 1867 to several hundred. Practically all of the regular employees of the Office are under the civil service laws. Each is regarded as an expert in his field.

Local school staffs should be aware of the assistance offered by the Office of Education. It renders valuable educational services which have not always been fully utilized.

THE UNITED STATES COMMISSIONER
OF EDUCATION

At the head of the United States Office of Education is the Commissioner of Education, who is appointed with the consent of the Senate by the President, upon the recommendation of the Secretary of Health, Education, and Welfare. He serves an indefinite term. Sometimes a change in presidents is followed by the appointment of a new commissioner, although only 13 commissioners have served under 18 presidents.

The Commissioner's duties are listed in the act that established the Office of Education. In addition, his duties have been expanded during the years to include special tasks assigned by the President and imposed by Congressional enactments, as well as voluntary cooperation with numerous educational agencies.

JUDICIAL CONTROLS

While public education is a matter over which each state is sovereign, there are certain limitations on state action. State educational policy is in a most vital way subject to control by the Supreme Court of the United States.

Any state legislation, including educational legislation, is subject to review by the Supreme Court. If the Supreme Court decides that the law violates a provision of the United States Constitution, the law is declared unconstitutional and invalid. The authority to invalidate legislation affecting education is derived chiefly from the following provision of the Fourteenth Amendment:

No state shall make or enforce any law which shall abridge the privileges or immunities of citizens of the United States; nor shall any state deprive any person of life, liberty, or property without due process of law nor deny to any person within its jurisdiction the equal protection of the laws.

The Supreme Court of the United States is the final judge as to whether a person has been deprived of liberty or property. Since the terms "liberty" and "property" are extremely comprehensive, all manner of social and economic legislation, including educational legislation, may be invalidated. Obviously, state educational policy is in a large measure subject to control by the judges of the highest of our federal courts.

Supreme Court decisions have influenced the states in such problems as the relationship between schools and religion, uniformity of treatment of different races in the schools, and the matter of contractual relations with teachers. None of these matters has to do with federal power over education, but rather with federal responsibility for protecting individual rights.

When the Supreme Court hands down a decision that affects the policies of public education, the decision itself constitutes an interesting public statement of educational policy. The decision is always accompanied by the reasoning and the analyses behind it. These matters, broadly circulated by the press, radio, and television, serve to educate the American public effectively about fundamental issues in public education. In this way the Supreme Court has served as an educator to all the people of the United States.

The McCollum decision (1949) is one example of a Supreme Court decision concerned with the relationships of schools and religion. It grew out of the protest of Mrs. Vashti McCollum, a professed atheist, that her seven-year-old son, who attended public schools in Champaign, Illinois, was being subjected to ridicule and scorn because he remained in the schoolroom when the other children left to take part in religious exercises and training currently provided by the churches of the city on time released by the schools for this purpose. The school authorities, and then a series of lower courts, ruled against her plea that "released-time" practices be outlawed. The case finally went to the Supreme Court, which ruled against the released-time practices followed in this particular school system.

Another decision with respect to religious education in the public schools was made in 1952 in the Zorach case in New York City. This decision declared the practice of released time constitutional. The opinions in the two cases were not contradictory. Public schools may not be used to promote religious instruction, as was thought to be the case in Champaign. But where the public schools do no more than accommodate their schedules to a program of outside religious instruction, as was the case in New York City, such action is deemed constitutional. Thus, religious instruction on released time is legal under certain conditions. Sometimes the distinctions between legal and illegal practices are so fine that only an experienced judge can make them.

Another conflict that has come to the Supreme Court is over uniformity of treatment of different races. The prevailing pattern of education in the states of the South has been separate schools for Negro children. Both white and Negro schools have been under the same board of education and the same superintendent of schools. They have been financed by a common tax structure. In many communities, however, there have been inferior buildings, old equipment, and poorly paid teachers for the Negro children. The pattern of separate schools was made more permanent when the United States Supreme Court, in 1896, handed down a decision in the famous Plessy v. Ferguson case. The theory underlying this decision, that separate but equal facilities did not violate the Constitution, gave the highest governmental sanction to the pattern of organizational segregation but not to any practice that denied Negroes equal educational opportunities with the white people. Any school district could segregate the races if it maintained schools that were equal. The separate-but-equal doctrine became the legal basis of segregated schools.

Many cases over the right to segregate the races have entered the courts since then. On May 17, 1954, the United States Supreme Court handed down a decision that declared an end to the segregation of school children on a racial basis:

> We conclude that in the field of public education the doctrine of "separate but equal" has no place. Separate educational facilities are inherently unequal. Therefore, we hold that the plaintiffs and others similarly situated for whom the actions have been brought are, by reason of segregation complained of, deprived of the equal protection of the laws guaranteed by the Fourteenth Amendment.

When Chief Justice Warren announced the decision, he said that the court realized the decree presented problems "of considerable complexity." Many of those "problems" still remain and will probably remain for many years, but in time desegregation in the American public schools will be practiced everywhere. By the fall of 1963 approximately 37 percent of the 1,119 biracial school districts in the South had a degree of desegregation. Of the 140 biracial districts that desegregated, 119 did so voluntarily.

On June 25, 1962, the Supreme Court registered a decision on the question of religion in the public schools. The Board of Education of Union Free School District No. 9, of New Hyde Park, New York, directed the district's principal to have the following prayer said aloud by the teachers and pupils at the beginning of each school day.

Almighty God, we acknowledge our dependence upon Thee, and we beg Thy blessings upon us, our parents, our teachers and our country.

This daily ritual was backed by action of the state board of regents, thus making it a statement of authority by the State of New York. The parents of 10 pupils brought action against the regulation, contending that it violated both the New York State Constitution and the Constitution of the United States. The state courts of New York ruled the regulation to be constitutional. The Supreme Court of the United States held it to be unconstitutional.

That the Supreme Court has a vital influence over education in the United States cannot be denied. It makes the final decisions in many important cases as to what the laws pertaining to education mean. Since most Americans believe that law and not men shall rule, that known rules of procedures and not the whims of politicians or powerful pressure groups shall control in all exercise of governmental power, the judges of the Supreme Court are the final authorities who settle many concrete educational issues.

THE FUTURE

Equalization of Education

There is strong sentiment among educators favorable to having the federal government expand its efforts to equalize educational opportunities throughout the nation through some program of federal grants to the states. There are, admittedly, great variations among the states in the quality of public education furnished and in their abilities to support public education. It is argued that the federal government has a responsibility to reduce such differences.

The quality of education furnished is not determined solely by the amount of money spent for education. The amount of money spent on education is, nevertheless, one very important factor. Perhaps it is the best single gauge to the quality of education. Those states that maintain inferior school systems are usually states that can raise little money, have little valuable school property, pay unreasonably low salaries to the teaching personnel, employ less well-qualified teachers, and assign large classes and excessive teaching loads to the teachers. According to data distributed by the NEA, New York spent $705 for each pupil in ADA (average daily attendance) in 1963–1964. During the same year Mississippi spent $241. The median expenditure in the United States was approximately $447. By no combination of compensating factors could Mississippi have offered its children educational opportunities equal to those of New York.

Considerable variation in wealth characterizes the states of the Union. For example, in 1961 Mississippi ranked fiftieth as measured in terms of per capita income. Its per capita income was $1,229, while in Delaware, which ranked first, the figure was $3,013.

In 1962–1963, 18 states paid annual salaries of $6,000 and above, while the average for the United States was $5,940. The discrepancy between the states paying the higher salaries and those paying lower salaries is shown on the chart, Fig. 13.2; the lowest average salary is only 49.3 percent of the highest.

States also vary in birth rate and the ratio of school-age children to the adult population. Here again Mississippi is in the least fortunate position. In 1960, Mississippi had the largest number of school-age children per 1,000 adults—660. In the United States as a whole

FIG. 13.2   ESTIMATED AVERAGE SALARY OF CLASSROOM TEACHERS, 1962-1963

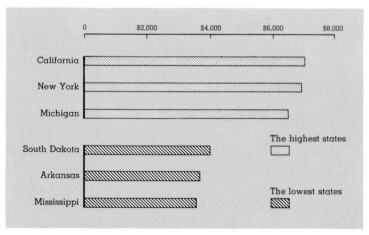

(Data from NEA Research Division, Research Report 1963–R12)

FIG. 13.3 ESTIMATED CURRENT EXPENDITURE PER PUPIL IN AVERAGE DAILY ATTENDANCE, 1963-1964

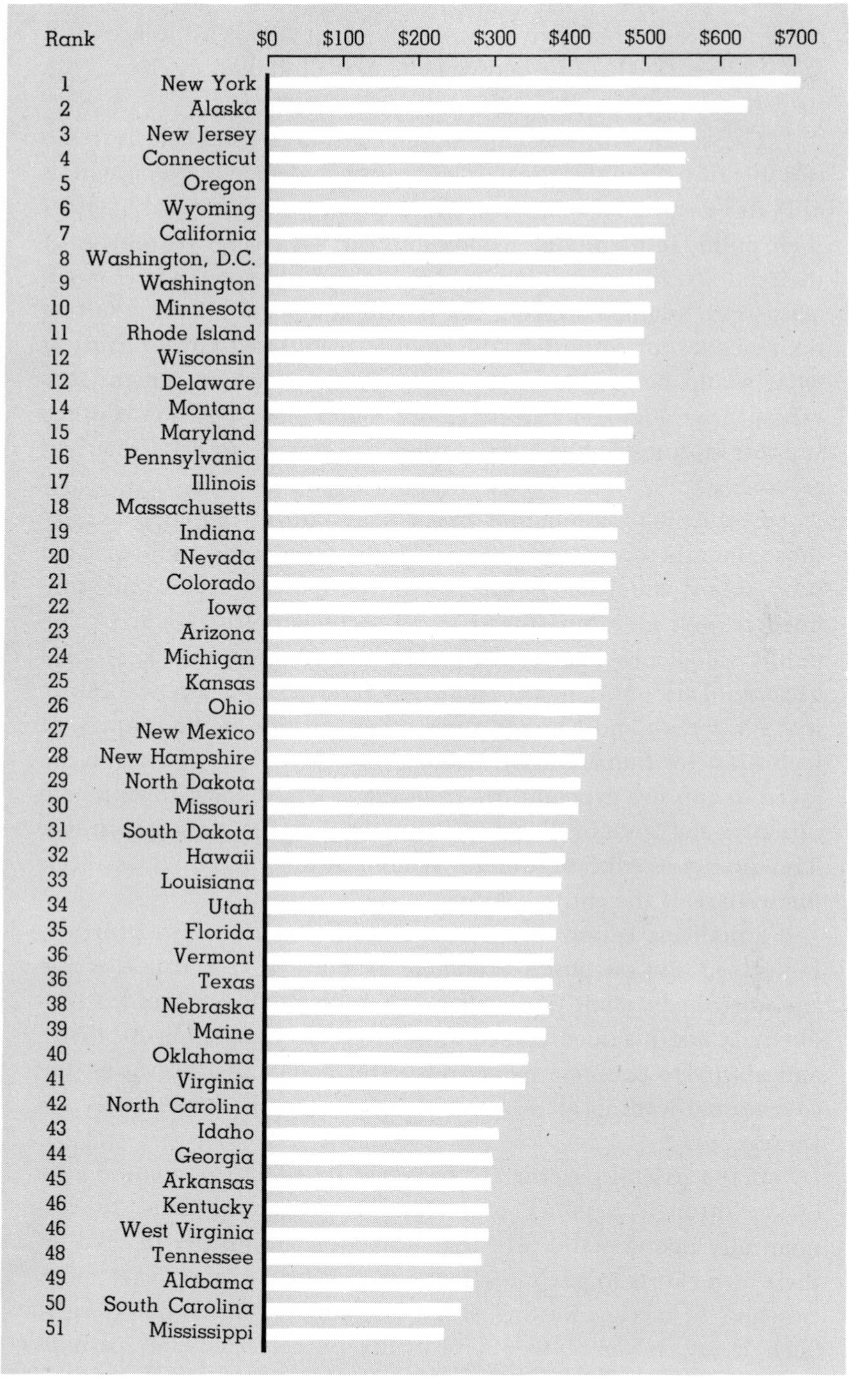

Rank		Expenditure
1	New York	
2	Alaska	
3	New Jersey	
4	Connecticut	
5	Oregon	
6	Wyoming	
7	California	
8	Washington, D.C.	
9	Washington	
10	Minnesota	
11	Rhode Island	
12	Wisconsin	
12	Delaware	
14	Montana	
15	Maryland	
16	Pennsylvania	
17	Illinois	
18	Massachusetts	
19	Indiana	
20	Nevada	
21	Colorado	
22	Iowa	
23	Arizona	
24	Michigan	
25	Kansas	
26	Ohio	
27	New Mexico	
28	New Hampshire	
29	North Dakota	
30	Missouri	
31	South Dakota	
32	Hawaii	
33	Louisiana	
34	Utah	
35	Florida	
36	Vermont	
36	Texas	
38	Nebraska	
39	Maine	
40	Oklahoma	
41	Virginia	
42	North Carolina	
43	Idaho	
44	Georgia	
45	Arkansas	
46	Kentucky	
46	West Virginia	
48	Tennessee	
49	Alabama	
50	South Carolina	
51	Mississippi	

(Data from NEA Research Division, Research Report 1962–R1)

there were 490 school-age children—children between the ages of 5 and 17—per 1,000 adults between the ages of 22 and 64. New York had the smallest number—410 per 1,000 adults.

The states with the most limited resources available for education must meet the greatest educational demand. Perhaps it is only to be expected that these states enroll a smaller percentage of their pupils in the public schools and carry a smaller percentage of their pupils to the completion of a high school education. Even if Mississippi adopted a model tax system and spent all the resulting tax revenues for education, the amount would still fall far short of what would be needed to support an average school system. It is evident from Fig. 12.4 that the poorer states make a greater effort to support education, but even so they are unable to raise sufficient revenue.

Because our population has a high rate of mobility and because the rate seems to be increasing, the social evils resulting from substandard education in one section of the country are not confined to that area but spread to all sections of the country. The public school problems of New York and Chicago are accentuated because of the substandard education received by many who move into New York and Chicago from other sections of the country. It is not just for humanitarian reasons that the people of Oregon are asked to approve expenditures from the federal budget to help education in the State of Florida. It is more than mere neighborliness. The quality of education in any section of the United States affects the welfare of the entire country.

Equalizing education on a national basis, it is argued further, is justified also on purely economic grounds. If it is true that the amount of education possessed by an individual increases his productivity and his other contributions to society as well as his desire and ability to consume more and better goods, then elevating the educational level in all sections of the country is economically advantageous.

If the federal government increases its efforts to equalize education through a policy of making larger grants-in-aid to economically poorer states, will that lead local authorities to relax in their own efforts to pay for schools? Will it be a case of "easy come, easy go," of careless wasting of federal money? This is one danger. Such laxity, however, would probably be corrected and perhaps prevented by an objective formula and a definite audit procedure. The Hoover Commission made this statement:

Fig. 13.4 Estimated Public School Enrollment as a Percentage of Total Civilian Population, 1961-1962

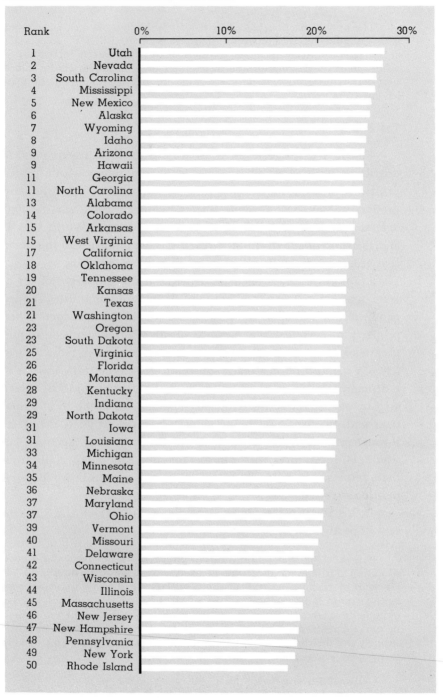

Rank		0%	10%	20%	30%
1	Utah				
2	Nevada				
3	South Carolina				
4	Mississippi				
5	New Mexico				
6	Alaska				
7	Wyoming				
8	Idaho				
9	Arizona				
9	Hawaii				
11	Georgia				
11	North Carolina				
13	Alabama				
14	Colorado				
15	Arkansas				
15	West Virginia				
17	California				
18	Oklahoma				
19	Tennessee				
20	Kansas				
21	Texas				
21	Washington				
23	Oregon				
23	South Dakota				
25	Virginia				
26	Florida				
26	Montana				
28	Kentucky				
29	Indiana				
29	North Dakota				
31	Iowa				
31	Louisiana				
33	Michigan				
34	Minnesota				
35	Maine				
36	Nebraska				
37	Maryland				
37	Ohio				
39	Vermont				
40	Missouri				
41	Delaware				
42	Connecticut				
43	Wisconsin				
44	Illinois				
45	Massachusetts				
46	New Jersey				
47	New Hampshire				
48	Pennsylvania				
49	New York				
50	Rhode Island				

(Data from NEA Research Division, Research Report 1963–R1)

The only restriction placed by federal legislation on such educational grants should be the provision that every State, when it accepts the grant, agrees to make each year to the federal headquarters for education a full report on all questions on which the federal headquarters for education may require information concerning the manner in which the State has used the grant.[3]

Tax Policy

For the federal government to tax wealth where it exists and to distribute funds where they are needed is in harmony with accepted principles of taxation. The federal government has tapped the most productive source of revenue—the individual income tax. A huge federal debt, made much larger by efforts to finance World War II and the subsequent continuing defense program, leads to the belief that federal taxes will probably be high for many years.

Local government agencies depend on the property tax for at least one-half of their total revenue. In most communities the expenditure for schools is the biggest item in the local budget. When property owners feel the pressure of adverse business conditions, they tend to demand relief first in property taxes. A reduction in school expenditures is a ready source of relief. The worst aspects of a demand for decreased school costs, it is believed, could be alleviated by having the states assume a greater share of the local school costs and, in turn, having the federal government assist the states through a policy of equalization of the cost burden. Such a plan would, however, meet with considerable opposition, especially from those reluctant to minimize local community responsibility for local public education.

In his State of the Union Message of 1949, President Truman said in part:

It is shocking that millions of our children are not receiving a good education. Millions of them are in overcrowded, obsolete buildings. We are short of teachers because teachers' salaries are too low to attract new teachers or to hold the ones we have. All these school problems will become more acute as a result of the tremendous increase in the enrollment in our elementary schools in the next few years. I cannot repeat too strongly my desire for prompt federal financial aid to the states to help them operate and maintain their school systems.[4]

[3] National Advisory Committee on Education, *op. cit.*, p. 38.
[4] As quoted in Malcolm S. MacLean and Edwin A. Lee, *Change and Process in Education* (New York: Holt, Rinehart and Winston, Inc., 1956), p. 182.

Truman was supported by the great majority of professional voluntary organizations and by leading laymen. He was backed also by his Commission on Higher Education, which said:

> The federal government assumes responsibility for supplementing state and local efforts in military defense against the Nation's enemies without; surely it may as justifiably assume responsibility for supplementing State and local efforts against educational deficiencies and inequalities that are democracy's enemies within.[5]

Of course, if the federal government's spending for education is increased without a corresponding increase in federal taxes, there must be a shift in spending. Money will need to be diverted from some other activities that are now publicly financed. Relative values will need to be reassessed. If we agree that education is vital to the welfare and defense of the nation, it should not be difficult to elevate education to a higher position on the scale of federal budget appropriations. To do this, however, will call for more than written reports from the commissions.

Statement of Basic Policy

If any one conclusion stands out from our review of the federal government's participation and activities in education, it is that there has, in the nation's past practice, been little consistency in procedures or purpose and little uniformity in policy. Grants-in-aid have sometimes been made without strings attached. In other instances the states have been asked to match federal funds granted. Grants have been made for higher education and for special fields on the secondary level. Grants have been made to ease emergencies in agriculture and other fields. Grants have been made to individuals. There seems to have been no pattern, no consistent trend, no emergent policy. It has been suggested that in order to aid in formulating future plans for the federal government in relation to education, a broad and basic statement of national policy be enunciated. This, it is believed, would serve as a guide to educators and legislators, contribute to stability, and lend direction and assurance to those involved in various aspects of the federal government's education program and activities.

What are some of the matters upon which clarification of posi-

5 U.S. President's Commission on Higher Education, *Higher Education for American Democracy* (Washington, D.C.: U.S. Government Printing Office, 1947), Vol. I, p. 103.

tion is needed? It would seem reasonable to expect that government aims should be stated. The statement of basic policy might state in broad terms what the federal government desires to achieve by way of educational opportunities for all children in the nation. The policy statement should also set forth general procedures and types of activities to be carried on in implementing the general aims. The basic and general terms of the statement of policy will give it qualities of endurance and make it adaptable to changing social conditions and to national emergencies. Such a statement of policy will provide a stable foundation and a guide for lawmakers and will encourage a measure of consistency in future federal participation in education.

The difficulties of formulating a statement of basic policy are numerous and sizable. In a democracy the frequent changes in Congress tend to result in inconsistencies and in activities that do not fit into a stable and long-term plan. Then, there is the question of who would draw up so important a statement of national policy.

Perhaps Congress, which has the final say, might itself issue a statement of policy with regard to federal participation in education. To date, however, there has been little unanimity among members of the Congress in this matter. Since World War I there has not been a session of Congress that has not had at least one bill providing money grants to the states for state school support. As yet, however, none of the bills has been enacted into law, although one of them passed the Senate in 1948 and again in 1949.

As we have stated, there has been considerable support for the proposal that a cabinet office be created to be solely devoted to education. The suggestion that a board of education at the national level be organized has received the support of the NEA and other influential groups. Perhaps the present organization, which includes a Commissioner of Education and an Office of Education under the Department of Health, Education, and Welfare, is potentially equipped to draw up a statement of federal policy. If this agency were endowed with adequate authority and were assigned considerable administrative responsibility, it could, perhaps, give the guidance that is needed and give it with sufficient weight to make it effective.

Another possibility is the appointment of a special group with specific responsibility for formulating a general policy and for making recommendations. This group might be something like the

Hoover Commission—a group of carefully selected individuals who were appointed by President Hoover. President Hoover in his annual message to Congress on December 3, 1929, said:

> In view of the considerable difference of opinion as to policies which should be pursued by the Federal Government with respect to education, I have appointed a committee representative of the important educational associations and others to investigate and present recommendations.[6]

In general, the recommendations that were made by the Hoover Commission are approved by the majority of educators today. Each president since the Hoover Commission made its report in 1931 has called together a special group to study the nation's education. The weakness of such commissions has been their lack of influence on the legislators. It is the lawmaking body of the federal government that ultimately decides on the future of education in our country. Any special group—a national board of education, a cabinet department, a strengthened Office of Education, or any other kind of functionary —can only be as effective as its impact on Congress.

This brings us to the responsibility of individual citizens—and particularly members of the teaching profession. The whole business of the federal program of education is not something remote, something complicated and removed from teachers and parents. Teachers owe it to themselves and to their profession to be acquainted with government activities in education on the local, state, and federal levels. It is important that teachers understand current political issues regarding such matters as federal support of education, taxation for education, and equalization of educational opportunities and that they be willing and able to discuss and interpret these issues for local citizens. It is this "grass roots" approach to the Congress through local voters that is the responsibility of individual citizens.

SUMMARY

It is generally agreed that the federal government should continue but improve its program of equalizing education throughout the nation. A broad statement of acceptable policy produced by a competent authority is a sound preliminary step to future plans. Such a statement will give direction and information to the Con-

---

[6] National Advisory Committee on Education, *op. cit.*, p. 1.

TABLE 13.1 DISTRIBUTION OF POWERS AND FUNCTIONS OVER SCHOOL MATTERS

LOCAL, STATE, AND FEDERAL LEVELS

	Local	State	Federal
Organization and Program			
1. Establishment of a school district	Actually establishes	Authorizes establishment	
2. Alteration of school district boundaries	Usually county superintendent	Authorizes procedure	
3. Selection of school district officials	Voters	Authorizes terms and procedures	
4. Foundation program		Specifies	
5. Program beyond foundation program	Decides		
Teaching Staff			
1. Minimum qualifications to teach		State law	
2. Issuance of teaching certificates		State superintendent	
3. Employment of teachers	Full control		
4. Teacher salaries	Determines	State minima	
5. Teacher tenure	Control in specific cases	State law regulates	
6. Dismissal of teachers	Control in specific cases	State law regulates	
7. Teacher promotion	Decides policies and promotes individuals		
8. Teaching load	Determines		
9. Maintenance workers	Employs		
Pupils			
1. Compulsory school attendance	Enforces	State law	
2. Assignment of pupils to school	Full control		

3. Admission policies	Determines		
4. Classification of pupils	Decides policies and classifies pupils		
5. Promotion of pupils	Decides policies and promotes pupils		
6. The curriculum	Determines	Sets foundation program	
7. Instructional methods	Determines		
8. Selection of textbooks	Full Control	Approved lists in some states	
9. Charges pupils pay	Decides	Decides in some states	
10. Expulsion of pupils	Full control		
11. Health regulations	Health department	Power to supersede	
12. Bus routes	Plans and operates	General regulations	
13. School lunch program	Administers		May finance in part
14. School census	Share	Share	

Finance

1. School levy of real estate taxes	Determines	May set limits	
2. School budget	Establishes	May review	
3. Finances for school budget	Important share	Important share	Minor share
4. Costs of academic instruction	Share	Share	
5. New school buildings	Decides location and design; finances	Minor share of costs	Share of costs in defense localities
6. Costs of vocational education	Minor share	Share	Major share
7. Education of exceptional children	Share	Share	
8. Education of the blind	Share	All in some states	
9. Education of the deaf	Share	All in some states	
10. Education of delinquents and incorrigibles	Counties in some states	Usually entirely	
11. Teacher pension system	Finances	Sets rules and eligibility	

gress, and from Congress will come decisions about the future of the federal government in the education picture.

QUESTIONS

1. What are some of the educational problems of the federal government that result from having three levels of government?
2. What legal principles have been developed by the federal government to guide it in its administration of education? How do you explain the lack of uniformity in these principles?
3. How is the education authority organized at the federal level? In what directions do you think improvement could be made?
4. What part does the United States Supreme Court play in shaping the policies toward education in the United States?
5. Do you consider the principal recommendations of the Hoover Commission with regard to federal aid to education to be sound? Why? How do you account for the small influence this report has had upon subsequent policy at the federal level?
6. How is the question of federal financing of education in the United States affected by the rapid growth in population?
7. How do you account for the extraordinary amount of attention that Congress has given to encouraging vocational education in the schools?

PROJECTS

1. Appraise the effect of the Morrill acts upon higher education in America.
2. Appraise the effects upon American education of the Smith-Hughes Act and other similar acts.
3. Analyze the arguments of the judges of the United States Supreme Court in some of their more notable decisions bearing upon education. Note particularly the social principles they used to justify their decisions.
4. Analyze the ranking of the states as given in Figs. 12.3 and 12.4 (pp. 308 and 309). Draw from this what you believe to be a justifiable conclusion with respect to the desirable federal policy toward grants-in-aid to education.
5. Show why property taxes have, under present conditions, ceased to be a satisfactory base for public school support.
6. Show how certain problems like Americanization and illiteracy are essentially national problems. Draw an analogy with education.

CHAPTER **14**

The nonpublic schools

M any schools in the United States may be termed "nonpublic," a classification covering a wide variety of institutions operating at all levels of education. Generally speaking, nonpublic schools are supported by private funds and their control is vested in private individuals or nonpublic organizations. In a few instances, control and support may be both public and nonpublic. A laboratory school in a state university is an example. To achieve simplicity and clarity we shall focus our discussion on those schools that are mainly privately controlled and supported. Although the state has legal authority over nonpublic schools, in practice it normally exercises only a minimum of control, confining the use of authority to such matters as the competence of the teachers and to the school's ability to satisfy minimum program requirements.

ENROLLMENTS

Elementary and High-School Enrollment

Enrollment figures are not available for all nonpublic schools. Little reliable data about specialized private vocational schools on the secondary level, for instance, is available. According to a report issued by the United States Department of Health, Education, and Welfare, in 1955–1956 approximately 13 percent of the elementary and secondary school enrollment in the United States was in nonpublic schools. In 1899–1900, only slightly more than 8 percent was in nonpublic schools. If the ratio continues to increase at the same rate, in 1965 the nonpublic schools will serve about 19 percent of the American elementary and high school pupils, or about one out of every six pupils.

The ratio of nonpublic to public school pupils varies from state to state. Approximately 70 percent of the nonpublic school pupils are enrolled in schools in 10 states. The 8 states that have the largest percentage of pupils attending nonpublic schools are: Rhode Island, New Hampshire, Wisconsin, Illinois, New Jersey, New York, Massachusetts, and Pennsylvania. In these 8 states the overall ratio of nonpublic school attendance to public school attendance is about 1 to 4. The percentages range from 27.9 percent in Rhode Island to 1.4 percent in North Carolina, showing, as one would expect, that the influence of the nonpublic schools in some states is much greater than in others.

Composition of Elementary and High-School Enrollment

In 1962–1963 the total enrollment in Catholic elementary and secondary parochial schools reached 6,700,000. This was approximately 19 percent of the total elementary and secondary school enrollment and 90 percent of the total enrollment of the nonpublic schools. Of the remaining 10 percent, 4 percent were in Lutheran parochial schools, 4 percent in nonsectarian schools, and 2 percent in schools under the auspices of other religious sects. Since little is known of the number of pupils enrolled in such nonpublic schools as the vocational, commercial, and technical trade schools that give training below the college level, the whole of the picture is not given by the above data.

College and University Enrollment

The ratio of attendance at nonpublic colleges to that of public colleges is approximately 40 to 60. The Office of Education estimates that by 1975 the ratio will be 30 to 70, provided the present trend continues. The ratio of resident attendance at nonpublic and

FIG. 14.1 NONPUBLIC SCHOOL ENROLLMENT AS A PERCENTAGE OF TOTAL ENROLLMENT IN ELEMENTARY AND SECONDARY SCHOOLS, 1959-1960

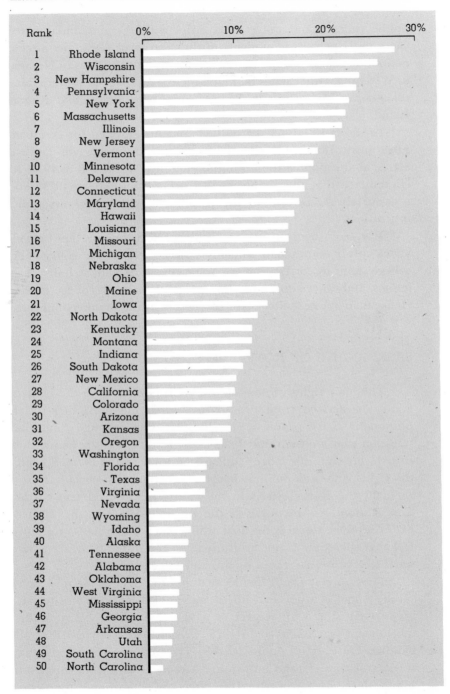

Rank		0%	10%	20%	30%
1	Rhode Island				
2	Wisconsin				
3	New Hampshire				
4	Pennsylvania				
5	New York				
6	Massachusetts				
7	Illinois				
8	New Jersey				
9	Vermont				
10	Minnesota				
11	Delaware				
12	Connecticut				
13	Maryland				
14	Hawaii				
15	Louisiana				
16	Missouri				
17	Michigan				
18	Nebraska				
19	Ohio				
20	Maine				
21	Iowa				
22	North Dakota				
23	Kentucky				
24	Montana				
25	Indiana				
26	South Dakota				
27	New Mexico				
28	California				
29	Colorado				
30	Arizona				
31	Kansas				
32	Oregon				
33	Washington				
34	Florida				
35	Texas				
36	Virginia				
37	Nevada				
38	Wyoming				
39	Idaho				
40	Alaska				
41	Tennessee				
42	Alabama				
43	Oklahoma				
44	West Virginia				
45	Mississippi				
46	Georgia				
47	Arkansas				
48	Utah				
49	South Carolina				
50	North Carolina				

(Data from NEA Research Division, Research Report 1963-R1)

public colleges and universities varies with the individual state. Close to 97 percent of students in the District of Columbia attend nonpublic colleges, while none attend nonpublic colleges in Nevada or Wyoming. Other states that rank high in attendance at nonpublic colleges are Massachusetts, Pennsylvania, New Jersey, and Rhode Island.

In the fall of 1963, 4.5 million students enrolled for credit in 1,985 institutions of higher education in the aggregate United States, almost double the 2.3 million enrolled in the fall of 1947. It is predicted that this number will reach 8.6 million by 1975. Approximately 30 percent of the enrollment will be in nonpublic institutions.

Many of the institutions of higher learning in the United States enroll nonresident students. Some of them give courses for college credit by correspondence. Some give short courses, individual lessons, and other adult education programs without college credit. Hence many more students are enrolled than the numbers indicate.

BASIC RIGHTS OF NONPUBLIC SCHOOLS

The basic rights of nonpublic schools to operate in the United States are derived from two sources. First, the prevailing social philosophy of the people is pluralistic. It is an accepted American tradition that a citizen may have many loyalties—to his family, his church, his club, his lodge—and still be loyal to the State. Second, the right of the nonpublic schools to function was officially recognized by the United States in the Fourteenth Amendment to the Constitution. As discussed in the previous chapter, the United States Supreme Court is the final arbiter when individuals or groups feel that some law is unconstitutional because it infringes on personal liberty as guaranteed by this amendment.

The Supreme Court has decided that the right to attend a nonpublic school is a personal liberty guaranteed by the Constitution. Its first decision with respect to a violation of the spirit of the amendment was rendered in 1925. Oregon had legislated that all children must attend public schools. The Court ruled that the law was a violation of the Constitution because it interfered unreasonably with the liberty of parents to direct the education of their children. It was further held by the Supreme Court that a law requiring attendance at a public school would destroy the value of the property owned by the nonpublic schools. The wording of the decision is worth noting. It is a pointed statement of America's belief in the pluralistic philosophy.

> The fundamental theory of liberty upon which all governments in the Union repose excludes any general power of the State to standardize its children by forcing them to accept instruction from public teachers only. The child is not the mere creature of the State; those who nurture him and direct his destiny have the right, coupled with the high duty, to recognize and to prepare him for additional obligations.

The policy in the United States with respect to the basic rights of nonpublic schools seems clear. Parents are protected in their rights to send their children to nonpublic schools. Freedom to choose is considered a fundamental right, one that is highly respected. The nonpublic schools are, in turn, protected in the ownership of their property and in their power to control that property.

REGULATION OF NONPUBLIC SCHOOLS

The nonpublic schools operate under the laws of the individual states just as the public schools do. The United States Supreme Court has consistently recognized the states' power to regulate schools. In the previously mentioned Oregon decision, the Supreme Court spoke as follows:

> No question is raised concerning the power of the State reasonably to regulate all schools, to inspect, supervise and examine them, their teachers and pupils; to require that all children of proper age attend some school, that teachers shall be of good moral character and patriotic disposition, that certain studies plainly essential to good citizenship must be taught, and that nothing be taught which is manifestly inimical to the public welfare.

In line with its rightful prerogatives, each state, as we have pointed out in a previous chapter, has passed laws governing the education that is conducted within its boundaries. These laws, as they affect the nonpublic schools, are of two kinds. There are general laws which apply to the activities of all individuals and organizations conducting businesses or charitable undertakings within the state. Unless specific exceptions are made, these laws apply to the nonpublic schools. Under these laws, an agency to which the state has delegated the responsibility, must enforce regulations concerned with building codes, health laws, fire prevention, workmen's compensation, welfare of children in boarding schools, motor vehicle codes, codes regulating cafeterias and other boarding places, and any other provisions designed to protect public welfare. In other words, nonpublic schools, which are incorporated, are subject to all of the general regulations that have been prescribed by the state for corporations.

A second kind of state law applies specifically to nonpublic schools although it may be general enough to apply to some other organizations within the state. The articles of incorporation of the nonpublic schools constitute a contract between each nonpublic school and the state. The Constitution of the United States prohibits the passage of any state law that violates the agreements made in the contract. The privileges accorded the nonpublic school under articles of incorporation usually extend to such matters as holding property, the right to sue and be sued, the right to make contracts, and such other agreements as may be deemed necessary to achieve the objects for which the institution was established. The articles of agreement always presuppose the principle of self-government under state regulation and thereby have proven to be the most popular and effective way a state has of regulating nonpublic schools. Incorporation also fully establishes the legal right of nonpublic schools to do what is deemed necessary to operate educational institutions under private auspices.

Besides basic legal regulations for nonpublic schools, state legislatures make interpretations that establish some limitations and privileges. The interpretations vary quite as much with respect to the conduct of nonpublic education as they do with respect to public education. These interpretations are found in the provisions made for education in the state constitutions, in the statutes passed by the state legislatures concerning nonpublic schools, and in relevant court decisions. This makes the state school code as important to the nonpublic school as it is to the public school.

Despite the variations among the states, two principles underlie state policy. The first is that, in general, a public tax may not be levied for the support of nonpublic schools. The second is that nonschool revenue may not be used for direct aid to nonpublic schools.

Even these principles, however, are subject to a variety of interpretations. Many of the differences arise in connection with the interpretation of the child benefit theory. This theory holds that benefits or services provided at public expense from revenue not collected for educational purposes should be given a child regardless of where he happens to attend school. Differences usually arise in a situation that involves indirect public aid to education, that is, the aid given to provide some service immediately for the individual pupil, not directly to the school. All children are entitled to the same free governmental services. In theory there should be no discrimination against children because they attend nonpublic schools. The question arises over whether the aid provided actually goes to the pupil or to the school. Among the services about which there has been this kind of disagreement are free textbooks, free transportation, health services, and other welfare services usually described as auxiliary educational services. If an auxiliary educational service is provided for all public school pupils, is it unjust discrimination to deny comparable services to all pupils in nonpublic schools? Some state legislatures say *yes*. Others say *no*.

Other services that have been centers of argument are commonly called quasi-instructional services. Examples of this kind of service are recreation; child accounting (the keeping of instructional and executive records of the child throughout the whole of his school life); psychological, psychiatric, and sociological diagnostic services; and placement and follow-up of high school graduates. Should a social service considered vital to the welfare of every child of school age in a community be denied a child because he happens to attend a nonpublic school?

Decisions on such issues are related to the interpretation each individual state legislature makes of the child benefit theory when it is applied to a specific educational problem. What the interpretation may be cannot be predicted. In general, it is agreed that the state or the federal government may not directly make state or federal financial grants to nonpublic schools. It is expected, however, that certain social services rendered by the state to individuals will not be denied to an individual pupil, even though he attends a nonpublic school. The child benefit theory holds that the services of the state are to follow the child wherever he may be.

CLASSIFICATION OF NONPUBLIC SCHOOLS

The great variety of nonpublic schools in the United States makes it difficult to arrive at a simple classification. The best we can do is to divide nonpublic schools into two main groups and state some of the features by which each group is identified. The parochial schools, one large group of elementary and secondary schools, are, as the name implies, operated by ecclesiastical organizations. A large majority of them are operated by the Roman Catholic Church which, in the past, has enrolled approximately 92 percent of all the pupils officially reported to be attending nonpublic schools in the United States. Because of the number and importance of these schools, more information about them is given in a subsequent section.

The second large group of nonpublic schools are private schools. The term "private school" in some educational publications is synonymous with nonpublic school. In popular usage, however, and in our discussion, the private school differs from the parochial school in that it is largely nonsectarian and is controlled by an individual or a self-perpetuating board of trustees. The two classifications of nonpublic schools might well be sectarian and nonsectarian. However, most educational publications use the words "private" and "parochial."

Parochial Schools

Parochial schools are those nonpublic schools that operate on the elementary and secondary level under the control and with the support of an ecclesiastical organization. The largest group of parochial schools are those operated by the Roman Catholic Church.

1. Roman Catholic Schools

a. *Origins.* The Roman Catholic Church has followed a policy of establishing elementary parochial schools in communities that have a Catholic population and organization sufficient to support such a school. Organizing schools as a regular and permanent feature of parish work began with the establishment of the first Catholic parish in Philadelphia in 1730. Philadelphia had a larger Catholic population than any other city in the country, and the system of parochial schools established there and throughout Pennsylvania became a model subsequently followed by Catholics throughout the country.

The schools were aided by the founding of teaching orders such as, for example, the Sisters of Charity, the Sisters of Loretta, and

A class is shown at work in the New Sacred Heart School, Pittsburgh, Pennsylvania. The room is air-conditioned and fluorescent-lighted, the air is sterilized with ultra violet rays, and the pupils write on green glass chalk boards. Some 1000 pupils are enrolled in this parochial school. (Wide World)

the Sisters of St. Dominic. Members of these orders established religious communities where some kind of productive activities, perhaps farming, made the community more or less self-sufficient. With the support of the religious order and of the Roman Catholic Church, the teachers were able to carry on their schools without aid from the state and to extend the Catholic educational system into new centers of Catholic life as fast as they became organized. Even before 1776, 70 Roman Catholic schools had been organized in the confines of what is now the United States. The Catholic Church expanded rapidly after 1840, when there was a rapid increase in the immigration of Catholics from Germany and Ireland. This increase in Catholic population, together with the action of the Third Plenary Council of Baltimore in 1885 making it obligatory for every parish to maintain a school, resulted in a rapid multiplication of Catholic parochial schools. The action of the Third Plenary Council made it clear that the church leaders considered education a vital factor in the internal development of the Roman Catholic Church in the United States.

b. Organization.   The Roman Catholics followed the lines of their dioceses in their school organization. A diocese is the area and the population that falls under the pastoral care of a bishop. Each diocese has its school system with the bishop at its head. The bishops are bound by the legislation of the Third Plenary Council of Baltimore, which not only made schools obligatory but also prescribed a definite form of school organization for all the dioceses. Thus, it is accurate to speak of Catholic schools as constituting a system, and it is this systematization of their schools that has provided a measure of unity and a source of strength.

Control over the schools in the diocese is in the hands of a board of education presided over by a bishop. The members of the board, except for a few lay people, are elected from the clergy. The executive officer of the school board is a priest, especially trained as an educator and school administrator. He serves as superintendent of schools in the diocese. The priest of the local parish generally serves also as head of the individual school supported by his parish. Beyond supervising the financial and religious matters, he delegates the direction of the school to a superior of the sisters or brothers in charge. This superior is, in practice, the actual principal who administers the school.

c. Curriculum.   The curriculum in the Catholic elementary and high schools is similar to the curriculum in the public schools in the same communities. The principal difference is in the emphasis upon religious education. The curriculum is planned to give a well-rounded general education and at the same time to give a special place to religious instruction, an area that is usually not recognized in the public schools, which must remain secular and nonsectarian.

d. Kinds of schools.   The elementary schools are all diocesan schools and constitute the main part of the Catholic parochial school system. Some of the high schools are organized in the parish and are also members of the diocesan organization. Others are independent and are conducted by one of the religious orders of the church. The Catholic University of America at Washington, D.C., established in 1887 by Pope Leo XII and the American Catholic hierarchy, has as one of its purposes the preparation of teachers for the entire Catholic educational system.

e. Enrollments.   In 1960–1961 enrollments in Catholic parochial elementary and secondary schools were 4,359,962 and 880,369,
respectively. The total attendance in 1920 was 1,795,673, and in
1880 it was 405,234. Thus growth in Catholic parochial school enrollments parallels growth in the total population.

f. Costs.   The costs of attending Roman Catholic elementary
and secondary schools, apart from services donated through the
church, is borne by the parents. The annual costs of the elementary
and secondary schools now exceed a billion dollars.

g. Attitudes of Catholic leaders toward public education.
Since those who send their children to Catholic schools must also pay
taxes for the support of the public schools, the attitude of the
Catholic leaders toward the public schools is of general interest. In
the main, the parents of the children who attend the Catholic
schools are appreciative of the privilege of freedom to make a choice
between two kinds of schools and of being permitted to provide
their children with religious education. The attitude both of the
parents and of the clergy is positive, intelligent, and constructive.
A short quotation will express the prevailing sentiment:

> Historically, we have had and, please God, we probably always will
> have a diversified system of education in this country. As American citi-
> zens, therefore, and especially as American educators, we must be interested
> in the improvement not only of our own unique kind of education, but of
> all kinds of American education—public, private, denominational—what-
> ever it may be. . . . The public schools, as a complementary system to
> private education, are absolutely necessary for the thousands of Americans
> who are content with a purely secular educational pattern. Such schools
> deserve the interest and support of our Catholic population.[1]

2. Protestant Schools

Some of the Protestant churches have, in recent years, conducted
nursery schools for children who are younger than compulsory school
and kindergarten age. These schools are operated by local churches
more as a service to the members of the church than for religious
reasons. Such schools diverge very little in their pattern of activities
from those conducted under public auspices.

It is not easy to state the Protestant position toward elementary
and secondary schools because no official position has been taken. In

[1] Very Rev. P. C. Reinert, S.J., "American Catholic Educators Face New
Responsibilities," *Proceedings and Addresses, Forty-Ninth Annual Meeting* (Washington, D.C.: National Catholic Educational Association, 1952), p. 59.

Although most Protestants do not promote the parochial school idea, they are favorable to parochial schools when member groups wish to organize them. There are well over 3000 such adequately supported schools. (Courtesy The Atlantic District of the Lutheran Church–Missouri Synod)

general, and with notable exceptions mentioned later, it is the position of the Protestant groups that the parent should send his children to the public schools and that the child should receive his religious education in the home and in the church. Protestants, as a group, do not favor parochial education as an answer to the problem of religious education. Nevertheless, they "defend the right of all religious groups to carry on church-related education at any level, elementary, secondary, or higher, and the right of parents to send their children to these schools if they so desire."[2]

Although the majority of Protestants believe in sending their children to the public schools, they are favorable to church schools if member groups desire to have them. There are above 3,000 Protestant day schools which enroll more than 190,000 pupils. In the main, these are supported by the Christian Reformed Church mem-

[2] D. Campbell Wyckoff, "The Protestant Day School," *School and Society,* LXXXII (October 1, 1955), 98.

bers, Missouri Synod Lutherans, Seventh-Day Adventists, Mennonites, Episcopalians, and Baptists.

3. Hebrew Day Schools

There are, at present, 293 elementary and secondary Hebrew day schools in the United States. Approximately half of these are in the New York City metropolitan area. About 55,000 pupils attend them. Inasmuch as each school is a unit, any generalizations about their programs are impossible. However, the general point of view, in common with other parochial schools, is that the Hebrew schools should follow the *same* curriculum offered by the public school in the community in which the school is located. The one element added is that with the regular education program some emphasis is given to Jewish learning. The words of one leader expresses this:

> By presenting the complete complex of general and Jewish learning to the child under one roof, that is, under one integrated program of education, the day school harmonizes Judaism and Americanism through a well-thought-out and complete philosophy of life. The stresses and strains

Hebrew parochial schools are growing. Some operate full time while others meet in the late afternoon for religious instruction. Most Hebrew schools utilize the most advanced knowledge in providing buildings and equipment. (Courtesy Jewish Education Committee of New York)

of living according to a religious *Weltanschauung* in modern society are ironed out gradually in a program of education dedicated to the development of the best ideals in Judaism and American democracy. Each approach enriches the other to produce a better Jew and a better American.[3]

Private Schools

The private schools are the most independent of the nonpublic schools. They are subject to very little public control and are permitted to operate with a minimum of state supervision. They are numerous, and they maintain widely varying standards.

1. Below-College Level

a. *Vocational schools.* Below-college vocational training, apart from the high schools, is almost exclusively the domain of the

Many private schools exist for a special purpose, such as educating the handicapped. (Courtesy Lexington School for the Deaf, New York City)

[3] Joseph Kaminetsky, "The Hebrew Day School Movement," *School and Society*, LXXXII (October 1, 1955), 106.

private school. Here vocational schools that are operated for profit prevail—technical institutes; business colleges; commercial or secretarial schools; art, interior decorating, drafting, design schools; charm, beauty culture, cosmetology, electrolysis schools; dramatic art, television, broadcasting, expression schools; trade, industrial, auto-mechanics schools; physical therapy, massage schools; baking, home economics, hotel management schools; jewelry and watch repairing schools. And there are many others that train specifically for some designated trade or commercial pursuit.

Information about such schools has not been collected thus far. Some notion of their magnitude, however, may be gained from estimates of enrollment made by the National Association and Council of Business Schools. It is estimated that during 1956–1957, a half million students attended these schools. One technical institute in Chicago, whose students were being trained to enter the field of electronics, enrolled over 20,000 post-high school students in 1963–1964. Undoubtedly, since the enrollments in these schools number into the millions their influence is tremendous. They provide a kind of education that receives little emphasis in the public schools.

b. *Parent-supported schools.* Another type of private elementary and secondary school is sometimes endowed and supported by wealthy parents. These are nonsectarian and serve approximately the same purposes as public schools of similar grade. The children often are selected so that they comprise a more or less homogeneous group in terms of economic or social background or special interests or problems. When the children are likely to attend college, attention is given to college preparation. Some of the secondary schools are endowed boarding schools. Some are known as "country day schools" where typically some of the pupils are boarding pupils and others live at home. The purpose or purposes that justify the establishment and support of each of these private schools varies from school to school.

c. *Academies.* The academies, in part parent-supported and in part endowment-supported, are an important group of private secondary schools. Some of the academies have an illustrious tradition and history dating back to the early days of our country. Originally intended to provide a curriculum more flexible and enriched than available elsewhere, the academies are now largely college preparatory. They are sometimes coeducational and are found in

Benjamin Franklin (1706–1790) is known to every American boy and girl as an American statesman, diplomat, author, scientist, and inventor. Few, perhaps, are conscious that he also influenced American education.

In 1749 Franklin voiced progressive ideas about education in *Proposals for the Education of Youth in Pennsylvania.* Two years later he opened the Franklin Academy which incorporated these ideas. His academy was far different from the other institutions of the time. Students applying for admission were offered a choice of three courses. They could enter one of what he called three schools—the English school, the mathematics school, or the Latin school. In typical Franklin manner he thus expressed his displeasure over the narrow classicism that characterized the Latin grammar schools of the time. Shortly after its establishment his academy was reincorporated as a degree-conferring institution. In 1779, three years after the signing of the Declaration of Independence, the University of Pennsylvania was established in its stead.

Franklin's intention was to displace the unsystematic practices of the private schoolmaster of the day with an institution organized and administered on a public basis. He attempted, also, to offer, so far as was possible at the time, a curriculum that was practical and useful. Even so great a man as Franklin, however, could not overcome the deep-seated prejudices favorable to educational emphasis on Latin. He saw English and other modern subjects gradually ousted from the curriculum of the school he had established in order to emphasize them.

Although Franklin's school was an initial failure, it was an expression of the progressive educational thought of the time. The Franklin Academy passed out of existence, but the ideas set in motion flowed on greatly to influence succeeding generations.

most parts of the United States. The military academies of high school grade emphasize military discipline.

d. Industry-supported schools. Private business has, in the past fifty years, greatly expanded educational opportunity in industries. This has resulted in another kind of private school. Large industrial corporations have provided extensive industrial training for their employees and, in some instances, have provided other kinds of education for the families of their employees. Some industries engage also in cooperative education programs with various engineering colleges in order to meet the nation's demands for citizens well grounded both in the common essentials and occupational abilities necessary to insure economic and industrial efficiency. The number of people attending such schools is large, and it fluctuates greatly from time to time.

Phillips Exeter is a boarding school for boys. Its magnificent plant serves some 750 boys. Qualitatively, the secondary school programs of some of these New England academies are unexcelled. They are among the oldest of America's secondary schools. Phillips Exeter was founded in 1781. (Courtesy The Phillips Exeter Academy, Exeter, New Hampshire)

Since so many of the private schools operate quite independently and since so little information has been assembled with regard to some of them, few generalizations are possible except to say that they are numerous and their influence great.

e. *Laboratory schools.* Schools for children at the nursery, elementary, junior high, and senior high school levels are conducted on many college campuses. These are variously called demonstration schools, experimental schools, training schools, or laboratory schools. When they are associated with nonpublic institutions, they are private schools. Sometimes, however, they are part of a public teachers college or public university. Then they are public schools which, however, differ from ordinary public schools in that they are not a part of any particular local school system. They are schools administered by the college or university for experimental and demonstrational purposes. Ideally, the laboratory school demonstrates the best modern educational theory in actual practice in the classroom. The philosophy of the school is carefully worked out; the curriculum is designed to meet the vital needs of its pupils; the

The academy was introduced into America in recognition of the need for a form of secondary education broader than that given by the Latin grammar schools which had dominated American secondary education for two hundred years with their highly restricted curriculum. The academy became the dominant institution in American secondary education from the latter half of the eighteenth century to well beyond the 1890's when the American four-year high school began its rapid growth.

One way to get a picture of the purposes, programs, and achievements of the academy and of its place in American secondary education is to read the history of one of the successful academies.* Phillips Exeter is an example of one of the earliest academies which continues to be a distinguished institution. Incorporated in 1781, Phillips Exeter now has a campus of 440 acres, 100 acres used for the school, 40 for playing fields, and 300 left in woodland. It has 75 school buildings and a faculty of 95 men to care for 763 boys coming from all the states.

While tax-supported high schools have grown rapidly in the twentieth century, the demands by able students for education at academies like Exeter have not dwindled. The quality of instruction offered by the academies has progressively improved. The function of the academies has changed. In 1781 few academy graduates went on to college, so the early academies provided terminal education. Today most academy graduates go on to college, many of them to private universities. For example, of the Phillips Exeter graduates of 1956 who went on to college, more than 65 per cent went to Harvard, Yale, and Princeton. The academies have, then, become largely college preparatory.

Although the academies in the United States are relatively inconspicuous in the total secondary educational picture, they perform a significant and unique function. The academies have offered a program consistent with ideals of high scholarship and have been dedicated to close, personal guidance of the individual pupil with particular emphasis on character development.

* For a vivid account giving traditions, support, and functions of the academies and imparting their spirit and ideals, see Myron R. Williams, The Story of Phillips Exeter (Exeter, New Hampshire: The Phillips Exeter Academy, 1957).

teachers are skilled artists in teaching; the organization and the administrative machinery demonstrate arrangements that best serve the pupils and teachers and that foster wholesome human relations; and the building and equipment are thoughtfully planned.

Laboratory schools have contributed significantly to the improvement of education in both private and public schools. One main difficulty is that they sometimes operate on insufficient budgets. To supplement their budgets, they frequently charge tuition. This

Many industrial concerns conduct vocational training schools in their factories. The class shown is at the Chrysler Corporation. (Chrysler Corporation)

tends to result in an economically and sociologically favored enrollment of pupils, which makes the results of laboratory school research less applicable to a typical cross section of the general population. In addition to their contribution through experimentation and research, the laboratory schools have improved teaching in America's schools by providing opportunities for teachers in training to observe and to have actual daily experience in much better than average classrooms.

2. College Level

a. *Colleges and universities.* No criterion has been established to guide in the classification of higher level institutions. The most dependable classification available shows that there are 132 universities in the United States, of which 70 are public and 62 are nonpublic. Since many public universities have numerous branches this 70 scarcely describes the true statistic.

The nonpublic four-year liberal arts college, usually called just "college," dominates the four-year college scene. There are well over five hundred such colleges in the United States, all of which are fully accredited. Very few such colleges are publicly controlled and supported. The dominance of the private liberal arts college is perhaps due in part to the fact that it was the earliest kind of organization for higher education in this country and also to the respect and faith that the American people place in these institutions.

The nonpublic institutions of higher learning have exerted and continue to exert great influence upon the thinking of the American people. Their programs penetrate almost every aspect of American life. Since these institutions in the fall of 1963 enrolled well over 1,800,000 students, it seems that the American people will continue to accord nonpublic institutions of higher education a prominent and permanent position in the educational system of the United States.

b. Technological institutes. There are between 60 and 65 private technological institutions of higher learning in the United States. Among them, to name a few, are such distinguished institutions as the Massachusetts Institute of Technology, the Carnegie Institute of Technology, the California Institute of Technology, the Case Institute of Technology, and the Illinois Institute of Technology. As their names imply, their contributions are mainly to the fields of science and applied science. The number of full-time students attending such institutions in the fall of 1962 was well over 250,000—a figure that attests to the general popularity of such institutions in the American scheme of education.

CONTRIBUTIONS OF NONPUBLIC SCHOOLS

The size and scope of the nonpublic school undertaking in the United States is, in itself, evidence of the high regard the people of the United States hold for nonpublic education. The debt the nation owes to nonpublic education is indeed very great. While it is not easy to assess the total contributions made by the nonpublic schools to the contemporary educational scene, a few of the more obvious contributions can be identified.

First, the nonpublic schools have furthered the preservation and strengthening of the cherished American ideal of freedom of choice and of the pluralistic philosophy which nourishes that ideal. Although in some communities competition between the public and nonpublic elementary and secondary schools creates a degree of friction, in most communities a healthy and friendly rivalry exists— rivalry to excel in the quality of services rendered.

Second, the nonpublic schools have educated so large a proportion of the American school population that they have appreciably lowered the burden of public support. Since the nonpublic schools seek to achieve all the functions striven for in the public schools, and, as is the case especially with the vocational schools, to answer certain needs not recognized in the public schools, the lessening of the costs to the public is accompanied by an actual increase in the breadth of education available.

Third, the nonpublic schools have made distinctive contributions to educational practice. Many of the forward-looking practices in the public schools have first been developed in the nonpublic schools. The nonpublic schools have contributed particularly to experimentation at the elementary level. Nursery school and kindergarten education were first tested in nonpublic schools. Vocational education in the high schools was first introduced and developed in the nonpublic schools. A great deal of research in scientific and professional fields has emanated from the nonpublic universities.

These are only a few of the contributions made by nonpublic schools. Enough has been said, however, to show that public and nonpublic education in the United States have advanced together, with a minimum of conflict and a maximum of mutual appreciation. In the minds of the citizens, both kinds of schools are essential to the preservation and continued advancement of American civilization.

QUESTIONS

1. Why has it been the policy of the various states to exert so little control over nonpublic education?
2. What would be some uses that could be served by the states collecting complete information about all the nonpublic schools operating under their jurisdictions?
3. What are the principal justifications for the establishment of nonpublic schools and nonpublic school systems in the United States?
4. What evidences are there that nonpublic universities exert a great deal of influence upon life in America?
5. Why are the four-year colleges in the United States predominantly nonpublic schools?

6. How do articles of incorporation operate to protect a nonpublic school?

7. How do the articles of incorporation of nonpublic schools serve as a control over nonpublic schools?

8. In your opinion, what will the future development of nonpublic education in the United States be like?

PROJECTS

1. From Fig. 13.4, page 337, show how the presence or absence of nonpublic schools in a given state affects your interpretation of the relative ranks.

2. Secure information on one of the industrial education programs conducted by some large industry. Appraise the nature of the program.

3. Read the advertisements of nonpublic schools as found in some influential magazine. Itemize the claims of the various institutions.

15

Units of school organization

ocal school units and the educational ideas that condition their
organization are the concern of this chapter. In examining the
local units of organization, either public or nonpublic, we should
remember that these units have emerged in response to certain ideas
about desirable educational practice which teachers have developed
and the public has accepted. Often the public is not ready to accept
a new form of organization approved of by educators. The educators,
until they have overcome such objections, have to function as dictated by the older, theoretically displaced forms.

THE NURSERY SCHOOL

The nursery school is the latest unit of educational organization
to bid for public recognition. Although it has not, as yet, been given
legal status by state legislatures, it has, nevertheless, been widely
established both as a nonpublic and public school unit. The theories
of education that have grown up around nursery schools have been
widely accepted.

The nursery school movement has received encouragement from
at least three directions. During the great depression, the Works

Progress Administration of the federal government sponsored nursery schools for the children of working mothers. By 1939, 1,500 such schools had been set up and some 300,000 children were enrolled. The federal government withdrew support in 1946. By that time it had demonstrated the value and need of nursery school education. It had also, by housing the nursery schools in public buildings, established a precedent for making nursery schools an integral part of the public school system. The federal government withdrew its support, not because it found the investment without merit, but because, traditionally, local and state school governments are the proper agencies to support and conduct public education.

Encouragement for establishing nursery schools has also come from child development experts whose studies have emphasized the importance of providing a suitable environment for the mental and physical development of children two to five years of age. Parents are a young child's most important teachers. They are with the child for a greater period of time than any other person, and the kind of activities they share cover a wide range of experience. Parents teach a child certain skills, like talking, and help him develop attitudes, emotional control, maturity in his relations with others, and the ideals that contribute to good living. Somewhere along the line, a transition must be made from the narrower environment of the home to the wider social environment of the school. The shift from home to school is a major environmental change in the life of a child. It is a time when he feels that his security is threatened, a time when he must make major adjustments. Psychologists tell us that skillfully directed nursery schools would make the transition easier for many four-year-olds and some three-year-olds.

The third source of encouragement comes from the public and private groups that have experimented with nursery schools. Such schools have been widely established in universities, in churches, in private homes, and within public school systems. Such schools have won the full acceptance of most who have been in close touch with them. Those conducted in the colleges and universities have been especially influential.

Nursery school education serves two broad educational purposes—childhood education and adult, or parent, education. The location and equipment must be suited to the two purposes. An appreciation of the facilities required for such education can best be gained by a visit to a well-equipped nursery school. One will find that the selection of the room and equipment is dictated by what child development specialists have learned is appropriate for three- and four-year-olds. Psychologists who have studied the effects of nursery school education upon children are agreed that a nursery school that is not properly equipped can do more harm than good. In a good nursery school, playground and schoolroom are a single unit, separate from units provided for older children. Playground equipment is specially designed. A roofed area just outside the room is provided for special outdoor activities. The room windows face the playground. The room is large, well lighted, and properly ventilated. The equipment is fairly expensive. It includes drinking fountains of suitable height, toilets and washrooms, sinks and other kitchen equipment, musical instruments, and facilities for caring for plants, animals, and birds. Cots are available for rest periods.

Nursery schools must also provide daily nurse's inspection. Medical examinations and dental care are essential. The help of a nutritionist and psychologist is also needed to guarantee adequate attention to the health needs. Most of all, of course, a specially trained teacher is needed.

Not all children will need or will profit from attendance at a nursery school. In deciding who shall attend, parents and teachers weigh many factors. Is the child an only child? Does he live in an apartment? Does the mother work? Does the mother feel that the child will do better if he is apart from her for some time each day? Does the mother feel that the child should have increased opportunity to expand his social adaptability? Attendance at nursery school is never required. It need not be regular.

It seems that the nursery school is here to stay. Social conditions such as increased employment of mothers, crowded housing, urbanization, poverty, and the like appear to justify both a continuation and an expansion of the movement. Apart from social expediency, future expansion of nursery school education can be justified in terms of the immediate value to the children who attend and to their parents who also participate in the program. Where nurserly schools facilitate the transition from home to school, where they help mothers understand and guide their children, where, all things considered, they help children make the adjustments required of them, the services and benefits justify the establishment and maintenance of nursery school units as a regular part of both the nonpublic and public school systems.

THE KINDERGARTEN

In an earlier chapter the idea of kindergarten education for children of preschool age was traced to Froebel, who demonstrated the practicality of the idea by conducting an experimental school. He moved his experimental school to Blankenburg, Germany, and in 1840 gave it the name "kindergarten"—a garden of children. So rapidly did the idea take hold that in the 25 years following Froebel's death kindergartens were established in the leading cities of Germany, Holland, Belgium, Switzerland, Austria, Hungary, Canada, Japan, and the United States. The name "kindergarten" has become synonymous, in many parts of the world, with the kind of education program suited to preschool-age children.

St. Louis made kindergarten education a part of its public school system in 1873. A demonstration kindergarten was established at the Philadelphia Exposition in 1876. These two ventures are credited with demonstrating to the American people, many of whom had previously been skeptical, the merits of kindergarten

Kindergartens are conducted somewhat as separate administrative units. The teachers are specially trained and the classrooms are specially equipped. (Hays from Monkmeyer)

education. Within 10 years, kindergartens had been established in all the major cities of the United States. All of these, with the exception of St. Louis, were under private control. As people became convinced of the value of the kindergarten, public schools enthusiastically adopted the unit.

Comenius had argued that at six the child was at the best age to enter school. We still accept six years as the logical age for entrance into the first grade. The kindergarten precedes first grade and, from the standpoint of organization, remains a more or less separate unit in the school system. The kindergarten is neither fully integrated with the nursery school unit, where one exists, nor with the first grade. The separation is not considered undesirable. Psychologists believe that rapid maturation takes place between the ages of four and five and between the ages of five and six, and that this must be taken into account in planning suitable programs for each of the three ages. For example, in contrast to the four-year-old, the child at five is clear and complete in his answers to simple questions. He is more adept at building with larger blocks, more skillful in acts of simple drawing, more critical of his own inability to do something he would very much like to do, more likely to finish what he starts, and more self-reliant in the performance of his personal duties. He is ready for wider experiences than either the home or the nursery school can provide. Since the kindergarten must provide an environment quite different from other school units, the rather general practice of keeping it as a separately organized unit, even though in the same building, probably will be continued.

All large cities in the United States now have kindergartens, at which attendance is voluntary. Since there is considerable variation in the ages of children who attend the earlier grades—all children do not arrive at the age of five on the same day—it is not easy to interpret data on kindergarten attendance. It appears, however, that slightly over half of the children of five years or thereabouts attend kindergarten. This means that not all of the communities in the United States that would be able to support kindergarten education do so, and also that not all parents are inclined to send their children to kindergarten even when one is readily accessible. It appears that the acceptance and development of kindergarten education, like nursery school education, will depend upon the wishes of the American public. Where kindergartens have been conducted according to the best-known educational standards of practice, experts report that some of the most effective education in the nation has been accomplished.

THE ELEMENTARY SCHOOL

The common school, district school, or grade school in the early United States enrolled pupils from first grade through the eighth. After that, if the pupil continued his schooling he transferred to a four-year high school. Since around 1910, there has been a strong tendency to reduce the unit of elementary education from eight to six grades. Even now, however, the eight-grade type of organization still enrolls more pupils than does the six-grade type. In discussing the education program at the elementary level, regardless of type of organization, it is common practice to consider the grades one through six as the logical unit.

The Curriculum

Elementary school pupils ordinarily follow a single curriculum, the chief aim of which is *general education*. In some schools the subject matter is classified under broad fields like language arts or social studies. In others the classification is more restricted, and reading, writing, spelling, penmanship, and grammar are classifications. This is discussed more fully in a later chapter. Since the elementary school must be adapted to the needs of children who vary widely both in abilities and interests, the curriculum is never considered a set one, a laid-out-in-advance path, to be followed at all costs. The curriculum is more a suggestion to the teacher of what is desirable. The teacher, in most American elementary schools, is given freedom to modify and adapt as the conditions in his classroom warrant. To the well-trained teacher this freedom to devise the most fruitful environment in terms of the needs of the pupils as he learns to know them is what makes teaching in the elementary school one of the most challenging of all teaching tasks.

The Teacher

The elementary teacher is a specialist in teaching at a particular grade level for which he must have well-rounded training and experience. This is recognized both within the profession and in the community. It has strong implications for preparation of elementary

These elementary school pupils are engaged in group research in preparation for their social studies class. (Kranzten Studio, Inc.)

teachers. The elementary teacher must teach a very wide range of subject matter. He must, therefore, strive for broad, well-rounded preparation in his own college work, which is sometimes difficult within the system of required majors and minors. The elementary teacher is so important an influence on the formation of early habits that help shape the future character of the pupils that the ideals he exemplifies must be part of a wholesome personality. He must have an understanding of how young children grow. He must be able to take their interests into account and make what he teaches continuous with what the child has previously learned. He must be prepared to confer with and direct parents. His relationships with parents place him in an excellent position to influence their thinking on educational problems.

The School Building

The modern elementary school building is typically designed along functional lines and is surrounded with attractively landscaped grounds and outdoor play facilities. It is one of the most attractive buildings in many American communities. By visiting such a building and noting the details that have been incorporated to serve the educational needs of pupils and teachers, one gets a reasonable appreciation of what modern architectural school-building science can contribute to the improvement of the elementary school.

Organization of the Classroom

The organization within the elementary school follows the self-contained classroom pattern, the service and resource-unit pattern, or some modification of these. In either case, the furniture in the classroom is completely movable so that discussion, laboratory activities, individual projects, and "research" by children can be conveniently cared for within the room. Many kinds of teaching-aid materials are available—not resting on shelves in neat arrangements but carefully catalogued and circulated throughout the school.

Although the self-contained classroom has a rather recently acquired name, it is the oldest form of educational organization in the United States. It is still considered by many educators to be the most desirable plan for elementary school organization. Under this arrangement, one teacher is responsible for the whole range of activities, and the equipment in the classroom is complete. Ideally, toilet and washroom facilities are included, as well as shop facilities, cupboards, work tables, art equipment, a piano, a record player, and perhaps a movie projector.

The service and resource-unit pattern may shift some responsibility for teaching from the classroom instructor. To facilitate instruction, teachers at least have access to a library, a workshop, an auditorium, and other specialized facilities. A specialized staff of resource persons also may be available to help all classroom teachers. This may include a teacher-librarian, a psychologist, a teacher of dramatics, of music, of art, of crafts, of physical education, and a remedial teacher. The efforts of specialists are coordinated with those of the classroom teacher who, with the help of the principal, plans the activities so there is no break in the unified development of the education program of a pupil. Coordination and scheduling of the use of the building and the personnel resources are the responsibility of the principal.

Whether the school is organized around the principle of the self-contained classroom, which is a more costly form of organization, or around the service and resource-unit pattern, or some variation of either, personnel organization is kept simple. All of the teachers are specialized but in different ways. Ideally, there are only two ranks among the staff, that of the teachers and that of the principal.

There are schools in the United States today that include all eight grades, all under the direction of one teacher and all housed in a one-room building. In some cities, grades seven and eight are included in the same building with the first six grades. In some instances the practice of having subject matter departmentalized and the instruction in each subject handled by a specialized teacher in that area is carried down as far as the fifth grade. Sometimes departmentalization is only partial. In these cases children may have one teacher for most of their schoolwork but have specialized teachers for something like music, physical education, or art.

Areas for Improvement

The elementary school is a fertile area for educational improvement. The success of any plan to build a continuous, organized, developmental program to serve all who attend schools through the twelfth grade is contingent upon the program built for children while they are in the elementary school. One indicated change in the elementary school is a better balance of men and women on the teaching staff. Elementary teachers now constitute about two-thirds of all the public elementary and secondary teachers in America. Women teachers in this group far outnumber men. Perhaps the growth of young children should be directed and stimulated by mature, emotionally well-balanced men *and* women. A number of changes in such areas as social attitude, salaries, and organizational pattern will necessarily precede this kind of improvement.

THE JUNIOR HIGH SCHOOL

The junior high school is the present-day answer to the problem of a unit that logically follows the one-curriculum elementary school.

Ideally, the junior high school embraces grades seven, eight, and

Henry Suzzallo (1875–1933), a distinguished educator of the earlier years of the present century and a former president of the University of Washington, expressed his thoughts on the constantly recurring social phenomenon, the criticism of the public elementary schools.

The argument for the adequate maintenance of our common schools does not require much repetition to insure acceptance; but the argument for much that goes on in their classrooms does. Nothing is more astonishing than the reforms which have been made in elementary education. The last decade or two have witnessed great changes, not all of them wise perhaps. For the most part, however, they have been worthy responses to changed conditions or to the demand for a larger realization of democratic ideals.

These modifications have been so rapid and extensive that the older generation often judges current practice by a personal experience which has been left far behind. The schools can scarcely be judged by such naïve methods. It would be just as fair to judge contemporaneous medical practice by that of a generation ago without knowing anything of intervening scientific discovery. Psychology and experimental teaching have developed many new scientific facts unknown to the teachers or parents of a generation ago. Sociological science, too, has indicated many new adjustments that have had to be made.

One constantly recurring criticism suggests that our present-day schools do not teach the fundamental subjects as well as earlier schools did, meaning that children cannot read as intelligently or as quickly as they once did, or that they cannot figure or spell as accurately as a previous generation.

While such statements are based on rather plausible deductions they are the product of a faulty psychology. The "good old days" have left most of their evils behind and the present remembrance of them is hallowed by a selective sentimentalism which retains only the agreeable. When based on any kind of reasoning, such conclusions assume that it would be impossible for a child to know the few basic formal subjects as well when they are pursued in connection with a half dozen other studies as when they were studied exclusively. Hence the inference, that so many new "fads and frills" are certain to interfere with a thorough acquisition of the fundamentals. The argument is plausible enough, but it happens not to be true to the facts as scientfically determined.

. . . Wherever it has been possible actually to compare past and present results, the comparison has been most favorable to current schooling.

From Henry Suzzallo, *Our Faith in Education* (Philadelphia: J. B. Lippincott Company, 1924), pp. 74–77. Quoted by permission of J. B. Lippincott Company.

nine. There are, however, many variations. Having the first eight grades together as one unit is typical of some agricultural areas and of some larger cities. In some states the grades that must be included in high school systems have been specified in state law. In Illinois and California, for example, the ninth grade in some communities is a part of the four-year high school. In some school systems grades seven and eight but not nine have been organized separately from the elementary and secondary schools. In all cases, however, the ideas characteristic of the junior high school have some influence on the teaching practices in grades seven, eight, and nine, and have guided the development of the movement toward the three-grade junior high school form of organization.

Typically, the junior high school cares for the educational needs of the twelve-, thirteen-, and fourteen-year-old children. It is an attempt to direct the movement away from a single curriculum, from a uniform program for all pupils, to an offering that provides the possibilities of choice and the opportunities for specialization that is characteristic of the senior high school. The possibilities for pupils to individualize their programs are moderately introduced in the seventh grade and are gradually increased throughout the eighth and ninth grades.

Wherever possible, pupils are provided with a wide range of direct exploratory experiences. Although exploratory experience is not peculiar to the junior high school—basic science at the college level, for instance, may be exploratory—it is introduced at the junior high school level as a special method of study. For the first time the pupil has the privilege of selecting an elective from such areas as general science, general shop, printing, crafts, art, electricity, music, dramatics, or a foreign language. The pupil surveys some broad area, accumulates first-hand experience, and discovers what is of interest to him. School marks are not usually given in the elective fields, or, where they are assigned, they are not considered to be marks of relative achievement. The teacher is on the alert to discover special interests, aptitudes, and skills and to guide and counsel the individual pupil.

Reading, general science, mathematics, general language, and social studies are all taught in the spirit of exploration. This consumes more time than conventional methods. Pupils are encouraged to observe, to read widely, to investigate independently, to write creatively, and to get a broad view of some field of learning before

The new mathematics and the slide rule are not strangers to this group of junior high-school-age pupils in a Chicago public school. (Chicago Public Schools)

entering detailed study of it. It is thought that the exploratory experience encourages more fruitful learning than is possible through older and more traditional practices.

Extracurricular activities in the athletic, social, musical, and dramatic fields are also provided. These and other features are especially designed to meet the needs of the preadolescent.

Junior high schools plan the work of the pupils around homerooms. The homeroom teachers generally combine the function of counseling with their teaching. One of the functions stressed both in their teaching and counseling is that of social living. The principal aim of the homeroom teacher, and of the other teachers as well but to a lesser degree, is to help pupils solve problems peculiar to their respective ages. The teacher must know what problems are typically associated with the dawning of a social consciousness. Mature guidance calls for mature insights into such problems. The problems dealt with cover almost the whole range of life—physical development, recreation, home relationships, religion, school relationships, personal conflicts, and the like. At the junior high school level it is particularly important that men teachers should be as well represented as women teachers.

A majority of pupils in the United States now attend some kind of reorganized secondary school that differs from the pattern typical of the traditional eight-grade elementary school. Studies by psychologists indicate that more attention should be given to finding better solutions to the ever-widening gap of individual differences that especially characterize pupils of the sixth-, seventh-, and eighth-grade age group. One of the weaknesses of the earlier junior high school programs was a tendency to veer too far away from the older one-curriculum program toward too much departmentalization. A pupil went from a six-grade, one-teacher, one-curriculum school into a school where his teachers sometimes numbered as many as six, each a specialist in a particular subject. Going suddenly from a uniform curriculum to a system of alternative subjects merely added to the pupil's problems of adjustment.

It may be said confidently that the attempt to build a new kind of school organization, one that will more fully provide for the needs of preadolescents, is well under way and that out of this effort will be developed better methods of meeting the problems posed by the children of the "in-between" ages. Psychologists and particularly the child development experts who have focused their studies and attention upon the children of these ages tell us that the physical, emotional, and intellectual characteristics of these youngsters leave little doubt that their needs and interests must be given special consideration. This is the period of early adolescence, a crucial period in the life cycle, a period marked by the child's growth toward physical and mental independence, a period of widening gaps in individual differences. The age is considered the most difficult from the standpoint of discipline. Teaching at the junior high school level calls for special understanding and for specialized teaching skills. It promises commensurate teaching satisfaction.

THE SENIOR HIGH SCHOOL

The senior high school, as we discuss it, embraces grades ten, eleven, and twelve, although some high schools include grade nine as well. Where the ninth grade is included as a part of the high school,

Detroit high school pupils arrange a bulletin board display of book jackets related to books they have read or books that they may be attracted to read. (Detroit Public Schools)

the attitudes toward the pupil and toward appropriate education for him are approximately the same as when the ninth grade is located in a junior high school. The pupil is still the same age and has the same psychological characteristics and the same educational needs.

Americans believe that an enlightened citizenry is necessary to the survival of our democracy. They believe that equal educational opportunity for all children and youth is a correlative requirement. This was not always so. At the beginning of the century many communities prided themselves because very few pupils who entered ninth grade ever finished the twelfth. Modern senior high school practices emerged from a social atmosphere where selection was a favored policy. At the beginning of the century, fewer than 8 percent of the seventeen-year-olds graduated from high school. The high schools actually were *high* schools. Only a few years ago the chances of graduating from high school were greater for those pupils who had intelligence quotients of 110 and above. A child's chances of obtaining an education were enhanced if he came from an economically favored home, if his parents were in the highest income brackets in the community. The high school program was planned with highly selected pupils in mind. Traditions that accompanied that kind of policy became very deeply established. Now, typically, at the completion of twelve years of school attendance each pupil receives a high school diploma. The diploma is the same for all, regardless of the quality of work or the subject matter studied. In most communities completion of the twelfth grade is the terminal point of education for many pupils. The activities of commencement are a universal recognition of this achievement.

With the extension of universal education it has become necessary to cut the academic cloth to fit the needs, abilities, and interests of every educable youth who may wish to take advantage of a senior high school education. If education at the senior high school level is to serve all American youth, then it must be so planned and administered that all American youth can profit from it. High school teachers have moved energetically in the direction of attaining this ideal. Though their progress has been commendable, the conflict of new with old continues partially unsolved. One obstacle to progress has been the deep-seated tradition, firmly intrenched in many minds of the older generation, that high schools should select the fit from the unfit. Another obstacle to fitting the high school program to all American youth is related to disrupting social crises— the depression of the thirties, World War II in the forties, and the sharp upturn in population growth in the fifties. A faculty may desire to make indicated changes but may be hampered by lack of funds and lack of available personnel. In times of international conflict, industry and the government tend to exert pressure for a special kind of training in the high school. The rapidity of social change scarcely gives the high school faculties a chance to keep up to date in their analyses of the adjustments currently needed.

The Curriculum

Typically, the modern high school is developed to serve the needs of students between ages 14 and 18. It offers in one administrative unit all of the programs for the education of all the youth who attend high school in a given community or school district. There are, however, some exceptions in a few of the larger cities. In New York City, for example, there are a number of specialized high schools, such as those giving vocational education. Specialized high schools generally are found in large, wealthy school districts. Most districts of ordinary size cannot afford them. Even though a high school may specialize in a particular kind of vocational training, it still remains comprehensive in that the pupils take a balanced program and can, therefore, continue on to college.

The problem of building a satisfactory curriculum to serve all American youth has two main facets. On the one hand, there must be a reasonable degree of specialized education and, on the other hand, a reasonable emphasis upon general education.

No term has been coined to designate the program that achieves an adequate balance between integration and specialization, between general education and specialized education. The pupil, with the help of his counselors, in most cases may select studies that will prepare him to enter some field of his own choosing. Sometimes this is referred to as fulfilling the preparatory function of the high school. The program of studies can be planned in terms of a future goal. Some high schools have been very ingenious in finding ways to meet the differentiated needs of the young adults. Others have not been ingenious enough. They have stressed certain kinds of preparation, such as preparing the pupil to enter college, but have not succeeded as well with meeting needs of pupils who wish to follow other lines of endeavor.

Every high school curriculum should also give reasonable emphasis to fostering cultural compatibility. It is not easy to say how a heterogeneous population of young adults should be educated so that they become sufficiently like-minded to guarantee the perpetuation and improvement of present American society. That is, nevertheless, a responsibility of every American high school.

The high school's answer to what it believes are the activities that lead to a well-integrated personality can be judged by what all the pupils are required to study. All pupils are usually required to study English for three years and United States history, civics, mathematics, science, and health and physical education each for one year. To this minimum or foundation program, the pupil can add, through his own selection, other courses in general or specialized education to complete his requirements for graduation. In other words, approximately one-half his program is general education and one-half is specialized education. The four subjects that carry the heaviest burden for achieving general education are, in order of the emphasis they receive, English, social studies, mathematics, and science.

The Core Program

One example of how high schools sometimes adjust to new demands has been the development of the core program, sometimes called core courses, corerooms, or core studies. The core program includes all the instruction thought to be needed by all pupils of a given grade level. For example, oral expression, written expression, and citizenship training would be integrated into a single course taught by the core teacher who has received appropriate special training.

Traditional subject matter is generally disregarded in planning work. The work may be planned around a study of the problems of the immediate community. A given project may reveal the important part individuals play in the community, the principles that underlie the American way of life, and problems connected with developing responsible citizenship. The project may teach how to cultivate the art of oral expression and how to participate in planning and conducting certain social activities. The group—the core teacher *with* the pupils—determines the aims of the project and the resources and activities needed to achieve them as the study progresses. The period of working together is longer than a traditional class period. This allows sufficient time for use of laboratory techniques and for pupil-teacher planning. It permits use of the community, makes it possible to complete comprehensive projects, and allows participation in activities necessary for a realistic program of citizenship training.

Work accomplished in core studies varies considerably from school to school. But in all schools it is recognized that the core teacher must be with the pupils longer and that he must know them well. He must be assigned a moderate teaching and counseling load. The core teacher will teach a heterogeneous group, not pupils classified in terms of native ability or academic achievement. He will be responsible for giving individual and group guidance to the pupils and will be free to plan the activities of the core program. Subject matter examinations will largely be replaced by an evaluation that is planned by both the teacher and the pupil. This newer evaluation will focus upon citizenship, work habits, and ability to solve problems, to contribute to group thinking and planning, and to master subject matter. While the coreroom is a unit in the high school plan of organization, it is also a unit of organization in which the teacher strives to fulfill certain functions with fairly definitely determined and generally accepted practices.

The core program is one recent attempt to improve the high school's effectiveness in achieving social integration. Other high school efforts at securing both specialized education and general education include the offering of extracurricular activities, counseling procedures, and special services like psychological testing. The American high school is becoming a truly comprehensive school. It is being modified to serve well the needs of all the young adults of the nation between the ages of fourteen and eighteen.

THE JUNIOR COLLEGE

Many communities in the United States have junior colleges which provide two additional years of free general education for those who wish it and free terminal education of the technical institute or semiprofessional type for those who do not plan to attend school beyond the fourteenth grade. It offers training that prepares students to enter strictly specialized study at the university level. The junior college also serves as a center for the administration of a program for adult education through evening schools, adult forums, and the like. All who graduate from high school are eligible to continue their education in the junior college.

At the beginning of the century, there were fewer than ten junior colleges in the United States and only one, the junior college established at Joliet, Illinois, in 1902 was public. By October, 1962, there were 424 two-year public and 277 nonpublic junior colleges. Some 816,375 students were enrolled. California, with 68 public and 6 nonpublic junior colleges leads the rest of the states with an enrollment in October, 1962 of 354,341 students. Of the 50 states, 39 now have one or more public junior colleges. From the picture of development of both public and nonpublic junior colleges, they have now attained a position of unquestioned public acceptance that suggests for them a prominent place in all the future plans for extending educational opportunities to the youth of America.

In college the library serves as the center for study and research. This interior of the library at the University of Wyoming shows the kinds of material libraries make available. In some areas, such as the Midwest, the universities cooperate, each university specializing in a field or fields. The research students in one university may use the resources of neighboring universities. Resources for study and research are thus multiplied many times over. (Ewing Galloway)

THE STATE UNIVERSITY

One of the most spectacular developments in American education is the state university, the apex of the public educational system. The state university—the answer to the American public's demand for higher education—has no counterpart in any other country. It is indigenous to the American cultural soil and suited to American tradition.

All the state universities have four-year colleges, which award a bachelor degree upon graduation. Superimposed on the college is the graduate school which (1) affords specialization beyond that given in the four-year undergraduate college, (2) awards degrees,

To most older people, Walter Hines Page (1855–1918) is remembered as the distinguished ambassador to Great Britain, an office to which he had been appointed by President Woodrow Wilson. Page also was a writer with a strong passion for democracy. One of the institutions that he believed would make democracy strong was the public school. In one of his speeches he describes "the school that built a town." This excerpt illustrates the trend of his thinking:

In the first period of Northwood's history, you will observe, the town carried the schools—carried them as a burden. The schools of the cultivated widow, the strenuous young lady and the old fashioned scholar and the young ladies' seminary, much as the several sets and sects each boasted of its own institution, were really tolerated rather than generously supported. The principals had to beg for them in one form or other. The public school was regarded as a sort of orphan asylum for the poor. The whole educational work of the town was on a semi-mendicant basis; or it was half a sort of social function, half a sort of charity. It really did not touch the intellectual life of the people. *They* supported *it*. It did not lift *them*. The town carried the schools as social and charitable burdens.

Now this is all changed. The school has made the town. It has given nearly every successful man in it his first impulse in his career, and it has given the comunity great renown. Teachers from all over the country go there to see it. More than that, many pupils go from a distance to enter the high-school. More than that, men have

the master's degree for one year of study beyond the bachelor program and the doctor of philosophy degree for three or more years of study and research beyond the bachelor program, and (3) offers numerous degrees designating fields of specialization—doctor of education, doctor of laws, doctor of science. The faculties are made up of highly trained specialists who combine teaching, scholarly writing, and original research.

Professional schools of law, medicine, dentistry, agriculture, library science, education, engineering, business, journalism, architecture, theology, and speech and a nonprofessional school of arts and sciences are all administered within the common university organization.

The public universities in some cases have become organizational giants. The comprehensiveness of their programs may be

gone there to live because of the school. They go there to establish industries of various sorts, because the best expert knowledge of every craft can be found there. The town has prospered and has been rebuilt. The architects are high-school men; the engineers who graded the streets and made a model system of sewers are high-school men; the roads were laid out by high-school men. There is a whole county of model farms and dairies and good stock farms. High-school men have in this generation made the community a new community. They conduct all sorts of factories—they make furniture, they make things of leather, they make things of wrought iron; they have hundreds of small industries. It is said that a third of the houses in the town contain home-made furniture after beautiful old patterns that the owners themselves have made. And there is one man who does inlaid work in wood. And all this activity clusters about the public schools. The high-school now not only affects but it may be said to dominate the life of the town; and this is the school that has built the town, for it has given everybody an impetus and has started nearly everybody towards an occupation. It has enabled them to find their own aptitudes.

Now there is all the difference in the world between the Northwood of this generation, and the Northwood of the generation before. It is a difference so great that it cannot be told in one morning. But the change is simply the result of a changed view of education.

From Walter Hines Page, *The School That Built a Town* (New York: Harper & Row, Publishers, Inc., 1952), pp. 59–60. Quoted by permission of the publisher.

inferred from their size. The University of California, largest of the state universities, as of January, 1964, had a full-time enrollment of 39,064 men and 23,176 women. The grand total of registrations, full-time and part-time, reached 101,064. The City University of New York, a municipal university, reached an overall total of 101,247. Twelve more state universities had full-time enrollments that exceeded 20,000, while 16 others exceeded 12,000. How large will they become by 1975 when the enrollment in public institutions of higher learning has been projected to exceed 6 million?

The combination of college and university instruction under a single administration is the principal distinctive characteristic of the American state university and is considered one of its chief sources of strength. In some cases, technical institutes within the university framework operate primarily for research purposes, for issuing learned publications under the direction of the teaching staff, for conducting programs contributing to the national defense, and for carrying on a variety of other undertakings deemed essential enough to call for recognition at the university level.

Many state universities have programs set up to serve special needs of the state. Extension divisions, organized in most state universities, provide credit and noncredit courses in various centers of the state for training in many fields. The state universities distribute visual materials and maintain lending libraries throughout the state, and offer short-course seminars, lectures, conferences, and other similar services.

Some state universities have branches in convenient centers in the state, making education more accessible and less costly to the people of the state.

State universities are supported mainly by direct taxation. They also, however, derive considerable revenue from endowments, alumni foundations, student fees, athletics, and the like. The annual expenditure for all state institutions is very large. Their plans are extensive. Their educational influence is very great. The state universities are large, colorful, liberally supported, constantly expanding institutions which make a very popular appeal to the people of the state. They are the capstones of the educational ladder.

THE EDUCATIONAL LADDER

The educational ladder in the American public school system has been the pride of the American people. It has made a major contribution to the maintenance and improvement of the American idea of civilization. The ladder constitutes a continuous chain of instruction from the kindergarten through the most advanced training given by the universities. In the main, the costs are borne by the public and the opportunity of advancing to the higher levels is constantly being extended to more people.

The elementary school, the junior high school, and the senior high school are viewed as institutions for everyone. The desire of the American people to extend educational opportunities at the higher level is answered in part by the junior college, the newest extension of free, popular education.

QUESTIONS

1. What factors should a parent consider before deciding whether to send his child to a nursery school?
2. How much should one expect a child's attendance at nursery school or kindergarten to contribute to his subsequent achievement in subject matter?
3. Why have the factors of continuity, gradation, and transition received such serious consideration in the establishment of school units of organization?
4. What kinds of specialized services would you expect to find in the better organized elementary schools?
5. What are some of the instructional resources you expect to find in the better organized elementary schools?
6. How is the transition idea reflected in the organization of the junior high school?
7. How has the movement to decentralize education affected the organization of the junior college?
8. What are some of the problems the high school faces when it attempts to provide an education for all American youth?

PROJECTS

1. From a table of ages of the children in some particular grade of a school system, generalize on what some of the problems of teaching in that grade may be.
2. Describe the expanding role of the junior college and estimate the future of this public school unit.
3. Set forth what you consider the principal problems of teaching caused by individual differences among the pupils in the different units of school organization.
4. In view of the fact that the federal government provides generous aid to nonpublic higher institutions, state the pros and cons for its providing aid to nonpublic secondary schools. To nonpublic junior colleges. To nonpublic elementary schools.

Stimulating and Growth

Directing
and Development

CHAPTER 16

Understanding pupils

In this Unit we discuss further the work of classroom teachers, focusing now on the teacher's most important responsibility, his responsibility to stimulate and direct the growth and development of pupils. In using the two words, growth *and* development, growth carries the idea of a process that results in gradual increase while development refers to the stage or product attained by the process of growing. One of the oft-repeated truisms in education is that a teacher is a better teacher if he knows his subject matter well. A less often repeated truism that is equally valid is that a teacher is also a better teacher if his knowledge extends beyond the narrow range of subject matter taught and includes also scientific knowledges about the nature and development of pupils. This chapter focuses on this latter kind of essential knowledge, a kind of knowledge that is antecedent to wise and effective stimulation and direction of the growth and development of pupils.

TWO ASPECTS OF UNDERSTANDING PUPILS

In order adequately to understand pupils they must be studied both as individuals and as interacting members of social groups. To be sure, learning by a pupil in school, as elsewhere, is an individual process. The pupil's interaction with his physical and social environment, however, significantly influences what he learns as an individual and how well he learns it. A pupil, for example, may enlarge his vocabulary through personal, independent reading. However, the actual meanings he attaches to the words he acquires, his pronunciation of them, his manner of speaking, and his conversational skills are largely the result of his interactions with those about him. Think of a pupil solving an arithmetic problem. He learns about arithmetic as he works the problem. He also, however, probably interacts with his teacher, with his fellow pupils, and, from the printed page, with the writer of the textbook. What results from working an arithmetic problem or reading a story is thus a complicated, personal, inner change, a change that embraces different kinds of learning. Simultaneously, while adding to insights into arithmetic or increasing vocabulary, the pupil develops certain social attitudes—likes, dislikes, prejudices, for instance. Thus to understand a pupil adequately the teacher must interpret each pupil as an individual and also in terms of the social environment that nurtures him, that determines to a considerable extent how he grows.

TWO KINDS OF INFORMATION ESSENTIAL

Generally speaking, a classroom teacher should know the technical meaning of the terms used in the schools that are related to information assembled about pupils. Each fact, quantity, or statement used to describe growth and development of pupils is concrete information about growth and development—the MA or the IQ, for example. Most schools in America collect comprehensive information about each pupil before attempting an assessment of his needs and possibilities. Collecting information about the pupils usually begins with the kindergarten and continues as long as the pupil is enrolled in school, perhaps through the twelfth grade. By the time the pupil leaves school a considerable amount of information about him has been assembled and recorded in what is generally called his cumulative record folder. It is important that the teacher know the meaning and implication of the technical terms used in making these entries.

It is also essential for teachers to know some of the important generalizations and conclusions regarding human growth and development that specialists have derived from research—especially from researches in the life sciences such as psychology, sociology, pediatrics, psychiatry, biology, dietetics, education, and others that have focused on some aspect of the growth and development of children and youth. Each valid generalization made by a qualified specialist serves as a background which the teacher can use to make an intelligent interpretation of the specific information that the testers, dentists, nurses, doctors, caseworkers, and others provide about pupils.

The language used by specialists to describe pupil growth and development provides teachers with a shared technical vocabulary. Teachers use, with precise meanings, such professional terms as maturation, readiness, learning, mental health, individual differences, achievement norms, motivation, adjustment, maladjustment, aptitude, attitude, intelligence quotient, mental age, age norm, grade norm, and other terms employed by specialists to describe pupil growth and development. Such terms are the everyday media of professional communication.

Without both kinds of knowledge—an understanding of the specific information about a pupil, and a comprehension of scientific generalizations that serve as a frame of reference—neither kind would be of practical value. Generalizations are derived from the averages of many pupils; they are representative of none. They serve principally as a basis for comparing one individual's performance with the average performance of many others. They may tell, for instance, the average reading ability of six-year-old pupils. In terms of that average the teacher interprets the information about a particular six-year-old pupil. With both kinds of information a teacher is equipped to judge the educational needs of each of his pupils, gauge more accurately his possibilities, influence his patterns of behavior, and with greater wisdom guide and stimulate his growth and development.

Knowledge about human growth and development continues to increase. In recent years, the psychologists, especially, have made significant contributions to this knowledge. Their scientific generalizations are now so well organized that they are readily available and easily understood by any interested teacher.

RESEARCH ON GROWTH AND DEVELOPMENT

Generalizations about human growth and development of special significance to teachers have resulted from researches in a variety of fields. Sociology, biology, psychology, and education are among the more important contributors. A few examples of scientific generalizations of special significance to teachers, generalizations that a classroom teacher could not possibly arrive at through his own study and observation, illustrate why the generalizations are of great importance to education.

Biology

Herbert Spencer's efforts to classify life's activities were described in Chapter 8. Spencer also proposed a classification of the sciences. He suggested that biology occupy a central place in any scheme of classification, biology with its foundations in chemistry and physics and leading on into psychology and sociology.

Many crucial problems of education have been clarified by the biologists and particularly by those biologists who have specialized in studies of heredity and evolution. Biologists, for example, have developed a deep concern for the great importance of recognition of individual differences in the education of oncoming generations.

To a biologist, one of the most remarkable features of the human population of this planet is its enormous variety. Here among the 250 million members of the one species, *Homo Sapiens,* we find no duplicates, except those rare cases of identical twins which since they arose from one egg count as one individual. Literally each person is biologically unique and declares this fact not only in his gross and obvious physical features, but in the individual properties of his blood and other body fluids, in the operation of his sense organs, and in numerous details of chemical constitution and behavior.

What is the biological meaning of this vast variety? The biological study of man and of other animal and plant species has established that it arises out of the interplay of two influences to which every living being is subject. One is the heredity transmitted to an individual by his parents through egg and sperm; the other is the varied conditions of life, the environments in which different individuals develop. The causes of hereditary variety are known in outline; they originate in accidents (mutations) which occur in the self-reproduction of the units, the genes, through which the continuous transmission of heredity takes place. The thousands of units which each parent transmits to the children are then shuffled and recombined in all possible combinations. . . .

The variety thus engendered is then acted upon by the sifting effects of the varied environments in which the species lives. . . .[1]

What is the implication for education?

. . . If increased ability to adapt by using our wits is the best hope of the future for human evolution, then the provision for varied opportunities for putting the great variety of human minds to use will be an important goal of future societies. Hardy, Weinberg, and their successors have shown us that human beings are never going to be uniform. Minds as well as bodies may be expected to retain their great variety. Any system of education based upon the assumption of uniformity will defeat its ends.[2]

It has not been easy for teachers to change deeply intrenched practices to accord with the implications of what biologists have concluded, namely, that, to use Dunn's words, "the social and cultural forms which man has evolved have the power to affect his biology . . ." (p. 146). Meredith Nicholson spoke of the schoolmaster of his time as "that ruthless forester who grafts and trims to make all trees uniform." As shown in the subsequent discussion, uniformity has become a sort of religion among America's high school youth. Will this emphasis lead to desirable growth and development as the rates of social, economic, and cultural change, so obvious in the recent past, accelerate still more in the future?

Since, as Spencer stated, biology leads on into psychology, sociology, and education, where its generalizations are often restated in various connections, a teacher's confidence in many of the generalizations made about education is bolstered by the knowledge that these generalizations have their origins in solid, scientific thinking. Some of the basic knowledges about some of the topics that are subsequently discussed in this chapter stem from biology. There are biological bases for understandings important to education, understandings about maturation, human growth, intelligence, environmental influences upon the human organism, and how the organism integrates parts into wholes. Although a study of biology is helpful, the teacher need not study biology because the basic contributions of biology are restated frequently by treatises that bear more directly upon specialized aspects of education.

[1] L. C. Dunn, *Heredity and Evolution in Human Populations* (Cambridge, Massachusetts: Harvard University Press, 1959), Chap. 1, "Variety," pp. 1–2.
[2] *Ibid.*, p. 146.

Sociology

The principal task of the sociologists is to explore social behavior and its products. Social organization, group control, institutionalism, collective behavior, social processes are examples of the subjects of their researches. Many of the generalizations stated by the sociologists are directly applicable to education. One research will illustrate.

In a research on adolescent society, the youth in 10 high schools of varying sizes in different kinds of communities were studied.[3] Answers were sought to questions like: What are the general interests of teen-agers? What activities do they engage in? How do boys and girls differ in interests and activities? What part do automobiles play in the lives of teen-agers? Who are the leaders? What effects does the teen-age social system have upon scholastic achievement? To what extent and why do teen-agers smoke? drink?

The following illustrates the nature of generalizations provided.

> . . . For both boys and girls, popularity with one's own sex is believed to involve good grades and school activities more than does popularity with the opposite sex. For popularity with the opposite sex, cars are more important for boys; and clothes, for girls. These two attributes feature prominently in dating, while good grades and school activities do not.[4]

Social theorists who deduce their generalizations from the other sociologists, in addition to those derived from their own observations, also set forth generalizations that are pertinent to the work of teachers.[5]

Psychology

The generalizations of the psychologists are so closely related to the problem of understanding pupils that most teacher education programs require a special course, Educational Psychology, devoted wholly to the applications of psychology to teaching. Psychology is an indispensable handmaiden to education.

The following quotation from a study of the growth of identical

[3] James S. Coleman, *The Adolescent Society* (New York: The Macmillan Company, 1961), pp. 368, vi, xi.
[4] *Ibid.*, p. 50.
[5] See, for illustration, an excellent statement by Talcott Parsons, *Essays in Social Theory* (New York: The Macmillan Company, 1958), Chap. V.

twins illustrates the kind of generalizations psychologists believe are important.

> . . . These studies implied that the development of the behavior of locomotion was the consequence of structural changes which were biologically paced and independent of the effects of the psychological environment. To a certain extent it was in this way that the concept of maturation was interpreted for some years. Additional research over a long span of time has indicated the impossibility of attributing the behavioral and inferred structural changes to one or other of these two conditions—biological predetermination or effects of stimulation—alone. We know now that we must always think in terms of interactions between these variables. An organism has the biological characteristics of its species and its parentage, but it must always grow up in an environment. The two cannot be completely isolated experimentally or in their behavioral effects.[6]

Education

As was indicated in the earlier part of the book, the word education carries many meanings. In this connection the term is used in a comprehensive sense to designate the broad field of educational theory and practice. It may encompass a number of areas of specializations such as English education, science education, educational philosophy, educational psychology, educational sociology, elementary education, secondary education, higher education, educational administration, comparative education, and so on. One who specializes in any one of these areas is generally known as an educationist. If properly trained he is a specialist in a given field, like psychology, and, in addition, is a specialist in its application to educational theory and practice.

Inasmuch as the field of education comprises many areas of specialization, the research contributions are extensive. The generalizations supplied to teachers may apply to reading, English, mathematics, school law, testing, school finance, school buildings, programmed learning, and many other aspects related to teaching. Studies by educationists touch practically every facet of American education.

A Teacher's Responsibility

In seeking to extend his understanding of pupils in order to achieve certain purposes such as to modify classroom practices so

6 Delos D. Wickens and Donald R. Mayer, *Psychology* (New York: Holt, Rinehart and Winston, Inc., 1961), p. 90.

as to give the most desirable direction to activities chosen to promote growth and development, the teacher should know what reliable sources he may consult and what he should do to keep reasonably informed about important new findings helpful to him. Fortunately, many teacher organizations in specialized fields like the National Council of Teachers of English and the Association of Childhood Education attempt through their publications to present significant research findings of special interest in their fields, including investigations devoted to matters related to understanding pupils.

INNER FORCES AND PUPIL GROWTH

A close relation exists between natural forces that operate within a pupil and his overall pattern of growth and development. As pointed out before, one cannot fully understand a pupil without recognizing that some characteristics of the growth of each pupil are biologically determined. A teacher's assessment of a pupil's achievement, and counsel offered in terms of this, must give appropriate consideration to the hereditary factor, to the inner forces that influence the course of his growth and development.

The growth and development that result from forces that are purely hereditary are maturative, that is, in a friendly environment they produce maturation. The mechanisms of heredity are now well understood and the reader might profit by spending a few minutes reviewing the basic knowledge biologists have supplied.[7]

The biological concept of maturation is that certain changes in the human organism are paced to a considerable extent by hereditary factors. Succinctly stated, this means that certain kinds of learning will not take place, certain kinds of behavior will not emerge, until structural changes within the organism make such changes possible. What a pupil obtains, then, from instruction, from stimulation and direction, from favorable environmental influences is determined by an inward, biological growth and development that are independent of environmental factors, that proceed at a rate that is *predetermined* by hereditary factors. What a pupil *can* learn at a

[7] See, for example, Douglas H. Fryer, Edwin R. Henry, and Charles F. Sparks, *General Psychology* (New York: Barnes & Noble, Inc., 1954), pp. 131–134 and 143–144. This is a condensed explanation of heredity and maturation in simple language.

given time is dependent in part upon the growth and development of certain mechanisms within him, upon his stage of biological maturation.

Psychologists have carried on many experiments designed to shed light upon the effects of maturation upon learning. Typical experiments have dealt with identical twins. Early training in walking, climbing stairs, swimming, skating, or some other kind of activity has been given one of the twins and withheld from the other for a period of time. In some of the experiments the durability of the effects was also studied. In some experiments the twins were alternated—the one used as a control taking the place of the one who received the training. Typically the control twin, the one who had not received the training, in a very short time acquired proficiency in swimming, skating, climbing stairs, equal to the twin who had received previous training. The experimenters concluded that the differences in speed of learning were the result of differences in the level of maturation; changes in behavior were the result of structural changes within the organism which, in turn, were the result, mainly, of biologically predetermined growth factors. Planned practice and training in advance of reaching a given level of maturation seem to make little difference in the final proficiency.

Because of biologically inherited characteristics related to maturation, pupils learn at different rates. In every sizeable age group learning rates range from slow to rapid, and as pupils advance from grade to grade the differentials in rates of learning result in progressively widening divergencies in learning achieved. The persistent and perplexing problem of giving adequate recognition to individual differences caused both by heredity and by previous learning experiences receives and will continue to receive major consideration in America's schools.

With the exception of identical twins, no duplicates are to be found among the people of the world. Each newborn child inherits a natural design from his parents; his intrinsic growth will follow a unique pattern. No pupil escapes developing in accordance with the law of heredity. Each was unique when he entered school; each will continue unique all his life.

In one regard, however, all pupils are alike. *One stage of growth follows the previous stage in a fairly well-defined sequence.* While all normal pupils can, within reason, progress and achieve the same developmental tasks, and when older, can master certain subject matter and develop particular skills, they will not arrive at the same stage of development at the same age because of the unique pattern of individual growth. Knowing the present stage of development of a pupil, a teacher can, within limits, predict what the next stage will be. Inasmuch as natural growth patterns are not uniform, however, he cannot predict very far in advance the specific time of full development in any area for a particular pupil. A child may be expected to creep or scoot before he learns to walk, but the prediction of the age at which a particular child will creep and then walk is subject to varying degrees of error. All normal pupils can, within limits, learn to perform similar tasks. Each, however, will learn in accordance with his own natural design.

Educationists use an inclusive term to describe the level of development of a pupil, an inclusive term—*readiness*. E. L. Thorndike, in 1913, stated that, "When an individual is ready to act in a particular way, it is satisfying to do so, and annoying not to do so; conversely, when an individual is not ready to act in a particular way, to do so is annoying." Thorndike called this the law of readiness. It gives recognition both to the factor of biological maturation and also to the willingness of the learner to learn—his desire, his mental set, the effects of environmental influences.

The theoretical explanation of the causes of readiness is irrelevant in the considerations of teaching practice; what is important is the *fact* of readiness. There are many kinds of readiness, one for almost every act: a readiness to walk, a readiness to talk, a reading readiness, a mathematical readiness, a writing readiness, and so on. A pupil will profit very little from instruction in subject matter for which he has not reached the appropriate readiness stage—the stage at which he can learn it with a reasonable amount of effort.

CULTURAL BACKGROUND OF PUPILS

The growth and development of a pupil are influenced by the social environment with which he is in constant interaction. As somebody has said, through continuous social interaction a child is "able to traverse in a short life-time what the race has needed slow, tortured ages to attain." In order to understand a pupil enough to direct his learning wisely, it is important not only to understand his ability to learn—his readiness—but also to know the nature of the cultural environment that has been and continues to be an influential factor in his growth. This cultural background includes material things such as superhighways, television, ranch houses, and swimming pools. It includes also nonmaterial things such as folk singing, birthday parties, church attendance, and loyalty to the Democratic or Republican Party. Throughout man's history a vast complex of social practices has evolved with so many variations that today cultural characteristics identify nations, others identify regions, and others are associated with class membership within a common community. These influence the social climate of even the smallest classroom.

Geographical Regions

The cultural differences that characterize various geographical regions of our country may be trivial or fundamental, ranging from marked differences in pronunciation, in preferences for certain kinds

In this Puerto Rican school where Spanish is the language of the community, teachers do not face the same problems as in some American cities, where the school population includes many non-English-speaking children. (Monkmeyer)

of food or clothes, to differences in attitudes toward classes, minority
groups, and in ways of earning a living. In moving from one section
of the country to another, a pupil becomes aware that he is different
from those who have spent their lives in the new location. To avoid
disagreeable tensions and to win approval of his peers, however, the
pupil usually adapts rather quickly and satisfactorily to his immediate cultural environment, even if by doing so he encounters family
disapproval. Regional cultural differences tend to create more of a
classroom problem in instances where a large migration results in a
block of "minority" group members—like the Cubans in Florida.

Class Membership

Cultural differences associated with regions do not usually, however, influence learning as much as differences that arise from membership in a particular class. Although many American citizens
hesitate to admit that their society has classes, one can discern on a
somewhat amorphous basis about six social classes: upper-upper
class; lower-upper class; upper-middle class; lower-middle class;
upper-lower class; and lower-lower class. Sociologists have identified
the distinguishing characteristics of each class and have observed
that class is important in determining, for example, an individual's
associates, living quarters, churchgoing habits, reading materials,
quality of clothes worn, and it greatly influences his educational
interests. In their choice of life plans, friends, leisure activities, and
educational goals, pupils reveal that they pattern after members of
their own social class. As one sociologist says:

> Everyone knows that students come to school with widely varying
> interests and aspirations, but the social categories to which these differ-
> ences are generally linked are less well known. The most important of
> these background differences, leaving race and ethnicity aside, is the socio-
> educational level of the family—a combination of father's (and mother's)
> occupation, income, and education.[8]

Studies of the specific attitudes and forms of behavior of middle-
class and lower-class children and of the effects of these upon learning show that there is an increased divergence among the classes
both in social attitudes and in specific forms of behavior as the
children grow older. Class differences influence in many ways the
motivation of pupils to learn.

[8] Burton R. Clark, *Educating the Expert Society* (San Francisco: Chandler
Publishing Company, 1962), pp. 58–59.

Although the number is diminishing, rural schools still exist in America. In such schools the teacher develops his own techniques in seeking to understand and direct the pupils. Since the number of pupils enrolled in the rural school is small, the teacher's methods are generally informal and his instruction highly individualized. (Monkmeyer)

America's schools are largely under middle-class leadership. Most classroom teachers reflect middle-class values and their instruction favors middle- and upper-class children. Children who come from middle-class homes have the values, manners, habits, and attitudes that teachers share and stress at school. The vocabulary used by the teachers is the vocabulary with which upper- and middle-class children and youth are familiar. Even tests typically contain items more readily recognized by children of the middle and upper classes than by children of lower classes.

Influences on the Curriculum

The curriculum being prepared by middle-class personnel contains a middle-class bias. In the lower grades, especially, the curriculum often includes material that gives little recognition to the cultural backgrounds of pupils from lower classes. One social psychologist made a study of 15 widely used readers.[9] The study revealed that the typical elementary school reader pictured a world oriented to middle- and upper-class traditions and also reflected an ethnic and class bias. The Americans are "almost exclusively north European in origin and appearance. . . . They are predominantly, almost exclusively, blondes. . . . Americans in these readers are all quite well-to-do." Not only does the material deal with ideas and experiences remote from the lives of lower-class children, it presents an ethnic bias that may lead children of Negro, Puerto Rican, South European, and possibly Jewish origins to feel as though they do not belong.

The pupil who comes from a middle- or upper-class home where reading is a common pursuit, where books, paintings, and music and the like are important parts of the home surroundings, has an educational advantage. Perhaps this weighting of the curriculum explains, at least in part, the positive correlation of high school marks with class membership.

Influence on School Attendance

Lower school attendance and dropouts are definitely greater among lower- and lower-lower-class children. This may be caused in part by the fact that pupils from the lower classes usually receive a greater proportion of the lower and failing grades. Studies of school records show that pupils who drop out of school early usually had a difficult time while in school. Studies also show that, on the average, the less competent the pupil has shown himself to be in meeting school tasks, the more quickly he is released to face out-of-school problems. The youngsters who are least able to acquire socially useful habits, information, and points of view without formal instruction are those to whom the school has given the poorest preparation. The exception to this general rule is the athlete. Because of success in athletics, a pupil, regardless of social class, is frequently given enhanced social recognition and his school attendance is likely to continue.

[9] Otto Klineberg, "Children's Readers: Life is Fun in a Smiling Fair-Skinned World," *Saturday Review,* February 16, 1963, pp. 75–77 and 87.

Adequate Recognition

The teacher must know the background of his pupils and appreciate its bearing upon learning. Otherwise, he may unknowingly permit his own cultural biases to color his interpretation of pupils' needs and interests. Each pupil must be recognized as the product of his family, school, and community. It must be remembered that his personality is in large measure molded by forces beyond his control and that what he believes should be the goals in life will be influenced by the goals and marks of success that dominate in his social environment. These will be different for lower-class and lower-lower-class families and for middle- and upper-class families. Clearly social factors such as mentioned must be taken into account in the aims and in the selection of curriculum materials and methods used in the classrooms, if America's schools are going to recognize individual differences adequately.

LEARNING

At the opening of this chapter it was indicated that a classroom teacher must know the technical meaning of certain terms such as mental age, intelligence quotient, and achievement norms to interpret accurately various kinds of information collected by the schools about the growth and development of pupils. It was also emphasized that a classroom teacher must know the important generalizations about human growth and development and be clear about the implications these generalizations have for teaching practice. Possessed of the two kinds of knowledge, specific information about each pupil and the scientific generalizations in terms of which to apply the specific information, a teacher has a valid basis on which to predict future behavior of his pupils.

One important term is *learning*. In a sense all the materials that follow—measurement, aims, subject matter, methods, and instructional aids—are all expansions of one basic concept, learning. What is learning?

Learning consists of the changes in behavior that follow behavior. When confronted by a situation a second time, one behaves differently than one did when meeting the situation the first time.

What is learning? What is the nature of the psychological process by which learning takes place? A psychologist explains the process as follows.

In many ways, learning is the most vital phase of the whole psychological process—vital for the occurrence of the necessary changes in the behavior of adjusting organisms.

The motivated organism senses its world, interprets it, responds to it, and then *responds to the consequences* of its own response. Once the organism has passed through this cycle, it is never again the same. Its first behavior has consequences; there is resultant comfort or relief or satisfaction. These consequences of its own behavior, registered and stored, become a part of the organism. It has gained experience. It is never again the same, and its behavior begins to show it. Tomorrow the organism interprets the world differently than it did today because it is different. It responds differently. It continues to register the consequences of its own behavior. It is well embarked on the spiraling, dynamic process of living, a process in which growth and change, over a period of time and with experience, plays a central role.

Filmore H. Sanford, *Psychology, a Scientific Study of Man* (Belmont, California: Wadsworth Publishing Company, Inc., 1962), p. 303.

To say this another way, learning is the modification in behavior that results from an earlier response to the same stimulus. A person responds differently to a stimulus situation because he profits from his previous experience. A child will not be likely to touch a hot stove a second time.

It is relatively easy to define learning and to provide simple examples, but some learning like, say, learning to be a truly great teacher, an outstanding novelist, a proficient surgeon, or a highly skilled mechanic, is very complex and occurs in many forms. To make the definition stated above more meaningful it must be expanded into a more general concept. One must know much more to be able to judge, for example, when learning is good and when bad, to know what conditions lead to the best learning, to conclude what factors are favorable to producing desirable learning. To achieve this a number of words are employed which, while in meaning they are not mutually exclusive, do help to explain the aspects of learning that commonly occur in everyday life—words that are part of everyday language. These words related to learning include: habit, skill, memory, forgetting, attention, motive, and capacity.

When used in the sense that the psychologist uses them, the concepts built around the words help to clarify the meaning of learning.

Habit

A habit is a form of learned behavior that is engaged in without conscious thought. It is a pattern of behavior that has become stereotyped and hence is highly predictable.

Habits are readily acquired; many of them, in fact, result from a single response. Since a pupil's first performance on a task may set the pattern for his later performances of similar tasks, it is important that, wherever possible, his first response should be a correct one. There is always the possibility that he will repeat his first performance over and over again. Obviously, the kinds of teaching each pupil receives in his earlier years and the habits he establishes are crucially important to the quality of learning that will result from his instruction in later years.

Since pupils form bad habits as well as good habits, teaching involves guidance in breaking undesirable habits. It is difficult for a pupil to break a bad habit, more difficult if it is of long standing. A pupil who habitually slouches in his seat may find it difficult to break the habit even when he strongly desires to do so. The older he is, the more difficult it is to break a habit. One's lifelong habits are deeply ingrained in one's organism.

The skilled teacher learns how to direct pupils away from the formation of bad habits by channeling their energies into directions that lead to the formation of good habits. The time-honored teaching device used to deter the development of bad habits and to encourage the building of good ones is punishment. Punishment in this connection does not always produce the results expected. To be effective, the punishment has to be severe and must be so timed as to interrupt the course of the act. Unfortunately, in school situations, punishment usually takes place some time after the response that it is expected to disrupt. Mild punishment may arouse interest and excitement among pupils and thereby actually reinforce bad habits. Punishment that is unnecessarily severe may lead to aversion, withdrawal, and other undesirable responses that may be worse than the bad habit the punishment was meant to correct. A good start to breaking a bad habit is for the pupil himself to recognize the cue that leads to action that he recognizes as unwholesome

Sometimes the behavior of children deviates from the normal to such an extent that the teacher needs help. Here a child guidance specialist helps to iron out a behavior problem. Although a teacher in an elementary school must know many things well, he cannot be expected to be a specialist in all of them. (Board of Education, Wilmington, Delaware)

and to substitute another response to the cue. He can start by saying to himself, "No!" to the wrong response—out loud if necessary—when he encounters the cue. "I misspell that word! I'm going to make sure I don't misspell it this time!" he says immediately when he encounters the word.

Skill

When a pupil has developed skill he has learned well that which enables him to arrive at a right result, create a desired product with a minimum outlay of energy or time. Whatever he does, if he possesses a skill, he does well. This holds true regardless of whether a skill is largely manual or highly refined and complex. The variations in rates of mastery of skills is as great as in the other aspects of learning.

Memory

Memory, like habit and skill, is another important aspect of learning. Memory is the recall of past behavior or, more accurately, behavior that is reconstituted, or mentally revived, or adapted. Some cue in the present environment, perhaps a substitute cue within the body itself, partially revives or reconstitutes some form of behavior that the learner has executed in the past. The recollection is available as knowledge, the possession of which prompts the individual to behave—differently, if the recollection is adverse, or in the same way, if the recollection is pleasant.

Ability to reconstitute past behavior is strengthened by repetition. The pupil strengthens his ability to recall an event or an experience through narration, by telling his parents about something learned in school, by repeating what is to be learned to himself, or by just thinking it. Intention to remember is here a factor also since the pupil will remember more vividly, verbalize more often, repeat more accurately, if he is aware that he is expected to narrate later what he learns.

Pupils are frequently required to memorize subject matter materials such as spelling words, definitions, rules of grammar; basic formulas in mathematics, chemistry, physics; vocabulary in foreign languages; and the like. Repeated verbalization, going over the material orally, silently, in writing, are indispensable reinforcements to efficient recall. Thorough, long-remembered learning is not a hurried process.

The teacher's methods as discussed in Chapter 19 have much to do with a pupil's success in remembering what is taught. Teachers can aid pupils to develop efficient habits of memorizing. In memorizing materials that have to be remembered verbatim, the teacher can help the pupils by explaining the advantages of distributive learning, that is by distributing memorization over a period of time. The more opportunities to verbalize, the better will material like concepts, processes, understandings, whatever must be remembered, be retained. The creative teacher can devise many ways to reinforce a pupil's memory through telling, orderly review, novel applications, using the old in new contexts, and the like. The teacher is always a factor in the successes and failures of his pupils to remember.

Forgetting

Forgetting, the inability to recall, is a kind of learning in which new learning weakens older learning. This concept of forgetting leads to practices different from those resulting from the concept that prevailed in earlier times—that memory is a kind of storehouse of knowledge and that forgetting is caused by a lapse of time between learning and attempted recall.

The current explanation of forgetting is that when a pupil makes two or more different responses to the same stimulus—assuming that the same stimulus recurs—the last response has a physiological advantage over the first. New and different responses to older stimuli diminish and eventually almost erase much of the earlier learning. What happens to what pupils learn in the early years of school depends, therefore, upon what they learn in the later years. A child may learn to say "am not" in school. If later he is constantly with people who say "ain't," he tends to forget the earlier learned response because when he makes the new response, using "ain't," the former response is weakened—forgotten. Thus we may conclude as Thorndike did at the beginning of this century, after many studies of forgetting, that "there is no validity in the assumption that there is some magical curve of forgetting which every function at every stage will somewhat closely follow." How much one forgets depends upon the new learning that takes place, the conditions under which it takes place, and how many new responses take precedence over old responses.

Attention

Attention—called *stimulus selection* by psychologists—is an essential factor in all learning. If the pupil's attention is given to a fly buzzing in the window instead of to the teacher's explanation of the meaning of a word, he learns about the fly and not about the word.

The teacher recognizes the importance of stimuli in the classroom and is alert to those which he may exploit to encourage pupils to give their attention. Stimuli that most favor attention are those most likely to arouse and hold interest, such as: change and variety, which have the greatest advantage in attracting attention; definite form as contrasted with degrees of vagueness; striking quality such as wisely selected, skillfully presented illustrations involving something extraordinary in color, sound, or shape; size at least sufficient to make clear the details (older textbooks presented the more technical and sometimes important materials in fine print that pupils usually skipped reading); strengths, such as a teacher who speaks with a clear, firm voice.

Repetition or frequency of response under many, but not all, conditions, may favor attention and reinforce learning generally. The more often a given stimulus is responded to within a limited period of time and under favorable conditions, the more firmly learning is established. The effectiveness of this principle is illustrated in politics and advertising where slogans, phrases, claims are repeated over and over again. In teaching (the reader may think here of learning to type or learning the multiplication table) the repetition of an appropriate response should occur under conditions that utilize other reinforcements such as words of approval from the teacher, concrete evidence of progress made toward attainment of the goal-object, desire on the part of the pupil to improve, and the like. Without these, repetition becomes dull and can lead to a decline in attention and in performance. In classroom practice, therefore, teachers construe repetition to mean the repeating of an appropriate response under conditions that afford the pupil other reinforcements when needed.

Since elementary teachers are with younger pupils throughout the school day and since the attention span of their pupils is short, sustained attention is not easy to obtain. Teachers of young pupils must give much thought to the problem of developing teaching skills.

As said before, the terms used in describing learning are not mutually exclusive. Skills are one kind of habit. Pupils can form the habit of making desirable stimuli selection, of giving attention to that which is expected of them, to learning what is most worth attending to, and, conversely, to learning not to attend to stimuli of little or no importance to them. The teacher, in addition to wisely selecting and managing the stimuli he uses, tries to get pupils to be conscious of their own responsibilities to form good habits of attention. In fact, teaching pupils how to study consists mostly of instructing them on how to develop good habits of attention.

It should be mentioned that undesirable behavior is often an effort to gain attention, and that redirecting attention is frequently dependent on a desirable learning climate in the classroom.

Motive

A motive is something that prompts a person to act in a certain way. The psychologist Woodworth defined motive as "a tendency toward a certain end-result or end-reaction, a tendency which is itself aroused by some stimulus, and which persists for a time because its end-reaction is not at once made." This seems to reduce the problem of teaching to the wise selection of a stimulus that arouses a strong tendency in the pupil, say, to read *Hamlet,* which persists until the reading of *Hamlet* is completed. How comforting! But, a qualification is in order! A pupil never has *a* motive. He has *many* motives, some of which harmonize, some compete, some conflict. Picture the teacher confronted with 30 pupils, each of whom may have a tendency to act in many different ways because he has a multiplicity of motives. It is this kind of situation that affords daily challenge to the efficient teacher. The teacher knows that he can more intelligently interpret the behavior of his pupils if he has some basic understanding about how motives operate to condition behavior.

Motives are closely related to and possibly emerge from the fundamental needs of the human organism, the more basic of which are air, food, water, sex, and perhaps exercise. Even these are not always of the same level, the same degree of urgency. At different times varying ones take priority over others. It is believed that when the basic needs are met, higher needs emerge. A ravenously hungry, growing boy will not be deeply interested in studying his mathematics just before lunch time. Nor will he be patient during a long wait in the lunch line. Food is the end result he seeks, and he does not like waiting to get it. The last period in the school day may seem dull to those pupils who feel a growing need for release of tension built up by a too-long period of inaction. Improper management of the motive-to-exercise sometimes leads pupils and teachers alike to look with a feeling of dread upon what they think of as the most difficult period in the day—the last one. Perhaps it has been preceded by too much physical inaction and the desire to exercise has intensified because the end-reaction has been too long delayed.

Human needs seem usually to follow a kind of hierarchical sequence in which the learner seeks to satisfy the lower ranking or more urgent needs first. Once the basic needs are satisfied, subsequent needs like the needs for physical security, affection, self-esteem, feelings of independence, desire for adult and peer approval, pride in superior achievement, may then receive attention. Somewhere in the upper reaches of this hierarchy come responses such as appreciation for the beautiful, desire to write creatively, intention to specialize in some field of interest to a point where one can utilize all his abilities.

Motivation originates in human needs. The psychologist explains the process:

Motivation, contrary to the popular usage of the term, is not a bag of tricks which the teacher uses to produce learning. Rather it is a process which belongs to the pupil. It is similar to vision in that it involves external stimulation, appropriate mechanisms of response, and an internal force which energizes the response. The basic substratum of motivation may be found in the needs of the child. The first important characteristic of motives is that they have an energizing function. They stir up behavior. Besides releasing energy, motives have a character of directionality. Energy produced by needs seeks a discharge in relevant incentives, or goal objects which satisfy needs. In brief, motivation may be described as a process in which energies produced by needs are expended in the direction of goals.

.   .   .

Motivation of school learning depends upon such factors as the learner's purpose or intent to learn, his self-concept and self-confidence, his levels of aspiration, and his knowledge and appraisal of how well he is doing in relation to his goals. It is the job of the teacher to create an atmosphere which provides desirable outlets for needs in the direction of worthwhile incentives—an atmosphere in which interests will as a consequence flourish.

From Glenn M. Blair, Stewart R. Jones, and Ray H. Simpson, *Educational Psychology*, Second Edition (New York: The Macmillan Company, 1962), pp. 208–209.

Capacity

Capacity means *potential* to learn. The term disregards the relative contributions made by nature and nurture to the development of this potential. It refers to the ultimate limit to which a pupil can develop a given function. A bottle holds only so much water; a limit is set. It is used by educators in such common statements as: "The pupil should work up to his capacity"; "Subject matter taught should match the capacity of the pupil."

TESTS

So far this chapter has been concerned with knowledge *about* growth and development, background knowledge that is general in that it is true of the many. To understand the individual pupil this general information must be supplemented by *specific* information about him. Both kinds of knowledge, that which is general about growth and development, and that which is specific about an individual, are essential. Much specific educational information collected about pupils is quantitative, consisting of the results of tests, either informal teacher-made tests or tests which have been standardized.

Functions of Tests

The main purpose of testing is to lead to a fuller understanding of the pupil. It is expected that this understanding will aid in directing instruction in terms of the pupil's educational needs. In this way tests serve as *instructional aids*. In the construction of any test, standardized or teacher-made, and in determining when and what kinds of tests to use, the function to be served should be the important criterion.

Perhaps the beginning student of education should not be left with the idea that educationists are all in one camp and agree upon the right functions and legitimate uses of tests. Dewey, for example, was never interested in *capacity* psychology. In his *How We Think* he took the position that individual differences in capacity are of far less importance to learning than is the fact that every pupil can be taught to learn and think far more effectively than he does.

There is the danger that tests may become ends rather than means to improved educational practice. Teachers may be tempted to concentrate more on evaluating a pupil's achievements than on gaining a better understanding of strengths and weaknesses in order more wisely to stimulate and direct his growth and development.

These and other considerations of the functions of tests the student will encounter later in his formal courses in educational psychology and, more particularly, in educational philosophy.

Standardized Tests

Standardized tests are tests prepared by experts who follow a definite procedure. After study and experiments with many test items, the experts determine the difficulty and value of the items and make a final selection. These test items are then administered to a so-called standardization group, usually a large group and one representative of those who will eventually be tested by the instrument as far as such factors as age, sex, socioeconomic background are concerned. The questions used in the test are "objective" in that the pupil does very little writing, if any, and the marking and scoring are done according to definite rules that do not require the scorer to make judgments. The test experts compute the averages made by the large standardization group in terms of the age or grade. These averages constitute the norms and any teacher administering and scoring the standardized test according to the methods prescribed in the test can compare the achievement of any pupil with the age and grade norms supplied by the experts.

1. Intelligence Tests

For a long time how to distinguish the dull pupil from the normal but unmotivated one posed a difficult problem for psychologists. A French psychologist, Alfred Binet (1857–1911), constructed the first individual mental examination. Originally published in 1904, it consisted of a series of tasks graduated into age levels on the basis of the accomplishments of children at each age level who were able to do the tasks.

The presently used standardized intelligence test is a composite one made of a number of parts, each of which has a high statistical correlation with indirect measures of mental ability, such as school marks. It is designed to measure how well an individual perceives relationships, his ability to interpret the meaning of abstract materials, his proficiency in the use of words. In other words, the tests measure *overall* mental ability.

What is included in intelligence tests is not determined through the application of some authoritative definition of intelligence but

Lewis M. Terman ranks as one of America's foremost educational psychologists. He revised the Binet individual intelligence test to make it applicable to American school children. He developed techniques for measuring the intelligence of children in groups. He was the first to make a comprehensive study of gifted children. The study, begun in 1910, followed the development of a thousand California school children with intelligence quotients of 140 or above through their subsequent periods of development, comparing their development with that of a control group of children of average intelligence.

implies rather that certain elements of learning are related to intelligence. Hence the cliché that intelligence is what intelligence tests measure. For purposes of this discussion of tests widely used in America's schools, the meaning of intelligence is assumed to be what the test makers represent it to be: the degree of ability represented by performance on a group of tests selected because they have proved their practical value in the prediction of success in academic work. In the main, careful studies of the results of intelligence tests reveal they are more dependable than subjective judgment and that they yield knowledge about pupils that, when properly used, is quite valuable.

a. *Assumptions.* Two Assumptions that underlie the construction of intelligence tests are: first, the pupils tested have had equal opportunity to be familiar with the tasks presented; second, the reactions of the pupils to the tests are independent of the kinds of schooling they have had. For practical purposes it is necessary to make these assumptions although they may not always be entirely true. For instance, the most common measure of intelligence used by makers of intelligence tests is pupil vocabulary. But nationwide uniformity in which all pupils enjoy equal opportunities to build vocabulary does not exist. Growth of vocabulary often depends on chance or accident. This means that even though tests are constructed and standardized with utmost care, final scores are subject to a degree of error. With an occasional pupil the error in an intelligence test score may be considerable. If a pupil takes two or more intelligence tests and makes different scores, it is generally assumed that his highest score is more nearly the correct one. It represents the level it is possible for him to reach; it indicates his potential.

b. *Two kinds.* The two kinds of intelligence tests are group and individual. Because of convenience and economy, group intel-

Edward Lee Thorndike (1874–1949) was a distinguished scientist in the field of educational psychology. His achievements were recognized by leading universities both in America and Europe who honored him with honorary degrees. His scholary writings and penetrating researches extended to many areas, as a listing of some of his publications shows. Among his more important contributions were: *Educational Psychology* (1904), three volumes; *Mental and Social Measurements* (1904); *Elements of Psychology* (1905); *Animal Intelligence* (1911); *The Original Nature of Man* (1913); *The Psychology of Learning* (1914)—a three-volume summary of his many researches on learning; *Psychology of Arithmetic* (1922); *Psychology of Algebra* (1923); *The Measurement of Intelligence* (1926); *Human Nature and the Social Order* (1940). He was also a professional lexicographer. From his researches on language development he compiled a dictionary which with some modernization by cooperating authors is still widely used. In 1942 he gave the William James public lectures* in which he applied his wide range of knowledge to topics of interest to students of language, political science, law, and sociology. Writing in the early stages of the development of educational psychology, he provided the education profession with an initial insight into methods of educational research that are still of considerable significance.

* Edward Lee Thorndike, *Man and His Works* (Cambridge, Mass.: Harvard University Press, 1943), p. 212.

ligence tests are more frequently used. They can be administered to large groups and scored by the regular teaching personnel. The administering and scoring, in fact, have been reduced almost to the level of clerical routine. In order not to add to teaching loads, special centralized testing bureaus often select, purchase, administer, and score all standardized tests. Information about tests is then routed to principals and teachers who, by position, are qualified to make intelligent use of it. This requires that the teacher have some understanding of the tests themselves and the implications of the test results.

c. Basic terms. It is necessary to understand one basic term, the mental age or MA, in interpreting intelligence test scores. A second important term, the intelligence quotient or IQ, is derived from the MA. Both have become part of the everyday, professional vocabulary of teachers.

To understand mental age, recall the procedure specialists follow in standardizing tests. If the final score a pupil makes on a standardized intelligence test is the same as the average scores made by children in the standardization group who have a chronological age of, say, 74 months, he is said to have a mental age of 74. All intelligence tests are gradated in months and MA's are expressed in months. If the average score of a pupil is the same as the average score made by the children in the standardization group who are the same age as he, his MA in months is the same as his chronological age. An MA of 78 affords no information on how old the pupil is chronologically; it simply means that his score is equal to the average child of 78 months in the standardization group.

The intelligence quotient or IQ is computed from the MA. It is simply the ratio, MA:CA. Because MA's are computed in months, usually in two-month intervals, both the MA and the CA are expressed in months. In order to eliminate dealing in decimals the result is always multiplied by 100. This may be better expressed by the formula
$$IQ = \frac{MA \text{ in months}}{CA \text{ in months}} \times 100.$$
Usually the MA and IQ can be read directly from tables furnished with the test. A teacher's main responsibility is to know how to administer and score the tests, and how to make intelligent interpretations of the data furnished by them.

d. Distribution of intelligence. Measures of intelligence of any large group representative of the population distribute according to the *normal curve of probability* the general form of which is shown in Fig. 16.1. The curve is bell-shaped, is *bilaterally symmetrical.* The same number of IQ's are above the average as below it. Since the curve is a mathematical continuum any division into groups must be wholly arbitrary. It is fortunate for education that the curve is bell-shaped so that by far the largest number of pupils constitute a small range cluster around the average of 100.

Psychologists have broken the distribution down into arbitrary classifications typically like the following:

Classification	IQ	Percent of Population
Genius or near genius	above 140	0.25
Very superior	120–140	6.75
Superior	110–120	13.00
Average	90–110	60.00
Dull	80–90	13.00
Borderline	70–80	6.00
Feebleminded	below 70	1.00

Fig. 16.1   The Normal Distribution of Mental Ability Compared
with the Distribution of Mental Ability Test Scores of 890
Sixth-Grade Pupils in a City School System

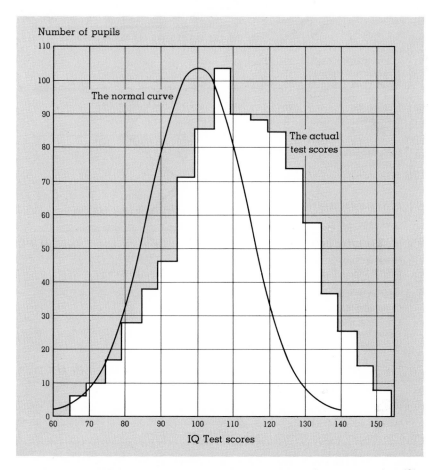

e. Interpreting the scores.   Each section of a group intelligence test measures a different aspect of native ability. Usually
scores made on the various sections are graphed into profiles such
as shown in Fig. 16.2. These pictographs reveal the strengths and
weaknesses of a pupil in various areas, as well as his total overall
ability. The graphs serve to aid the teacher in comparing and interpreting the scores.

The intelligence quotient expresses the pupil's *potential* rate of
learning. Since pupils with higher intelligence quotients learn more
rapidly than those with lower quotients, the divergencies between

FIG. 16.2   INDIVIDUAL MEASUREMENT OF MENTAL MATURITY

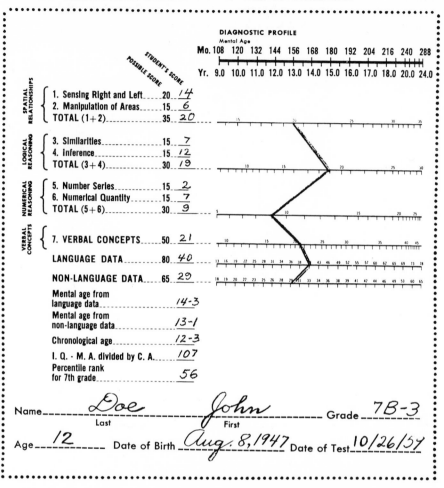

Generally, mental maturity is measured by a standardized test. The scores of an individual pupil are drawn on a diagnostic chart like the sample above. (Adapted and simplified from a California Short-Form Test of Mental Maturity, Junior High Level, '57 S–Form.) The various achievements of a given pupil are measured by standardized tests very much like intelligence tests. Compare the profile chart shown on page 425 with the aptitude chart above. (Adapted and simplified from a California Achievement Test, Intermediate Form AA)

mental ages increase as educational experiences multiply. The following chart (Fig. 16.3) illustrates the increase in the differences of the mental ages of three pupils with IQ's of 80, 100, and 140. In the kindergarten, when they are 5 years or 60 months old, their mental ages, expressed in months, are 48, 60, and 84. The discrepancy be-

Fig. 16.3   Divergence in Mental Age of Three Pupils with IQ's of 80, 100, and 140, as They Grow Older

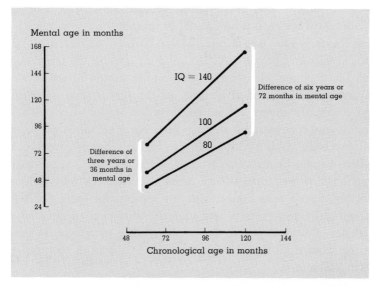

(George G. Thompson, Eric F. Gardner, and Francis J. DiVesta, *Educational Psychology*, p. 8., copyright © 1959, Appleton-Century-Crofts, New York)

tween the youngest and the oldest is 36 months or 3 years. In the fifth grade, when they are 120 months or 10 years old, their mental ages are 96, 120, and 168. The discrepancy between the youngest and the oldest then is 72 months or 6 years.

Knowing the position of each pupil on a group intelligence test helps a teacher judge what each pupil is able to learn; it reduces the guesswork in estimating what a pupil should be expected to accomplish.

2. Achievement Tests

Standardized achievement tests measure a pupil's knowledges, skills, understandings, and the like in a given subject matter field such as mathematics or English and cover the whole range of ages from kindergarten through the twelfth grade. They are, for instance, used in the kindergarten to determine reading readiness, they are used near the end of high school, the so-called College Entrance Examinations, to aid nonpublic colleges and universities in selecting students for admission, and at all points between for ability grouping and guidance.

Achievement tests have been constructed to test achievement in almost every subject taught. Some of the tests—usually referred to as batteries—measure several types of subject matter and may yield separate scores for each kind of subject matter.

a. *Kinds.* The two kinds of standardized achievement tests are speed tests and power tests. In the speed tests all the items are of equal difficulty, and the score is the number the pupil answers correctly in a specified period of time. In the power tests, sometimes called *scales,* the items are scaled in order of difficulty, with the easiest-to-answer questions coming first. No time limit is set, the pupil proceeds as far up the scales as he can, and his score is the number of items he answers correctly. Some tests are a combination of speed and power tests. Where speed and accuracy are considered important, speed tests concentrate on testing the basic skills like reading, while power tests test understanding and ability to use knowledge. Power tests test the pupil's ability to reason, to derive meaning from the printed page, to arrive at solutions to problems, to form judgments.

b. *Norms.* Although no great skill is needed to administer and score standardized achievement tests, some knowledge about the tests is helpful in drawing justifiable inferences from the test results. The teacher needs to understand 1) the nature and significance of norms; 2) how to make and interpret a pupil's profile.

Norms are supplied by the publisher of standardized achievement tests. Without norms a raw score would be practically meaningless. As pointed out before, the norm is a statistical average computed by the maker of the test from the scores of many pupils who have taken the test. The norms enable the teacher to compare the scores of his individual pupils with those of others.

The three most commonly used achievement test norms are age, grade, and percentile norms. The age norm is the average achieved on the standardized test by pupils of a given age. The grade norm is the average made by pupils of a given grade. The percentile norm is the point on a scale of 100 points that indicates the percentage of those taking the test who made a score equal to or less than the value of that point. If the score is on the 72nd percentile it means that 72 percent of the scores fall at or below this score.

As with intelligence scores, the distribution of achievement test scores conforms fairly closely to the normal curve of probability (Fig. 16.1). The teacher can locate the scores of his pupils on the distributional picture furnished by the test manuals.

FIG. 16.4 INDIVIDUAL MEASUREMENT OF ACHIEVEMENT

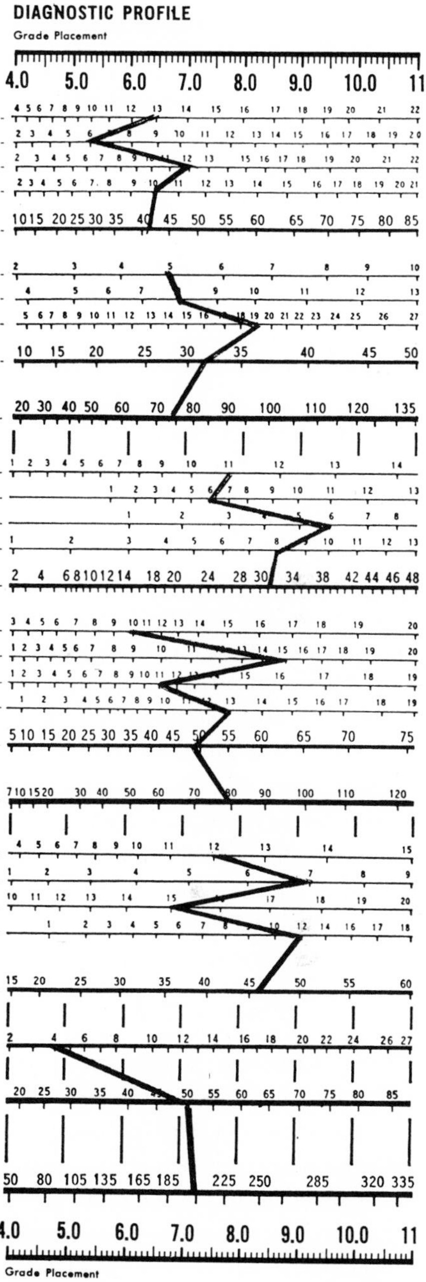

DIAGNOSTIC PROFILE — Grade Placement (4.0 5.0 6.0 7.0 8.0 9.0 10.0 11)

		POSSIBLE SCORE	STUDENT'S SCORE
READING VOCABULARY	A. Mathematics	22	13
	B. Science	23	6
	C. Social Science	23	12
	D. General	22	10
	TOTAL (A+B+C+D)	90	41
READING COMPREHENSION	E. Following Directions	10	5
	F. Reference Skills	15	8
	G. Interpretations	30	19
	TOTAL (E+F+G)	55	32
	TOTAL READING	145	73
ARITHMETIC REASONING	A. Number Concept	15	11
	B. Symbols and Rules	15	6
	C. Numbers & Equations	10	6
	D. Problems	15	8
	TOTAL (A+B+C+D)	55	31
ARITHMETIC FUNDAMENTALS	E. Addition	20	10
	F. Subtraction	20	15
	G. Multiplication	20	11
	H. Division	20	13
	TOTAL (E+F+G+H)	80	49
	TOT. ARITHMETIC	135	80
MECH. OF ENGLISH AND GRAMMAR	A. Capitalization	15	12
	B. Punctuation	10	7
	C. Words and Sentences	20	15
	D. Parts of Speech	20	12
	TOTAL (A+B+C+D)	65	46
SPELLING	TOTAL SPELLING	30	4
	TOTAL LANGUAGE	95	50
	TOTAL TEST	375	203

Name __ Doe __ / __ John __   Grade __ 7B-3
Last / First

Age __ 12 __   Date of Birth __ Aug. 8, 1947 __   Date of Test __ 10/27/59

The distribution of test scores and the establishment of norms that inevitably conform in general to the normal curve of probability may seem to some teachers to reflect a fatalistic philosophy of education. By the way test scores distribute, some pupils will inevitably rank high, others low. The distribution, however, reflects the pattern of nature and its form cannot be changed any more than the nature of human beings can be changed.

c. Individual profiles. Graphic techniques are often used to make vivid the relative achievement level of a given pupil or a class of pupils. Pictographs, called profiles, are line diagrams of the norms made on different tests or on different sections of a test. Examples are reproduced in Figs. 16.2 and 16.4. From a brief study of such charts teachers can gain considerable information about a given pupil or class of pupils.

3. Other Kinds of Standardized Tests

Standardized tests have been constructed for purposes other than measuring intelligence and achievement. Interest tests measure a pupil's likes and dislikes; aptitude tests indicate such pupil potential as musical, mathematical, or mechanical ability; personality tests measure some aspect of a pupil's personality; prognostic tests predicate a pupil's promise of success in a given line of endeavor; and diagnostic tests discover pupils' weaknesses in a narrow subject matter field with a view to directing the teachers in remedial instruction. Usually tests like these are used by specialists or supervisors in the schools. The standardized intelligence tests and the standardized achievement tests are the instruments most commonly used by classroom teachers.

4. Effects of Standardized Testing Upon Educational Practice

Although standardized tests have been very widely used in America's schools, it is not easy accurately to assess their effects because many variables complicate the picture. The following developments seem to have resulted, in part at least, from the standardized testing movement.

a. Recognition of individual differences. The vast amount of data that has accumulated on many traits and in almost every area of learning has made the teaching profession conscious of the complexity of the problem of giving adequate recognition to the wide range of individual differences characteristic of every classroom. The test data about pupils makes questionable such established practices as having all pupils enter school at the age of six, progress at the same rate, study the same subject matter, receive marks on the same scale of achievement, and advance through the first twelve years of school in lock-step style. The extent of differences has indicated the need for flexibility in meeting the needs of each individual, and innovations have been introduced—some of these are described in chapters that follow.

Among changes that may have arisen in part as a result of the testing movement are flexibility in class size; programmed learning; team teaching; ungraded schools; educational TV; special classes for extreme deviates such as those who suffer from physical defects or inadequacies like low learning ability, or those who possess very high IQ's. Some states give extra state aid to local school systems to enable them to employ a specially trained staff and to provide special equipment for such exceptional children as the crippled, those with hearing or vision handicaps, or the mentally retarded educable children.

Social attitudes of sensitivity, resentment, or discouragement may be accentuated by test scores that emphasize pupil differences. Parents, for instance, sometimes feel that having a slow-learning child is a reflection upon the family, and they are embarrassed to admit the fact.

Standardized testing is often basic to ability grouping. A consciousness of individual differences has also led schools to use the test results early to diagnose pupil difficulties. The profile may show clearly where a pupil is having initial difficulty and special help may be given at that point before some form of abnormal behavior arises through frustration.

b. Classroom practice. The increase in dependence upon standardized tests in making such decisions at the high school level as those related to admission to "honors" classes, "advanced placement" classes, "college level" classes, and to recommendation for admission to colleges and universities influences teachers to teach what is believed will help pupils show up well on tests. Thus schools are influenced by tests to remain conservative. This may not be entirely unwholesome since the achievements on standardized tests are presumably those that the specialists believe most importantly related to future academic success. For a long time, for instance, specialists in the field of English education have decried the time spent on teaching formal grammar in the junior and senior high schools. English teachers at these levels have been reluctant to curtail work in formal grammar, partly because they were not convinced that it is not closely related to proficiency in writing and speaking, partly because it is a relatively "easy" branch of English to teach, and partly because it seems to impress parents with the value of English instruction. When teachers discover, however, that formal grammar is not an important part of achievement tests, they tend to be influenced in the direction of more emphasis on usage, writing, appreciation, and interpretation. Generally speaking, however, the wide use of standardized tests does not strongly encourage progressive teaching practices.

c. *Social effects.* Sociologists have given some study to the social effects of establishing rank orders among human beings, the kind of rank orders schools use in classifying pupils into levels in terms of standardized intelligence and achievement tests. It is difficult to appraise the effects of these practices upon pupils or their parents. One can never judge with certainty the reactions of a pupil to being, say, constantly assigned to a position of subordinate status within his group, or a position of prominence at the head of his group. Teachers are aware that some pupils who are regularly assigned to low ranks in the schools sometimes resort to bizarre behavior, reveal feelings of inferiority by behavior that is overtly aggressive. The so-called "hoods" have usually experienced many frustrations in school. The pupil who is regularly on the 99th percentile must also inevitably make adjustments. The causes of various overt behaviors cannot with certainty be traced. Perhaps no two are affected alike. Whatever the effects are, they are usually shared in some degree by parents and other pupils.

d. *Influence on curriculum.* It is known that some high schools, both public and nonpublic, place strong emphasis upon curriculum materials dictated by such examinations as the College Entrance Examinations that are required for entrance to many nonpublic colleges and universities. To what degree the use of standardized tests influences schools toward standardizing the curriculum is debatable. Using standards to compare the intelligence and achievements of pupils does not necessarily legislate that teaching materials and practices be standardized. Nevertheless, the tests have had this effect to some extent. In other words, the test movement, designed to reveal the extent and nature of individual differences among pupils so that the curriculums could be differentiated to meet the needs of all pupils, has, to some extent, led to the opposite result.

Teacher-Made Tests

1. Objective Tests

Experience with standardized tests tends to encourage classroom teachers to construct tests of their own that are like the standardized tests in that they are objective and easy to score. Since these are made by the teacher they can be definitely related to the current work in the classroom. The more commonly used types are short answer tests that can be mechanically scored, such as true-false tests, completion tests where the pupil fills in missing words needed to complete a sentence or paragraph, matching tests where related items are paired, and multiple-choice, in which the pupil selects a correct answer from among five plausible answers.

Typically the teacher-prepared objective type test possesses low reliability when used to determine pupil rank. Further, it tends to condition a pupil's study habits so that he attempts to outguess the teacher. When studying, the pupils tend to concentrate on items that they predict may be on the objective test, regardless of relative importance; to pay insufficient attention to organizing what they learn; and sometimes to stress rote memorization to the detriment of reasoning.

Seemingly, the teacher-made objective tests serve their most useful purpose when used to test the pupils' mastery of basic knowledges and skills or the degree to which they can recite material that must be reproduced verbatim.

2. Essay-Type Examinations

The examination or test that calls for essay-type answers must be prepared with considerable thought and care, and close concentration is called for in scoring or evaluating. Sometimes the time and energy required make the essay-type test exceedingly burdensome for the teacher with large classes. The essay test does, however, have some advantages over other kinds of tests. It can be designed to measure achievement of the objectives of the teaching—the understandings, interpretations, and appreciations. At the same time it encourages the pupil to organize his materials and to write his re-

Much information about students can be gained from examinations. The written examination is only one type. (Chicago Public Schools)

actions in paragraphs that are coherent and unified. Some studies have shown that pupils who study for essay-type tests do better on objective tests than do those who study only for objective tests.

Perhaps the general conclusion about the use of teacher-made tests is that the effective teacher uses different kinds, trying as best he may to design tests to fulfill the various purposes he has in mind. Generally speaking, it is desirable that the purpose of the test be clear to both teacher and pupil.

INFORMAL METHODS OF GAINING AN UNDERSTANDING OF PUPILS

In addition to information from various kinds of tests, the teacher gets help in understanding pupils from such sources as school records, school nurses, counselors, notations of former teachers. Most importantly, the teacher always depends on his own observation and insight. The profile, test results, and comments of others take on meaning primarily as supplements to the teacher's observation of the pupil in the classroom, the lunchroom, on the playground, and in informal conferences.

Although more attention has been given here to the specific information about pupils that comes from tests of various kinds than to the information from informal methods the teacher uses regularly, this is not meant to disparage the importance of the informal methods. They are numerous and varied and do not lend themselves to the kind of analysis that is appropriate here. In gain-

While this student teacher teaches the class, the regular teacher spends her time gaining valuable information about her pupils from information collected and recorded. Such technical information supplements what she learns about the pupils from her own skilled observation. Possessing this information she still has the problem of how best to use it in stimulating and directing the learning of each individual pupil. (University of South Florida)

ing information and in interpreting information to aid in understanding pupils, direct teacher observation is indispensable.

UNDERSTANDING PUPILS ESSENTIAL TO SUCCESSFUL TEACHING

This chapter is the first of four that deal with aspects of the central problem of all formal education—that of stimulating and directing the growth and development of pupils.

To fulfill his teaching responsibilities with reasonable skill the teacher must understand each pupil, and to do this he must be in command of two kinds of information considered fundamental. He must have a reasonable grasp of the nature of human growth and development in general. He must, in addition, be able to interpret the meaning of each of the specific items of information assembled about the pupils.

Informal methods and social situations are often avenues to a better understanding of pupils. (Shelton from Monkmeyer)

QUESTIONS

1. Give examples of educational practices that recognize and examples of practices that seem to disregard the principle of variety as explained by the biologist.

2. State what the concept of readiness implies for: age of school entrance; uniform subject matter for all pupils; school marks; promotion.

3. List some of the distinguishing characteristics of schools in economically depressed areas. Explain why these have been allowed to persist from generation to generation.

4. What are some forms of behavior that distinguish lower-lower class children in city schools from upper-upper class pupils?

5. Show how the following definition for education, proposed by Dewey in his *Democracy and Education* (1916), accords or does not accord with modern theories of growth and development.

    It (education) is that reconstruction or reorganization of experience which adds to the meaning of experience, and which increases ability to direct the course of subsequent experience.

6. In what ways may forgetting be a constructive aid to learning?

7. How may the older concepts of learning as passive absorption and memory as a kind of storehouse for knowledge still be identified in modern practice?

8. What are the principal differences between the pupil who learns lines from a Shakespearean play to reproduce them in writing on a classroom test and the pupil who learns the lines to act the part in the play?

9. Why was Binet's application of the standardization principle to measurement of intelligence considered a monumental invention?

10. In what ways do the materials of this chapter reflect the principle enunciated by Rousseau that education to be effective must be in accordance with nature?

PROJECTS

1. In terms of a hypothetical fifth-grade pupil show the steps required to derive his mental age. Describe the significance of this MA to his teacher.

2. List some of the important educational tests you have taken and tell at what point in your career you took these tests. Evaluate the effect of these tests upon your learning. Show how they influenced your education.

3. Draw up a check-list for evaluating observable study habits. Evaluate the study habits of two or three college students as observed for a brief period in the college library. List conclusions about the habits of attention of these students.

4. List some specific classroom practices at a particular grade level that reflect teacher consciousness of the psychology of learning.

5. In terms of a particular economically depressed area you know or may read about, list steps that might be taken in order to improve education in that area.

6. Describe the activities of a particular teacher that show the influence of a knowledge of the generalizations contributed by science about human growth and development.
7. Tell how your own concept of understanding pupils has been affected by study of the materials in this chapter.

17

Aims in American education

The comment has been made that the most useless bore is the person who is *merely* well informed. Why should a person who is considered "well informed" be a bore? He may be a bore because he is filled with bits of information that are unrelated and unorganized. His information may be like so many scraps of metal in a junk yard, an accumulation without purpose. He may be a man of motion without direction. The man is judged inefficient and uninteresting.

On the other hand, a man who possesses much knowledge, who has organized his knowledge around some purpose, and who has acquired his knowledge with foreseen direction is probably a man who is highly esteemed and respected by people who know him. He enjoys social prestige.

The two men differ not in the *amount* of knowledge each possesses but mainly in their motivation. The efficient person, as he learned, organized his knowledge with definite purposes in mind. His aims gave direction to what he learned and to what he did with what he learned.

Many successful men, some of lasting fame, have been self-educated men. They demonstrate that some men can realize high achievement without benefit of formal education. They have earned no college degrees, yet they are men of good judgment and eminent practical achievement. Since some self-taught men have succeeded as well or better than others who were formally educated, we may conclude that the value of education is not determined by the place in which it is received. Is it the motivation of the self-made man that gave direction and drive to his activities and made him successful? If so, aims or objectives are likely to influence the direction of learning, whether it is inside or outside the school.

WHAT DETERMINES EDUCATIONAL AIMS?

Individual Teacher's Philosophy

The teacher's aims are related to his values, to his philosophy. He will seek, within the limits discussed in Chapter 5 and later in this chapter, to achieve those ends which to him, personally, are worthy and practicable. Some of the teacher's aims will be broad and sweeping. He may seek, for instance, to promote attitudes of fair play. Such aims underlie all his teaching. In addition, he will have immediate aims associated with what he seeks to achieve in a single activity. He may also have a specific aim for a particular child. For example, he may set as a goal for one child the development of the habit of paying attention to instruction. The teacher might have a conference with this child during which the wording of this goal could be worked out by the child. Checking with the child on the advancement toward that goal might occur weekly. When the goal is satisfactorily achieved, another goal may be adopted. Such immediate and specific goals give direction to effort and provide a measure for judging progress.

Sometimes the work in a specific area of teaching is organized in a unit. Such a plan includes a statement of aims to be achieved in the unit. The aims, in this case, help the teacher to select relevant material and to unify teaching. In such a unit in English, for instance, the aims might be (1) to participate courteously in a group discussion, (2) to build up understanding and consideration of others, and (3) to use concrete and vivid words in speaking and writing. The teacher is guided usually by *sets* of aims, not by a single aim. These aims, moreover, will be ineffectual if the pupils do not share, whenever possible, in their formulation. The teacher's individual aims must always be flexible so that they can be readily modified in terms of the unexpected, in the light of changed conditions.

The teacher, however, is not always completely free to decide on his aims. Various influences and pressures affect his choice. Some of these are from external authorities—the school board, the local teaching group, state and federal government, and accrediting agencies. There are also pressures from various groups, from the home, and from commerce and industry. The press may exert a strong and significant influence. Professional commissions set up to establish general educational aims may also affect what the teacher attempts to do in his classroom. Sometimes, in fact, except for details related to an immediate situation, the choice of goals is made *for* the teacher, rather than *by* the teacher. When the influences do not operate in a consistent direction, a measure of confusion is introduced and then each teacher must decide, in his own way, to which influence he shall yield.

External Authorities

1. Professional Groups

In order to promote unity and give consistency to the direction of teaching a given grade level or a particular subject, a group of teachers, or their representatives, frequently get together and produce a general plan of work. The plan is typically preceded by a statement of aims or objectives which the group agrees should be striven for and toward the promotion of which the curriculum or other material worked out should lead. Often an instructional group looks for guidance to some national organization, like the American Society for Childhood Education or the Modern Language Association.

As an example, representatives of the English teachers in three junior high schools drew up a proposed English curriculum in which they set forth the following objectives:

1. Instruction in the language arts should prepare pupils to use efficiently the skills of listening, speaking, reading, and writing requisite to effective learning.
2. The language arts are avenues to all learning; therefore, a good language arts program should (a) integrate the language arts courses, (b) integrate with other courses of the school, (c) enrich personal living.

3. All good teaching in the language arts results in the development of individual personalities in the direction of their highest potentialities.[1]

Although such aims are general in the sense that they must be interpreted by the individual classroom teacher, they are sufficiently specific to give direction to the teacher's immediate aims.

2. School Staffs

In many cases individual school staffs formulate statements of aims for their own school. Such goals will have an influence on the aims adopted by individual teachers. The following is an example:

We aim to help each pupil:
1. to succeed in school.
2. to learn to get along in the school where he is and in the classes of which he is a part and with the people with whom he works.
3. to form the habit of doing what has been taught and is known to be right.
4. to be of service to each other and to the needs of the school.
5. to expect to abide by the rules and regulations that are made for the good of all.
6. to recognize and use the abilities, talents, and creative thinking of individuals in all lines to make an interesting school.

Sometimes this kind of statement of school aims is worked out by pupils in collaboration with faculty and perhaps with parents.

3. State and Federal Government

The aims of the school and of the individual teacher are influenced significantly by state and federal government. The federal government, we have noted, has often exerted its influences on aims when it made grants-in-aid under such acts as the Smith-Hughes Act. You will remember that under this law, states receive grants for vocational education on the secondary level, providing the schools meet certain federally established requirements. Such requirements actually determine, to a large extent, what aims are to be achieved in such fields as home economics, agriculture, and industrial arts. In addition to determining the activities of a high school by setting up requirements for federal grants, the federal government influences the aims of the schools through official statements of desirable aims and pronouncements from such groups as the White House Con-

[1] These objectives were based on the teachers' interpretation of the philosophy expressed in *Language Arts for Today's Children*, National Council of Teachers of English (New York: Appleton-Century-Crofts, 1954), Vol. 2.

ference on Education. This conference, which has been called together from time to time by several of the presidents of the United States, comprises widely representative professional educators and influential lay people.

State legislatures and state educational authorities also influence the aims of the school. For example, state laws stipulate that schools teach, and pupils study, certain subjects. In some states it is required that American history be studied for a full year in high school. In some states pupils in the elementary school are required to participate in physical education for a stated number of periods each week. Sometimes, through the office of the chief state school authority, the states have been prescriptive in the matter of study required of teachers who desire certification. The state foundation program is an influence on the aims of the school. Each governmental act is motivated by an aim, and the act in turn, almost, if not entirely, legislates an aim for teaching.

4. Institutions of Higher Learning

Colleges and universities exert some influence on the aims and objectives of the high schools by their admission requirements. Sometimes high school pupils feel that the all-inclusive aim of their high school education is to prepare for college board examinations. Pressure on the high school from institutions of higher learning may be cause for the high schools to attempt to influence what is taught in the junior high schools and even in the elementary schools.

It has been stated that high schools tend to credit the colleges with being more of an influence than they actually are. In defending the emphasis placed on the study of grammar in high school, for instance, it was said, "Our children must be well prepared in grammar in order to do well on the college entrance examinations." A review of some of the college entrance examinations used showed that there was actually little stress placed on formal grammar. Some high schools were using college entrance examinations to justify something they were including in their teaching for some other reason.

5. Accrediting Agencies

Accrediting agencies like the North Central Association of Colleges and Secondary Schools determine to some extent what subjects a pupil in high school must pursue for graduation. In this sense, they, too, have an influence on the school's aims and on the aims of the individual teacher.

Societal Pressures

Pressure groups, as discussed in Chapter 10, are characteristic of modern America. Many of the groups exert their influence on the school. In addition, pressures come from such agencies as the home, industry, the press, and professional commissions.

1. Home

If the home does not fulfill certain needs related to achieving maturity, then the school will be expected to add the fulfillment of these needs to its aims of instruction. The home or the community may, for instance, expect the school to undertake activities related to sex education, social dancing, grooming, or the like. In some instances the objectives of the school will be tied in with certain activities in the home. In a rural community, for example, the school may teach the conservation of food by correlating work in methods of freezing, canning, and otherwise preserving food with the materials and facilities the children have in their homes and the instruction they have received at home.

2. Industry

When certain vocational preparation, certain skills or foundations, are in demand in industry, the pressure will be felt in the schools to adopt corresponding preparatory vocational aims. The pressure may be direct or subtle. Work experiences in industry may be added to high school experiences. Scholarships for advanced study, awarded by industry, may influence high school work. Contests for prizes or national prestige influence what the high school does.

3. Press

Journalists, television commentators, and news analysts exert pressure on the public and also directly on the schools to shape their programs to fulfill objectives that come into public limelight, usually because of current crises. When Russia surpassed the United States in the development of space satellites, journalists led the hue

Vocational preparation is one of the specific aims of education in America. (Evanston Photographic Service)

and cry for education to be patterned more on the Russian plan. Our assumed inferiority to Russia was attributed to inadequate education. "Our children should work harder, be more serious." "Stress mathematics and science and foreign languages." "Select the gifted children early; see that they are adequately motivated to pursue the required subjects."

One trouble with journalists is that they tend to be dramatic, to distort the true picture. They may overemphasize some of the aims of education because they are devoted to promoting a "cause." Often they are not completely informed about education but make an impression on the public by mounting emotional or irrational assaults on the waste of school funds in elaborate school buildings, on the school's failure to teach Johnnie to read, on the school's failure to keep America abreast of Russia in technical advances—matters that lend themselves to the journalist's art. Often, however, the effect of journalistic efforts—urging, for instance, that teaching be made more attractive as a means to alleviate teacher shortages—are socially very desirable. The restrictions of authoritative external bodies and the pressures of official statements, the press, and industry will be greater in fields of specific subject areas, especially in vocational fields. In the areas of general education—the basic education that is given to all children, that is, the education of the elementary school and that portion of the high school program that is not differentiated—the teacher has more freedom in making the final decision as to aims and the subject matter that he believes is potentially most profitable in terms of those aims.

4. Professional Commissions

From time to time groups of outstanding educators have taken up the task of formulating statements of the aims or purposes for education in America. Such statements may contain many helpful suggestions for the teacher. They may indicate what the teacher should emphasize, what results he may expect, what kinds of materials are best to choose, in what directions the pupils' energies may be influenced, and the like. The Educational Policies Commission of the NEA issued *The Purposes of Education in American Democracy* in 1938. This is a classic statement generally endorsed by public schools.[2]

THE OBJECTIVES OF SELF-REALIZATION

The inquiring mind. The educated person has an appetite for learning.
Speech. The educated person can speak the mother tongue clearly.
Reading. The educated person reads the mother tongue efficiently.
Writing. The educated person writes the mother tongue effectively.
Number. The educated person solves his problems of counting and calculating.
Sight and hearing. The educated person is skilled in listening and observing.
Health. The educated person understands the basic facts concerning health and disease.
Health habits. The educated person protects his own health and that of his dependents.
Public health. The educated person works to improve the health of the community.
Recreation. The educated person is participant and spectator in many sports and other pastimes.
Intellectual interests. The educated person has mental resources for the use of leisure.

[2] Quoted from pages 50, 72, 90, and 108 by permission of the National Education Association.

Building a healthy body is stressed at all levels of education. Most states demand that the schools require courses in health education for graduation. (Evanston Photographic Service)

Aesthetic interests.   The educated person appreciates beauty.
Character.   The educated person gives responsible direction to his own life.

THE OBJECTIVES OF HUMAN RELATIONSHIPS

Respect for humanity.   The educated person puts human relationships first.
Friendships.   The educated person enjoys a rich, sincere, and varied social life.
Cooperation.   The educated person can work and play with others.
Courtesy.   The educated person observes the amenities of social behavior.
Appreciation of the home.   The educated person appreciates the family as a social institution.
Conservation of the home.   The educated person conserves family ideals.
Homemaking.   The educated person is skilled in homemaking.
Democracy in the home.   The educated person maintains democratic family relationships.

THE OBJECTIVES OF ECONOMIC EFFICIENCY

Work.   The educated producer knows the satisfaction of good workmanship.
Occupational information.   The educated producer understands the requirements and opportunities for various jobs.
Occupational choice.   The educated producer has *selected* his occupation.

Learning to get along with others is another school aim. Some schools employ specially trained teachers to direct social activities in the schools. (Lincoln Public Schools)

Occupational efficiency. The educated producer succeeds in his chosen vocation.

Occupational adjustment. The educated producer maintains and improves his efficiency.

Occupational appreciation. The educated producer appreciates the social value of his work.

Personal economics. The educated consumer plans the economics of his own life.

Consumer judgment. The educated consumer develops standards for guiding his expenditures.

Efficiency in buying. The educated consumer is an informed and skillful buyer.

Consumer protection. The educated consumer takes appropriate measures to safeguard his interests.

THE OBJECTIVES OF CIVIC RESPONSIBILITY

Social justice. The educated citizen is sensitive to the disparities of human circumstance.

Social activity. The educated citizen acts to correct unsatisfactory conditions.

Social understanding. The educated citizen seeks to understand social structures and social processes.

Critical judgment. The educated citizen has defenses against propaganda.

Tolerance. The educated citizen respects honest differences of opinion.

Conservation. The educated citizen has a regard for the nation's resources.

Social applications of science. The educated citizen measures scientific advance by its contribution to the general welfare.

World citizenship. The educated citizen is a cooperating member of the world community.

Law observance. The educated citizen respects the law.

Economic literacy. The educated citizen is economically literate.

Political citizenship. The educated citizen accepts his civic duties.

Devotion to democracy. The educated citizen acts upon an unswerving loyalty to democratic ideals.

Understanding world relations has become a major aim of the schools. A group of sixth-grade pupils is pictured in the public lobby of the United Nations ready for a guided tour of United Nations headquarters. (United Nations)

STATEMENTS OF AIMS

One of the first difficulties encountered in attempts to state the aims of education in American schools is terminology. The words used have had various meanings.

Terminology

In various lists of aims prepared as guides to teaching, many different kinds of terms have been used. This has led to some confusion and misunderstanding. Because of the subtleties of learning it may be that some confusion is unavoidable.

Consider the basic word "aim." The meaning of this word seems clear when one uses it to describe a physical object at which one is shooting a gun, or when, in war, the object is to destroy a certain bridge. When the act, however, is a mental one, no one word can describe all of the different kinds of objectives, and sometimes

John Dewey emphasizes that aim and means are related, that ends are always pluralistic, and that all the consequences of an act, not just one, must be considered.

. . . ends arise and function within action. They are not . . . things lying beyond activity at which the latter is directed. They are not . . . termini of action at all. They are terminals of deliberation, and so turning points *in* activity. . . .

In being ends of *deliberation* they are redirecting pivots *in* action. . . .

A mariner does not sail towards the stars, but by noting the stars he is aided in conducting his present activity of sailing. . . . Activity will not cease when the port is attained, but merely the *present direction* of activity. The port is as truly the beginning of another mode of activity as it is the termination of the present one. . . . We know without thinking that our "ends" are perforce beginnings. . . .

Common sense revolts against the maxim, . . . that the end justifies the means. There is no incorrectness in saying that the question of means employed is overlooked in such cases . . . that overlooking means is only a device for failing to note those ends, or consequences, which, if they were noted would be seen to be so evil that action would be estopped. Certainly nothing can justify or condemn means except ends, results. . . . Not *the* end—in the singular —justifies the means; for there is no such thing as the single all-important end. . . . It is not possible adequately to characterize the presumption, the falsity and the deliberate perversion of intelligence involved in refusal to note the plural effects that flow from any act, a refusal adopted in order that we may justify an act by picking out that one consequence which will enable us to do what we wish to do and for which we feel the need of justification.

From John Dewey, *Human Nature and Conduct* (New York: Holt, Rinehart and Winston, Inc., 1922), pp. 223, 225, 226, 228, 229. Quoted by permission of the publishers.

different words are used interchangeably to describe precisely the same objective. In most instances where mental processes are concerned, each of the various terms used carries a slightly different emphasis. Let us note how this is true in the following sentence: The student whose *aims* are worthy, whose *aspirations* are high, whose *designs* are wise, and whose *purposes* are steadfast may reach the *goal* of his *ambition* and surely will win some *object* worthy of life's *endeavor*. Writers who attempt to describe the direction education should take by stating what it should seek to achieve have to make a choice among such terms. All of the terms refer to mental acts in which aim plays a part. The choice of a particular word, however, results in slightly different emphasis.

It is, perhaps, not surprising to find writers in education using such phrases as "purposive learning," "objectives of education," "object lesson," "purposeful effort," "ends in view," and others that reflect a philosophical viewpoint toward the relation of aim to teaching. It would be easier, of course, if all the writers used the same terminology. In the present stage of terminology development, however, the best we can do is remember that all of these phrases are related to aim and not attempt to disentangle the meanings or to distinguish shades of emphasis. In all the lists the attempt has been to do the same thing—to make carefully formulated suggestions to guide teaching practices in schools, even though there have been different approaches that have led to different kinds of statements.

Although there have been a number of approaches to arriving at official statements of the aims of American education, two approaches have been most favored. The first approach involves the activity analysis method, a method similar to the vocational analysis method described in Chapter 2. The second approach emphasizes growth of the learner.

Activity Analysis Method

In "What Knowledge Is Most Worth," an essay published in 1859, the English philosopher Herbert Spencer first proposed the use of the activity analysis method for arriving at aims of teaching. He classified the activities of life in which adults engage under five categories: (1) those related to preserving life and health; (2) vocational activities, or those related to earning a living; (3) domestic activities, or those related to family duties or care of children; (4)

social and political activities; and (5) leisure activities, art, etc. The school, he said, should improve the preparation of children to perform the activities related to each of these areas of adult life.

This method of arriving at the guiding aims of education was widely followed by groups in America. In 1918, for example, a commission of leading American educators was appointed by the NEA to formulate an official statement of the aims of American education.

The eminent child development psychologist John E. Anderson, after directing the Child Welfare Research Institute at the University of Minnesota for many years, arrived at the conclusion that the principal goal of education should be the enhancement and enrichment of personality.

It is difficult, indeed, for one who has followed children and has seen at first hand the vitality, energy, and strength of the young human being to believe that their existence is without purpose and that humans are tiny bits of matter in a universe that is without meaning and significance. Through and through, the developmental process seems to be creative; the problems and situations which are old and hackneyed to the adult are new and interesting to the child. And the social organization of adolescents, even though they are like those of earlier generations, are new creations to those who form them. Neither the person nor society is quite the same at successive moments—life goes on even while we think about it.

In the enhancement and enrichment of personality and the mutual creation of a good life for all is found the measure of a full life. Some make money a symbol of a good life; some make power, some material goods, some social position. As more is learned about personality, the primary goal becomes the desirability of using the capacities of persons to the fullest degree, and of searching out the talents which all possess and giving them opportunities to manifest themselves. Society proceeds most rapidly when it utilizes its human resources most fully and gives each member some opportunity for self-realization through the essentially creative process of broadening his own life space and finding in interests and activities the opportunities for development and appreciation. Wasted ability is forever lost, both for the person and for society. Emphasis, then, goes to living a full life, not so much in terms of status and rewards as in terms of contribution, development, and personality enhancement. Thus, we seek a society in which there will not only be a concept of the dignity of the human being, but also the opportunity for the person to manifest that dignity.

From John E. Anderson, *The Psychology of Development and Personal Adjustment* (New York: Holt, Rinehart and Winston, Inc., 1949), p. 675. Quoted by permission of the publishers.

The commission, known as the Commission on the Reorganization of Secondary Education, prepared a report that was published by the United States government under the engaging title, "The Cardinal Principles of Education." The report proposed that the following seven objectives serve to guide the teaching process in American schools: health, worthy home membership, vocational efficiency, citizenship, worthy use of leisure time, ethical character, and command of the fundamental processes. Since 1918, attempts have been made to improve upon the statements contained in this report. In essence, the same activity analysis technique has been followed. The aims so derived generally bear some resemblance to the cardinal principles.

Those who are critical of this method point out that the activities analyzed and classified are typical of the society of the

> The goals of a curriculum in American schools in the middle of the twentieth century are determined finally by the purposes for which the schools are established. It is clear that the American people want the children and youth of the nation to be educated to the extent of their highest potentialities; that they want them to be self-reliant individuals who are at the same time good cooperating members of society; and that they want them to be able to make their own livings. In other words, the major purposes of American education are in general: (1) cultivation of satisfying and wholesome personal lives, (2) development of social sensitivity and effective participation in the life of the local community, the nation, and the world, and (3) preparation for vocational competence.
>
> From *The English Language Arts,* prepared by the Commission on the English Curriculum of The National Council of Teachers of English. Copyright 1952, The National Council of Teachers of English. Reprinted by permission of Appleton-Century-Crofts.

adult world outside the school. The objectives are not stated in terms of learners, are not indigenous to classroom situations, do not recognize the active, participatory nature of learning.

Growth Concept Approach

Another and widely different approach begins with focus on the learner and his desirable growth. The all-inclusive aim of education is the development of continued capacity for growth. In the words of John Dewey, who contributed much to a clarification of this approach, "the aim of education is to enable individuals to continue their education—or that the object and reward of learning is continued capacity for growth."[3]

The growth concept requires that the teacher take conditions in his classroom into account and rely upon his knowledge of the pupils in his formulation of aims. Daily aims worked out in terms of this growth philosophy of education (or its sister, the developmental psychology of human development) would be too numerous to list and too varied for classification. Growth, self-direction, and self-control are very general and all-inclusive aims that must be implemented through the selection of more specific goals.

The student council in session in Evanston Township High School provides a forum for discussion of problems close to the hearts of the pupils. The development of social and civic responsibility is one of the aims stressed in statements made by the Educational Policies Commission of the NEA. (Evanston Photographic Service)

CRITICISMS OF AIMS

Abstractness and Impracticality

Statements of aims based on an analysis of activities should be expressed as specifically and concretely as possible, as are the aims quoted on pages 442–445. In this kind of sociological approach the aims are classified and divided into categories. Typically, the categories are kept at a minimum, somewhere between 4 and 10, a

[3] John Dewey, *Democracy and Education* (New York: The Macmillan Company, 1916), p. 117.

number thought small enough to preserve the unity of the educative process but large enough to include all important phases of adult life. In the Educational Policies Commission statement there are four main classifications: (1) self-realization, (2) human relationships, (3) economic efficiency, and (4) civic responsibility. Each of these four main divisions is broken down into more specific statements. It was hoped that this arrangement would suggest aims to teachers of all grades and would provide guides for daily tasks and assistance in selecting subject matter, in evaluating pupils, and in directing extracurricular activities.

Still, some teachers feel that even a detailed classification, like the one quoted, is too general. Health or citizenship are abstractions. As they are stated they seem nebulous and isolated from the needs and capacities of individual boys and girls. In addition, they are considered by many too philosophically neutral, too subject to personal interpretation. Some teachers feel that they need help in applying these objectives to work with individual children in the classroom. Others discount such statements as idealistic wishes of adults rather than day-to-day guides for practical use. For these reasons, partly, the general trend has been toward greater use of the growth concept approach, toward stating only the general objective of education and allowing the aims to grow out of the classroom situation.

Quantity of Subject Matter

One common criticism of teaching aims is that American schoolteachers sacrifice a desirable concern with the total product of their teaching—understanding, interest, desirable attitudes—to a concern with covering a certain amount of prescribed subject matter. In literature, pupils are expected to read a specified *quantity* of material; in algebra, the ninth grade pupils are expected to advance rapidly enough to arrive at quadratics by the end of the year. Teachers are criticized for adopting too completely the aim to "cover so much ground in so much time."

Promotion Policies

Sometimes a teacher whose principal concern is with the total needs of an individual child will promote a pupil without giving primary attention to the subject matter mastered. The teacher's aim is influenced, of course, by the objectives of the school. Formerly as many as 10 to 30 percent of the pupils were retained in a given grade. In recent years the tendency has been to pass on to the next grade all those who promise to profit more by promotion than by being required to repeat the grade. The practice has greatly reduced the number of failures in each grade of the elementary school.

Schools where pupils have been promoted freely have been criticized by some for "wholesale" promotion. Criticism stems from a difference in philosophy—a difference in conception of the aims of the school. Should the teacher follow practices deemed desirable in terms of the total growth needs of the child? How about the needs of the group being taught? To what degree should the achievements of a group be subordinated to the needs of an individual child? Can individual needs be fully met without unduly sacrificing the needs of a group? Before proceeding with his age group, should a child be required to master certain subject matter? Should the aims be in terms of this required mastery, or should they be wholly in terms of the individual's total needs? In terms of social needs? Should aims be formulated by the individual teacher or dictated by external authority? These are questions which, obviously, do not lend themselves to easy, offhand answers.

Scope of Social Studies

Teachers who turn to the social sciences for sources of teaching materials rather than to one specialized field, such as history, are sometimes criticized for diluting the materials of history when history, in the critic's opinion, should receive the main, if not the sole, emphasis. Those who favor placing the main emphasis upon history or economics or political science argue that it is better to probe one subject intensively than to skim the surface of a number of them. Arguments like this one sometimes become quite heated.

Teachers who follow a generalized approach to social studies maintain that they do not disparage the contribution of history or any subject to the understanding of modern social problems and interpretation of modern social movements. They feel, however, that social problems, economic problems, labor issues, political issues, and the like should be studied in their modern setting, too.

What should the aim of social studies teaching be? If the social studies teacher aims to cultivate the pupil's understanding of present-day issues and social conditions, then, perhaps, it does not matter from which of the major social science disciplines the subject matter comes. Those who feel that the stress should be on one particular social science will, of course, question the validity of the teacher's approach.

Purpose of Examinations

When examinations have been used to diagnose pupil's weaknesses, to reveal individual needs, when they have aided the teacher in increasing his effectiveness with individual pupils, in other words, when they have facilitated learning, examinations have been favorably viewed as helpful instruments of learning. When examinations have been used to compare the achievements of one pupil with another, to select the fit from the unfit, to classify and stratify the pupils, to determine who shall receive highest approval and honor awards, then they have come in for considerable criticism.

American educators, by and large, favor an increased use of examinations *as instructional aids*. This aim, it is contended, should guide the construction of examinations and determine how and when they shall be used. This is what a critic of examinations in English schools had in mind when he wrote:

> . . . no educational system is possible unless every question directly asked of a pupil at any examination is either framed or modified by the actual teacher of that pupil in that subject.
>
> .   .   .
>
> The best procedure [of examination] will depend on several factors, . . . namely, the genius of the teacher, the intellectual type of the pupils, their prospects in life, the opportunities offered by the immediate surroundings of the school, and allied factors of this sort. It is for this reason that the uniform external examination is so deadly. We do not denounce it because we are cranks, and like denouncing established things. . . . Our reason of dislike is very definite and very practical. . . . When you analyze in the light of experience the central task of education, you find that its successful accomplishment depends on a delicate adjustment of many variable factors. . . . The evocation of curiosity, of judgment, of the power of mastering a complicated tangle of circumstances, the use of theory in giving foresight in special cases—all these powers are not to be imparted by a set rule embodied in one schedule of examination subjects.[4]

CONCLUSION

It is perhaps obvious that teaching aims cannot be static, rigid, or fixed. As one aim is achieved, the next aim is defined. Each accom-

---

[4] Alfred North Whitehead, *Aims of Education* (New York: The Macmillan Company, 1929), pp. 7–8. Quoted by permission of The Macmillan Company.

plishment leads to a definition of the next aim. When one end is achieved, it becomes the means to the next. Ends that are worthy function to free learning activities, to direct them, but never to freeze them.

This generalization is true of aims that are set by the school, by government authorities, by nations. History tells the story of Greece, a nation at one time alive with new and noble ideas that engendered aims that led the whole nation to socially desirable action. At a later time the people of the same nation found themselves no longer motivated by appropriate and collective aims. The nation lost direction and floundered. For education to have direction it must be guided by aims, but the aims must be appropriate, must make an appeal strong enough to evoke strong individual and collective action. The failure to recognize that effective aims are not static explains in part why Greece flourished at one time in its history and floundered at another.

Forward-looking and active institutions sometimes, with passing years, become stagnant and lose their strength and popular appeal. The early leaders in the schools of the Christian church were inspiring teachers. Later, much of the teaching by churchmen became pedantic, catechismic, formal, and uninspirational. Such deterioration is due, in part at least, either to adherence to aims outmoded and therefore inappropriate, to the adoption of new aims inappropriate for some reason, or to a change in social conditions that render all the general purposes of the institution obsolete.

Aims will influence education, will constitute a challenge to action only when the aims are acceptable because they can be and are adapted to current conditions. The dynamic nature of the complete educational picture calls for a constant reinterpretation and reappraisal of the aims sought. Changing social conditions bring new educational demands into focus. Changing conditions in the classroom bring new demands into focus also. Conditions are never static. Effective aims also cannot be static.

QUESTIONS

1. How does the advancing age of the pupils affect the aims of instruction?
2. How are the teachers to formulate aims that reflect the social viewpoints of the people when these viewpoints are sometimes in conflict?
3. How are the aims of education in American schools affected by the character of the community?

4. What functions are served by having carefully formulated statements of aims by official bodies?

5. Under what conditions are educational aims apt to be static in nature? Dynamic?

6. How do you account for the great variety in manner of stating aims? Would it be advantageous to have a single statement of the aims of education? How can one select from among the many statements?

7. When may a statement of educational aims be an aid to teaching? A hindrance?

PROJECTS

1. Explain how one's educational philosophy shapes the character of his educational aims.

2. Give an example that illustrates the interrelationships of aim, subject matter, and method.

3. Summarize how one of the official statements was derived and show how the validity of the aims is established.

4. Illustrate by example how an educational aim directs the whole of the educative process.

5. State the aims that guide you in your professional study. Justify your professional studies and activities in terms of these aims.

CHAPTER **18**

Subject matter in America's schools

Subjects of study probably date back to the earliest schools. The Babylonians had schoolhouses in 2100 B.C.; other civilizations may have had them earlier than that. Archaeologists have established that one of the skills taught in the early schools was writing. Words and phrases and, later, complete sentences and quotations were copied from old documents. Inasmuch as the documents were available for copying, writing—using symbols—must have predated even these very early schools. It also can be assumed that someone had been taught to read these early documents and that there were some who could teach others to read. In all likelihood, when the earliest schools were set up over 4,000 years ago, they aimed to perpetuate and extend the ability to read, to write, to interpret, to appreciate, and eventually to add to the store of manuscripts. No doubt these ancient manuscripts were the earliest forerunners of the subject matter in today's schools.

As time passed and it was recognized that certain social groups —especially at first the priests—needed knowledge in particular areas before beginning their work, pertinent information and skills were selected and organized for instructing potential members of these groups. It appears now that the advance from barbarism to civilization was marked by stages of development in the classifications of knowledge—classifications made partly to facilitate instruction of an oncoming generation.

The orderly organization of subject matter into classifications that were generally considered appropriate for young pupils was quite advanced by the time America began to be a settled country. When the first colonial schools were opened, there was available a great deal of material that those in charge felt was ideally suited to their aims.

EVOLUTION OF SUBJECT MATTER IN THE UNITED STATES

In Elementary Schools

Initially, American elementary schools borrowed their classifications from Europe. Our first educators and those who supported the schools were religious leaders and other church members. Children were viewed as the children of the Church. Schools were established to teach children to read and write so that they might read the Bible which, in turn, might lead them to be better church members.

Many different churches set up schools that varied somewhat because of differences in religious beliefs. By the time the Declaration of Independence was signed, however, the elementary schools were essentially alike in that they all emphasized the study of reading, writing, spelling, and arithmetic. In all these subjects, they utilized scriptural quotations and moral platitudes.

After the passage of a half century, there were discernible changes in the common subjects. Although reading, spelling, writing, and arithmetic remained the chief subjects, modifications took place within each, both in content and in organization. English grammar became a separate subject equal in importance to the others. Knitting and sewing were included for girls in some schools.

By 1876, the subject matter of the elementary schools was greatly expanded. Conditions had changed and some of the new ideas from European educators had filtered into practice. Following a trend toward secularization in the schools, education became less concerned with religion. In teaching reading the teachers helped the children not only to develop proficiency in reading the Scriptures but also to develop skill in reading and appreciating literature other than the Bible. Declamation, oral language, geography, United States history and the Constitution, elementary science, music, drawing, and physical education were now among the subjects. Many textbooks were rewritten. In addition to textbooks, actual objects were used for instruction. Such direct experiences as field trips and laboratory experiments were added.

The expansion of subjects of study continued, and by the end of the century, manual training, nature study, and a new outgrowth of reading—a subject called "literature"—made their appearance. In fact, by the beginning of the present century, all the elements of the modern subjects had been introduced into the elementary schools. As our aims, our conditions, our knowledge, and our understanding change and increase, the evolution continues and our classifications, our emphases, and our textbooks continue to change.

In Four-Year High Schools

The evolution of subjects in the American four-year high school constitutes a story almost as independent of the evolution of the subjects in the elementary schools as though the two never belonged to the same family of institutions. When the Declaration of Independence was issued, the subjects in the high school were almost exclusively Latin and Greek. The dominance of what was studied is implied by the name of the school—Latin grammar school. The aim of the secondary school was largely vocational—to prepare individuals for further study for entrance into the ministry of the church. The transition from elementary school to high school was so abrupt that it amounted to an almost complete break.

Fifty years after the Declaration of Independence, high school subjects had undergone considerable change. By 1825, the Boston Public Latin School, for example, included in its program such well-defined subject matters as arithmetic, algebra, geometry, trigonometry, geography, declamation, reading, English grammar, English composition, debating, chronological history, and the constitutions of the United States and of Massachusetts. Slowly but surely the subjects covered by the high schools continued to undergo modification.

The influence of the Latin grammar schools waned after 1800, and the private academy became the dominant secondary school institution. The number of subjects expanded amazingly, reflecting the rapid development of new subject matter, especially that related to the development of the specialized sciences. By 1837, the academies in New York State offered 73 different subjects, including architecture, astronomy, chemistry, botany, conic sections, embroidery, civil engineering, French, geology, analytic geometry, German, Hebrew, Italian, law, logarithms, vocal music, instrumental music, mineralogy, political economy, painting, statistics, surveying, Spanish, trigonometry, and principles of teaching.

After 1890, the date that coincides with the end of the American frontier movement, the private academy ceased to be the dominant institution and its influence rapidly waned. The four-year public high school became the prevalent institution. As the high schools grew in number and enrollment, new subjects were rapidly introduced into the curriculum. The passage of the Smith-Hughes Act of 1917, which gave federal grants-in-aid to those high schools giving training in vocational education, spurred expansion of vocational education programs. In some high schools, the entire program of some pupils was built around study in one of the areas of vocational education. The new subjects included motor mechanics, machine shop, radio, advanced electricity, agriculture, business law, stenography, beauty culture, commercial cooking, and aeronautics. Music and art subjects also multiplied. The older fields, e.g. English, science, mathematics, and foreign languages, also were expanded. As many as 19 different subjects were offered under the broad heading of "homemaking." Not all of these, of course, were offered in a single school. Driver training and mathematics for nurses are further examples of the trend both toward completeness in curriculums to meet today's needs and toward selecting subject matter specifically and directly related to an explicit aim.

No attempt has been made here to establish relative importance or prominence among the many subjects offered. This is partly because no reliable data showing the percentage of pupils enrolled in the various subjects are available. Moreover, since there is no consistency in high school policies in requiring the pupils to pursue certain subjects, generalizations about their relative prominence would be unreliable.

SELECTION OF SUBJECT MATTER

The brief review of the history of subject matter in the schools in the United States reveals great changes over the years in scope, content, organization, and emphasis. What has determined these changes? What criteria have operated in the selection of subject matter?

Subject matter is a tool designed and selected to help children move in the direction defined by a school's educational goals. The relative values of various areas of subject matter have always been judged in terms of their probable potential contribution to the desired ends. As the aims, from colonial times on, changed for various reasons, subject matter likewise changed.

When educators began to state aims for education and were asked to justify subjects in terms of aims, the question of the relative values of different subjects also came up for serious consideration. Even assuming that all the subjects had value, the extent of that value, the relative value of one subject as compared to all the others, had to be determined.

If, as the great English philosopher John Locke (1623–1704) believed, the mind at birth is like a blank piece of paper with nothing written upon it, a *tabula rasa,* with inherent powers that can be strengthened by "exercising" with subject matter, then it could be argued that certain kinds of subject matter better serve this need for exercise than others. From this, it follows that subject matter for all pupils should be uniform. Having each learner receive the same spelling, or grammar, or mathematics would be all right because these subjects provide the best kind of mental exercise for all learners. "The faculties of our souls are improved and made useful to us just after the same manner as our bodies are . . . would you have a man reason well, you must use him to it betimes, exercise his mind in observing the connection of ideas and following them in train."[1]

Actually, the "blank paper" theory was not accepted for very long, so it does little to explain the selection of subject matter. Another belief that came to be known as faculty psychology had more of a following. It explains, in part, some of the perplexing lack of direct value in subject matter, especially in the high school.

[1] John Locke, as quoted in Paul Monroe, *A Brief Course in the History of Education* (New York: The Macmillan Company, 1907), p. 265.

John Locke is usually accorded the distinction of being the most influential of all the English writers who addressed themselves to education. If the degree of his influence is rivalled by that of Herbert Spencer it should be recalled that he preceded Spencer by almost two hundred years.

First of all, Locke was a great philosopher and it is easy to minimize his importance by singling out his view toward education and presenting it as though it were the whole of his philosophy. His views on education did not accord with his philosophy, and this should be kept in mind in judging the contributions of the man.

He revealed his conception of the intellectual aspect of education in his *Conduct of the Understanding.* The entire treatise was a defense of the idea that the intellect is best trained through exercise and discipline, and that mathematics is the most suitable kind of subject matter to furnish the desired kind of discipline. ". . . Nothing does this better than mathematics, which therefore I think should be taught all those who have the time and opportunity *not so much to make them mathematicians, as to make them reasonable creatures. . . .*"

For instance, early spelling textbooks contained many words that would never be useful to most of the pupils, even in adult life. English grammar, emphasizing sentence structure, seemed to have little connection with developing powers of expression. Those who were faculty psychologists believed that the mind is composed of a series of distinct and separate faculties—such as thinking, memorizing, feeling, willing—and that each of these could be trained through exercise just as a muscle could be strengthened through exercise. Moreover, it was assumed that training received in one area of subject matter is transferred to another. This meant, for instance, that the powers developed through memorizing poetry would be transferred to memorization of grammar or multiplication tables. The study of Euclidean geometry was considered particularly valuable because it developed prowess in logical reasoning which could be used in studying other subjects and in out-of-school activities. When we recall that Euclid's *Elements,* a very early textbook on geometry, has served as a model for all the later textbooks on the subject, we get some notion of how long this approach to geometry survived.

Knowledge about how children learn, about the nature of child development and growth, and about differences in capacities and interests influences the selection of subject matter. Currently the trend is to select subject matter that is as flexible as possible and is *directly* related to the achievement of aims. Knowledge and insight are required in deciding what subject matter will contribute most. Usually the teacher in the classroom has more or less broad boundaries of subject matter determined for him by the school district, the school, or some other authority. Where textbooks are supplied or prescribed, the extent of teacher choice is further limited.

American people tend to become progressively more dependent upon formal education to educate youth for citizenship obligations. Education reflects this need to train large numbers of young people for everyday democratic living. In earlier times much of the education of the young was received outside the school. At that time, because of social conditions, advanced education was highly selective, largely on the basis of ability to pay. Higher education was almost monopolized by specially privileged people who used graduation from higher institutions as a stepping-stone to rising on the social scale. That tradition is gradually disappearing in the United States. Formal education is becoming a requirement for entrance to many average adult activities. Nowadays, the trend is toward greater attention to what graduates of high schools and colleges have learned or have learned to do and less attention to how long the graduates have attended school or from what units they have been graduated. There is greater interest in *what* children in the elementary and high schools study and in the degree to which efficient learning is promoted. The future promises even more emphasis on the practical values of the subjects provided in our schools.

CLASSIFICATION OF KNOWLEDGE

Perhaps one of the greatest advances man has made in his attempts to achieve a high level of civilization through education has been in the classifications he has made of accumulated knowledge. His ability to organize and to systematize his knowledge into such classifications as physics, geology, and mathematics has contributed to research, to the preservation of knowledge, and to learning. Man's future, it seems, will depend largely upon the uses he makes of his accumulations and classifications of knowledge. These uses hinge, in part, upon the way educational institutions teach young people to apply knowledge.

Bertrand Russell is a distinguished English philosopher. The following excerpt from one of his books suggests his viewpoint on subject matter.

. . . For the first time in history, it is now possible, owing to the industrial revolution and its by-products, to create a world where everybody shall have a reasonable chance of happiness. Physical evil can, if we choose, be reduced to very small proportions. It would be possible, by organization and science, to feed and house the whole population of the world, not luxuriously, but sufficiently to prevent great suffering. It would be possible to combat disease, and to make chronic ill-health very rare. It would be possible to prevent the increase of population from outrunning improvements in the food supply. The great terrors which have darkened the sub-conscious mind of the race, bringing cruelty, oppression, and war in their train, could be so much diminished as to be no longer important. All this is of such immeasurable value to human life that we dare not oppose the sort of education which will tend to bring it about. In such an education, applied science will have to be the chief ingredient. Without physics and physiology and psychology, we cannot build the new world. We can build it without Latin and Greek, without Dante and Shakespeare, without Bach and Mozart. That is the great argument in favour of a utilitarian education. I have stated it strongly, because I feel it strongly. Nevertheless, there is another side to the question. What will be the good of the conquest of leisure and health, if no one remembers how to use them? The war against physical evil, like every other war, must not be conducted with such fury as to render men incapable of the arts of peace. What the world possesses of ultimate good must not be allowed to perish in the struggle against evil.

. . . What I suggest is that, where a difficult technique is indispensable to the mastering of a subject, it is better, except in training specialists, that the subject should be useful. In the time of the renaissance, there was little great literature in modern languages; now there is a great deal. Much of the value of the Greek tradition can be conveyed to people who do not know Greek; and as for the Latin tradition, its value is not really very great. I should, therefore, where boys and girls without special aptitudes are concerned, supply the humanistic elements of education in ways not involving a great apparatus of learning; the difficult part of education, in the later years, I should, as a rule, confine to mathematics and science.

From Bertrand Russell, *Education and the Good Life* (New York: Boni and Liveright, Inc., 1926), pp. 26, 27, 28, 30. Quoted by permission of Liveright Publishing Corporation and George Allen & Unwin Ltd.

For Research

Logically classified categories of subject matter serve as a ready reference for those who wish to extend the range of human knowledge. Diligent and systematic research demands a previously well-organized body of subject matter to serve as a springboard for new discoveries.

For Preservation

Preservation of knowledge is essential to the continued existence of any civilization. Classification and organization of knowledge into logical, usable, understandable systems are essential for its preservation and transmission to succeeding generations. In botany, for example, material may be classified into progressively more select groups beginning with broad divisions and proceeding to successively smaller units such as class, order, family, genus, species, and, finally, variety. Geology or zoology or history will follow some other pattern, appropriate to its own field. In each of the divisions, organization is a value in itself. The practical purpose served is determined by the one who uses it. The more logical the classification and the more logical the various divisions within the organization, the more suitable is the whole for preservation for the future.

For Learning and Transmission

The major classifications of knowledge have formed the bases of the subjects offered by the schools. Modifications in classifications have been evolved to make them more practical and more usable in teaching the young. By the end of his first grade, the pupil is aware of fairly sharp distinctions between reading, writing, spelling, and arithmetic. As he advances through the grades, he rapidly learns to distinguish numerous other subjects. Usually the distinctions are emphasized by the way the subject matter is prepared for his use—in textbooks, workbooks, study guides, and the like.

It would be a mistake, of course, to conclude that all the child learns in school is a result of exposure to what is ordinarily thought of as subject matter. What the child learns before he begins school and what he learns in school apart from the materials in the subjects of study are thought by teachers to be quite as important as what he learns through association with organized subject matter.

There is one division of subject matter that is quite different from the rigid, logical classifications associated with the preservation of knowledge and the advancement of research. This is the classification of subject matter in terms of its relation to direct and indirect experiences of the child. Subject matter in books, for instance, would be classified as part of the indirect experience material. The subject matter is part of direct experience, however, if the child comes into direct contact with the original material. For instance, the child learns as he sees a house burn down, climbs a mountain, watches a plane take off, observes a mother bird feed her young. His growth is promoted along desirable lines by the opportunity to preside at an assembly, to make a dress, dissect a frog, or write a poem. The subject matter may be unorganized, lacking in sequence, and unplanned. It is not, however, without momentary or even long-range purpose. Learning in this way is natural and, perhaps, most rapid and most efficient.

The second approach utilizes subject matter that is more or less systematically arranged in a way to facilitate learning. The pupil learns through vicarious, not direct, experience. He reads, listens, observes. He learns through participating in the experiences of others.

Both kinds of learning, both kinds of subject matter, have a place in the school. In the earlier grades, particularly, direct learning, associated with personal experience, is emphasized. In the field of science, for example, the pupils work with objects at firsthand, experience them as concrete realities. As the child progresses through the grades, the subject matter tends to be related more to indirect experience. Gradually a conceptual order in subject matter is introduced as a substitute for the perceptual order that preceded it. The important point to remember is that the perceptual precedes the conceptual.

There is a natural limit to the amount of subject matter that can be learned through firsthand experience. It becomes necessary to expand the world of the pupil through learning subject matter that depends upon language, pictures, mathematical symbols, stories, historical episodes, and maps. Sufficient direct learning experience makes the indirect learning more meaningful. A perceptual background is a sound base for a conceptual understanding. In arithmetic, for instance, pupils can learn about symbols in such a way that symbols have no meaning apart from purposes associated with the arithmetic lesson. In science, pupils may work with subject matter that has little relation to their everyday lives. On the other hand, the symbols used in arithmetic can be so related to direct experience that they will be meaningful. If the materials of science provide an opportunity for direct experience in observation and manipulation, are related to, or are built upon, direct experience in the everyday life of the child, then the child has a background for the understandings that are conceptual. He can read and understand and learn about the matters of science. He has a background of percepts from direct learning upon which he builds. Thus, the two kinds of subject matter are complementary. When learned with a reasonable balance, the one reinforces the other.

ORGANIZATION OF SUBJECT MATTER

Terms

In discussing organization of subject matter we use such terms as "integration," "correlation," and "core" to refer to plans for unification. In addition the two terms "curriculum" and "course of study" are frequently used and should be understood.

1. Curriculum

The term "curriculum" is now commonly used to include all the activities and experiences that have been planned for the child in school, or that are sponsored by the school, to advance his desirable growth. Originally "curriculum" referred only to those activities that had been planned for the classroom. This left outside-of-the-classroom activities to be "extracurricular." The child had to maintain a basic level of achievement in the classroom to be "eligible" for extracurricular participation. The current trend is to consider the entire school experience of the child as a unit and to determine the emphasis on any particular kind of activity in terms of the needs of an individual child. As progress has been made in discovering children's needs and adapting to their needs, the curriculum, the total school offering, has been enriched by visual aids, plays, excursions, and various types of pupil activities in and out of the school. A specific plan of organization is implied when we talk about core curriculum, subject matter curriculum, or integrated curriculum.

2. Course of Study

A course of study is usually worked out in a particular subject area. It may be an area like United States history or a broader area like social studies. Often it is developed by the teachers and supervisors, sometimes together with curriculum specialists, in a particular field or grade level. Typically it begins with a statement of aims for the course of study and then in more or less general terms makes suggestions for the teaching materials and methods that might be used. A course of study may set a minimum common denominator for a grade level or a certain subject within a school system or a school. It is an aid to teachers in integrating the subject matter taught because they can discover, in general, what has been covered in the preceding year of a child's schooling and what he will probably attempt in the following year. The course of study is a service tool for guidance workers who counsel high school pupils in their choice of subjects. The course of study becomes an educational hazard when it is overly specific instead of suggestive, when it is too mandatory to allow for adaptation in terms of all the aspects of the learning situation.

Language Arts

The emphasis in this broad field is upon the word "language." The raising of language to the level of an art signifies the attempt to cultivate language so that it may be used as an expression of beauty, be appealing, and have more than commonplace significance. Language arts is concerned mainly with developing skills in expressing ideas and in receiving ideas from others, both through the written and spoken word.

In earlier American schools, subject matter was suited to developing the mechanical skills of reading, speaking, spelling, and writing. Listening, appreciations, and habits were largely disregarded. The current trend is toward selecting subject matter that will contribute to much wider growth. It is assumed, for example, that the development of the powers of communication is closely related to the development of a rich, attractive, well-adjusted personality. The trend is toward emphasizing the values as well as mechanics of communication in the wider aspects of social living.

Electronic devices used in foreign language laboratories have changed teaching techniques. (Board of Education, St. Louis)

As the broader concept of the language arts has been adopted, subject matter has been increasingly diversified. As yet, no clear agreement has been reached among America's language arts teachers as to the relative emphasis different aspects of the program should receive, nor has a logical sequence in specific areas been developed. Some teachers deviate very little from the older practices of teaching reading, writing, and spelling as separate mechanical skills. Others place the greatest emphasis upon well-rounded development. Most teachers feel that a realignment of the subject matter of the language arts field is inevitable.

Science

In America's schools, children very early come into contact with subject matter relating to the physical and material world. The approach is first through the avenue of direct experience and, in the early grades, is almost entirely lacking in logical organization. The method of teaching is highly informal. The subject matter is much what the teachers and the pupils wish it to be. Kindergartners, for example, use plants, animals, herbariums, and aquariums. Later, perhaps in the fifth grade, well-equipped science laboratories as well as textbooks, visual aids, and the like are utilized. Typically, science throughout the first nine grades is general science, with subject matter drawn from one or several specialized fields of science. There is

Formal grammar was greatly emphasized in the early elementary schools. The following is an excerpt from a text that was widely adopted and generally used in the seventh and eighth grades.

EXERCISE 72

Study the pronouns in the following sentences and:
1. Classify each into the smallest known class.
2. Decline it.
3. Give its antecedent.
4. Give its gender.
5. Give its number.
6. Give its person.
7. Give its use in the sentence.
8. Give its case.
9. Tell how you determined these properties.
10. Explain any irregularity which you may discover.

[Thirty sentences are given. These are representative.]

10. He desired to pray, but it was denied him.
11. He has squandered his money, but he now regrets it.
17. It thundered as it seemed to me.
19. Well, then, Mistress Dudley, since you will needs tarry, I give the Province House in charge to you.

From John B. Wisely, *An English Grammar* (Boston: Atkinson, Mentzer and Company, 1906), p. 236.

little agreement as to grade-placement for any of the subject matter. The problem of sequence is frequently left entirely in the hands of the individual teacher or those who administer the science program in an individual school.

The subjects of study from the tenth year on are progressively more specialized. Typically, biology comes in the tenth year, physics in the eleventh, and chemistry in the twelfth. In each instance, however, the subject tends to be introductory. Realistic situations and numerous examples of application are used.

In attempting to continue the general education plan, the general science pattern is also followed in some colleges. A nonspecialized course for freshmen called "Basic Science" is given. The course is constructed to give insights into the nature of the physical world for those students who do not plan to pursue further study in any specialized science.

Science materials used earlier in American schools were poorly

Note how the character of subject matter has been changed by the addition of modern electrical equipment in this complex demonstration system used in a high school classroom. (Lincoln Public Schools)

suited to educate the pupil about his physical and biological world. Likewise, the highly specialized subjects studied by some teachers in college courses designed to prepare them for teaching science in the lower grades have not been appropriate. College courses, more often than not, are organized to train specialists—chemists, biologists, geologists, physicists—rather than to educate teachers who plan to teach science. Unfortunately, institutions of higher learning have made little attempt to meet pre-service needs for teachers of general science at the elementary and high school levels. It seems logical to argue that great scientists will never be educated unless great teachers are first educated to teach them and that the best of instruction, including instruction in science, should begin when the child first enters school.

Mathematics

Subject matter in mathematics has been more nearly standardized than in any other area. Arithmetic is a standard subject through-

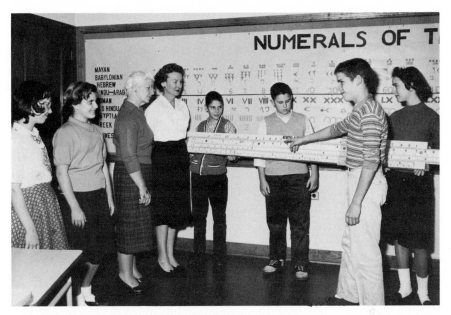

The slide rule is used to help pupils gain a better understanding of mathematics. (Evanston Photographic Service)

out the first six grades of the elementary school and, in many schools, throughout the first eight grades. It is typically taught as a specialized subject. Most arithmetic teachers in the elementary schools closely adhere to the adopted text. The writers of the textbooks in arithmetic and also in the more specialized mathematics of the four-year high school exert, therefore, a considerable influence in determining the kind of subject matter pursued.

Mathematics is a required subject for general study until the ninth year, and, in many schools, until the twelfth year. In the ninth grade the subject matter is sometimes differentiated into two kinds of mathematics—algebra of the traditional type and general mathematics. General mathematics is usually the more immediately practical of the two.

The emphasis given mathematics through all the early grades in America's schools is a response to the belief that mathematics contains much that is of a general educative value, that it contributes to enriching the daily lives of pupils. It is also generally believed that mathematics fosters ability to think and express oneself precisely.

American schools have had comparatively little success with

teaching mathematics. Many believe that more skill and under-standing could be achieved if improved subject matter were avail-able. Others insist that mathematics must be related more to the pupils' everyday lives. Still others advocate a complete realignment of subject matter to emphasize the central, the basic concepts com-mon to all specialized areas of mathematics.

In recent years there has been a strong reaction among mathe-matics educators against mathematics presented to the pupils mainly as a collection of techniques and manipulations, giving simple, basic concepts little attention. Experiments are now going on in universities and in many public schools in developing what is called The New Mathematics. This does not invalidate the older theories of mathematics. However, concepts that constitute the central theme of mathematics are introduced very early, and the subject matter in the grades and high school is realigned and augmented. In some cases terms previously common only in college mathematics are now introduced in the early grades. Unifying ideas, like sets (any well-defined grouping of distinguishable objects) receive consider-able emphasis. The pupils are, in fact, introduced to sets of objects, pictorially perhaps, before being introduced to symbols. First learn-ing of a basic idea is through direct experience; the symbols and terminology are introduced later. Structure is another concept intro-duced early. This refers to subject matter that treats of the basic principles and properties common to all systems of mathematics. A child sees a line as an infinite number of points. He grasps the idea of infinity at once. Other examples of unifying ideas that may be introduced much earlier than heretofore are measurement, systems of enumeration, the meaning of operations, logical deductions, graphical representations, drawing valid generalization, and as the pupil progresses, other unifying themes. Throughout current experi-ments with subject matter, the effort is directed toward stressing from the beginning the unifying themes and ideas common to all mathematics.

Contemporary mathematics is undergoing rapid, drastic change, but at this writing so rapid has been the revision that curriculum organization, textbooks, and properly trained teachers have lagged behind what the mathematics educators advocate. As one mathe-matics educator said, "We may not yet have the perfect new math that will work with all children, but the important thing is, we're working on it!"

Social Studies

As long as social studies was confined to a study of only one aspect of social living, the classification into specialized fields like geography or history was considered quite adequate. Teachers became increasingly aware, however, that within such a scheme of classification many important phases of social living were not even being touched. They reasoned that pertinent subject matter related to the whole of a current social process, not just a small segment of a process, should be included if pupils were to develop an intelligent appreciation of the broad area of human relations in modern society. In locating materials that would shed light upon crucial and urgent present-day social problems it was necessary to investigate all fields, not just the social sciences. The reorganized subject matter, focused upon selected problems of social living, was called the *social studies*.

The trend is for teachers to formulate the course pattern, to direct the selection and organization of the subject matter, and to use any materials that promise to develop insight into human relations problems, to promote a better understanding of the nature of the social processes, and to build competence in living and dealing with one's fellows. This means the subject matter is selected to develop competence in intergroup relations, skills in group action, concern for the welfare of others, tolerance for the viewpoints of others, respect for and ability to work with others who have different cultural backgrounds, and understanding of the elements that contribute to the increasing interdependence of human beings everywhere. In other words, the social studies emphasize skills, traits, attitudes, and understandings needed for the improvement of human relations everywhere.

Subject matter of the social studies in the elementary and secondary schools has perhaps departed more radically from the older and more specialized patterns of organization than has any of the other fields. This is, it seems, partly because social problems are so numerous and varied that they, more obviously than other problems, can be approached only through the avenues of more than one kind of specialized subject matter.

Social studies in our schools, however, have never been organized uniformly according to any definite scheme or pattern or logical sequence. This is one criticism made by those who advocate the more traditional, specialized, schematic arrangement.

Fine Arts

The fine arts include the dance, painting, music—any mode of expression thought to be significant and beautiful. The expression may be in the form of both appreciation and actual production or creation. Fine arts are emphasized throughout the elementary school, including the kindergarten, and also through most of the grades of the secondary school. They are recognized, also, as important in adult education.

The attention given to the fine arts at all levels of education in the United States is a recent phenomenon. In the past the tendency was to consider the fine arts as a "frill." Music in the nursery school and kindergarten, rhythms for younger children, handicrafts for all ages, including those who are handicapped or suffering from some nervous ailment, are now typical. Perhaps the pressure of social changes—shorter work week, mandatory retirement, mechanical

Pupils develop appreciation of the fine arts by viewing the work of artists. By this experience, pupils are encouraged to express themselves creatively. (Evanston Photographic Service)

housekeeping aids—bringing about increased leisure have been responsible, in part, for the upsurge of interest in the fine arts.

The subject matter of the fine arts, drawn from many fields, is neither highly systematized nor standardized at any of the levels of education. In selecting and organizing the subject matters, interests and the maturity levels of the pupils serve as the main criteria. Thus, a ninth-grader with no background in art and a fourth-grader who studied art in second and third grades might be able to handle the same subject matter. The subject matter is determined largely by the needs of the individual pupil as they are revealed to the teacher, not, as is the case with mathematics, upon a progressively increased level of difficulty arbitrarily settled in terms of grade levels.

Children, particularly those in the elementary school, use a great variety of forms of expression—drawing, painting, singing, listening to good music, acting out stories, playing in a school orchestra, playing musical instruments they have made. The subject matter may include almost anything thought to be beautiful and aesthetic, anything that will provide an outlet for children to communicate in a creative or in a receptive, appreciative way.

Health

In all the official statements of aims of education in the United States, high priority is given to health. Sometimes the aim is divided into two aspects—physical health and mental health. This is one of the dualisms first introduced into educational philosophy in the Middle Ages. The use of the two terms indicates the emphasis desired in the education program and probably causes little harm, providing one remembers that the two terms merely designate the health aim from two different angles. Health is health of an organism. When there is a threat to good health, the whole of the organism is involved.

Study in the health area is varied. Children in the grade schools often make a special study of diets, record and rate their own diets, study the relative numbers of illnesses pupils have, and look for a relationship between illness and diet. Study of science at some grade levels will also include nutrition. It is not unusual for elementary school pupils, in their home economics classes, to carry on projects in nutrition. The classroom and the school building with its light-

Health is an important subject in the elementary school. (Conried from Monk-meyer)

ing, sewage disposal, and the like may also provide subject matter for health education. Sometimes the health services of the school are used as source material. School dental services have led science classes to study the fluoridation of water, the relation of diet to good teeth, and the relation of eating sweets or drinking sweetened liquids to the preservation of teeth.

Much of the subject matter of health studies involves direct experience from actual activities. Free play, particularly in the elementary school, may, for instance, make a significant contribution to self-control, fair play, and physical efficiency.

Health, as a major object of education, cannot be achieved by studying logical categories of subject matter. It is an aim that embraces the needs of every pupil at all levels of education. What is studied in health education even in a single grade cannot be standardized. Perhaps in this field more than in any other, expert planning is of paramount importance. The subject matter must be flexible—adaptable to the growth characteristics and primary interests of the individual pupils.

General Trends

The trend in organizing subject matter is toward larger units. Traditional organization is in terms of more or less isolated subjects. The teacher in the elementary school conducts a class in reading, a class in arithmetic, or a music class. In the high school one teacher has a class in geography, one a class in algebra, and another a class in chemistry.

To overcome the disadvantages of too great emphasis on the separateness of subject matter, to move from fragmentation toward greater unity, various plans have been followed. One such plan is called "correlation." Interested teachers working together discover relationships in their subject matter. The teacher of literature, for instance, may correlate Dickens' *Tale of Two Cities* with the history teacher's treatment of the French Revolution. Teachers and administrators tend to like this plan since no subject loses anything and traditional organization is not basically upset. Actually, the barriers between the subjects are not eliminated. Rather, they are adjusted to; teacher-planning achieves some unification despite them.

Another approach to unifying small areas of subject matter is called "integration." This type of organization is more readily adapted to the lower grades of the elementary school than to the secondary school. The teacher selects, or directs the selection of, projects that will give the child experiences educationally desirable, promote learning specifically suited to his academic level, and provide an opportunity for the teacher to give the kind of guidance that promises to lead to social and personal maturity. If, for instance, the project selected is the operation of a grocery store, in setting up the store and running the business the children would read, draw, add and subtract, and engage in many learning activities that ordinarily are taken up separately. They would also have such experiences as planning and working together, sharing, and cooperating.

Sometimes the fragmentary character of traditional subject matter organization is lessened by combining areas and having an expanded unit. Typical large divisions are social studies, general science, language arts, health, physical education, general mathematics, and general arts. The subject matter area known as "unified studies" and embracing English and social studies is an even broader kind of classification.

The core program as a part of the junior and senior high school organization was described in Chapter 15. The term "core studies" is used to describe another plan for unifying work in the elementary school. Under this plan, a basic unit or problem on such subjects as housing, family, or civil liberties is the "core." Children who pursue the core give to this phase of their work all the time that is allocated to "general" education, that is, to education that is common to all students as differential from specialized education or vocational training. In working on the basic problem children use material from any subject. Emphasis is upon pupil activity. A wide range of reading materials as well as the resources of the community are used.

Within the general plans called correlation, integration, unified studies, and core studies, the variations are numerous. They all mark the trend toward organizing subject matter in larger units. They are of increasing interest to those who wish to improve our instructional programs.

SUBJECT MATTER IN AMERICAN SCHOOLS

At Grade Levels

Subject matter has long been organized into levels paralleling the grades of our schools. In the Middle Ages, subject matter was limited to the knowledge systematically organized in books somewhat like encyclopedias for the purpose of being learned. Eventually the easier parts of accumulated, organized knowledge became the subject matter of the earlier grades. The more abstract, the more conceptual, and the more difficult to comprehend became the subject matter for the later grades. The most difficult to assimilate was to be taught by the graduate schools in the universities. Grade-placement of subject matter was decided upon an empirical basis. Eventually, for example, Euclidean geometry was placed regularly in the curriculum for sophomores in high school. Adaptations of Euclid's textbook are still used in high school geometry classes.

It was believed that subject matter, in time, found its own natural level and settled there. Its natural level was that stage of educational advancement at which it could be understood. Any other reasons for why it should be studied at a predetermined level were never probed. From earliest time a systematic, arbitrary arrangement of subject matter was accepted as appropriate apart entirely from utilitarian or interest values. It is related that even about 300 B.C. a pupil, having learned the first proposition of demonstrational geometry, raised the question of what he would get by learning these things and was answered by Euclid who called his slave and said, "Give him three pence since he must needs make gain by what he learns."

In ninth grade, algebra begins with the intuitively conceived axioms and proceeds to quadratics. Demonstrational geometry, which follows, is a tenth-grade subject and also takes a full school year to learn. Advanced algebra is learned in the first half of the eleventh grade, and solid geometry is learned in the second half of the eleventh grade. The subject matter of Latin is grammar in the ninth grade, Caesar's *Commentaries* in the tenth, Cicero's *Orations* in the eleventh, and Virgil's *Aeneid* in the twelfth.

Subject matter in American schools thus becomes crystallized. Materials in numerous fields have been systematically sifted, sorted, and organized, and their pedagogical uses have been prescribed according to grade-level sequence.

Total Learning

A somewhat expanded notion encompasses as subject matter *all* that a pupil learns. This concept does not exclude the idea that subject matter is organized in grade levels or that it includes what is in the textbooks. Subject matter, however, is not limited to that which is in a book. It also includes what goes on within the pupil, the reaction to what is studied. In this case the subject matter consists of the facts and ideas that are communicated to the pupil. Here the subject matter is only that which the pupil assimilates. In this sense no two pupils ever study the same subject matter, even though they use the same textbook and are taught by the same teacher.

Purposive Learning

Clearly, an individual's belief about what the subject matter of a school is, is directly related to what he thinks the aims of the school should be. If he believes that learning should contribute to purposes shared by the teacher and the pupils, then he might define subject matter broadly as the "facts observed, read, recalled, and talked about, and the ideas suggested, in course of a development of a situation having a purpose."[2] This definition emphasizes that a classroom constitutes a special place for deliberate education and that there is more to the mastery of subject matter than learning what is included in the textbook. Importance is placed upon the management of a situation so that learning proceeds with a purpose. It is the aim or purpose that is uppermost in the minds of the pupils and the teacher and that dictates what and how subject matter shall be learned. In this concept, the subject matter varies with the individual pupil, since individual reactions to what is read or talked about will vary. In addition, it is recognized that how the pupil organizes what he learns depends upon various factors only some of which are within the pupil himself.

THE TEACHER AND SUBJECT MATTER

In our discussion of the qualifications, training, and experience necessary for teaching, it was pointed out that the successful teacher has acquired a breadth of knowledge far wider than that possessed by even the most advanced of his pupils. This knowledge is like a huge reservoir—it stands ready at all times to be drawn upon as needed.

The teacher's knowledge is a necessary complement to textbooks. Frequently, textbooks are divided into sections, and perhaps into subsections, for purposes of organization, reference, clarity, and emphasis. The textbook is a tool, and the divisions, sometimes quite minute, may be a definite aid to instruction. If, however, the teacher does not have a wide range of knowledge, the textbook with its detailed subdivisions tends to give subject matter a quality of rigidity, to make it less adaptable to momentary situations and less appropriate to teaching with a purpose. The teacher's knowledge must extend beyond the limits of the subject matter established in the textbook, limits unavoidable in the preparation of specialized books. The boundaries of a textbook are never the boundaries of the most fruitful subject matter.

2 John Dewey, *Democracy and Education* (New York: The Macmillan Company, 1916), p. 212.

The chances are that the teacher will organize his knowledge in a way somewhat paralleling the organization of subject matter of the specialist because the teacher has studied under and mastered that kind of arrangement. The physics teacher, for instance, tends to think of physics around words like measurement, mechanics, heat, static electricity, electricity-in-motion, sound, light, and invisible radiations.

The pupil's orientation to subject matter is different from the teacher's. The pupil's organization, growing out of his past experiences, is inchoate. The successful teacher is aware of the discrepancy. He is alert to the opportunities and to the importance of providing avenues for a pupil to follow in developing his own organization and application. In drawing upon the reservoir of knowledge, the teacher will not be influenced by the kind of organization characteristic of his own school experience. He will tend to draw from any area, whether in textbooks or in the world of practical affairs, appropriate to achieving the end desired. For instance, the teacher's knowledge may influence the subject matter of the literature class to include something that might traditionally be classified as history, philosophy, economics, or something else. In our review of the current trends in the organization of subject matter, it will be noted that the importance of organizing subject matter in larger units is recognized.

Subject matter, it has been pointed out, may include direct experience and indirect or vicarious learning. In advancing educationally the tendency is to move from emphasis on the direct toward progressively greater emphasis on the indirect. A learning situation may include both direct and indirect features in varying degrees. In the biology laboratory the pupil may have such direct experiences as learning about circulation by dissecting a rabbit. He will also use the textbook, library reference materials, and perhaps filmstrips and movies. Sufficient direct experience is necessary to make indirect learning effective. The indirect must be associated with the direct by meaningful symbols, vocabulary, and examples. The successful teacher is resourceful in making appropriate connections. For instance, in teaching arithmetic, it will be less difficult for a farm boy to make a meaningful connection between the symbols of measurement applied to a bushel of oats or an acre of ground than it will be for a city pupil who buys oats in a cereal box and thinks of land divisions as city blocks and fifty-foot lots.

Unfortunately, students often arrive at college, even at the graduate level, without having built firsthand experiences with quantitative subject matter sufficient for clear understanding of the meanings various words and symbols are expected to convey. For enjoyment or real appreciation, a meaningful connection between subject matter and human living is essential.

PATHS TO PROGRESS

What paths to progress have been indicated in our study of subject matter in America's schools? The selection of materials, the organization of subject matter, the teacher's background, and other factors play a part in determining the quality of the subject matter in schools. All of them are interwoven in their causes and effects and mutual impact. All offer a challenge for improvement.

At present, subject matter designed to promote specialized and vocational competences tends to be relatively adequate and satisfactory because the specialized areas have immediate and definite aims and the subject matter appropriate to advancing these aims is readily available. The path of progress leads toward selecting subject matter potentially more significant in advancing the aims of general education. There is a current tendency to give unwarranted emphasis to specialized subject matter and to give too little emphasis to subject matter that contributes to the aims of general education, to a sound cultural background. Chemistry teachers, for instance, tend to stress the kind of subject matter that prepares chemists, not the kind that makes citizens intelligent about the physical world. Unfortunately, there is a continuing lack of agreement about what subject matter best contributes to general education of all learners. The development of materials appropriate to the general education in all subjects, selection of suitable subject matter, and planning adequate curriculums are important areas for study and leadership.

Another path to progress is unmistakably indicated in the selection of subject matter that is more adaptable to the vast range of children's learning abilities. Balanced reading programs, textbooks suited to different levels of ability, and workbooks that permit pupils to advance at individual rates are becoming increasingly effective. Including more direct experience, particularly in the high school, is another improvement in the selection of subject matter that may be profitably extended.

Present trends indicate that in the future, organization of subject matter will continue to be progressively more in terms of unity and less in terms of specialized, fragmentary fields. Specialists in the psychology of learning, in child development, in social psychology, and in social biology have effectively challenged the soundness of a theory in which education is viewed mainly as the acquisition of material as it is arranged in textbooks.

Regardless of the way subject matter is selected or organized, its value in the educational experiences of the child depends largely upon the effectiveness of the teacher. Progress here lies in the direction of improved training and experience. In order to exploit fully the potentialities of the entire learning situation, the teacher must not only understand the learning process and be thoroughly acquainted with children; he also must have both a broad, general background and an extensive reservoir of information and understanding in the particular field in which he is teaching.

QUESTIONS

1. What is your definition of subject matter?
2. What is the curriculum? The course of study? A subject of study?
3. How may one judge relative values of the various subjects of study?
4. What should be the relationship between school textbooks and the subject matter used in a given classroom?
5. What are the characteristics of a suitable textbook?
6. How, in your opinion, is continuity in a subject such as the fine arts or social studies to be achieved?

PROJECTS

Consult some specialized publication on the subject matter of your chosen field. Set forth what seem to be the principal trends in the selection of subject matter.

CHAPTER **19**

Methods of teaching in America's schools

Three kinds of understanding are essential to effective teaching: first, basic understandings, knowledges, and generalizations about pupils; second, knowledge that is classified as appropriate subject matter; third, understandings related to methods, procedures, and skills required to utilize effectively, in directing learning, the knowledge of subject matter and understandings about pupils. In a sense, these three kinds of understandings constitute a trilogy in that they are inextricably interrelated, each constituting one component of the educative process.

For a teacher-in-preparation or an experienced teacher to keep informed about educational developments it is important that he maintain a reasonably balanced interest in all three aspects. Since each kind of understanding is of such breadth and magnitude as to sustain a lifetime of study, it is relatively easy, even tempting, for a teacher to allow his interests to become one-sided. That a balanced interest in the three essential aspects—knowledge of pupils, of subject matter, and of methods—is a valuable goal for teachers-in-training and for teachers-in-service cannot be overemphasized.

484

METHODS, A DEEPENING CONCERN

Problems relating to teaching methods have become a matter of expanding interest in recent years. This seems due, in part at least, to an intensified awareness by experienced teachers that all they know about human growth and development and about subject matter to be learned can be translated effectively into learning only with wise use of skillful methods. Without the ability to select and utilize appropriate procedures, the position of a teacher is somewhat analogous to a family with a swimming pool which serves only as an ornament because no one in the family can swim.

The expanded interest in teaching methods is due in part also to the accelerated change in curriculum, to the expanded background of interests and experiences of pupils, and to the extensive variety of teaching aids now available. A teacher today looking back at the pre-TV, pre-plane travel, pre-automated manufacturing, pre-Cold War international maneuvering times, recognizes at once that many classroom methods geared to conditions of a decade ago are now out-of-date. In the wake of current rapid change, teaching methods are inexorably swept along.

That the teaching profession is responding to the current demand for improvement in methods of teaching is attested by the attention given to this area by numerous groups of educators—for instance, the National Council of Teachers of English and the National Council of Teachers of Mathematics. Information about teaching problems, experiments, recommendations, and innovations are widely disseminated by such organizations through their national publications. A teacher will find among these much material to stimulate his interest in teaching methods and also to guide him in determining the methods and procedures appropriate or adaptable to his classroom.

Approaches to Study of Methods

One may approach a study of methods of teaching by focusing on so-called general methods. General methods include the basic principles, generalizations, and concepts that are, presumably, applicable to teaching in general, to the teaching of all subjects. In his five formal steps to conducting the recitation, for example, Herbart assumed that teachers in general conduct recitations and that they could use the five formal steps as a guide regardless of the subject matter they are teaching. Likewise, Dewey in his *How We Think* assumes that all teachers are attempting to help pupils learn how to think. All teachers are assumed to ask questions, evaluate pupil achievement, engage in telling, and the like. A study of general methods would be expected to cover what teachers do in general to stimulate and direct the learning of pupils.

Another approach to the study of methods focuses on special methods. This relates to problems inherent in the teaching of a specialized subject matter field or in the teaching of a particular age group, usually very young children. This assumes there are methods that apply particularly to teaching English, mathematics, and the like, and that these can better be studied in special courses. The study of special methods is thought to have the added advantage of providing an opportunity for logical combination of study of teaching methods with a study of subject matter. Thus, colleges now give such courses as Intermediate Mathematics, Physics for Teachers, Chemistry for Teachers. Furthermore, in some universities study of special methods and student teaching in the subject field are closely correlated.

No attempt will be made here to evaluate the two approaches to the study of methods. It seems that both have certain advantages. There is some advantage in the broader approach that gives consideration to such topics as the aims of education, how rewards and punishments operate to condition learning, how interests, motivation, and other affective factors can be utilized. On the other hand, concentration on a study of the problems peculiar to the primary or preschool level is likely also to result in certain advantages. Certainly it is profitable to explore under the guidance of a skilled college teacher problems related to any special field. Both approaches indicate that a study of methods of teaching is a comprehensive field. Perhaps study of both general and special methods may be needed for a satisfactory command in any one field.

A Comprehensive Field

Methods of teaching cover a comprehensive field. This is due first to the fact that education is established for the very complex purpose of promoting human improvement itself. As pointed out in the chapter on Understanding the Pupil, this involves a twofold

Paul Monroe (1869–1947) was a thorough student of the history of education. His influence over education was considerable at the beginning of the present century. The following paragraph shows his view on the meaning of method.

Method is the process of using this culture material so as to produce the desired development of the child. This development must include the expansion of his own powers, the creation of control over them and the direction of them to the necessary, to the useful, and to helpful social activities. Method is the guidance of the child in his activities by the teacher so that he may incorporate into his own experience that portion of the experience of the race which, to those who have the direction of his education, seems valuable; that is, suitable for his stage of development and similar in complexity to his own interests and activities. The sole effort of the teacher should be directed toward the guidance of this process; his sole interest should be in the expanding consciousness of the child, in furnishing experiences appropriate to the power of the child and properly related to his interests and activities. The teacher should be so equipped by previous training that he can give undivided attention in this process. Hence the necessity of *method*, as the term is ordinarily used. This method should be possessed by the teacher, but it is of most value when most unconsciously used. Method in the broader sense requires upon the part of the teacher a knowledge of the child; a knowledge of his existing interests, activities and possessions; a mastery of the material or the subject-matter dealt with; and understanding of the process through which the child incorporates the novel experience into his own; and an ability to use and to make subordinate the machinery of the schoolroom and the technique of the process of instruction. This last one is considered method *par excellence*, but it is only one phase of method.

From Paul Monroe, *A Brief Course in the History of Education* (New York: The Macmillan Company, 1907), pp. 407–408. Quoted by permission of The Macmillan Company.

continuing problem, on the one hand problems related to the biological character of each human being, the character of whom is the outcome of the interaction between the individual and his environment, and on the other hand problems related to the environment, including the school with everything that makes it an important part of that environment.

The great breadth of the area of teaching methods is also due to the extended range of subject matter, each element of which presents its own novel teaching problems. Take, for example, the field of English. Some of the questions a teacher might need to answer are: What is the best method for the study of words? Children seem to learn slang terms easily, but have difficulty learning legitimate words. Why? How should punctuation be taught? Will a single method like phonemics suffice? Can a poem be taught to high school pupils by programmed instruction? If so, how does one program a poem? One might similarly proceed to other elements of English such as reading, writing, grammar, spelling, listening, viewing, mass media, only to find that each presents peculiar problems of teaching, none of which is easy to answer. In seeking an answer, a teacher may recognize the need for knowing, in general, about available teaching aids, team teaching, programmed learning, curriculum construction, program evaluation, and so on.

Since methods of teaching is such a comprehensive field of study, the survey that follows in this and the next chapter makes no attempt to deal with concrete analyses of the many problems of teaching method. The treatment here is necessarily limited to overall trends in various subject matter fields.

TEACHING SUBJECT MATTER

Language Arts

The aim in teaching language arts is twofold—the development of abilities to express ideas and feelings and to receive and interpret messages. Writing and speaking constitute the media of expression of ideas and feelings. Listening and reading constitute the media through which the ability to receive and interpret messages is developed.

1. Written Expression

After judging a pupil's present capacity to write clearly and effectively, the teacher next concentrates on finding ways to encourage growth in this skill. Growth is emphasized rather than expertness which is held in mind as a remote goal. The pupil should always have a clear notion of the next step in the development of his abilities.

The material best suited for study, discussion, and rewriting are the sentences and paragraphs from a pupil's own written expression.

The following is an excerpt from a lecture to prospective teachers given by William G. Perry, Jr.

Now since the teacher is someone who has been hired by the community to engage full-time in this transmission of the culture, you will find that you are not just a Ganymede or a Hebe standing at the fountain of knowledge with a little cup, but rather you will find that your students are quite properly responding to you as if your other hand, the one you have behind your back, had brass knuckles on it. They will be responding to you as you were saying, as you must say —as you cannot escape saying whether you put it into words or not—not only, "come and drink from the fountain of knowledge," but also, "And while you are at it, bud, you do it our way on time; if you don't, you will not only not get these lovely things, but you will be sent shamefully home, a failure."

Now what do people do under stresses and threats like that? They resist, just as Sally resists eating those beans, not because she doesn't like beans, but because she is afraid that by liking them, now that you have told her to eat them, she will somehow be losing something. She doesn't know quite what, but she feels that something dreadfully important will be lost. So what students do in their resistance is to conform to the letter of what you say. They will eat two spoonfuls of beans, with one bean on each. They will say the letter of what you require them to repeat, but they will reject the spirit, even if they think it will be good for them.

.   .   .

It is in the student's sense of the warmth of being understood, of being therefore personally related, that he is set free from his anxiety so that he can do his academic work productively.

And it is not impossible that it is through the warmth that you may convey this way that the student may come to feel that it may be worth while to grow up. If grown-ups are impersonal, authoritative, and intellectual, then it is perfectly clear that being mature means to give up having fun. It means to the student that to grow up and be a Self must carry with it an absolutely intolerable loss, the discard of all his impulses and desires, and that to be a Self will not ony mean to be alone, but to be lonely indeed. But if you are warm and attentive to your students' feelings, then they will realize that you, too, put some value on feelings, and that maybe it would be possible to grow up and still have feelings and still have fun. In that case, since you eat beans, maybe they will try them, too.

Reprinted by permission of the publishers from William G. Perry, Jr., "Conflicts in the Learning Process: The Student's Response to Teaching," in A Handbook for College Teachers, ed. Bernice Brown Cronkhite (Cambridge, Mass.: Harvard University Press, 1950), pp. 20 and 35.

Variations in word meanings receive attention, with a view to selecting words that express the precise meaning desired. Published paragraphs, which may be read by the pupils at home and serve as examples of better forms of written expression, are also discussed in the classroom. The contributions made to expression by correct spelling, punctuation, and grammatical structure are made an integral part of the instructional procedure.

How does the assignment contribute to the growth of an individual's powers of expression? This is the paramount criterion for the selection of a method. For example, teachers help their pupils see that socially acceptable forms of written expression are important, not because they represent the ends of good written expression, but because they make a pupil a more effective social individual. Younger children are taught to know words, to use them, and to write them in proper context. Knowing words helps them to think and adds to their development of capacity to deal with other persons and to provide solutions to individual personal problems. A pupil learns that his potential powers cannot be developed in a day, that they, with some effort on his part, will develop gradually.

One of the problems in attempting to promote growth in the abilities of written expression is the pupils' lack of interest. To encourage them to develop their capacities, teachers use as many lifelike situations as possible. Pupils write useful letters, prepare scripts for an assembly program, devise school posters, or originate captions to announce special events in the school. Pupils may be asked to read a written digest of something they have read in order that the class may also know about it, to write an occasional verse just for fun, to write a formal composition in order to demonstrate how one should be written, or to take notes on a talk they will hear in order to transmit effectively and faithfully the ideas of the speaker to the class. The use of lifelike situations has been effective because it brings into play the pupils' interests and helps the pupils to see that they write in school for the same reasons that people write outside school. Resistance to writing is easier to overcome if the pupils are encouraged to write about things of concern to them and if writing can be done in ways of some immediate use.

The question of methods in teaching spelling, punctuation, grammar, and handwriting often arises. Teaching written expression includes all these subject matters. Spelling is combined with, and is a part of, written expression, but the central emphasis is upon word study—the meaning of words and the form in which they convey the meaning. Both the words studied and the spelling of the words are taken from the words the pupils use. Meaning and structure are considered together. A word wrongly spelled usually does not carry its true meaning. "It reigned yesterday" is an example. Teachers focus attention upon words. A number of words are examined, analyzed, and reviewed each week but always by a method that leads to growth in the powers of expression. Both punctuation and grammar are given careful attention but, again, as means to developing powers of written expression.

2. Oral Expression

In helping pupils develop the powers of oral expression, teachers must realize the importance of full recognition of the child's native resources and his level of maturation. The native capacities are developed by putting natural organs—ears, vocal chords, larynx —to use. The way the child is taught to use the organs determines the nature of the development that takes place.

Teaching speech in school is important because speech is man's basic mode of expression. It is his most effective way not only to give expression to his wants but to preserve his techniques and knowledge and to pass them on to the next generation.

Unfortunately, methodical teaching of speech in the schools has been somewhat neglected. This may be, in part, a legacy from the past when schools were places where children were forced to be quiet. Studies show that a four-year-old speaks ten thousand words a day, a five-year-old speaks twelve thousand words a day, and the longest period for either age group without audible speech is nineteen minutes. The average length of periods of inactivity—and these are infrequent—is four minutes. Children are naturally highly stimulated to talk, and if silence is not enforced, speech in the schoolroom is almost a continuous process. The methods for correcting, modifying, and directing the pupils' speech are continuously in use.

Considerable attention is given to the development of a speaking vocabulary. There are many differences between a speaking and an understanding vocabulary, and the problem of developing one differs from the problem of developing the other. Each entails different methods.

Training the voice has received much attention. Schools often provide specialists to direct the speech instruction of pupils with

A distinguished American philosopher, George Herbert Palmer (1842–1933), analyzes the doctrine of giving praise.

. . . When is conduct praiseworthy? When may we fairly claim honor from our fellows and ourselves? There is a ready answer. Nothing is praiseworthy which is not the result of effort. I do not praise a lady for her beauty, I admire her. The athlete's splendid body I envy, wishing that mine were like it. But I do not praise him. Or does the reader hesitate; and while acknowledging that admiration and envy may be our leading feelings here, think that a certain measure of praise is also due? It may be. Perhaps the lady has been kind enough by care to heighten her beauty. Perhaps those powerful muscles are partly the result of daily discipline. These persons, then, are not undeserving of praise, at least to the extent that they have used effort. Seeing a collection of china, I admire the china, but praise the collector. It is hard to obtain such pieces. Large expense is required, long training too, and constant watchfulness. Accordingly I am interested in more than the collection. I give praise to the owner. A learned man we admire, honor, envy, but also praise. His wisdom is the result of effort.

Plainly, then, praise and blame are attributable exclusively to spiritual beings. Nature is unfit for honor. We may admire her, may wish that our ways were like hers, and envy her great law-abiding calm. But it would be foolish to praise her, or even to blame when her volcanoes overwhelm our friends. We praise spirit only, conscious deeds. Where self-directed action forces its path to a worthy goal, we rightly praise the director.

From George Herbert Palmer, *The Nature of Goodness* (Boston: Houghton Mifflin Company, 1903), pp. 241–242. Quoted by permission of Houghton Mifflin Company.

exaggerated defects. Methods that have proven very effective in speech correction are adaptable to teaching the normal school pupil. In normal classroom situations, a few simple rules are followed. Good speech calls for good listeners. The teacher sets an example with his own speech habits. A pupil is directed to speak plainly and loudly enough to be heard. He speaks to the class, not just to the teacher. Good articulation is striven for. Careless speech, even in the most informal discussion, is discouraged. The pupil is made conscious that he is speaking his thoughts, that others are thinking with him, and that they are occupied with the thoughts he is trying to arouse, not with their own thoughts.

Most of the methods teachers use are informal and are selected to help a certain pupil or to fit some special situation. As with written expression, as many true-to-life situations as possible are used, such as assemblies, announcements, presiding over the class, and discussion. Teachers find the tape recorder particularly helpful.

3. Reading

Reading is language development that interprets what is seen on the printed page. Reading English is the obverse of writing and speaking English. Writing and speaking are processes in which meaning is translated into words, while reading is a process in which words are translated into meaning. Both are active processes but they differ, hence the methods of teaching the two must differ.

The discovery of printing brought reading into prominence. Printed symbols cause one to think. Ideas come to the pupils through their eyes rather than through the medium of sound. The response a pupil makes to a symbol depends upon the ideas and emotions that are aroused in him by the sight of the symbols. No two pupils make the same response to the same symbol because the same symbol carries different meanings to different people.

How children are taught to read obviously influences the nature of their ability to comprehend and to interpret what they read. Reading is not taught as an absorptive process. It is treated as an active process in which the reader expresses himself through the interpretation of what he reads. It is a process that stimulates his thinking, feeling, and acting.

Powers of expression, whether oral or written, expand as the ability to read develops. The development of this ability is a constant and continuous process. It begins when the small child first points to a picture in a book and continues throughout the course of his life. Growth patterns in ability to read, to comprehend what is read, and to interpret more meaningfully what is read vary in different individuals. Thus the student who reads with ease the most difficult technical treatise is one who has gradually sharpened his powers of distinction, enlarged the scope of his knowledge of meanings, and developed a highly specialized vocabulary. What he reads may be easy for him and difficult for someone else. A pupil's ability to read depends not only on how well he has learned to read previously, but also on the lines along which growth has been directed. He may read one kind of material expertly and read and comprehend another kind poorly. In reading, the over-all growth pattern of each pupil is unique. A method of teaching that takes into account the natural design of the learner gives promise of contributing the maximum to the development of the ability to read.

In view of the nature of reading development, the efforts made in earlier schools to classify reading into grade levels and to establish standards for each of the grades seem rather hopeless gestures. The range of reading abilities in each of the grades is inevitably very wide. Method, to be effective, must take into account the extensive differences among pupils of the same age in reading interests, abilities, and all-around reading competence.

Teachers in the lower grades of the American schools have developed and use highly successful methods of teaching reading, principally because they have accepted the guidance of child development specialists. The quality of teaching reading deteriorates somewhat in the higher grades; teachers too often use methods that largely disregard the findings of the psychologists. Consequently, high school and college students do not read as well as they should. Their progress in language facility has been slower than it should be, considering the amount of training these pupils have had. Since the methods of teaching have been partly responsible for the situation, language arts teachers at all levels have made the study of methods one of their goals.

Specialists have noted the trend away from narrower techniques like the alphabet method, used almost exclusively in early times, the word method, and the method of having pupils read orally. Following World War I, teaching children to read silently became almost the sole objective of teachers of reading. The present stress is on the use of a wide variety of methods. Reading is viewed as but one aspect of language development. Both silent and oral reading are deemed important. Emphasis is placed upon reading to get meaning. Methods are used that assist the pupil to understand, assimilate, interpret, and evaluate what he reads. Children are given the opportunity to react to what they read. The teacher starts his teaching of reading by having the pupil read stories about familiar experiences. Later instruction is adapted to the interests of the pupils. Emphasis is placed upon balanced reading. Modern textbooks, library materials, and the like are adapted to this need.

4. Listening

Attentive, sympathetic listeners are necessary to the cultivation of good oral expression. Listening is also a form of expression by the one who listens. It is a somewhat neglected area of language arts. In teaching children to be good listeners the teacher is concerned with the impact the spoken word makes upon the listener, the ideas it arouses, and the reactions to which it leads.

Pupils are taught that listening may have different purposes, for example, listening carefully to a question to answer it, to a record just to be entertained, to a persuasive advertisement on the radio to cricize the logic of the argument, or to the reading of a beautiful poem to appreciate it. Life presents many opportunities for listening, and the school has an obligation to encourage growth and development in the skills of listening quite as much as in the skills of reading. Just as, at times, spelling, punctuation, and sentence structure are made the focus of direct instruction, so also is listening. The subject matter is carefully chosen, the purpose is agreed upon, and the procedures are defined just as carefully as they would be in any other language arts instruction.

5. Trends

Language arts teachers are aware of the individual differences among their pupils and that the differences expand as growth in language arts progresses. Individual needs are given as close attention as are group needs. Much thought is devoted to choice of material and to deriving ways whereby subject matter may be effectively directed toward desired ends.

Language arts teachers carefully analyze the language development of preschool children, of children in the primary grades, and so on up through the graduate school of the university. Observation of growth of large numbers does not obscure their vision of individual differences. It does help in setting up levels that can be used as standards or guides in planning instruction.

The language arts teachers, whose methods are based on current educational theories, tend to be nonconformists in the profession. They ignore some practices that were sacred to the older language arts teachers—such practices as adhering to established grade-placement of subject matter and demanding standard achievement for promotion. These teachers insist that good language arts teaching can proceed only when the individual pupil is fully understood, when an attempt is made to discover his individual requirements. Only then can appropriate subject matter and methods be selected.

Language arts teachers are not, however, the educational rebels they are sometimes pictured. Instead, they are realists. They are practicing psychologists. They are convinced by their studies of human growth and development that their methods of teaching are better, that they are essential to the proper promotion of human growth.

A broadened range of social experience also widens the range of the subject matter that can be used in teaching language arts. Language is a social instrument. The language arts teachers seek, therefore, to coordinate their classroom work with the social experiences of the school and with the experiences the pupils may have in other subjects like geography and social studies. When correlating the language arts with other subjects, the language arts teachers may be accused of overlapping the other fields. If they do, it is with a distinct instructional aim in mind. When pupils read, they cannot just read "reading." Growth in reading implies a broadening of the range of experiences as well as growth in reading skills.

The language arts teachers have been especially resourceful in choosing functional subject matter. In reading, for example, schools have placed great emphasis upon having suitable library materials readily accessible to teachers and pupils alike. The librarian, who is usually also a language arts teacher, serves mainly as a resource person to help teachers or pupils. Single textbooks for reading have almost disappeared from the better schools. The wide range of pupil needs, interests, and abilities demands a wide range of reading materials. Efforts are made to develop balanced reading programs. A wide range of sources is made available. The differences in cultural backgrounds, interests, and abilities of the pupils are taken fully into account. This change in methods has impregnated many language arts classrooms with new spirit, has ventilated them with a breath of fresh air.

All teachers in the school are, in a sense, language arts teachers. Pupils are taught to read in mathematics and science classes. There they learn the use of specialized words. Language arts teachers attempt to coordinate the language arts of all the classes. When school work has been compartmentalized into rigid divisions of subject matter, the work of the language arts teachers to coordinate language arts skills with other school subjects tends to be more difficult. Critical reading, vocabulary building, spelling, sentence structure, and collateral reading become submerged in many of the

An informal discussion is one method of stimulating student interest. (Encyclopaedia Britannica)

classes in specialized subject matter because of the dominance of other aims. The trend at all levels, however, is to stress growth in the communicative arts through the conscious efforts of the teachers of all the subjects.

Planning a sequence in the language arts area remains an unsettled problem. There is agreement, however, that methods should place greater emphasis upon written and spoken communication, less upon isolated drill. Speaking opportunities should far outnumber writing opportunities. Overt attention should be given to developing the skills of listening. Both practical and imaginative writing should be taught. What a pupil reads should be in answer to his interests, needs, and abilities. The teaching of reading should emphasize reading with purpose. Ordinarily the purpose of reading for information and enjoyment should outweigh, but not obviate, reading to improve the mechanics of reading. Pupils should share their reading experiences with others as often as possible. To set forth in advance specifically what is to be covered in the language arts instruction or to define the methods of directing the instruction is not possible. Much is left to the intelligence of the well-trained language arts teacher.

Science

A precipitately heightened interest in science education among the American people has been reflected in the school program. Our discussion deals with the methods of teaching science only in the area of general education, where all pupils, regardless of interest or ability, are studying the same subject matter.

Much thought and effort have been devoted to the formulation of a developmental program of teaching science. The old problem of sequence is still unsolved, but instruction in science now begins in the first year of school and continues as general science up to the seventh grade. In the seventh, eighth, and ninth grades, science is usually still general science, but the instruction is given by a specialized teacher. The subject matter after that becomes more specialized. There are classes in physics, chemistry, and biology.

Teaching general science has two principal purposes: (1) to lead the student to an accurate understanding and appreciation of the physical world and (2) to cultivate the student's ability to use the scientific method.

One of the age-old stumbling blocks to teaching in this area is the complex form in which the sciences have been organized by the specialists. The connections of the highly systematized subject matter with the experiences of everyday life have often been hidden from both the pupils and the teacher. Teachers in the earlier grades now teach science without the use of textbooks. Much attention is given at first to obtaining concrete experience and to connecting the subject matters studied with those experiences. Even in the first grade, the pupil begins to recognize the nature of a lever or the relationship between sunlight and life. The teacher begins with what the pupil has learned from his previous experience and develops from that experience the proper modes of scientific treatment. Time is sacrificed to understanding and to fostering a vital interest. The cue to method is that nothing is learned by the pupils unless they understand it fully.

The teacher in general education never assumes that he is obligated to produce a scientific specialist. He leaves that to the later years when selection operates. He does assume that everyone should learn something about the method scientists have used to perfect their knowledge as well as something about the results they have achieved. A pupil's understanding grows as he learns *how* to look and for *what* to look.

Facilities for teaching science, generously furnished by most schools, are as highly varied as the methods that they are expected to serve. Laboratories, library materials, visual aids, books suited to the age of the pupils—all contribute to and influence the teacher's methods. The selection of science teaching methods is ideally left to the discretion of an able teacher who has considerable knowledge of pupils' needs.

Mathematics

Methods in the teaching of mathematics in America's schools might have been included in the preceding discussion, except that American schools treat mathematics as a specialized subject apart from science. This specialization begins in the very early grades and continues through all the remaining grades. The subject matter of mathematics is usually organized in relatively narrow areas like algebra and plane geometry, although some leading mathematicians now advocate organization in more comprehensive fields.

Perhaps in no field of teaching have the results been more subject to critical scrutiny. If current criticisms are heeded, a great deal of change will likely be made in teaching mathematics in the years that lie ahead. One of the common criticisms is that most pupils at the elementary and high school levels do not learn mathematics well unless parents aid them. Another common criticism is that, as mathematics is taught in our schools now, the subject matter is largely forgotten by the pupil when he leaves school and enters his life work. A third criticism is that in studying mathematics many pupils develop a fear of mathematics or an antagonistic attitude

Kindergartens still follow the principle enunciated by Froebel—for the very young, self-activity is the surest road to sound education. (Children's Bureau, DHEW)

toward doing any kind of quantitative thinking. Perhaps this can be traced to the teacher's convincing the pupils that mathematics is a very difficult subject.

Teachers are the first to admit that the methods of teaching mathematics for the purposes of general education have not been as efficient as desired. Efforts to improve these methods are being made. Traditions, however, have a strong hold and changes are not easy. If, as some contend, the teachers of mathematics have placed too much emphasis upon manipulation, such as applying formulas, and upon getting the right answers, rather than upon processes of thinking out answers, then a key to progress seems to be a change in the emphasis of teaching. Setting up equations in the ninth grade will become just as important as solving an equation that has been set up. Teachers complain that in systems where city-wide standard-ized tests are administered, the tests are scored right or wrong, sometimes with a machine, according to the correctness of the an-swer, regardless of whether pupils can think through the processes or not. This places a pressure on teachers to emphasize rapidity and manipulation rather than thought processes. The emphasis is shifting to methods that train pupils to think quantitatively as well as to manipulate accurately and rapidly. The accuracy and speed is considered a follow-up to thinking rather than a precedent.

The subdivisions of mathematics—algebra, geometry, and the like—have been taught in the general education programs as isolated, distinct, specialized subject matter, related neither to one another nor to the experience of the pupils. Current stress is, therefore, on the development of a unified mathematics field which emphasizes relationships and attempts to make all that is taught meaningful. It has become more important to have the children comprehend basic structures than to have them advance through established, gradated steps, often going on to a new step without mastery of what went before. The emphasis is now being placed on developing an understanding of mathematical concepts, rather than on studying specialized arithmetic, algebra, or geometry. The trend is to strive to have the pupil fully understand those fundamental mathematical concepts that are part of his own living and those that are common to mathematics generally. There is also an

Elements of realism, social cooperation, and self-activity are present in this excursion of two junior high school pupils in applied science and mathematics. (Kranzten Studio, Inc.)

increased concern with the child's growth pattern, with his background and his readiness. Teaching conceptual thinking without regard to whether the concept should be labeled algebra or calculus is a path to progress in teaching mathematics. All children, with adequate instruction, can learn mathematics and many will enjoy it. Meaning, relationships, and processes will serve as a truer guide than emphasis on the so-called fundamentals so necessary to the manipulative tradition.

Social Studies

The social *sciences* are the orderly, systematically arranged bodies of knowledge that deal with various aspects of social living. The social *studies* of the elementary and high school consist of portions of the subject matter of the specialized fields that have been selected and organized for instructional purposes in general education.

Although the content of the social studies is similar to that of the social sciences, the methods of teaching are different because the purpose is different. The subject matter in social studies is simpler, less compartmentalized, and less logically organized. The methods of teaching social studies strive to utilize broader generalized interests of the pupils rather than the specialized interests that may later develop.

One area of life in which the teachers of the social studies seek to promote growth is that of social relationships and understandings. Obviously, this area cannot be wholly separated from the language arts. Nor can the social studies assume the whole of the responsibility for achieving growth in social development. They can merely give more emphasis to the problem. The methods of the social studies teacher will be selected to help pupils develop greater maturity in the socialized aspects of their behavior.

The affective factors involved in social development present one of the most difficult problems of method. Teachers and pupils alike have social attitudes, feelings, prejudices, and biases which they bring to school with them. Recognizing deep-seated predispositions among pupils, social studies teachers promote social interaction in the classroom that leads pupils to consider the bases of their opinions, beliefs, and prejudices and to understand and respect differences. The teachers attempt to bring about the kinds of social change in which camping leaders have been so successful. Children who attend summer camp for a period of weeks seem to mature rapidly in ability to get along with others and to manage their own affairs. The methods used in camping give teachers a clue to the kinds of experiences that lead to growth in social skills. Firsthand experiences are needed to supplement the formal subject matter of the school. Emphases on formal reports, library reading, abstract discussions, and the like have not added greatly to growth in socialization.

Social studies teachers have developed considerable skill in dealing with controversial problems. The technique is one of getting the pupils to understand both sides of a question and to render their own decision. This teaches pupils to deal intelligently with controversial aspects of life. The teacher is free to express his bias, but purely as a matter of opinion.

Social studies teachers at all levels of education have many opportunities to use lifelike situations. They make contact with issues in home life, study firsthand the operations of the police, fire, judicial, and other departments of local government, study the safety department programs and school board and municipal elections, participate in school government and other school activities, and hold mock political conventions. Study of such situations is combined with the study of the more formal kinds of subject matter. The two kinds of activities are complementary. Study of the causes of poverty, for example, may lead to a trip to several sections of the city where poverty is most prevalent, to the clubs, community organizations, settlement houses, and the like that work with the poor. Pupils are carefully prepared for the trip in advance through the study of pertinent books and pamphlets and by discussions. After the trip a scheduled follow-up lesson is devoted to reviewing what was learned on the trip, to making conclusions and generalizations, and perhaps to applying the generalizations to other situations or problems.

As mentioned earlier, the problem of developing a logical sequence in the subject matter of the social studies is similar to the problem encountered by the language arts teachers, and the same generalizations apply. There is a trend in the school to integrate the subject matter of social studies and language arts for the purposes of general education. The core program of the junior and senior high schools, which was described in Chapter 15, is an attempt to do this. The student of education will encounter a considerable amount of

Play acting, a method liked by all children, is a favored technique for encouraging self-expression. (Illinois State University)

discussion of this trend in his future courses. The integrated approach evidenced by the increase in titles of integrated studies and core programs seems likely to continue. The movement now reaches from the first years of the elementary school through college.

Fine Arts

The purpose of the fine arts is to develop the pupil's sensitivity to and appreciation of what creative artists seek to express. The teacher of fine arts seeks to provide an environment appropriate to this end and to cultivate the powers of expression.

We have noted that the logically organized subject matter of mathematics is used in directing pupils to develop their powers to think and express their thoughts quantitatively. In marked contrast, when directing growth in the area of the fine arts, loosely organized, and sometimes unorganized, subject matter is used.

The trend among teachers of the fine arts at all levels of education is to stress direct participation as a means to enlarging the scope of the aesthetic experiences of the pupils. Painting, singing, acting, and playing instruments can add a great deal to the pupils' understanding and appreciation of what the arts are about. Listening and observing, too, have their place, but overly emphasized they can dull the pupils' interest in the fine arts. They can have a superficial, or even a negative, effect.

While the emphasis in the fine arts is upon creativeness and participation, the element of the technical is not omitted. As the children work to improve their acting in the play, or to sing in unison, or to perfect the rendition of instrumental music, they, of course, consider with the teacher the technical problems involved. As they study the technical aspect of the art, however, it is not just to learn more about the art. Always the purpose of technical study is to develop a higher level of expression.

Aesthetic responsiveness and expression are closely bound up with emotions. The teacher, therefore, takes into full account the personal nature of responsiveness and expression and their emotional foundation. Respect for personality should be high on the scale of values of the teacher of fine arts, and his methods and the complete learning environment, at all times, should reflect this. Children will not sing or paint or act if they are ashamed or embarrassed or

A group activity can be both instructive and fun. (Kranzten Studio, Inc.)

fearful. Teachers of the fine arts, themselves conscious of the values that lie in the arts, tend to demonstrate what teaching is like when teaching is viewed as an art. They follow their own, perhaps untraditional, methods in creating conditions most productive of the kind of pupil growth they seek to achieve.

When teachers of other subjects imply that fine arts is a somewhat inferior or unnecessary field of study, it is usually because they do not understand the purposes of the teachers of fine arts. Persistent traditions associated with other fields of teaching tend to set fine arts apart. For example, if a teacher of fine arts attempted to give pupils numerical or letter grades in music or art appreciation, not only would he find it impossible to evaluate a child's appreciation of music or of art, but he would damage the climate for advancing such appreciation by introducing competitiveness, desire to please the teacher, anxiety, and other undesirable attitudes. The moment a teacher of fine arts attempts to emulate the evaluation techniques of, say, the mathematics teacher, his effectiveness in achieving growth in fine arts starts to wane. Creativeness, free expression, and appreciation of the beautiful flourish only in a sympathetic atmosphere.

QUESTIONS

1. What are some of the dangers in separating method from subject matter for purposes of analysis?
2. What purpose is served by an acquaintance with several methods of teaching in a given field?
3. Why is a teacher more likely to be effective with his teaching methods if he knows the subject matter well?
4. What is remedial instruction? When should it be used?

PROJECT

Analyze a recent publication of a subject matter professional organization such as the National Council of Teachers of Mathematics or National Council of Teachers of English. List the suggestions made upon methods of teaching. State your conclusions as to what experienced teachers deem to be of greatest significance.

CHAPTER 20

Instructional aids

C lassroom teachers in America's schools typically strengthen teaching by using various instructional aids. That the use of aids is growing in popularity is attested by the great number of aids constantly added to an already long list of tried, tested, conventional ones.

Popular interest in instructional aids stems from a conviction that teaching methods need considerable improvement and that wide use of such aids may help achieve this. Certain instructional aids may help to bring teaching more closely in line with factors that psychologists say encourage effective learning, may help instruction to capitalize on factors of attention and reinforcements to learning, and also may help to make possible a fuller recognition of wide divergencies in learning rates. Instructional aids, teachers and pupils alike agree, tend to make both teaching and learning more interesting. Every year shows an increase in their popularity, in confidence in their effectiveness.

The kinds of teaching aids available are very numerous. One college textbook devotes 500 printed pages to describing audio-visual aids. Several manufacturing companies list hundreds of such usable items as long-playing records, filmstrips, tape recordings, and models. One company alone lists, for example, 52 long-playing records that reproduce Shakespearean plays as recorded by the most famous Shakespearean actors. Another company specializes in making records for the elementary schools that reconstruct history through dramatizations, dramatizing such themes as Riding the Pony Express, the California Gold Rush, and the first continental railroad. Each year more than 6,500 sound-motion pictures are produced and adapted by several manufacturing companies for use in every grade and in almost every subject matter field. Perhaps this stress on variety and quantity in instructional aids stems from a heightened recognition of the part played in effective learning by the senses, from an increasing knowledge of how perceptions are formed and of how perception and thought are related. The accepted assumption—that mental images result from sensations—reinforces the belief that variety in the stimulation of the senses in the classroom greatly enriches learning, and hence contributes to more reliable and mature thinking.

When the teacher makes his selection and decides on the use of instructional aids, he is guided by the same consideration of definite and worthy purpose which guides in all other decisions related to the stimulation and direction of learning. Some aids are designed to serve but a single purpose; a slide rule is for computation; a lifelike model of the human heart to explain the design and physiological functioning of the heart. A chalkboard, on the other hand, is an instructional aid adaptable to many purposes. The discussion of instructional aids in this chapter is to acquaint the student with some that teachers use, to give an overview. For obvious reasons the purposes that guide teachers in the selection and use of aids are omitted.

CLASSIFICATION

Instructional aids discussed are classified as follows: library and library materials, textbooks, audiovisual materials, programmed learning, and aids that require certain organizational modifications within the school. This arbitrary classification is followed purely as a matter of convenience.

LIBRARY AND LIBRARY MATERIALS

The typical elementary and secondary school has a central library within its own building, often one of the most inviting places in the building. In larger schools the school library is administered by a trained teacher-librarian; in smaller schools a classroom teacher doubles as school librarian. The resources housed in the library for both pupils and teachers vary with the policies of administration. In some the resource materials are limited to books and graphic materials, while in others they include teaching aids such as films and records.

In general, school libraries are administered by trained individuals who fulfill a coordinating function, serve teachers and pupils in many ways. Supplementary materials flow from library to classroom and back again. Pupils use the library for round-table discussions, group study, individual reading, research, and study, and as a place to learn to locate and use such resource materials as indexes, reference books, bibliographies, catalogues, encyclopedias. Pupils have the opportunity to browse among many books. They are guided and encouraged to choose books in harmony with their individual interests and abilities.

Administrators, teachers, and librarians cooperate to make the library a rich center for many kinds of resources and educational activities. Wisely coordinated, the library and the teacher-librarian are indispensable adjuncts, one might say handmaidens, to effective classroom teaching, vital in wisely planned programs of every classroom.

TEXTBOOKS

The well-prepared teacher uses textbooks and workbooks as valuable aids to his teaching. He does not make the mistake of thinking that within the pages of the textbook he will find subject matter complete. He will not use the textbook and workbook as substitutes for his own knowledge or resourcefulness. He will, instead, use the textbook as a supplement, a guide, and a source of suggestions. In addition, the teacher usually does not restrict himself to one textbook but selects one book as a basic text and several others for the

It has been said that with the exception of the Bible no books had more influence over the lives of early Americans than McGuffey's readers and spellers. These series of books, begun in 1836, were revised many times and the last copyright was issued in 1901. It is said that the sales of the books totaled over one hundred million copies.

The Reverend William Holmes McGuffey (1800–1873), who edited the books, was a Presbyterian minister and a professor at Miami University, Oxford, Ohio. McGuffey grew up with the frontier. He was born near the western edge of Pennsylvania and moved with his family to Ohio.

McGuffey believed the child should be taught to read from the start and should not begin with spelling as had been customary. He used many illustrations and adapted the material to the level of the pupils. As the replica of a page from his spelling book illustrates, he emphasized correct pronunciation and the precise use of words in everyday speech.

His stories combined experiences of the frontiersmen with traditional types of stories for children in a way that appealed to the entire frontier population. From the standpoint of education, the new West was a simple country. There were few books, but there was zeal for a kind of education that combined learning to read with learning the dominant cherished virtues—thrift, hard work, morality, temperance, and religion. Many of the stories McGuffey included in his books were so told as to unmistakably emphasize a moral or extol a virtue.

"If you find your task is hard,
Try, try again;
Time will bring you your reward
Try, try again."

Since McGuffey's books were the principal reading material for the average American of the time, the extent of McGuffey's influence upon reading tastes, points of view, common standards of conduct, morals, propriety, and attitudes can well be imagined. His influence persisted for a long time and extended to many facets of everyday life.

classroom reference shelf. The pupils use the basic textbook for study and the others as supplementary reading materials.

How are textbooks selected? In approximately half of the states the local school district has jurisdiction over textbook selection. Usually a committee made up of teachers, supervisors, and administrators selects one or more books in a field or level. Unfortunately, under this plan there is no uniformity of textbooks so children who move from one district to another may be handicapped because they have become used to different books. In the remaining half of the

Lesson 62.

DICTATION EXERCISES.

Dost consider that dust thou art? He paid the servant his hire, and the wages were higher than last year. With whoop and hurra they tore the hoop from the barrel. The mower will cut more grass to-morrow. The foreign consul took counsel with the enemy, and called a council of war. English consols are high. Kings are sometimes guilty of flagrant wrongs. Many a fragrant flower blooms unseen. He tore his clothes in a struggle to close the door. His course toward that coarse lad was wrong.

Lesson 63.

Words accented on the first Syllable.

cŏn′taet	nŏs′tril	cŭr′ry	pŭn′ġent
fŏr′est	prŏd′uet	fŭl′erum	rŭs′tie
hŏb′by	prŏb′lem	hŭd′dlė	rŭb′bish
lŏft′y	rŏs′ter	pŭb′lie	sŭlk′y
lŏġ′ie	tŏr′rent	pŭb′lish	sŭl′try
ăf′flux	băṇk′rupt	kĭn′dred	serĭb′blė
ăm′bush	eăm′phor	pĭck′et	trĭp′let
ăn′them	hăv′oe	tĭck′et	trĭck′lė
ăn′nalṣ	hăġ′ġard	wĭck′et	lĭz′ard
ăs′peet	hăṭch′et	ĭn′voiçė	vĭl′là

states, statutes require uniform textbooks throughout the state. In some of these states, the state department or an authorized committee selects several books or series of books for each subject, leaving the final choice from among these to the local district.

To aid in selecting textbooks, committees frequently use a check list containing such items as authorship, date of publication, content, vocabulary, organization, suggested pupil activities, recommended teaching aids, illustrative material, format, and durability. No matter how high a particular book may rate on all the check list items, however, the most important deciding factor will be how well it will contribute to the needs of the pupils who will use it.

The textbooks today are far superior to those used even fifty years ago. In early America the hornbook, a paddle-shaped contrivance which hung from the pupil's neck, usually contained the Lord's Prayer and the alphabet. *The New England Primer* is an example of the small, morally slanted, compact textbook also used in colonial days. McGuffey's *Eclectic Readers* emphasized the Bible and morals by means of interesting stories. The author of today's textbooks determines content through experiment based on knowledge of child psychology. He attempts, as nearly as the pages of his book will permit, to enter the classroom and assist in the instruction. As with other teaching activities, the author sets up his goals and then draws upon his knowledge and experience as a teacher to meet the goals. The better present-day textbook is proficiently written, attractive, usable, and long-wearing. The improvement in appearance, format, durability, and illustrations has come about through research and advancement in publishing generally. The modern textbook is an invitation to learning.

AUDIOVISUAL MATERIALS

The human organism constructs images that are a consequence of seeing and hearing. Since the nature of one's perceptions is closely related to one's ability to think, learning from a wise use of audiovisual materials in the classroom may be of paramount importance to effective teaching. From the images constructed by the pupils upon being exposed to wisely selected audiovisual material, understandings of the true nature of external objects and of spatial, social, and temporal relationships are expanded. Furthermore, the learning so derived tends to be vivid and lasting. Perceptions resulting from effective audiovisual experiences are integrated by the human organism through some process the nature of which as yet is unknown. It is upon some such reasoning as this that the wide use of audiovisual materials in American education has been justified.

In recent years, and particularly in the elementary schools, serious attention has been given to encourage good habits of listening. Besides being an effective learning experience in general, good listening is precedent to effective speech. Skill in communication is considered closely related to habits of listening. Many audiovisual aids are so designed as to utilize to the fullest the advantages of good listening.[1] The Shakespearean records and the recorded dramatized historical incidents previously mentioned, for instance, are excellent examples of a kind of device that promotes understandings and appreciations while also encouraging the habits of good listening.

The following cursory overview of some kinds of audiovisual aids that are frequently used by classroom teachers gives an idea of the great variety and educational potential of these aids. Teachers, guided by the purposes they have in mind, of course, use discrimination in selection of particular devices.

Maps and Globes

Maps and globes are a part of the everyday equipment of the classrooms in America's elementary schools and in many classrooms in high schools. The maps and globes are made in attractive, contrasting colors to show areas of the earth or, as in case of globes, the whole earth itself. They are constructed so as to be readily accessible for classroom use, are attractive and easy to read. They are accurately drawn to scale and can conveniently be used for such activities as locating places, measuring distances, computing areas, tracing great circle air routes, ocean currents, and wind systems, showing the number and position of heavenly bodies, or the division of the country in the War between the States.

Manufacturers of school maps and globes recognize the principle of readiness through gradation of their product in detail and complexity. They make materials for younger children that show fewer details and acquaint the child with only basic map symbols. For older pupils all standard map symbols are used for details like elevation, rivers, falls, cities, railways.

The art of map making for educational purposes has been highly developed by a number of manufacturers who combine their know-how in the manufacture of maps with the knowledge and skill of professional cartographers and educational specialists. Through cooperative efforts a great variety of maps is available to serve in such special subject matter areas as history, economics, and literature, as well as almost any particular branch of geography from world climate to geological evolution.

1 See the section on listening on p. 494.

Models

Models, among the oldest of instructional aids, are still considered by teachers to be among the most helpful. Models appeal to all ages; children from infancy have played with them in the form of toys; adults flock to view and manipulate them in museums of science and industry where they are used on an elaborate scale to elucidate a wide range of subjects.

Models are designed for use in elementary and secondary schools to aid in teaching in almost every subject matter field and to serve a wide variety of purposes. True models are manufactured on an accurate scale and usually are three-dimensional representations of some principle, fact, or idea. An exact replica, for example, of an automobile or of any of its working parts is available to the high-school teacher of auto mechanics to make clear his explanations or the explanations given in the text. A model may illustrate how the human heart functions or how the blood circulates in the body. With a skillfully designed model a pupil virtually "sees" the explanations.

Manufacturers often modify true models—called mock-ups—in order to make clearer certain kinds of explanations. In the mock-up they resort to certain exaggerations, such as in size, color, or transparency. Thus, in the Chicago Museum of Science and Industry a viewer can stand inside a modified model of the human heart and study at leisure each working part. Another kind of modified model, the best examples of which are found in museums, is the diorama. It consists of a combination of figures, background pictures, actual specimens, and symbolic materials, which with the ingenious use of direct and indirect lighting make the scene appear almost real.

In larger cities classroom teachers may supplement their own use of models with field trips to museums where skilled lecturers instruct the pupils on a great variety of subjects.

Models available in the schools usually are readily accessible, easily assembled and disassembled, and therefore conveniently adaptable to any logical teaching plan.

Flat Pictures

Flat pictures have been the means for centuries for effectively conveying a message, expressing an idea, portraying an event, reproducing the historical likenesses of persons and scenes. Pictographs in ancient caves and the large circulation of modern pictorial magazines attest to the everlasting appeal of flat pictures. Quite naturally, classroom teachers utilize all the advantages of their universal appeal.

Usually teachers in subject matter areas like geography, social studies, history, literature, and science have a continuous but changing display of appropriate pictures in the classroom. Many such pictures are attractive, accurate as to detail, and instructionally sound. The pupils know what Ann Hathaway's cottage or the birthplace of Robert Burns looks like, and the same holds true of many historical figures and places and scenes in the world. The clever use of color in modern photography has added to the vividness of the pictures.

In addition to real pictures, there exists a vast array of pictures that are wholly imaginative. An ancient battle, the sorrows of a displaced people, illustrations of literary themes are often depicted by artists' imaginative drawings.

Among the advantages of using flat pictures as instructional aids is their easy availability and the almost inexhaustible supply. They can be secured from many sources with little or no cost.

Projections

Many classrooms in America are equipped with projectors. Since these projectors will flash an enlarged image of many kinds of materials, printed or in the form of slides or a series of slides called filmstrips, the kinds of images that can be projected are almost limitless. The so-called "overhead projector" can be utilized by the teacher from the front of the room while facing the class.

Slides and filmstrips may be purchased from many companies. Some teachers do their own photography and have the film companies prepare slides for them. The advantages of still slides are many. A whole biology class, for instance, can see in a greatly enlarged picture what each would see under an individual microscope. A mathematics teacher can encourage rapid mental computation by rapidly flashing number combinations, fundamental factoring processes and the like on a screen. An explanation of a mathematical process can be flashed on a screen to be seen by all the pupils. The teacher can call attention to the parts that are especially significant or are likely to give particular difficulty. A teacher of geography, for instance, may use a three-dimensional, colored slide showing a stereographic, lifelike view of an entire mountain scene and focus the attention of the pupils on such features as the terracing of farms on the mountain sides.

Chalkboards

If a classroom had a "symbol" it would probably be the chalkboard. Chalkboards are indispensable aids and standard teaching aid equipment in classrooms everywhere. Chalkboards are frequently spoken of as blackboards because they were formerly made of slate. Through manufacturing processes that utilize plastics, the modern chalkboard has been greatly improved over slate. Using steel coated with a vitreous material or with plywood, it is possible to have a chalkboard of a soft color that fits in with the decor of a room.

Teachers give considerable attention to developing skill in using the chalkboard. They learn such skills as lettering, stenciling, drawing to scale, and free-hand drawing like cartooning and caricaturing, using tools such as variegated colors in chalk, stencils, magnets, rulers, and compasses.

Having pupils use the chalkboard often helps to reveal difficulties and build understandings.

Radio

The radio is a part of the everyday environment of every American child. At home, at the beach, or in the family car, the radio is likely to be his constant companion. In the 1930s American educators began to focus attention on the possibilities of using the radio in the classrooms to develop better habits of listening. Many school systems now have access to FM and AM broadcasting systems over which programs suitable for classroom listening are broadcast. A part of the teaching, perhaps a more specialized part, may be accomplished through radio. By radio, schools have an almost unlimited choice of controlled programs ranging from the finest of plays and music to the voices of many prominent historical leaders speaking at the time of most crucial historical events.

No conclusive appraisal of the benefits of radio education in the school has been made. Such questions as "What are its effects upon learning?" "Does use of the radio in the classroom improve the listening habits of pupils?" "What conclusions have been reached as to the best uses of radio in the schools?" and similar questions remain unanswered.

Tape Recorder

While surveys show that the tape recorder has not become a widely used instructional aid in American schools, it is well suited for some teaching purposes. It can contribute, for example, to improving the writing, speaking, and listening habits of pupils. It is an excellent device for helping pupils to improve their selection, pronunciation, and enunciation of words, to develop their writing skills by preparing scripts, to pronounce and understand a foreign language, to increase speed in shorthand, mathematical computation, reproduction of science formulas and the like.

Perhaps the great advantage of tape recorders lies in their versatility. Almost every kind of perception that is or can be conveyed by the sound medium can be imprinted for convenient reproduction on tape. Some state universities maintain comprehensive

A note of realism is introduced into learning by aids utilizing sight and sound such as are being used by these boys. (Kranzten Studio, Inc.)

lending tape-recorded libraries to encourage the use of tape recorders in the classroom. They issue catalogues of available recordings that include valuable hints on how teachers can profitably use the recordings. The National Education Association, especially, has an extensive tape-recording library located in the Audio-Visual Division of the University of Colorado. The great encouragement received by classroom teachers from agencies such as the NEA and the state universities attests to the confidence those agencies have in the as yet largely unexploited educational values of tape recorders.

LP Hi-Fi Records

School systems, public libraries, extension divisions of universities, and other public agencies maintain extensive collections of long-playing high-fidelity records to be lent to teachers and schools. These supplement tape-recorded programs and are also used independently in connection with literature or music. The advantages of this device are its ready availability and general high quality of artistry. The themes that are faithfully reproduced by great artists are almost limitless.

The Language Laboratory

The language laboratory now found in many high schools is an instructional aid to foreign language teachers who stress building conversational skills. The equipment in the language laboratory enables pupils to listen to the spoken word and to repeat it in return and then listen again to their own pronunciation, thus comparing their own language with that of the expert.

It is general procedure to have the lessons taped and for all the pupils to listen to the same materials through individually provided earphones. The teacher also can join in with explanations. Each pupil may imitate what he has heard and have his own voice recorded. He may then play his version back, judge his response, then repeat the procedure until he is satisfied. As the reader perhaps knows, tapes can easily be erased and used over many times. The language laboratory permits each pupil to proceed on his own and to practice building conversational skills in accordance with his own needs.

Tachistoscope

The tachistoscope is a device for projecting words, phrases, sentences, number combinations, formulas and the like for short durations, for durations as low as one-hundredth of a second. The image is reproduced on either a small viewing screen or flashed as a lantern slide on a larger screen. The viewer is warned when the shutter is about to be tripped, he looks at the screen, and then reproduces what he has seen. As a rule, the device is used for remedial work, to speed up the reading of slow readers or to increase the rate and accuracy of computational skills.

Sound-Motion Pictures

As physiologists have pointed out, though the human organism operates in terms of specialized functions like hearing, seeing, feeling, and the like, the organism is constituted to tie together, to integrate, what it receives through each of these senses. Any teaching technique or device, therefore, that appeals simultaneously to more than one of the senses, to say hearing and seeing, has an increased potential as an instructional aid. The sound-motion picture is a device that takes advantage of native tendencies that tend to attract and sustain attention.

The sound-motion picture is perhaps the nearest man has come to realistically reproducing an actual scene or human event. A series of still pictures moving at the rate of 24 pictures per second gives the illusion of continuous motion. Sound synchronized with the moving picture is registered on the same film. Microphotography and films that reproduce actual colors make the 16mm sound film commonly used in schools applicable to many teaching purposes. Frequently large commercial organizations like Bell Telephone, Ford Motor, or American Oil will produce excellent educational films and supply them without charge to the schools as a part of their public relations program.

At present most schools have available sound-motion equipment. In larger schools usually a teacher or a teacher-librarian or one who specializes in the use of sound-motion pictures serves as coordinator. Coordination is necessary partly because films and projectors are so expensive that their maintenance and use must be systematically provided for and partly because it is wise to have someone in the school who knows what films are available and takes the responsibility for previewing, obtaining, and returning them.

Television

Among the communication media undreamed of at the beginning of the century is the one most subject to current exploration and discussion with reference to classroom teaching possibilities, television.

While classroom use of TV indicates that television can be used to improve the effectiveness of classroom teaching in all subject matter fields, so far the most valuable results have been achieved in the areas of literature and science. Extensive experimentation is now being carried out to discover the most advantageous ways of using the new medium.

Teachers utilize television in a number of ways, but the most common procedure is to tell pupils about programs they wish them to see. Sometimes a bulletin board is utilized to call the attention of pupils each week to the programs of educational value. Since programs are announced a week in advance any teacher has at hand a listing of a great many programs, some of which are likely to include the kind of material he desires the pupils to see. When commercial programs are of special interest to schools, the sponsors make available carefully prepared printed materials that can be placed on the bulletin board. Often, subsequent to a TV projection of an educational program, the material will be available on film for teacher use on a movie projector in the school.

Some schools have television sets used for regular class viewing of suitable programs, including those produced by commercial and those by educational stations. Some high schools have equipment, called closed-circuit, that enables them to produce live programs for school viewing.

In some areas of the country selected schools are equipped with special receivers to receive programs that are prepared and transmitted especially to fulfill a specific instructional purpose at a particular grade level.

Experimentation with television as a medium of classroom instruction is being carried on extensively throughout the country. At present the trend is for the schools to obtain from both commercial and educational television stations special tapes or recordings that can be transmitted on the school's own closed-circuit equipment in

This teacher combines the second and third grades in teaching pupils to read and write, by using the overhead projector. Better schools throughout America are experimenting with teaching aids at all levels of education. (William R. Simmons, Ford Foundation)

any desired way or at any time. As another example of current experimentation, one school system is experimenting with teaching a foreign language to younger children by closed-circuit television. In this case a teacher teaches pupils in a television studio and the lesson is carried by telephone cable to selected classrooms where pupils see and hear the lesson on television sets.

The effectiveness of instruction by television, both from an educational and a relative cost standpoint, has not been assessed. It is a live innovation that promises to receive increasing emphasis.

PROGRAMMED LEARNING

Programmed learning is learning achieved by using subject matter materials that permit an individual pupil to study efficiently

Coordinated classroom television instruction by closed circuit enables the television teacher to teach very large classes in a selected area. A successful television teacher must be able to meet tasks that demand unusual teaching skill and preparation. The design of classrooms in the future may have to be changed to accommodate new teaching devices. (Illinois State University)

without the continuous help of a teacher and independent of membership in a study group. To enable a pupil to learn independently, the subject matter to be learned is broken up into a series of small, psychologically related segments that are logically arranged in steps. With the aid of a teaching device, such as described subsequently, a pupil proceeds independently, at his own rate, through each of the steps.

Justification for Programmed Learning

Since in programmed learning the pupil learns at a rate commensurate with his ability, individual differences in learning rates are fully recognized, even though, theoretically, all pupils will eventually achieve the same standard of mastery. Programmed learning is more satisfying to the pupil than learning through traditional processes because the results are immediately known by him. Since the programmed learning activity is an individual one, a pupil who learns slowly does not feel the sting of competitive comparisons that make him feel inferior. Finally, programmed learning utilizes the advantages of motivation. As one psychologist says:

> Human behavior is remarkably influenced by small results. Describing something with the right word is often reinforcing. Other simple reinforcers are to be found in the clarification of a puzzlement or simply in moving forward after completing one stage of activity.[2]

The proponents of programmed learning in America's schools —a rapidly growing number—believe that it is an important step to correcting past omissions. Why, say the educational psychologists, do schools put forth such prodigious efforts to gain understandings of pupils, to discover their more urgent needs, and then give so little attention to their individual needs? Why should teachers learn about the psychological bases of education and then teach as though such bases do not really exist? If these omissions have been due to

This junior high school pupil is studying modern mathematics by self-teaching through programmed learning. Note the various aids that supplement the materials in the programmed textbook. (Kranzten Studio, Inc.)

[2] B. F. Skinner, "Teaching Machines," *Scientific American*, Vol. CCV, No. 5 (November, 1961), p. 97.

the lack of a practical method, then, it is contended, programmed learning will contribute to eliminating that lack.

Problems

Two difficult problems in programmed learning are related to, first, selecting the kinds of material that can best be taught by this method, and second, arranging these materials into a series of steps that are reasonable and are psychologically related. Obviously, all kinds of subject matter cannot be taught by the programmed method. The selection must be carefully made. It is only by actual experiment with pupils that the soundness of the steps in a program can be evaluated. Many attempts are now being made in America's schools to select suitable subject matter and to program it. Although the method is relatively new, the results have been most promising.

Automated Instruction

Once the difficult tasks of programming are completed—the materials are selected and the logical steps for learning devised—the question remains: How shall the materials be presented to the pupil?[3] Two means of automated instruction have proven popular, the programmed textbook and the teaching machine.

1. Programmed Textbooks

The programmed textbook is an incomplete textbook that the pupil completes by filling in key sentences, words, or numbers in so-called frames. He checks his own answers by comparing them with the correct answers given elsewhere in the book, usually on the succeeding page where he also finds his next frame. Many attempts are being made currently in universities and in lower schools to produce improved automated textbooks. This calls for extensive tryouts of the materials and careful study of the results to refine the materials and improve the sequence.

The number of programmed textbooks published for use in the schools is rapidly increasing. The books cover a wide range of subjects. Each presents the basic skills and information to be learned,

---

[3] See, for example, the explanation of difficulties encountered by an astute book editor in "An Adventure in Programing Literature," *The English Journal,* Vol. LII, No. 9 (December, 1963), pp. 659–673.

allows each pupil to proceed at his own rate, evaluate his own progress, and correct his own weaknesses.

2. Teaching Machines

With teaching machines, instead of marking an answer in a frame in a book, a pupil responds to the programmed subject matter by making the response on a machine that indicates immediately whether he has chosen the correct answer. He cannot proceed to the next step until a correct response is registered to the current one. A right response is always a prerequisite to the next task. Like the programmed textbook, the value of teaching machines depends upon the skill in selecting the subject matter and in arranging it in a logical series of steps. Like experiments with programmed textbooks, experiments with teaching machines are being conducted in many schools, and there is considerable confidence that many kinds of learning can be achieved through their proper use. In fact, numerous manufacturing concerns have planned ambitious expansions and are building newer and better teaching machines.

Left, this teach–test–reward machine, first exhibited at the 1925 meeting of the American Psychological Association, was devised by the psychologist S. L. Pressey of Ohio State University. In the window appears a four-choice question, which the pupil answers by pressing the key corresponding to the answer he thinks correct. If it is, the next question turns up at the window. But if it is not, the initial question remains before the pupil, and he must try another answer (press another key) until he finds the correct one. Meanwhile, a counter in the back counts all tries. By simply lifting the lever, the machine was changed to a self-scoring device: a new question was turned up whatever key was pressed, and only rights were counted. Further, if the pupil did well, a "life-saver" candy came down the chute to reward him! (Ohio State University)

Right, a teaching machine, like a textbook, conveys information. When a machine such as the tachistoscope is used to teach pupils to read or to master the fundamentals of mathematics, no distinction is made between what is method and what is subject matter. They are inseparable aspects of the educative process. (Grolier, Inc.)

AIDS REQUIRING ORGANIZATIONAL MODIFICATIONS

Ability Grouping

The prevailing pattern of grouping children in America's schools is by age-grade. Ordinarily, children enter the kindergarten at age 5, then advance together from grade to grade, graduating from the high school at about 18 years of age. Ability grouping refers to classifying and grouping pupils of a given age grade for teaching purposes. This is usually done more or less in terms of ability to learn, in terms of relative intelligence.

For classification purposes within a grade level, intelligence scores are usually used for younger pupils. Achievement test scores such as described in Chapter 16, together with measures of intelligence, are generally the bases for classifying older pupils, those above elementary-school age.

No set pattern has been followed in the high schools in ability grouping. In some large high schools pupils who rank high on achievement tests are assigned to advanced placement. For them the subject matter studied is more advanced and the rate of progress is stepped up. College-level subject matter may be studied and college credit given for work in the last two years of high school. A second-level group may consist of the moderately gifted, who are assigned to courses, perhaps called "honor" courses, which are also advanced, both in subject matter studied and in rate of progress, but less so than the advanced placement classes. The third level, which may comprise as many as two-thirds of the pupils of a given grade in high school, is more conventional in curriculum and methods of teaching. The lowest group is the smallest, and for this group the studies are largely limited to basic skills and vocational subjects.

Ability grouping in the lower grades is usually three, four, or five groups within one classroom. These groups may work at different rates on reading, spelling, and arithmetic. The teacher works with one group while the others proceed with their individual activities. In the intermediate grades practices may vary from school to school and from subject to subject within the same school. For instance, classification and grouping may be used in mathematics and science but not in social studies or English.

Numerous attempts have been made to evaluate the results of grouping children on the basis of ability. For younger children the findings of the studies are inconclusive. Younger pupils seem to learn as well in heterogeneous groups as in ability groups. Seemingly, many variables must be considered in judging the worth of the practice, especially for younger pupils. In larger high schools teachers and administrators indicate that the practice encourages a higher degree of achievement, and in most larger high schools the practice is taken for granted.

Certain questions have been raised about the practice, questions that remain unanswered. What are the effects of the practice upon the social attitudes of the pupils? Of their parents? Will those who are always labeled inferior come to dislike those who are considered by school officials to be superior? Will those labeled superior become smug? What is the effect upon a slow learner of the constant fear of being failed or not promoted? How do parents feel about having their children labeled slow learners, or fast learners? These and other similar questions are not easy to answer.

It appears that, in general, the American people look with favor upon ability grouping in the schools when it is done to meet the educational needs of the more extreme deviates such as pupils with very high IQ's and those with very low IQ's. The attitude toward the practice for pupils between these extremes is not clear. Perhaps it is mixed.

At this writing ability grouping in American schools is a matter for wide experimentation. It continues to be used at all levels but most generally in the high schools. There is no indication of a lessening emphasis on this instructional aid. Teachers indicate that they find it makes teaching easier, more challenging, and that it enables them to depart from the practice of teaching all the pupils the same kind of subject matter and of judging them by the same standards. At the same time all recognize that the practice has unmistakable disadvantages, which, to the present, schools have been unable to obviate.

Team Teaching

Team teaching is a rather recent term used to designate the practice long used in universities of having a number of teachers, each with a different but related specialty, teach certain courses as a team. In the high schools as many as a hundred pupils may be taught by a team of perhaps half a dozen teachers whose training, interests, and talents supplement one another. Oftentimes the pupils are a select group. The length of the class period is typically flexible and usually the larger group is broken into smaller groups, perhaps with each smaller group meeting with one teacher of the team. Pupils may be grouped and regrouped in such a way that teachers may work with the whole group, with any part of it, or just with individuals.

In the elementary schools where there are several sections of the same grade, say fifth grade, all the fifth grade teachers work as a team, each taking responsibility for some particular aspect of the work and using any special talents, interests, or training. Even where the facilities do not permit combining the classes for actual team work, interchange among the teachers is often worked out.

Team teaching requires modification of the traditional school organization in physical facilities, use of audiovisual and other aids, subject matter materials, and teaching methods. Currently in those schools where organizational adaptations have been possible, teachers, parents, and pupils feel that team teaching promises considerable improvement over traditional practices. Although at present it is being experimented with in relatively few school systems, team teaching gives promise of further development. Beginning with the 1964–1965 school year, for example, approximately 7500 elementary school pupils in New York City schools were enrolled in team teaching programs in 41 participating schools. In the previous year only 7 schools and 900 pupils had participated in the experimental program. Where it has been used, the reactions to the procedure have been generally favorable.

Opportunity Room

Opportunity room is the name given to a special room in a school set aside and specially equipped for the instruction of pupils who possess marked handicaps that make it impossible for them to learn in classes enrolling normal pupils. These handicaps may be either physical or mental.

In some states, Illinois for example, a very successful state program affords leadership at the state level through a policy of financial aid and certification of specially trained teachers for the handicapped. Some school systems have specially designed buildings, provide suitable transportation, furnish teachers' helpers, and in other ways make the education of handicapped children a profitable and pleasant experience. At the same time, the removal of handicapped pupils from regular classrooms is an aid to teachers who, with many pupils to teach, would find caring for the handicapped a wearing responsibility.

Some schools have handicapped pupils spend part of their time in the regular classrooms and part time in the opportunity rooms. This is advocated on the grounds that handicapped pupils should have as great an opportunity as possible to be a normal part of school life, since they will someday have to take a place in the everyday life of the community. There is also educational value in having normal pupils learn proper regard for the handicapped.

CONCLUSION

Large sums of money are being spent on instructional aids to help teachers, make classroom teaching more rewarding, and encourage more effective and more significant learning. Instructional aids do not lighten the load of classroom teachers although they do help teachers to teach more effectively. Instructional aids emphasize the responsibilities of classroom teachers to adapt to methodological change. The traditional pattern of teaching was face-to-face verbal presentation and response. Today new media of communication require of the teacher additional specialization and extra preparation before teaching his pupils. All this requires extra time and energy. Instructional aids are not contrivances that lessen the work teachers do. Other ways must be found to accomplish this.

QUESTIONS

1. What are some of the factors that must be considered by a classroom teacher in making a selection of teaching aids?
2. In what ways do teaching aids add to the direct experiences of the pupils?
3. What are some of the teaching advantages of mock-ups?
4. What are the advantages of programmed learning? What are the possible dangers?
5. Which do you consider to be the better teaching device—programmed textbook or teaching machine? Explain why.
6. To what extent do you believe that teaching methods will be changed by the introduction of automated learning materials in the classroom?

PROJECTS

1. After paging through a textbook on audiovisual aids write some of your conclusions about their uses in the classroom.

2. List the skills you feel you must develop while training to be a teacher in order to use teaching aids effectively.

3. Examine a textbook on programmed learning such, say, as Sullivan's *Programmed English*. Write your evaluation of this book.

4. Write your analysis of Martin Mayer's criticisms of the use of newer teaching aids as set forth in his article in the *Saturday Evening Post*.

5. Write the principal conclusions to be drawn from your study of the analyses of the twenty specialists writing in the *Phi Delta Kappan* on programmed instruction.

6. Give reasons why the 16mm motion picture film has played and continues to play an important role in classroom learning.

7. Examine a teaching machine. Write what you conceive to be the advantages of teaching machines over other aids.

8. Some elementary schools are experimenting with ungraded rooms. Explain how this kind of grouping is achieved. Explain the advantages over ability grouping.

C H A P T E R   **21**

Fields of further study

The principal aim of this book has been to describe what the American people have done to provide adequate education for all American citizens and, particularly, for those who attend the schools. Trends in development have been noted and, in some instances, future trends have been indicated. Selection of aspects of education to be included was made in the light of two criteria: the material chosen should contribute to an *overview* and should serve as an *introduction* to American education, especially for the reader getting his first view of American education. For some readers this book may be a terminal point. For others—students who have decided to enter teaching or who, for various reasons, wish to explore professional education further—the following brief view of some more specialized fields in education may be helpful. We have in mind here the freshman or sophomore, i.e., the student who has a few years of undergraduate work to do before entering teaching.

As described in our discussion of how the teacher qualifies, college programs for teacher preparation are made up of three parts. One is the general education, the liberal education, the common cultural knowledge and understandings expected of all college graduates. Another is specialized education. This includes work specifically selected to contribute to a specialized field of teaching. If the subject for specialized study is one that is included in the general education of all students, the courses pursued are more advanced than those required of all students. The third is devoted to professional training. It is to this third part that we now turn our attention.

ORGANIZATION OF PROFESSIONAL STUDY

Professional education differs from other areas of study in three general ways. First, the subject matter is professional in nature. The aim is definitely vocational. It is assumed that the student has chosen teaching as his future vocation, as his chief means of earning a living. Second, the content of specialized methods courses in which the student learns to teach in his field of choice is not ordered on the principle of gradually advancing difficulty in the same degree as is content in fields like mathematics, physics, a language, or history. For example, a course dealing with the teaching of arithmetic may use some simple mathematical materials that were learned by the teacher-to-be long ago. The course in the teaching of physics in high school may use very little of the content materials studied in advanced physics. The whole field of physics, or any part of it, whether it is advanced or not, may be drawn upon for illustrative material for professional study. Attention is directed to the problems involved in teaching physics, which, of course, may be of advancing difficulty. Learning physics is a minor objective. The assumption is that the student already knows the material to be taught and that he will continue to learn more about it. The third difference lies in the backgrounds of the professors of education in the college or university. In addition to their college work which includes advanced training in professional education, they have had considerable practical schoolteaching experience on the elementary and secondary levels. Their principal function is to help the teacher in preparing to become a *successful* teacher.

AIMS OF PROFESSIONAL STUDY

The all-inclusive aim of the professional program is to develop competent and interested teachers. Professional study is not always fully understood. Some students have an adverse attitude toward professional study and resent its being required. To them the courses seem theoretical, impractical, and irrelevant to their future needs. They feel that they are capable and can depend upon their native intuitive qualities. If their native insight does not suffice, then they expect to provide answers to their problems by guessing, by trial and error, by taking chances. These students are not strongly motivated to study. Other students, whose attitude is almost a complete opposite, expect the courses in professional education to provide them with all the correct solutions to any future teaching problem. They do not have the slightest doubt but that experts in educational procedures can tell them how best to teach arithmetic or social studies or to handle a difficult disciplinary problem. They expect to follow a rule-of-thumb method given by specialists in their teaching fields. When they begin teaching and find that they do not have ready-made answers, they tend to deny the value of any and all professional study and may lose interest in teaching.

A third attitude is that professional study leads to improvement of teaching. Professional education, as is true of any field, is an absorbingly interesting field to the student who is not willing to follow the path of caprice and is not satisfied to follow a path of routine procedures he has read about or discussed. He will study professional education in order to improve his understanding of all aspects of teaching and to become a more effective teacher.

Thoughtful professional study tends to reduce the serious errors that sometimes occur as a result of lack of educational understanding and experience. Also, professional study usually increases the satisfactions that accrue from teaching. A teacher who thoroughly studies the mental, emotional, and social growth of children, who knows the nature of the development in children of powers of self-expression and the relationships between maturation and learning, and who recognizes what is involved in developing a practical pattern of teaching is likely to avoid mistakes and pitfalls.

It is a common observation that, on the whole, no people are more seriously devoted to their work than teachers. It is the teacher with a sound professional background who receives the greatest satisfaction from teaching. It is he who gives teaching serious study and who contributes most, not only to his own satisfactions, but to the satisfactions of those whom he teaches.

Teachers who have not developed professional maturity teach as though their work was planned *for* them by others. They like the course of study to be handed to them, the textbooks to be selected for them. They follow the practices of an earlier day, when even the daily topics of classroom work were selected for teachers and pages to be covered each day were indicated by overseeing authorities. They, in common with many teachers in early America, may rightfully be considered to be of small professional stature. The teacher who has studied his profession cannot be expected to behave as though only his superiors know how to teach school. His responsibilities have broadened as his capabilities have increased. He has become the one who decides, within limitations, what the pupils will study, how much ground they will cover, how he will coordinate his work with that of his colleagues, and what his relationships with parents shall be. In general, he will decide how he will advance the achievement of the aims he selects.

Professional study helps teachers to direct the long-term progress of education more wisely. People in the United States have all kinds of ideas for the improvement of education—some wise, some foolish, some constructive, some selfish. The American schools are not all they should be. They fall far short of what the teaching profession and the American people would like to have them. Many old teaching traditions are, admittedly, outmoded. Methods of taxation need revising. Organization of schools needs overhauling. The curriculum needs reconstructing. Methods of teaching require improvement. Well-educated members of the teaching profession, though they may not dominate the future trends in American education, certainly must furnish some of the significant insights to help the American public make decisions.

FOUNDATION COURSES

All the beginning courses in any phase of professional education are foundational in character. This means that they provide an introduction to a particular field. They open the door to more advanced study in the area. The undergraduate student will have "foundation" courses in philosophy of education and in child growth and development, for instance. In each of these areas, work advanced beyond the semiprofessional level will be offered to the undergraduate who is specializing in a professional area and to the graduate student who is doing work on a higher level. The more highly specialized courses, devoted to such topics as taxation, school law, school buildings, educational statistics, advanced child development, school supervision, and school administration, are designed for experienced teachers.

Colleges and universities vary in their requirements of study in foundation courses. The foundational fields—history of education, philosophy of education, educational sociology, psychology of human development, methods of teaching, and student teaching—will, however, at some time and in some form be part of any program of professional preparation. In general, students will take at least the beginning course in these areas.

In some schools the courses named History of Education, Philosophy of Education, and Human Development or Educational Psychology together with an Introduction to Education in America are combined in a series of units each lasting for a semester and known as "Foundations of Education." Usually such an integrated course is taught by a group of specialists. It also uses appropriate materials from sources like social psychology, sociology, political science, and anthropology. The integrated course has proved a successful base for more specialized professional study.

SPECIALIZED COURSES

History of Education

In some teacher education programs a foundation course in the history of education is taught as a separate course. In others the historical aspects of some phase of education are included in the separate course devoted to that phase of education. If reading is studied, for instance, the student may begin with material related to the historical development of our present practices in teaching reading. Either kind of course, if taught by an able teacher, may achieve the desired understandings.

The general purpose in studying history of education is to make clear that the education of one generation is influenced by the education of the generation that preceded it. The student learns that it is profitable to study the thinking and practices of able educators throughout history, and he realizes that the key to what comes after is often found in what went on before.

An eminent specialist in the field of history says:

On every hand the past controls us, for the most part unconsciously, and without protest on our part. We are in the main its willing adherents. The imagination of the most radically minded cannot transcend any great part of the ideas and customs transmitted to him. When once we grasp this truth we shall, according to our mood, humbly congratulate ourselves that, poor pygmies that we are, we are permitted to stand on the giant's shoulders and enjoy an outlook that would be quite hidden from us if we had to trust to our own short legs; or we may resentfully chafe at our bonds and, like Prometheus, vainly strive to wrest ourselves from the rock of the past in our eagerness to bring relief to the suffering children of men. . . . Whether we are tempted to curse the past as a sort of chronic disease, or bless it as the giver of all good things, we are inevitably its offspring; it makes us its own long before we know enough to defend ourselves. It is almost all that we have, and to understand it is to understand ourselves, our possibilities of achievement, our frustrations and perplexities.[1]

Education is a fundamental influence in the development of all civilizations, and the continuity in the development of education is a fundamental historical fact. Citizens of today, for instance, hear much about the educational crash programs of the national government, the programs of expediency, those that are suddenly put into operation without any forward-looking planning. Yet this is not a new government attitude. The Morrill Act in 1862 was a crash program, as was the Smith-Hughes Act of 1917. Numerous other examples could be cited. The old traditions, like tenacious bulldogs, tend to hang on long after reason says to let go. The history of education indicates that the traditions of the past will only be changed after enlightenment is sufficiently widespread to make acceptable the fact that there are other and more efficacious ways of solving educational problems.

Study of the history of education could easily be dull unless attention is focused upon the future of education as it is understood in the light of the past. History of education points to what education in the United States has been as well as upon what it may become. Knowledge and interpretation of the history of education can throw light upon difficult educational problems and bring encouragement to those who might, without this understanding, be completely discouraged. A study of the history of education can do a great deal to improve our understanding of present education and to accent the challenge ahead.

From a historical perspective we get a notion of the relationship between an educational event, situation, or problem and

---

[1] James Harvey Robinson, *The Ordeal of Civilization* (New York: Harper & Row, Publishers, Inc., 1926), pp. 3–4. Quoted by permission of the publishers.

certain other social events, situations, or problems. Further, we see the relationship between the educational events, situations, or problems and the whole of the American educational scene. By studying the history of education or some aspect of it, we get a picture of the relative place of education in the present scheme of social life in the United States.

Philosophy of Education

The philosophy of education is a comprehensive, critical evaluation of the principles that underlie the practices in education in the United States. When organized into a system, these principles serve as a guide to intelligent practice. The study of educational philosophy helps each of us to formulate a consistent and comprehensive viewpoint toward education so that we may know why we do what we do and so that we are able to give reasons for all that we do and are willing to examine our practices critically in order to assure ourselves that our practices are well founded. In other words, the philosophy of education is studied for the purpose of helping us clarify our own educational viewpoints.

The study not only will help the student formulate a comprehensive viewpoint toward education and educational practices but it will also help him resolve within his own mind the conflicts that exist between the varied viewpoints Americans hold toward education. Some of the conflicts are rather troublesome to the beginning student in education and, as he begins teaching, may be a source of worry. The conflicts exist not only among the citizens of a community but also among the members of the educational profession. Sometimes the sharpest critics of educational viewpoints and classroom practices are themselves teachers. At times the editors of popular, influential magazines and newspapers develop a philosophy of education for their publications and attempt to sway the American people to accept their views. These views are expressed with a positiveness and persistency that attract the attention of the public but that may disturb many classroom teachers whose fundamental views toward education are in direct conflict. Does a study of philosophy help resolve such conflicts?

After all, in the field of human relations the human race seems to have made little progress in the last two hundred years either in improving the quality of human relations or in working out universally accepted and generally effective ways of resolving conflicting social viewpoints. We must accept the fact that conflicts in viewpoints on almost every social issue exist. These a single individual cannot resolve. What he can do, however, is to resolve his own conflicting viewpoints. He can formulate a philosophy of education that, to him, is both justifiable in the light of what he knows and defensible in terms of its consequences.

There are three steps used by the educational philosopher in arriving at his judgments about what is the best educational theory and practice. The first is the establishment of a standard of values. The educational philosopher places a higher value upon the path of action he follows than upon the one he does not follow. He directs his actions in terms of widely accepted basic values such as democracy, morality, and so on. We constantly engage in selecting values to guide our action in everyday life. The process of establishing values and of evaluating education in terms of the values is no different in the school than outside, except perhaps that we formalize the process to a greater extent in the schools.

The second step involves a critical and methodical examination of the assumptions of each educational practice and an evaluation of these assumptions in terms of our chosen standards of value. What assumptions underlie using coercion? Administering standardized tests to all pupils of a particular grade? Giving marks to pupils? Giving examinations? Unionizing teachers? Requiring demonstrational geometry in the tenth year of school? Every requirement in the school and every technique of administration or of teaching is based on some fundamental assumption related to values.

The third step used by the educational philosopher is to evaluate what is done in the schools in terms of its actual or possible effects. Before one decides what is good to do in school, one considers what the consequences may be in terms of one's standard of value. The teacher who contemplates keeping a student after school to study his algebra must think of all the consequences. Might this student be led thereby to dislike algebra, to dislike the teacher? All educational philosophers are interested in the effects of what is done in the schools upon the character and personality of the pupils. They therefore consider the possible outcomes of what is done in the schools and judge the merit of what is done in terms of all the possible outcomes.

The practical and common problems of everyday classroom teaching are a rich source of subject matter for educational philosophy. What are the ordinary beliefs of the members of the teaching profession about what is good education? What philosophical generalizations about teaching do teachers draw from the knowledge of child growth and development? Upon what kind of educational philosophy do practices rest—such practices as marking pupils, classifying or refusing to classify children into ability groups, awarding honors, withholding honors, using the results of standardized tests, punishing children?

Educational philosophy examines all teacher activities critically, with the purpose of testing the validity of all that is done. This does not mean that teachers of educational philosophy find fault with everything that is done. Criticism is developed as a method of philosophy. It is pursued methodically. Familiar practices are investigated beyond what is ordinarily known about them. Inconsistencies in thinking are revealed, confusions dissolved, conflicts resolved, and order, clarity, and consistency introduced in knowledges, beliefs, and practices. The philosopher in education goes to many fields for his information and ideas. He examines the information and ideas critically, and as he does this, he evolves both a method of criticism and criteria to use in criticism.

Some of the greatest professional philosophers have addressed themselves to educational philosophy. Some of the works of such men as Charles S. Peirce, William James, Josiah Royce, John Dewey, Bertrand Russell, A. N. Whitehead, Herbert Spencer, and others, including even Plato, were directed to a discussion of education. It may well be that this linking of education and philosophy occurs because education is viewed as an organized, deliberate, conscious attempt to mold the viewpoints and the dispositions of the young. Truly professional philosophers can scarcely refrain from considering a matter that is of such social significance and ethical importance.

Educational philosophy can be as trivial or as deep as one wishes to make it. The foundation course, however, can only be the beginning of a study of a very extensive field. As a rule, the beginning courses deal with such philosophical topics as the aims of education, the nature of subject matter, appraisals of the methods used in teaching, and the various practices related to the organization and the administration of schools. Among the ideas that are critically examined may be those of grouping pupils, of promoting and failing pupils, of giving examinations, and many other practices commonly associated with teaching school.

The student who wishes to develop the art of critical thinking, who favors constructive change, who wishes to chart the paths to future progress, who believes that interests, attitudes, and emotions are factors to be considered in the education of people, who feels that what has been discovered by the specialists in human development and in the other fields of the social sciences should affect the practices followed in educating the young, will find his future study of educational philosophy a highly fascinating, practical, and significant experience. Above all, he will receive from such study help on one of the most important problems, one for which he must formulate a workable solution. That is the problem of his own reasoned, defensible point of view toward what the education of a growing, developing human being should be.

Human Development

Human development is a fascinating field and one of undeniable importance to the individual who wishes to teach intelligently and to derive a great degree of personal satisfaction from his work.

The scope of the field of human development is wide. As a professional field of interest to teachers, however, the focus of the course, regardless of title, is on using education to promote growth in the quality of human behavior. Behavior and development of behavior patterns receive pronounced emphasis. A study leading to understanding of the learning acquired by the infant, the nature of childhood fears, the source of attitudes, the way children learn to talk or read or think or reason is helpful in planning classroom activities that promise maximum desirable growth among children.

The typical college textbook on human development devotes considerable attention to learning, growth, individual differences, personality development, emotions, attitudes, and the like. Perhaps the most fundamental idea underlying all the concepts is that of the total development of the pupils. Hence the textbooks include such topics as growth in ability to make generalizations, the effects of repetition upon learning, how emotions promote or inhibit growth, what has been learned about memory, habit formation, the breaking of bad habits, the effects of approval, the effects of punishments and rewards upon learning, how growth in skills is effected, how intention affects learning, how growth in habits of attention is encouraged, what the nature of thinking is, and so on. Each of these topics relates to factors that shape the character of total growth of the human individual. The subject matter of the course in human development may be almost as broad as life itself. All the topics included apply not only to the learners in the school, but to everyone who learns. It is, however, only when these findings are made directly applicable to the problems of learning in the school that we call the course "Educational Psychology."

STUDENT TEACHING

As mentioned in the chapter on "How Teachers Qualify," in his last year of training the student customarily spends part of his time as a student teacher. The course in student teaching is the most obviously practical of all the professional courses because it gives the student an opportunity to do on a limited scale what he has looked forward to doing and has prepared himself to do. The nature of the course varies greatly from institution to institution. The student teacher usually is assigned to work with some teacher in a

Beginning teachers learn a great deal about teaching having studied how successful, experienced teachers work. (Roy Stevens, Ford Foundation)

public school as an assistant or cooperative teacher. What the student does, of course, depends upon the teacher with whom he cooperates. Usually, the senior teacher has been selected because he is a successful teacher and because he is interested in helping in the education of teachers.

Under the immediate supervision of the classroom teacher, the student teacher gradually assumes more and more responsibility and engages in a constantly expanding number of practical activities. As he teaches, he continues to study with the object of personal and professional improvement. If the time is spent wisely, the student builds skills and understandings and develops a feeling of confidence that will be of inestimable value when he enters school as one of the regularly employed teachers.

ADVANCED STUDY

Following the completion of the courses giving the foundation in education, or some of them, the student will find many avenues open for advanced professional study. A university catalogue lists specialized courses that are given in departments and schools of education dealing intensively with almost every problem the teacher-to-be is likely to encounter. The teachers of nursery school, kindergarten, and the primary grades may study one kind of course grouping, the middle-grade teachers another, and the junior high school teachers still another. Courses are designed specifically for each of these levels in the teaching of reading, arithmetic, social studies, geography, creative dramatics, arts and crafts, music, speech, and physical education. All such courses, when taught by able teachers, afford many insights into the handling of rather narrowly classified but important problems connected with the promotion of child growth. In the light of his interests and his choice of a field for specialization and with the aid of his adviser, a student will decide what advanced courses to pursue.

In contemplating future fields of study, if the student can select courses that are compatible with his vocational plans, he will not only enjoy them more but his profit will be much greater. By and large, the later courses in education, pursued for the purposes of professional preparation, combine both subject matter and methods of directing the subject so as to promote human development to a

Language arts teachers confer as a group on how to improve their language arts skills. Group conferences on mutual problems are a favored means of promoting mutual understanding, for getting suggestions for further study, and for mutual help. (Seattle School District)

maximum degree. Some may, however, emphasize one aspect much more than another.

Most students find the more specialized courses in professional education a source of great interest, perhaps because these courses are then more closely related to the student's vocational objective and are usually taught by specialists who themselves are deeply immersed in their subject. If one is going to teach reading, for example, then a course in the teaching of reading, taught by an inspiring psychologist who has specialized in that aspect of child development, can indeed be most rewarding. The same holds true in other fields.

PERSPECTIVE FOR THE FUTURE

In analyzing American education—what educators and the people are doing to provide American youth with an adequate formal education—we have examined primarily the past and the present. It is appropriate as this book closes to set forth some observations and conclusions that look to the future.

Despite crosscurrents in educational theory, conflicts in educational philosophy, numerous diversions such as wars and depressions, distractions, intrusions, and criticisms from dissatisfied elements in the body politic, education in America has gradually and unmistakably improved from generation to generation. So deep-seated is the pride of the American people in their educational institutions today that no amount of effort to weaken or destroy the character of these institutions could, by any stretch of the imagination, succeed.

If American education is to be further improved, it seems clear that the American people must become more sensitive and better informed about the problems and needs of education. Since the people are dependent upon the teaching profession for intelligent educational leadership, the primary responsibility for keeping the citizens reliably informed rests upon the members of the teaching profession. If the profession is to be effective in discharging this responsibility, it must view the problems and needs of education with unselfish and far-seeing perspective.

What has been discussed has been no more than a beginning of a study of educational needs and problems. Persons who eventually hope to become leaders in the field of education will recognize at this stage that they have simply made a beginning, albeit a sound one. The reader who explores further the topics of this book will reach in time intelligent and informed convictions about what should be done further to advance the cause of education in America.

It seems clear that an increased concern on the part of the American people for the welfare of education will lead to a willingness to provide more adequate financial support. While financial support of education has never been even close to a level considered sufficient, the situation is improving. In the last generation, political statesmen and civic leaders have seriously addressed themselves to the problems of financing American public and private education. Although their lengthy and vociferous disagreements about sources of revenue and means of distribution may have led now and then to a stalemate, there are, nevertheless, unmistakable signs of an awakening consciousness of the importance of resolving the problems of financial support of education.

The American people's developing interest in education should result in greater efforts to encourage more talented young people to choose teaching as a permanent career. Particularly is there an urgent need to have outstanding young men and women enter teaching at the now somewhat neglected elementary level, a level that is critically important because it is basic to all later education.

Currently it is encouraging to see achievements in cooperation between the teaching profession and the public. The profession itself can also profit by making earnest and concerted efforts to cultivate improved cooperation between various segments of its membership. The profession now suffers somewhat from a lack of professional unity.

Since the beginning of the nation, reflective writers in every domain of intellectual, ethical, and aesthetic thought have independently come to the conclusion that, in the development of America, education is a vitally important foundation stone. Past accomplishments, however worthy, must be but a prelude toward still greater educational achievements. Such an aim may be discerned, not only among intellectual leaders but in local communities, civic organizations, and at the state and federal government levels. The future of American education is bright with promise.

Every individual can be a force in shaping the future of education. Each person can be confident that whatever he does constructively will help attain a worthy cause—a cause that demands active and unselfish participation.

The reader will pardon me, I am sure, if I close this book on a personal note. I wish that I were young again, starting a lifetime career in teaching. No work, no profession, offers a richer and more satisfying life for the person who genuinely wants to serve society well and proudly. What an exciting position, what a stimulating prospect, to have before you!

SUGGESTED READINGS

The references which follow have each been selected to supplement some topic in the text. They are intended to direct the student to articles currently being published in leading magazines, journals, and newspapers and to alert him to special reports by professional organizations. The titles have been gleaned from a variety of sources readily available in a college library. Many of the articles, from the popular nonprofessional periodicals with a large circulation, mirror the deep and wide-spread interest the American people have in education. For the most part the references are to nontechnical articles, and the range of subjects is broad. Their sources will undoubtedly continue to provide provocative articles related to education.

UNIT ONE

BROGAN, D. W. "Unnoticed Changes in America," *Harper's Magazine,* Vol. 214 (February, 1957), pp. 27–34. A foreigner notes observable changes in America which he believes remain unnoticed by the masses of American people. He concludes, "The new and puzzling aspects of the America of 1957, as compared to 1925, are problems of education—education in a far deeper and more important sense than the discussions over illiteracy and technology."

BROOM, LEONARD, and PHILIP SELZNICK. *Sociology: A Text with Adapted Readings,* 2d ed., Harper & Row, New York, 1958. Pages 104–112 describe the social effects accruing from the fact that public education has become a basic social institution in present-day society.

CALDWELL, SARAH. "Teaching Is Hard Work," *Atlantic Monthly,* Vol. 194, No. 5 (November, 1954), pp. 40–48. An experienced teacher explains why teaching has strong attractions for an individual.

COLE, FAY-COOPER. "A Witness at the Scopes Trial," *Scientific American,* Vol. 200, No. 1 (January, 1959), pp. 120–130. Describes the scene of a trial in which a teacher is tried for teaching the theory of evolution to his classes in biology and gives a realistic picture of the ways in which legislators and pressure groups sometimes influence American education.

CONANT, JAMES B. *The Education of American Teachers,* McGraw-Hill, New York, 1963. In Chapter 6 (pages 112–117), Dr. Conant sets forth what he believes to be four components "of the intellectual equipment that would be a prerequisite to the development of teaching skill."

GOOD, CARTER, V. (Ed.). *Dictionary of Education,* 2d ed., McGraw-Hill, New York, 1959. A dictionary concerned with the specialized terminology of professional education wherein the newer terms found in current educational literature are defined. This is a dependable reference book.

HUBBARD, FRANK W. "Millions of Children," *NEA Journal,* Vol. 52, No. 3 (March, 1963), pp. 52–54. A study of class size in America's urban elementary schools. "In the opinion of classroom teachers, the 'breaking point' is reached when we begin to put more than 30 pupils in one room." The study finds that only 28.8 percent of America's urban school children are enrolled in classes of fewer than 31 pupils; it considers the effects of the overload on teachers and on teaching effectiveness.

HUGHES, MARIE M. "What Teachers Do and the Way They Do It," *NEA Journal*, Vol. 53, No. 6 (September, 1964), pp. 11–13. Discusses some of the ways of doing things in the classroom that can make a difference in the overall quality of teaching.

JERSILD, ARTHUR T. *When Teachers Face Themselves*, 2d ed., Bureau of Publications, Teachers College, Columbia University, 1957. Discusses the satisfactions and disappointments that enter into a teacher's life.

JOHNSON, HENRY. *The Other Side of Main Street,* Columbia University Press, 1943. This is different from those schoolteacher autobiographies that are in the spirit of the great tradition or that reveal a spirit of disappointment or pessimism. Henry Johnson has a great depth of understanding built on a variety of teaching experiences. He was a professor of history and also of the teaching of history. His book reveals a picture of Main Street different from that portrayed by Sinclair Lewis. Both authors were from Sauk Center, Minnesota.

KVARACEUS, W. C. "The P.T.A. Is a Waste of Time," *The Saturday Evening Post* (May 2, 1964), pp. 6 and 10. Shows that the P.T.A. should not be abolished because of the way it functions, but that it can and must function more efficiently in more worthwhile ways.

LAMBERT, SAM M. "Angry Young Men in Teaching," *NEA Journal*, Vol. 52, No. 2 (February, 1963), pp. 17–20. Explains why so many young men leave teaching for other kinds of work.

MEAD, GEORGE H. *Mind, Self and Society,* The University of Chicago Press, 1934. A distinguished social philosopher explains the theory behind the establishment of social institutions. Pages 260–273 afford an insight into the relationship between the community and the institutions it establishes. This is an earlier but still quite up-to-date development of the theory of social institutions.

MURRA, WILBUR F. "The First Century of the National Education Association," *School and Society*, Vol. 85 (May 11, 1957), pp. 157–160. A history of the organization of the NEA, covering the first one hundred years of its existence.

NAGEL, ERNEST. "Charles Sanders Peirce, a Prodigious but Little-Known American Philosopher," *Scientific American*, Vol. 200, No. 4 (April, 1959), pp. 185–192. A critical review of the man and his works by a professional philosopher. ". . . there is a fair concensus among historians of ideas that Charles Sanders Peirce remains the most original, versatile and comprehensive philosophic mind this country has yet produced."

NATIONAL EDUCATION ASSOCIATION, Department of Classroom Teachers. *Conditions of Work for Quality Teaching,* Washington, D.C., November, 1959. Chapter 1 explains why good teaching is the work for a professional practitioner. It sets forth specific conditions that give the concept of "profession" a clear-cut meaning.

NATIONAL EDUCATION ASSOCIATION, Research Division. *The American Public School Teacher, 1960–61,* Washington, D.C., 112 pages. Discusses what duties the teachers perform, and the amount of time spent on them.

NEA JOURNAL. "We Had No Idea," Vol. 50, No. 10 (October, 1961), pp. 47–54. Describes the many services rendered to the teaching profession by the NEA.

OOSTING, BERNARD R. "Faculty Housing," *The Nation's Schools,* Vol. 60, No. 6 (December, 1957), p. 39. Explains how the Board of Education of the Hinsdale-Clarendon Hills area of Illinois builds and rents homes to provide houses for married teachers with families.

PETERSON, HOUSTON (Ed.). *Great Teachers,* Rutgers University Press, 1946. A compilation of descriptions of great teachers as seen by their students.

RASEY, MARIE I. *It Takes Time,* Harper & Row, New York, 1953. The autobiography of one who, as a young girl, chose to become a teacher.

RETTIG, SOLOMON, and BENJAMIN PASAMANICK. "Status and Job Satisfaction of Public School Teachers," *School and Society,* Vol. 87 (March 14, 1959), pp. 113–116. A study of status and job satisfaction by two medical men. Analyzes why public school teachers seem to have an inferiority feeling and suggests remedies.

ROSS, LILLIAN. "Dancers on the Green," *The New Yorker* (July 18, 1964), pp. 35–90. A description of the work of a fifth grade public school teacher in New York City. This is a rather long, but highly readable, photographic-style picture of what a dedicated teacher did; with some overtones on what she was paid, how she lived, and the like.

SATURDAY REVIEW (September 21, 1963), "The Magnitude of the American Educational Establishment (1963–64)," p. 63. The basic statistics are interestingly summarized and pictorially presented. The information is from estimates by the U.S. Office of Education and the NEA.

SATURDAY REVIEW (October 19, 1963), "A Summary of NEA Recommendations," p. 60. Sets forth fifteen recommendations emanating from a three-year NEA project for the improvement of the instructional program in the schools throughout the United States prepared by a national committee of distinguished educators. A clear statement of what teachers feel their true functions to be and what their attitudes should be toward the many innovations now being introduced into school instruction.

SCANLON, JOHN. "Strikes, Sanctions, and the Schools," *Saturday Review* (October 19, 1963), pp. 51–55 and 70–74. A careful appraisal of the efforts of teachers working through organizational channels such as the NEA and the AFT to gain recognition for their claims to better working conditions. The author contrasts the methods of the AFT in New York City with those used by the Utah Education Association in their demands for increased salaries.

SCHILPP, PAUL ARTHUR. *The Philosophy of John Dewey,* 2d ed., Tudor, New York, 1955. Pages 3–45 contain an excellent biography of John Dewey written by his daughters and edited by his daughter Jene. Gives a realistic view of the times as reflected in the education of one man.

WARREN, EVA. "Earth Being So Good Would Heaven Seem Best," *NEA Journal,* Vol. 53, No. 3 (March, 1964), pp. 8–10 and 83, 85, 87. A free-lance writer and editor surveys what teacher associations are doing to provide homes for retired teachers. "From my contacts with retired teachers in these communal residences, I am convinced they are . . . some of the happiest."

UNIT TWO

ADAMS, JAMES TRUSLOW. *The Epic of America,* Blue Ribbon, New York, 1931. Chapter 10 tells the story of the end of the frontier.

BLACKWOOD, PAUL E. "Migrants in Our Schools," *Educational Leadership,* Vol. 14 (January, 1957), pp. 207–212. An investigation reveals that all occupational groups in the United States are approximately equally mobile.

BREASTED, JAMES HENRY. *The Conquest of Civilization,* Harper & Row, New York, 1926. Chapter 15 contains a scholarly description of Athens in the Age of Pericles. Shows how education was related to the training of citizens.

CLARK, BURTON, R. *Educating the Expert Society,* Chandler, San Francisco, 1962. Chapter 2, "Education, Occupation, and Status" explains how education defines the "life chances" of individuals and groups.

DEWEY, JOHN. *Problems of Men,* Philosophical Library, New York, 1946. In Chapter 5 Professor Dewey sets forth the reasons he believes teachers should be organized.

EBY, FREDERICK, and CHARLES FLINN ARROWOOD. *The History and Philosophy of Education, Ancient and Medieval,* Prentice-Hall, New York, 1940. This thorough and authoritative treatment constitutes an excellent source for reference to any specific period. The effects of the three social movements described in Chapter 7 of this text—the Athenian, the Christian, and the Renaissance—are covered in the best of scholarly tradition. The student should consult the table of contents for specific reference.

EGGLESTON, EDWARD. *The Hoosier Schoolmaster: A Story of Backwoods Life in Indiana,* Orange Judd, New York, 1871. A novel that gives an authentic description of a frontier school.

FRANKEL, CHARLES. *The Case for Modern Man,* Harper & Row, New York, 1955. Chapter 10 contains an excellent analysis of the causes and effects of modern social change. In just thirteen pages Frankel shows the impact of contemporary social change upon institutions.

HAVIGHURST, ROBERT J. "Social Class and the American School System," in George Z. F. Bereday and Luigi Volpicelli, Eds., *Public Education in America,* Harper & Row, New York, 1958, pp. 79–90. Shows in what ways the American education system is related to social structure.

HOLLINGSHEAD, AUGUST R. *Elmtown's Youth,* Wiley, New York, 1949. A sociological study. Pages 168–172 describe the effects of teachers' class bias on the education of pupils in one small community.

JAMES, MARQUIS. *Andrew Jackson,* Bobbs-Merrill, Indianapolis, 1933. Chapter I gives a vivid picture of the kind of environment in which many children of early settlers developed.

NEA JOURNAL. "Education and the Disadvantaged American," Vol. 51, No. 4 (April, 1962), pp. 8–12 and 33–40. Shows that there are still schools

in America as barren as the worst of the frontier schools. Heavily illustrated pages 33–40. This is a summary of an extensive report by the
Educational Policies Commission of the NEA. It shows that some of the
problems of providing satisfactory education to the disadvantaged are
beyond the powers of the educators alone.

PAGE, WALTER HINES. *The School That Built a Town,* Harper & Row,
New York, 1952. Reprints of two addresses and one article by Walter
Hines Page which explain the basis for his strong faith in democracy,
and in education to strengthen democracy. An example of the kind of
thinking done by the most intelligent of lay leaders.

PARKER, SAMUEL CHESTER. *A Textbook in the History of Modern Elementary Education,* Ginn, Boston, 1912. Chapter 5, "Development of
American Secular School Systems," is an excellent treatment showing
how the schools became secularized during the frontier period of
American history. Parker's description of secularization as it took place
in New York State is especially revealing.

PASSOW, A. HARRY (Ed.). *Education in Depressed Areas,* Bureau of Publications, Teachers College, Columbia University, 1963, pp. 1–5. A con-
cise summary of the problem of providing a satisfactory education to
children who live and learn in depressed areas.

REMMERS, H. H. and D. H. RADLER. "Teenage Attitudes," *Scientific American,* Vol. 198, No. 6 (June, 1958), pp. 25–29. A report of a study
of the attitudes of teenagers showing them to be conformists. "The
future of our democracy is not promising unless we restore a social
climate which will reward independent thinking, personal morality and
truly enlightened cooperation in place of going along with the crowd."

ROBINSON, JAMES HARVEY. *The Ordeal of Civilization,* Harper & Row,
New York, 1926. Pages 184–193 describe the Italian cities of the Renaissance in which learning and art developed to a height undreamed of
north of the Alps.

ULICH, ROBERT. *History of Educational Thought,* American Book, New
York, 1945. Pages 61–71 contain an excellent discussion, by a historian,
of Jesus Christ as a teacher.

WEBB, WALTER PRESSOTT. *The Great Frontier,* Houghton Mifflin, Boston,
1952. Chapters 1 and 12 and pages 84–85 contain, respectively, an
analysis of the frontier factor in modern history, a description of education in its relation to the corporate age, and a discussion of how the
frontier influenced education.

WEST, JAMES. *Plainville, U.S.A.,* Columbia University Press, 1945. In this
well-known sociological study, West vividly describes the impact of the
schools upon a rural society on pages 75–81.

UNIT THREE

ALSCHWEDE, ARTHUR M. "The Protestant Schools," *Phi Delta Kappan,*
Vol. 45, No. 3 (December, 1963), pp. 136–140. Explains the purposes,
programs, and methods of financing protestant schools.

BROWN, FRANK B. "The Non-graded High School," *Phi Delta Kappan,*
Vol. 44, No. 5 (February, 1963), pp. 206–209. Describes the organization

of the Melbourne, Florida, high school which operates on a non-graded plan. Achievement tests are used to determine where pupils will be classified.

BROWNELL, BAKER. *The Human Community,* Harper & Row, New York, 1950. Part VI analyzes the relationship between school and community with particular reference to the small, mainly rural, community. The effects of what the author refers to as "the great consolidation" upon communal values is discussed. See especially pages 155–160.

COLES, ROBERT. "How Do Teachers Feel?" *Saturday Review* (May 16, 1964), pp. 72–73 and 90. A research study by a child psychiatrist who spent two years in the deep South studying the problems of classroom teachers in desegregated schools.

FLEMING, THOMAS J. "The Crisis in Catholic Schools," *The Saturday Evening Post* (October 26, 1963), pp. 19–24. A survey of the problems facing the Catholic parochial schools in the United States along with various solutions being proposed and certain solutions being tried.

FRANKEL, CHARLES. "Philosophy," *NEA Journal,* Vol. 51 (December, 1962), pp. 50–53. A scholarly review by a professional philosopher of what the study of philosophy is about. Prepared expressly for classroom teachers.

GOODLAD, JOHN I., and ROBERT H. ANDERSON. "The Nongraded Elementary School," *NEA Journal,* Vol. 47, No. 9 (December, 1958), pp. 642–643. Presents an up-to-date report on the movement of some American communities to set up schools without following a grade level pattern. This is a movement presently on the upswing.

GOSNELL, CULLEN B., LANE W. LANCASTER, and ROBERT S. RANKIN. *Fundamentals of American Government,* McGraw-Hill, New York, 1957. The student of educational organization may wish to review some dependable text in political science that sets forth the fundamentals of American politicial theory. Natural rights, popular sovereignty, the separation of powers, and judicial review are all treated briefly in Chapters 1 through 4.

HAZELTON, PAUL. "Education and Politics," *Saturday Review* (June 15, 1963), pp. 62–63 and 81–83. An analysis of the relationship between politics and the conduct of education.

HOLT, HOWARD B. "Are School Boards Necessary?" *School and Society,* Vol. 91 (November, 1963), pp. 349–350. An old question about the wisdom of placing the control of education in the hands of amateur citizens is analyzed. No one seems to have come up with a better practice.

KAMINETSKY, JOSEPH. "The Jewish Day Schools," *Phi Delta Kappan,* Vol. 45, No. 3 (December, 1963), pp. 141–144. ". . . Jewish Day Schools today are the fastest growing and the most dynamic of all Jewish schools. There are 293 Jewish Day Schools . . . as compared to a mere 16 such schools in 1935." Explains the values seen in the nonpublic Jewish school movement.

KOHLBRENNER, BERNARD J. "Some Practical Aspects of the Public Character of Private Education," *School and Society,* Vol. 86 (October 11, 1958), pp. 348–351. An examination of state constitutional and statutory provisions reveals that there is little public control over teachers in nonpublic schools.

Koos, Leonard V. *Junior High School Trends,* Harper & Row, New York, 1955. Pages 143–144 contain an extended interpretation of the junior high school by one who has followed its development throughout its history.

McManus, Msgr. William E. "The Administration and Financing of Catholic Schools," *Phi Delta Kappan,* Vol. 45, No. 3 (December, 1963), pp. 132–135. "There can be little doubt that the administration of the nation's Catholic schools has been more than adequate. They successfully meet the same standards as the public schools. . . ."

McMurrin, Sterling M. "The U.S. Office of Education: An Inside View," *Saturday Review* (February 16, 1963), pp. 78–81. A former Commissioner of Education discusses some of the problems that confront that office.

Medsker, Leland L. "The Junior-College Picture," *NEA Journal,* Vol. 47, No. 9 (December, 1958), pp. 628–630. Explains the nature of the junior college and mentions several of its problems.

National Education Association, Research Division. *Rankings of the States,* an annual bulletin that ranks the states in terms of teachers' salaries, relative wealth of the states, the financial effort made by each state to support schools, per pupil expenditure, and the like.

Parkman, Francis. "The 'Typical' Independent School," *Phi Delta Kappan,* Vol. 45, No. 3 (December, 1963), pp. 128–131. Explains the administrative structure, nature of financial support, attitude toward federal aid, and other characteristics of nonpublic schools.

Robinson, Donald W. "Commissioner of Education, Our Least/Most Important Government Post," *Phi Delta Kappen,* Vol. 44, No. 3 (December, 1962), pp. 106–115. A scholarly analysis of the work of the Commissioner of Education: what he does; why the Office has so many vacancies; why the Office is ineffective; some of the proposals to improve the work of the Office of Education.

Sheed, Wilfred. "Don't Junk the Parochial Schools," *The Saturday Evening Post* (June 13, 1964), pp. 6 and 10. A young journalist makes a plea that America continue to permit its pluralistic philosophy to govern the education of its children.

Silberman, Charles E. "Give Slum Children a Chance," *Harper's Magazine,* Vol. 228 (May, 1964), pp. 37–42. Proposes an answer to the question, "Can the nation afford a public school system which is failing to educate between 50 and 80 per cent of its Negro and slum white children?"

Stellhorn, A. C. "Schools of the Lutheran Church-Missouri Synod," *School and Society,* Vol. 87 (May 9, 1959), pp. 225–227. A statement of the educational program of this denomination. "Lutherans believe— and the other supporters of church schools share this view—that, besides greatly benefiting the individual and the church, they are rendering the state the best possible service. . . ."

UNIT FOUR

Aldrich, C. Anderson, and Mary M. Aldrich. *Babies Are Human Beings,* Macmillan, New York, 1939. These noted pediatricians reflect considerable insight into the psychological problems involved in stimulating and directing human development.

ANDERSON, JOHN E. *The Psychology of Development and Personal Adjustment,* Holt, Rinehart and Winston, 1949. Chapter 10 contains an excellent discussion of the problems of motivation, by a specialist in early childhood education.

BALLINGER, STANLEY E. "Of Testing and Its Tyranny," *Phi Delta Kappan,* Vol. 44, No. 4 (January, 1963), pp. 176–182. A review of a book by a professor of mathematics called *The Tyranny of Testing.* The review gives substantial analysis of the testing movement, reveals the major strengths and weaknesses of the movement.

BENNETT, MARGARET. "Teaching Is Better With," *Saturday Review* (February 16, 1963), pp. 82–83. A classroom teacher who began teaching without courses in Education concludes, "My attitude toward education courses can be summed up with a paraphrase of that old saying about money: 'I have taught with education courses and without education courses, and, believe me, *with* is better.' "

BERKMAN, DAVE. "You Can't Make Them Learn," *Atlantic Monthly,* Vol. 210, No. 9 (September, 1962), pp. 62–67. Analysis of the problems confronted by teachers who teach in schools in economically depressed areas.

BERLIN, I. N. "Desegregation Creates Problems Too," *Saturday Review* (June 15, 1963), pp. 66–68. Explains the problems created by teaching children who have widely divergent sociological origins.

BETTELHEIM, BRUNO. "Stop Pampering Gifted Children," *The Saturday Evening Post* (April 11, 1964), pp. 8 and 10. "Segregating the gifted, I am convinced, harms both the advanced student and the not-so-advanced." A psychologist's analysis of the effects of ability grouping.

BLOUNT, NATHAN S. "Fructify the Folding Doors; Team Teaching Reexamined," *The English Journal,* Vol. 53, No. 3 (March, 1964), pp. 177–179 and 195. Views team teaching as "the most exciting prospect in English." Explains why.

BROWNELL, JOHN A., and HARRIS A. TAYLOR. "Theoretical Perspectives for Teaching Teams," *Phi Delta Kappan,* Vol. 43, No. 4 (January, 1962), pp. 150–157. A rather complete analysis of what is required for team teaching, written by two men who are involved in an extensive experimental program of team teaching.

CICOUREL, AARON V., and JOHN I. KITSUSE. *The Educational Decision Makers,* Bobbs-Merrill, Indianapolis, 1963. Chapter 5, "High School Bureaucracy and Social Mobility." A study that attempts to answer the question of how the search for talent with the increasing emphasis upon testing and counseling and the bureaucratization of such activities in the school system affect the maintenance of education as the major channel of contest mobility in American society.

CRONBACH, LEO J. "What Research Says About Programed Instruction," *NEA Journal,* Vol. 51, No. 9 (December, 1962), pp. 45–47. A clear explanation of what is involved in the current attempts to build well-designed programs of instruction, and some discussion of the difficulties encountered in arriving at a fair appraisal of the educational results.

DREWS, ELIZABETH. "The Four Faces of Able Adolescents," *Saturday Re-*

view (January 19, 1963), pp. 68–71. An analysis of the efforts of the schools to locate the talented, and an appraisal of their efforts to teach them.

DuBridge, Lee A. "Physics," *NEA Journal,* Vol. 52, No. 9 (December, 1963), pp. 24–28. In simple language shows the changes that are taking place in the field of physics and explains how the changes lead to many new developments.

Dunn, L. C. *Heredity and Evolution in Human Populations,* Harvard University Press, 1959. Chapter 1, "Variety," and Chapter VII, "A Look Ahead." An intelligent discussion of the problems of man from the viewpoint of a biologist. "We now know that mankind has not only a biological but a social unity arising from the interdependence of human beings in societies and of societies with each other. Consequently, our inventions have to deal with a problem common to all men; they have to be conceived in social terms for social ends."

Eldred, Donald M., and Maurie Hillson. "The Non-Graded School and Mental Health," *Elementary School Journal,* Vol. 63 (January, 1963), pp. 218–222. Discusses advantages of non-graded schools from the standpoint of mental health.

Fisher, Mildred Ogg. "Team Teaching in Houston," *The English Journal,* Vol. 51, No. 9 (December, 1962), pp. 628–631. Describes the plan for modified team teaching which is working successfully in Houston.

Gibb, E. Glenadine. "Some Approaches to Mathematics Concepts in the Elementary School," *NEA Journal,* Vol. 48, No. 8 (November, 1959), pp. 65–66. Analyzes the nature of the current discussions centering around the question of developing a better sequence of subject matter in mathematics.

Gibel, Inge Lederer. "How *Not* to Integrate Schools," *Harper's Magazine,* Vol. 227 (November, 1963), pp. 57–66. The writer, who is a mother in a large city, analyzes the effects of school policy, such as ability grouping, having mostly middle-class teachers, and the like, upon the education of children.

Goslin, David A. "The Social Impact of Standardized Testing," *NEA Journal,* Vol. 52, No. 7 (October, 1963), pp. 20–22. A sociologist analyzes the effects of standardized testing both upon the individual and upon what is taught in the school.

Grobman, Harold. "Biology Is Changing, Too," *Saturday Review* (September 21, 1963), pp. 67–69 and 75. Describes the new instructional practices and materials in biology that are being introduced into the schools, beginning with first grade and extending through the basic courses in college. Stresses particularly the trends in vitalizing the instruction at the high school level.

Handlin, Oscar. "Are the Colleges Killing Education?" *Atlantic Monthly,* Vol. 209 (May, 1962), pp. 41–45. A professor of history analyzes the stifling effects of the stress given to competition in college instruction.

Kliger, Samuel. "The Workbook and the Programed Text," *The English Journal,* Vol. 52, No. 9 (December, 1963), pp. 674–676. Are programmed textbooks merely old workbooks in new format? Answers the question from the programmer's point of view.

KLINEBERG, OTTO. "Life Is Fun in a Smiling, Fair-Skinned World," *Saturday Review* (February 16, 1963), pp. 75–77 and 87. An analysis of basic reading textbooks. Shows how they concentrate on representing Americans as well-to-do groups of Caucasian descent. Analyzes the attitudes built up in the children by the nature of the illustrations in the readers.

LANGE, PHIL C. "Selection and Use of Programed Learning Materials," *NEA Journal,* Vol. 53, No. 4 (April, 1964), pp. 28–29. Sets forth the assumptions about teaching procedure that underlie programmed learning.

LEAR, JOHN. "What the Moon Ranger Couldn't See," *Saturday Review* (September 5, 1964), pp. 35–40. Shows the rapidity of change in the world of subject matter to which school children are exposed.

MANNING, JOHN. "Discipline in the Good Old Days," *Phi Delta Kappan,* Vol. 41, No. 3 (December, 1959), pp. 94–99. A professor of humanities vividly and authentically describes how our ancestors handled the problems of school discipline not so long ago. The carefully documented references may serve as a bibliography on the subject.

MARKLE, SUSAN MEYER. "Inside the Teaching Machine," *Saturday Review* (November 18, 1961), pp. 58–60. Explains in detail the problem of programming instructional materials.

MAYER, MARTIN. "Last Chance for Our Schools," *The Saturday Evening Post* (September 14, 1963), pp. 24–36. A comprehensive report on the present state of education in America as concluded by the author after ranging over 32 states. He describes the newer methods he found in use and explains some of the more recent developments in teaching. He also points out the obstacles that he contends rob America's school children of the education they deserve.

MICHELS, WALTER C. "The Teaching of Elementary Physics," *Scientific Monthly,* Vol. 298 (April, 1958), pp. 56–64. A new approach which emphasizes the understanding of basic principles. "The history of physics and mathematics supports the amalgamation of the two subjects."

MUELLER, THEODORE. "Psychology and the Language Arts," *School and Society,* Vol. 87 (October 24, 1959), pp. 420, 422, and 427. Shows why effective language training must center in audio-oral work.

MUSS, ROF E., and OTHERS. "Discipline," *NEA Journal,* Vol. 52 (September, 1963), pp. 9–22. A series of discussions on the problem of discipline in the school.

NATIONAL COUNCIL OF TEACHERS OF MATHEMATICS. *An Analysis of New Mathematics Programs,* Washington, D.C., 1963, 68 pp. Analyzes the nature of eight experimental programs in which mathematics has been revised.

NATIONAL COUNCIL OF TEACHERS OF MATHEMATICS. *The Revolution in School Mathematics,* Washington, D.C., 1961, 90 pp. Describes a number of the new programs being experimented with in the schools. Explains what has caused the current revolution in mathemetics education, what is being done to implement the revolution, and what decisions are involved for local schools.

NEA JOURNAL. "Teacher Opinion Poll," Vol. 53, No. 6 (September, 1964),

p. 25. Maintaining pupil discipline remains one of the most persistent problems teachers face. It appears that keeping order in the classroom has become a more difficult problem than it was in past years.

OPPENHEIMER, ROBERT. "The Tree of Knowledge," *Harper's Magazine,* Vol. 217 (October, 1958), pp. 55–60. Explains the problem of adjusting to the new knowledges that accumulate so rapidly. Advocates "some hard and concentrated work in the specialized traditions. . . . It means a major change in the way in which we look at the world and in our educational practices. It means that an understanding of the scope, depth, and nature of our ignorance should be among the primary purposes of education."

PHI DELTA KAPPAN. "Programed Instruction," Vol. 54, No. 6 (March, 1963). This issue is devoted entirely to the subject of programmed instruction. Twenty specialists write on the contributions programmed instruction can make to learning.

POSTMAN, NEIL (Ed.). *Television and the Teaching of English,* Appleton-Century-Crofts, New York, 1961, 138 pp. A report made by the Committee on the Study of Television of the National Council of Teachers of English. Part I deals with the educational significance of television. Part II deals with classroom study through television.

PRESSEY, S. L. "A Simple Device Which Gives Tests and Scores—and Teaches," *School and Society,* Vol. 23 (March 20, 1926). The author of the first teaching machine explains how it works.

REED, JERRY E., and JOHN L. HAYMAN, JR. "An Experiment Involving Use of English 2600, an Automated Instruction Text," *Journal of Educational Research,* Vol. 55 (June, 1962), pp. 476–484. From this, one gets an idea of what an automated textbook is like.

REID, JAMES M. "An Adventure in Programing Literature," *The English Journal,* Vol. 52, No. 9 (December, 1963), pp. 659–673. A veteran book editor explains the programming of poetry after what he calls "his two-year adventure" in programming literature.

ROWLAND, HOWARD S. "Using the TV Western," *The English Journal,* Vol. 52, No. 9 (December, 1963), pp. 693–696. Shows how a teacher may use TV "Westerns" to build a foundation for critical viewing.

SAVELAND, ROBERT N. "Whatever Happened to Geography?" *Saturday Review* (November 17, 1962), pp. 56, 57 and 77. Points out that geography has been neglected in the high school and elementary school curriculum. "An objective survey will in many cases indicate the desirability of restoring geography to the position it merits in the school curriculum."

SCHRAMM, WILBUR. *Programmed Instruction for Today and Tomorrow,* Fund for the Advancement of Education, New York, 1963. Describes the many ways in which programmed learning is contributing to the enrichment of learning.

SCOLLON, KENNETH M. "Why Art in Education?" *Saturday Review* (February 15, 1964), pp. 70–72 and 80. States many reasons why it is important to emphasize the fine arts in the schools.

SHARP, EVELYN. "The New Math: You Don't Count on Your Fingers Anymore," *Saturday Review* (January 19, 1963), pp. 65–67. Describes the new mathematics being introduced into the modern school curriculum.

SKINNER, B. F. "Teaching Machines," *Scientific American,* Vol. 205, No. 5 (November, 1961), pp. 90–102. Explains how teaching machines promote effective learning by enabling "the student to learn in small but rigorous steps, each of which is rewarding," and how they may introduce a new element in methods of teaching.

STEVENS, MARTIN, and WILLIAM R. ELKINS. "Designs for Team Teaching in English," *The English Journal,* Vol. 53, No. 3 (March, 1964), pp. 170–176. Description of team teaching in high school in which experiments have been conducted with different methods.

STREHLER, ALLEN F. "What's New About the New Math?" *Saturday Review* (March 21, 1964), pp. 68–69 and 84. Explains why mathematics as taught in the schools is being revised and explains why there is some confusion among the educators as to what directions the revisions should take.

SULLIVAN, W. W. *Programmed English,* Macmillan, New York, 1963, 427 pp., 1783 frames, 5523 oral responses. A reusable textbook for teaching grammar. The books are given the pupils. Teacher is available to answer questions. Pupils respond orally, quietly, individually. They complete the tests as indicated in the textbook. Class participation is used for reviews. An example of the better planned programmed textbooks.

SWANSON, REYNOLD A. "Improving Instruction Through Materials Centers," *The American School Board Journal,* Vol. 139 (October, 1959), pp. 47–48. Describes how teachers are aided through a school resource center.

THORNDIKE, EDWARD LEE. *Man and His Works,* Harvard University Press, 1943. Chapter 8, "The Psychology of Punishment," analyzes the psychological effects of the use of coercion.

TRAXLER, ARTHUR E. "Using Tests in Schools," *The American School Board Journal,* Vol. 139, No. 1 (July, 1959), pp. 11–13. A specialist in testing explains how standardized tests, for students and for teachers, may be used to contribute to the efficiency of teaching, and also how they may serve as a detriment to good teaching.

UNDERWOOD, BENTON J. "Forgetting," *Scientific American,* Vol. 210, No. 3 (March, 1964), pp. 91–99. An experimental study of forgetting. "Summing up these observations in the form of a general theory, we can say that all forgetting results basically from interference between the associations a man carries in his memory storage system."

WATSON, GOODWIN. "What Do We Know About Learning?" *NEA Journal,* Vol. 52, No. 3 (March, 1963), pp. 20–22. A brief, readable summary of what psychologists believe to be true about learning.

WILSON, CHARLES H. "The Average Child," *NEA Journal,* Vol. 51, No. 3 (March, 1962), pp. 28–29. A school superintendent raises the question of what is an "average" child.

WITTY, PAUL A., and P. J. KINSELLA. "A Report on Televiewing in 1961," *Elementary English Journal* (January, 1962), pp. 24–32. A comprehensive review of the television viewing habits of elementary school children.

WOODRING, PAUL. "The Editor's Bookshelf," *Saturday Review* (November 17, 1962), pp. 70–71. The educational editor of *Saturday Review* analyzes two books which attack the testing movement in American life and education. His analysis gives a good picture of the testing movement as seen by an educational psychologist.

INDEX

Ability grouping, 526–527
Academies, 359–362
Accreditation, 48–51
Achievement, measurement of, 423–426
Activity analysis, in arriving at aims, 447–449
in study of teachers' work, 36–39
Adolescent society, 398
Adolescents, attitudes of, 239
behavior of, 246
Aims of professional study, 532–534
societal pressures and, 440–445
statements of, 442–450
Aims of teaching, from activity analysis method, 447–449
criticisms of, 450–453
determination of, 436–445
external influences on, 437–440
from growth concept approach, 449–450
as guide to subject matter, 480
meaning of, 435–436, 446
Aldrich, Anderson C., 246
Aldrich, Mary M., 246
American Federation of Teachers, 89–90
Anderson, John E., 448
Associations, teachers', 83–91; American Federation of Teachers, 89–90; National Education Association, 84–86
Athenian movement, 153–159
Attention, 412–414
Audiovisual materials, 512–521
Automated instruction, 524–525
Automation, 236–238

Beard, Charles A., 207
Beard, Mary R., 207
Beecher, Dwight E., 61
Binet, Alfred, 417
Biology as basis for understanding pupils, 396–397
Blair, Glenn M., 415
Boards of education, local, 279–283
functions and powers of, 282–283
members of, compensation of, 281; qualifications of, 281–282; selection of, 280; terms of office of, 280–281
size of, 281
Boston Public Latin School, 458
Breasted, James Henry, 158

Cajori, Florian, on Galileo, 169
Capacity of pupils, 415–416
Career days, 78
Carr, William G., 84
Carter, James G., 222
Certification of teachers, 46–49
Chalkboards, 516
Child benefit theory, 350–351
Christian movement, and early education, 371
and ethical behavior, 159–160
and professional education, 161–162
and secular education, 162–163
Civilian Conservation Corps, 320
Clark, Burton R., on class membership, 404
Class membership, 404–407
Classrooms as units of administration, 26–27
Coleman, James S., 398
Colleges, accreditation of, 48–51
private, 363–364
Comenius, John Amos, 174–179
Great Didactic, The, 177
influence on textbooks, 176–177
Commager, Henry S., 227–228
Common sense, 111–113
Community, relationships in, 246–247
resources, use of, 27–28
Conant, James B., 5
Copernicus, 167
Core program, 383–384
Corporate trend, 241
Course of study, definition of, 466
Critical thinking, and Athenian movement, 153–159
in education of citizens, 154–155
in formulating a philosophy, 106–107
and level of civilization, 157–158
as method in education, 155–157
in modern education, 158–159
Curriculum, definition of, 466

Demosthenes, 154
Desegregation, Supreme Court decision on, 332
Dewey, John, 121–122, 134, 181–182, 416, 446, 449–450, 480
Dickens, Charles, on education, 190–191, 477
Dictionary of education, 23
Discussion, influence of, on group membership, 141–142

Punishment, 409–410

Pupils, ability grouping of, 526–527
  growth and development of, attention and, 412–414; capacity and, 415–416; cultural backgrounds and, 402–407; forgetting and, 412; habit and, 409–410; inner forces and, 400–412; memory and, 411–412; motive and, 414–415; pattern of, 401–402; research on, 396–399; skill and, 410–411
  information about, from achievement tests, 423–426; from intelligence tests, 417–423; from teacher-made tests, 429–430; from use of informal methods, 430–432
  understanding of, information essential to, 394–395; two aspects of, 393–394
  variety among, 396–397

Puritans, 214–219

Quintilianus, Marcus Fabius, 40

Radio, 516–517
Radler, D. H., 239
Readers, McGuffey's, 510
Readiness, law of, 402
Reading, methods of teaching, 493–494
Reinert, Very Rev. P. C., S.J., 355
Religion, as source of philosophy, 113–114
Remmers, H. H., 239
Renaissance, characteristics of, 163–164
  classical language and modes of thought of, 164–166
  and inductive method, 166–170
Robinson, James Harvey, 258, 536
Rockefeller report, 238
Roman Catholic parochial schools, 352–355
Roper survey, 323
Rousseau, Jean Jacques, 174, 179–185
Russell, Bertrand, 463

St. Louis school system, kindergartens in, 370
Salaries of teachers, 96–100
Sandburg, Carl, 215
San Francisco Unified School District, salary policy of, 100
Sanford, Filmore H., 408
School bus, 273–274
School district, Bellflower, California, 275
  definition of, 266
  Pike County, Illinois, 276

School districts, public, city, 271
  common, 267–268
  community, 276–277
  consolidation of, 272–276
  county, 270
  desirable characteristics of, 278–279
  intermediate, 270
  local traditions and, 265
  number of, 270
  patterns of, 267
  reorganization of, 277–278
  state-centered, 272
  town and township, 268–271
School Lunch Act, 320
School systems, typical pattern of organization of, 269
Schools, doctrine of free, 225–226
  and free lands, 226–228
  frontier, 213–225
  as institutions, 129–135
  one-teacher, 270
Science, methods of teaching, 498–499
  as source of philosophy, 114–117
  subject matter of, 468–470
Senior high school, 379–384
Simplicity postulate, 22
Simpson, Ray H., 415
Skill, 410–411
Skinner, B. F., 523
Smith-Hughes Act, 316–319
Social movements, effects of, upon education, 170–171
  as sources of ideas, 151–153
Social studies, methods of teaching, 502–504
  scope of, 452–453
  as subject matter, 473
Sociology, 398
Socrates, 155–157
Sophists, 154–155
Sound-motion pictures, 519–520
South, early education in the, 223–225
Spencer, Herbert, 174, 200–201, 296, 397, 447–448
Standard of living, 243
Standardized tests, 417–426
State, board of education, 295–297
  chief school officer, 298
  constitutional provisions, 291–292
  department of education, 298–299
  educational authority, 295–297
  financial aid, 306–307
  fiscal policy, 302–303
  foundation program, 301–302
  and judicial review, 293–294
  legislatures, 292
  minimum standards, 300–301
  programs of education, 299–309

67 68 69 70   11 10 9 8 7